Interoperability for Enterprise Software and Applications

Proceedings of the Workshops and the Doctorial Symposium of the Second IFAC/IFIP I-ESA International Conference: EI2N, WSI, IS-TSPQ 2006

Edited by
Hervé Panetto
Nacer Boudjlida

First published in Great Britain and the United States in 2006 by ISTE Ltd

ISTE Ltd
6 Fitzroy Square
London W1T 5DX
UK

ISTE USA
4308 Patrice Road
Newport Beach, CA 92663
USA

www.iste.co.uk

Library of Congress Cataloging-in-Publication Data

IFAC/IFIP I-ESA International Conference: EI2N, WSI, IS-TSPQ 2nd: 2006
  Interoperability for enterprise software and applications: proceedings of the workshops and the doctorial symposium of the second IFAC/IFIP I-ESA International Conference: EI2N, WSI, IS-TSPQ 2006/edited by Hervé Panetto, Nacer Boudjlida.
     p. cm.
  Includes index.
  ISBN-13: 978-1-905209-61-3
  ISBN-10: 1-905209-61-4
  1. Computer software--Development. 2. Application software--Development.
  3. Internetworking (Telecommunication) I. Panetto, Hervé. II. Boudjlida, Nacer. III. Title.
  QA76.76.D47I345 2006
  005.1--dc22
                                                                          2006018170

British Library Cataloguing-in-Publication Data
A CIP record for this book is available from the British Library
ISBN 10: 1-905209-61-4
ISBN 13: 978-1-905209-61-3

Printed and bound in Great Britain by Antony Rowe Ltd, Chippenham, Wiltshire.

Second International Conference
I-ESA'2006
Interoperability for Enterprise Software and Applications

Bordeaux, France, March 22nd – 24th, 2006

Supported by INTEROP NoE (IST-508011) and ATHENA IP (IST-507849)
Co-sponsored by IFAC and IFIP

The interoperability in enterprise applications can be defined as the ability of a system or a product to work with other systems or products without special effort from the customer or user. The possibility to interact and exchange information with internal and external collaborators is a key issue in the enterprise sector. It is fundamental in order to produce goods and services quickly, at lower cost, while maintaining higher levels of quality and customisation. Interoperability is considered to be achieved if the interaction can, at least, take place at the three levels: data, applications and business enterprise through the architecture of the enterprise model and taking into account the semantics. It is not only a problem of software and IT technologies. It implies support for communication and transactions between different organisations that must be based on shared business references.

The I-ESA conference aimed at bringing together researches, users and practitioners dealing with different issues of Interoperability for Enterprise Software and Applications. The conference focused on interoperability related research areas ranging like *Enterprise Modelling* to define interoperability requirements, *Architecture and Platforms* to provide implementation frameworks and *Ontologies* to define interoperability semantics in the enterprise.

General Co-Chairs
>   Guy Doumeingts, ADELIOR, France
>   Rainer Ruggaber, SAP, Germany

Program Co-Chairs:
>   Gérard Morel, CRAN UMR 7039, Nancy-University, CNRS, France
>   Jörg P. Müller, Siemens Corporate Technology, Germany

Workshops, Tutorials & Invited Sessions Co-Chairs:
>   Hervé Panetto, CRAN UMR 7039, Nancy-University, CNRS, France
>   Nacer Boudjlida, LORIA UMR 7503, Nancy-University, France

Doctoral Symposium Co-Chairs
>   Jolita Ralyté, CUI, University of Geneva, Switzerland
>   Giovanna Di Marzo, Birkbeck College, University of London, UK

Local Organization Chair
Bruno Vallespir, LAPS, University of Bordeaux 1, France

Local Organization Committee
Thècle Alix, LAPS, University of Bordeaux 1, France
Séverine Blanc, LAPS, University of Bordeaux 1, France
David Chen, LAPS, University of Bordeaux 1, France
Nicolas Daclin, LAPS, University of Bordeaux 1, France
Yves Ducq, LAPS, University of Bordeaux 1, France
Tania Oger, LAPS, University of Bordeaux 1, France
Mathieu Roque, LAPS, University of Bordeaux 1, France
Nabila Zouggar, LAPS, University of Bordeaux 1, France

Workshops International Program Committees

Workshops General Chairs:
Panetto Hervé   CRAN UMR 7039, Nancy-University, CNRS, France
Boudjlida Nacer   LORIA UMR 7503, Nancy-University, CNRS, France

EI2N'2006: Enterprise Integration, Interoperability and Networking
Workshop co-chairs:
Berio Giuseppe   Università di Torino, Italy
Panetto Hervé   CRAN UMR 7039, Nancy-University, CNRS, France
IPC co-chairs:
Molina Arturo   Tecnológico de Monterrey, Mexico
                     Chair of IFAC TC 5.3
Panetto Hervé   CRAN UMR 7039, Nancy-University, CNRS, France
                     Vice-Chair of IFAC TC 5.3
IPC Members:
Albani Antonia   Delft University of Technology, The Netherlands
Berio Giuseppe   Università di Torino, Italy
Chapurlat Vincent   LGI2P, France
Chatha Kamran   Lahore University of Management Sciences, Pakistan
Chen David   LAPS, University of Bordeaux 1, France
Chen Pin   Department of Defence, Australia
Goranson Ted   Old Dominion University, USA
Jaekel F-Walter   Fraunhofer IPK, Germany
Jochem Roland   University of Kassel, Germany
Opdahl Andreas   University of Bergen, Norway
Ortiz Angel   Polytechnic University of Valencia, Spain
Pingaud Hervé   Ecole des Mines d'Albi Carmaux, France
Shorter David   IT Focus, UK
Vallespir Bruno   LAPS, University of Bordeaux 1, France
Whitman Larry   Wichita State University, USA
Zelm Martin   CIMOSA Association, Germany

WSI'2006: Web services and interoperability
Workshop co-chairs:
Söderström Eva   University of Skövde, Sweden
Backlund Per   University of Skövde, Sweden
Kuehn Harald   BOC Information Systems GmbH, Austria
IPC co-chairs:
Backlund, Per   University of Skövde, Sweden
Söderström, Eva   University of Skövde, Sweden
IPC Members:
Ågerfalk Pär J.   University of Limerick, Ireland
Boncella Bob   Washburn University, USA
Charalabidis Y.   Singular Software, Greece
Hedbom L.-Åke   Volvo IT, Gothenburg, Sweden

Henkel Martin	University of Stockholm/KTH, Sweden
Johannesson Paul	University of Stockholm/KTH, Sweden
Karagiannis D.	University of Vienna, Austria
Karsten Martin	University of Waterloo, Canada
Kjebon Jana	SEB IT, Stockholm, Sweden
Kühn Harald	BOC Information Systems, Austria
Lillehagen Frank	Troux Technologies, Norway
Schmitt Jens	University of Kaiserslautern, Germany
Wangler Benkt	University of Skövde, Sweden

IS-TSPQ'2006: Interoperability Solutions to Trust, Security, Policies and QoS for Enhanced Enterprise Systems
Workshop co-chairs:

Kutvonen Lea	University of Helsinki, Finland
Linington Peter	University of Kent, UK
Morin Jean-Henry	University of Geneva, Switzerland

IPC Members:

Chadwick David	University of Kent, UK
D'Atri Alessandro	Luiss Guido Carli University, Italy
DiMarzo Giovana	Birkbeck College, University of London, UK
Goedicke Michael	University of Duisburg-Essen, Germany
Goranson Ted	Old Dominion University, USA
Guth Susanne	Open Digital Rights Language Initiative
Jacob M.-Eugenia	Telin, The Netherlands
Jonkers Henk	Telin, The Netherlands
Kabilan Vandana	Stockholm University and KTH, Sweden
Khadraoui Djamel	CRP Henri Tudor, Luxembourg
Krogstie John	NTNU, Trondheim, Norway
Heiko Ludwig	IBM TJ Watson, USA
Merabti Madjid	Liverpool John Moores University, UK
Mertins Kai	Fraunhofer IPK Berlin, Germany
Mukherji Jishnu	Hewlett-Packard, USA
Pawlak Michel	University of Geneva, Switzerland
Rifaut André	CRP Henri Tudor, Luxembourg
Sadighi Babak	SICS, Sweden
Scannapieco M.	Università "La Sappienza" di Roma 1, Italy
Shrimpton David	University of Kent, UK
Söderström Eva	University of Skövde, Sweden
Soley Richard M.	OMG, USA
Tsalgatidou A.	University of Athens, Greece
Weigand Hans	Tilburg University, The Netherlands

I-ESA'2006 Doctoral Symposium
Doctoral Symposium co-chairs:

Ralyté Jolita	University of Geneva, Switzerland
Di Marzo Giovana	Birkbeck College, University of London, UK

Reviewing Committee:

Backlund Per	University of Skövde, Sweden
Berio Giuseppe	Università di Torino, Italy
Di Marzo Giovana	Birkbeck College, University of London, UK
Goossenaerts Jan	Technical University of Eindhoven, The Netherlands
Heymans Patrick	University of Namur, Belgium
Léonard Michel	University of Geneva, Switzerland
Ralyté Jolita	University of Geneva, Switzerland
Söderström Eva	University of Skövde, Sweden

CONTENTS

Editorial

The second I-ESA international conference, supported by the INTEROP NoE (Interoperability Research for Networked Enterprises Applications and Software Network of Excellence, http://www.interop-noe.org) and the ATHENA IP (Advanced Technologies for interoperability of Heterogeneous Enterprise Networks and their Applications, http://www.athena-ip.org) and sponsored by IFAC and IFIP, offered a workshops program comprising three workshops and a Doctorial Symposium. The objective of the workshops held on March 21st, 2006 was to strengthen some key topics related to interoperability of enterprise applications and software. The workshops organisation left time slots for brainstorming among the attendees in order to come out, at the end, with possible new research directions. The Doctorial Symposium provides an open forum for students involved in the preparation of their PhD to discuss their research issues and ideas with senior researchers.

It is a fact that enterprises need to collaborate if they want to survive in the current extreme dynamic and heterogeneous business world they are involved in. Enterprise integration, interoperability and networking have been disciplines that have studied how to enable companies to collaborate and communicate in the most effective way. Enterprise Integration consists in breaking down organizational barriers to improve synergy within the enterprise so that business goals are achieved in a more productive and efficient way. The 2nd IFAC TC 5.3 Experts Workshop on "Enterprise Integration, Interoperability and Networking" (**EI2N'2006**) aims to identify current research and practical issues on applications interoperability for enterprise integration.

One of the main domain related to interoperability concerns architectures. Technology such as Web services promises to facilitate the interaction between IT systems and enterprise applications. The 2nd workshop "Web Services and Interoperability" (**WSI'2006**) gathered researchers and practitioners in order to explore various aspects of web services and their benefits to the interoperability problem, according to a technical perspective as well as a business one.

However, interoperability of enterprise software and application concerns also trust and security of the exchange process. The objective of the "Interoperability Solutions to Trust, Security, Policies and QoS for Enhanced Enterprise Systems" (**IS-TSPQ'2006**) workshop was to explore architectures, models, systems, and their utilization for non-functional aspects, especially addressing the new requirements for interoperability.

And finally, a Doctoral Symposium has given the opportunity for students involved in the preparation of their PhD in any area of Interoperability for Enterprise Software and Applications to present and discuss their research issues and ideas with seniors' researchers to better understand the interoperability context and issues.

We would like to express many thanks to the workshops chairs and committees for their contribution to the scientific success of these events.

Nacer Boudjlida, *LORIA UMR 7503, Nancy-University, CNRS, France*
Hervé Panetto, *CRAN UMR 7039, Nancy-University, CNRS, France*

Entreprise Integration,
Interoperability and Networks

EI2N Workshop Chairs' message

After the successful first edition of the workshop, in 2005, the second edition of the EI2N workshop has been organised in the context of the I-ESA06 International Conference by the *IFAC Technical Committee 5.3* "Enterprise Integration and Networking". The workshop aims to identify current research and practical issues on applications interoperability for enterprise integration that should be fully developed in the future works.

In response to the call for papers, 13 papers have been submitted; each paper has been reviewed by three reviewers, members of the international programme committee. Only 6 papers have been accepted and 5 have been presented. Other than the presentations of the accepted papers, to involve and to understand impact on the workshop participants, two groups have been organised to discuss on the topics addressed in the presented papers. These two groups have finally reported the results of the respective discussions.

The workshop has then been organised around three topics addressed by the accepted papers: UEML (Unified Enterprise Modelling Language), ontologies for application interoperability and, finally enterprise interoperability. The first two papers on UEML, i.e. *UEML: systematic approach for the determination of elementary constructs* and *Comparison of goal-oriented languages using the UEML approach* present two distinct proposals towards the definition of such a UEML. The former focuses on how to define, starting from existing modelling languages, constructs that can be considered as part of each language (and referred to as elementary constructs in the paper). The latter focuses on how to use the UEML approach 2.0 proposed in INTEROP network of excellence, for representing two languages, GRL and KAOS, well-known in the (software) requirement engineering community; then, based on the proposed ontological representation, the paper provides correspondences between the constructs belonging to these two languages.

The paper *A multi-views business process ontology for flexible collaboration* addresses web service ontologies and how one of these ontologies can be used for composing (in processes or business processes) web services.

Finally the two last papers, i.e. *GRAI and SCOR Meta-model and Design Principles for Interoperability* and *Framework for enterprise interoperability* address what is interoperability between enterprises and how enterprise interoperability can be characterised; specifically, the first paper is about principles (defined by using SCOR as the main reference model, well-know in supply chain, together with a decisional framework represented by a GRAI grid) to design enterprises taking part to a network. The second paper aiming at defining enterprise interoperability and structuring the related research domain, provide a framework to classify solutions and to understand barriers (conceptual and technological) to make interoperable enterprises.

It has been a great pleasure to work with the members of the international programme committee who dedicated their valuable effort for reviewing, in time, the submitted papers: we are indebted to all of them. We are also indebted to Michael Petit (Facultés Universitaires Notre-Dame de la Paix, Namur, Belgium) and Thomas Knothe (IPK-Berlin, Germany) who moderated and reported the discussions within the workshop groups, and to Nacer Boudjlida (LORIA, France) who kindly accepted to chair one session. Finally, we would like to thank the INTEROP Network of Excellence (European FP6 IST-508-011, http://www.interop-noe.org) for its great support.

Giuseppe Berio, *Dipartimento di Informatica, Università di Torino, Torino, Italy*
Hervé Panetto, *CRAN UMR 7039, Nancy-University, CNRS, France*

Session 1:
UEML for Enterprise
Applications Interoperability

UEML: Systematic Approach for the Determination of Elementary Constructs

Matthieu Roque* — **Bruno Vallespir*** — **Guy Doumeingts****

*LAPS/GRAI, University Bordeaux 1, ENSEIRB, UMR 5131 CNRS
351 cours de la Libération, 33405 Talence Cedex, France
Matthieu.Roque@laps.u-bordeaux1.fr
Bruno.Vallespir@maps.u-bordeaux1.fr

**Groupe ADELIOR
Paris, France

ABSTRACT: *Nowadays, one of the important objectives of research in the enterprise modelling domain is the development of a unified language, often called UEML (Unified Enterprise Modelling Language). This paper is focused on one of the more illuminating aspects of UEML: the comparison of the constructs of the enterprise modelling language. In previous work we identified some situations which can occur when we want to compare some modelling constructs belonging to different languages. We investigate in more detail this problem of comparison, using a formal approach based on the set theory.*

KEY WORDS: *Interoperability, enterprise modelling, models transformation, constructs, UEML.*

1. Introduction

Since the first development in the area of enterprise modelling that started in the US in 1970s (for example, SADT, SSAD, IDEF0, Data Flow Diagram,…), many enterprise modelling languages have been elaborated world-wide. We can mention for example, Entity Relationship model, MERISE, GRAI grid and nets, CIMOSA constructs and building blocks, OMT, IEM, ARIS method, IDEFx,… (Petit *et al.*, 2002), (Vallespir, 2003), (Vallespir *et al.*, 2003), (Vernadat, 1996). It is generally recognised that there are too many heterogeneous modelling languages available in the "Market" and it is difficult for business users to understand and choose a suitable one. Main problems related to this situation are (Chen *et al.*, 2002):

- difficulties (impossibility in some cases) in translating a model built using a language to a model expressed in another one;

- difficulties for an enterprise in using a software tool if it is based on languages which are different from the ones adopted by the enterprise;

- difficulties for a user in selecting the relevant languages to resolve a particular problem.

However, it seems that the elements behind these various languages are similar or differ only slightly in details. Thus, it is natural to think about the development of a Unified Enterprise Modelling Language. One of the principal benefits to have a Unified Enterprise Modelling Language is to be able to transform a model of an enterprise built in a language in another one (Chen *et al.*, 2002), (Doumeingts *et al.*, 1999), (Vallespir, 2003), (Vallespir *et al.*, 2003), (Vallespir *et al.*, 2001), (Vernadat, 2001). Moreover, requirements about UEML have been stated during the UEML project (IST-2001-4229) (Knothe, 2003). The third most important requirement stated was the expectation for an "invariant and unique behavioural semantic" language. Thus, the language UEML is used like a "pivot" language and thus allows avoidance of one-to-one transformation (Chen *et al.*, 2002), (Berio, *et al.*, 2003).

2. Roadmap

Several approaches can be considered for elaborating our unified language like the bottom-up approach which starts with an analysis and then synthesis of existing enterprise modelling languages. Indeed, for the moment, it seems to be more efficient to use the principle which consists of integrating existing languages (Chen *et al.*, 2002), (Vallespir *et al.*, 2003), (Vallespir *et al.*, 2001).

This approach is composed of the following steps:

1) Choice of existing languages.
2) Build meta-models of the languages in order to have the constructs and the links between them for each language.

3) Study of the intersections between the constructs of each language in order to identify the common constructs and to allow to define the elementary constructs.

4) Do the union of elementary concepts.

5) Establishment of correspondences rules.

3. Meta-modelling

In this paper, we focus only on the determination of the common constructs in order to find the elementary constructs. Thus, only the steps 2) to 5) above are presented. In our approach, we consider the meta-modelling as a lens by which a unified enterprise modelling language may be defined. Thus, we use the meta-modelling like a technique of dialogue, by describing the constructs of the different languages. The objective is to "to exceed the terminological problems and graphic conventions, in order to identify their common points and those [that diverge]" (Oussalah, 1997). Some approaches like XML (DTDs and Schemas), MOF, Telos, can be used as meta-modelling language. These techniques are content-independent (applicable for the definition of any language). Others meta-modelling languages are content-dependent (and sometimes domain-specific): for instance, XMI is an exchange format based on the UML metamodel in XML designed for enabling exchange of UML models. Accordingly, a UEML could be defined as a content-dependent domain-specific meta-model through a content-independent meta-model. The UEML might just use content-independent meta-modelling techniques as a way for its definition (Panetto et al., 2004). Finally, the meta-modelling that we use is the UML (Unified Modelling Language) class diagram (OMG, 2003) because it seems sufficient to deal with our problem which is, in the first place, to describe the syntactical aspects of the languages. For each language, a meta-model is built with the class diagram and, all the constructs of the language and the links between them are represented. With these meta-models we can compare the constructs of the different languages.

4. Definition of the elementary constructs

In previous works, the concept of elementary construct has been introduced and we highlighted that its determination is not easy (Roque et al., 2005). The objective, of this section is to propose a formal approach in order to facilitate the determination of the elementary constructs. The definition of the elementary construct is recalled below.

**A construct is an elementary construct, if it exists completely or not at all
for each considered languages.**

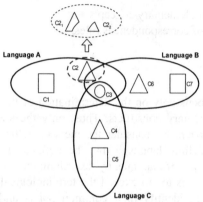

Figure 1. *Elementary constructs*

For instance, in Figure 1, we can see that all the constructs are elementary constructs except the construct C2. Indeed, all the others constructs belong completely or not all to the language A, B and C. The construct C2 belongs completely to the language A but only a part of this construct belongs to the language B. Thus, it is not an elementary construct.

4.1. Constructs comparison in the case of two constructs

If we consider the comparison of only two constructs A and B belonging respectively to two different enterprise modelling languages, we can distinguish three kinds of relationships between the two constructs. In Figure 2, Figure 3, and Figure 4, we consider the two constructs and we indicate what constructs we have to integrate in UEML.

4.1.1. *Case 1: no connection*

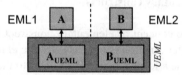

Figure 2. *"No connection" relationship*

$A_{UEML} \equiv A$ and $B_{UEML} \equiv B$

4.1.2. Case 2: equivalence (A ≡ B)

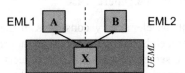

Figure 3. *"Equivalence" relationship*

$$X ≡ A ≡ B$$

4.1.3. Case 3: A and B have a shared part

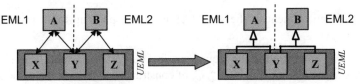

Figure 4. *"Have a shared part" relationship*

The three constructs X, Y and Z^1 (Y = Shared part, X = A-Y, Z = B-Y) are created in the UEML meta-model. However, what is really the meaning of the "has a shared part" relationship. Indeed, the concept of "set" in mathematics is very general. A "set" can indicate any collection. The objects which are in a bedroom can be qualified of a set even if it is heteroclite and which is defined by the property "being an object located in the bedroom of someone at this time". However, one can say that a person is a set, and that its arm belongs to him according to a set relationship. One can answer yes, because of the general information of the set concept; but it is not necessarily relevant because that does not correspond to what one wanted to model. When we think of our left arm, we do not consider it like an element of a set where it would be similar to others, but like an organ which belongs to an organisation or an element where it deals with her specific function, in relation to others organs. For instance, the directions of an enterprise compose the enterprise. This vocabulary can be used to qualify the link which exists between an arm and a person. It is a UML "composition" or an "aggregation" and not an inclusion in the sense of the set theory. However, in this paper, we focus only on the generalisation relationships which seem to be the more frequently relationships. In this case, the constructs X, Y and Z allow recomposing the constructs A and B by generalisation relationships.

To elaborate the UEML meta-model we have to generalise these results about two constructs to any number Nc of constructs.

---

1 In this paper each class property is considered as independent. This assumption is valid because assuming independence gives the worst case for the number of combination of constructs to be considered.

4.2. Constructs comparison in a general case

In order to define all the elementary constructs in the case of any number of constructs we use an approach based on the set theory approach. Indeed, the concept of class and the concept of set are very similar. The objects instances of a class share general characteristics, expressed in the class in the form of attributes, operations and constraints. We call $P(A)$ the characteristic property of the set A corresponding to the cartesian product of "n" sets corresponding to the "n" properties of the class A [1]. Thus, we have:

$$P(A) = P_1(A) \times P_2(A) \times \ldots \times P_n(A) \tag{1}$$

and $p_n(A)$ is an element of the set $P_n(A)$ and corresponding to an instance of the property $P_n(A)$.

Thus, we can write some equations in order to determine the elementary constructs in the case of a number "N_c" of constructs and how the constructs of each of each language can be recomposed.

4.2.1. Definition of the elementary constructs

We define in the first time the set **E** corresponding to the union of the N_c constructs [2].

$$E = \bigcup_{i=1}^{N_c} (C_i) \tag{2}$$

Thus, we can define N_{EC} elementary constructs (EC_i) corresponding to all the sub-sets which is possible to create with the intersections of all constructs. To determine these elementary constructs it is useful to use a truth table as in Boolean algebra where each "0" corresponds to the complementary of the set (equal to $[E - (C_i)]$ noted ^cC_i) in the set E and each "1" corresponds to the set. Thus, each combination of the truth table defines an elementary constructs. However, the first one does not need to be considered because $^cC1 \cap {}^cC_2 \cap {}^cC_3 = \varnothing$. In the case of 3 constructs we can define 7 elementary constructs. Then, we can write the equations corresponding to the 7 elementary constructs and their characteristic property (Table 1).

Elementary constructs	Correspondences rules
$CE_1 = {}^cC_1 \cap {}^cC_2 \cap C_3$	$C_1 = CE_4 \cup CE_5 \cup CE_6 \cup CE_7$
$P(CE_1) = P({}^cC_1) \cup P({}^cC_2) \cup P(C_3)$	$P(C_1) = P(CE_7) \cap P(CE_6) \cap P(CE_5) \cap P(CE_4)$
$CE_2 = {}^cC_1 \cap C_2 \cap {}^cC_3$	$C_2 = CE_2 \cup CE_3 \cup CE_6 \cup CE_7$
$P(CE_2) = P({}^cC_1) \cup P(C_2) \cup P({}^cC_3)$	$P(C_2) = P(CE_2) \cap P(CE_3) \cap P(CE_6) \cap P(CE_7)$
$CE_3 = {}^cC_1 \cap C_2 \cap C_3$	$C_3 = CE_1 \cup CE_3 \cup CE_5 \cup CE_7$
$P(CE_3) = P({}^cC_1) \cup P(C_2) \cup P(C_3)$	$P(C_3) = P(CE_1) \cap P(CE_3) \cap P(CE_5) \cap P(CE_7)$
$CE_4 = C_1 \cap {}^cC_2 \cap {}^cC_3$	

$P(CE_4) = P(C_1) \cup P(^cC_2) \cup P(^cC_3)$
$CE_5 = C_1 \cap {^cC_2} \cap C_3$
$P(CE_5) = P(C_1) \cup P(^cC_2) \cup P(C_3)$
$CE_6 = C_1 \cap C_2 \cap {^cC_3}$
$P(CE_6) = P(C_1) \cup P(C_2) \cup P(^cC_3)$
$CE_7 = C_1 \cap C_2 \cap C_3$
$P(CE_7) = P(C_1) \cup P(C_2) \cup P(C_3)$

Table 1. *Elementary constructs and correspondences rules*

Thus, we can define N_{EC} elementary constructs in a case of N_C constructs [3].

$$N_{EC} = 2^{N_C} - 1 \qquad [3]$$

We can write equation [4] and [5] which respectively determines all the elementary constructs and the corresponding characteristic properties.

$$\forall i \in [1, N_{EC}], \ EC_i = \bigcap_{j=1}^{N_C}(C_j)' \qquad [4]$$

$$\forall i \in [1, N_{CE}], \ P(CE_i) = \underset{j=1}{\overset{N_c}{X}} P(C_j)' \qquad [5]$$

where $(C_j)'$ is either equal to (C_j) or to $[E - (C_j)]$ noted $^c(C_j)$. All the combinations of (C_j) have to be done. When $(C_j)'$ is equal to $^c(C_j)$ then we have to delete $P(C_j)'$ in the equation of $P(EC_i)$.

IF $\forall i \in [1, N_{EC}], \ EC_i = \bigcap_{j=1}^{N_C}(C_j)' = \varnothing$ **THEN** the equation giving $P(EC_i)$ has no

sense and has to not be considered.

4.2.2. Correspondences rules

In order, to find the originating constructs we have to use equations [7] and [8] below:

$$\forall i \in [1, N_C], \ C_i = \bigcup_{j=1}^{N_{CE}}[(CE_{j/i})] \qquad [7]$$

$$\forall i \in [1, N_C], \ P(C_i) = \bigcup_{j=1}^{N_{CE}}[P(CE_{j/i})] \qquad [8]$$

where $EC_{j/i}$ is either equal to EC_j, if C_i appears in the equation of EC_j, or to the empty set in the others cases.

IF $EC_{j/i} = \varnothing$ **THEN** $P(EC_{j/i})$ has to be not considered in equation [8].

4.2.3. *Approach for defining the elementary constructs*

Finally, we can define three different steps in order to determinate the elementary constructs.

1) Write the equations in order to define all the elementary constructs for the considered number of constructs.

2) Interview the providers of the languages in order to define the intersections between the constructs of the languages.

This step is really not obvious. Indeed, most of the languages have not a formal definition of their constructs. In this case, the comparison is mainly based on informal comparisons where each construct is only defined by a textual description. In the UEML project (Berio *et al.*, 2003) which provided UEML 1.0, this comparison had been performed by using a scenario. This scenario had been modelled in each considered enterprise modelling language. The study of the intersections between the constructs had been done on the bases of this scenario. Even if, this approach do not provide a formal approach in order to compare the constructs, the lack of formal definition of the constructs, do not permit to use a formal and automatic method. The UEML 2.0 (Berio, 2005) undertakes a very different, eventually complementary approach. Indeed, it requires to fully model the languages in their three conceptual components: abstract syntax, semantic domain and semantics. These three components are organised according to a meta-meta-model: any language is represented by constructs, in turn associated to some meaning provided by a semantic domain. However, the subject of the paper is not to discuss on the way to get the different equations which represent the intersections between the constructs.

3) Resolve the equations according to the results of the preceding step.

5. Illustrative example

Let us assume that we want to deal with the transformation between only two pieces of languages: the activities in SADT and GRAI languages (Roque *et al.*, 2005) as shown in Figure 5.

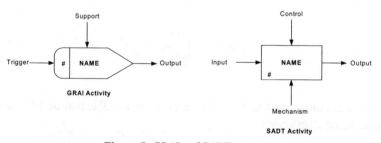

Figure 5. *GRAI and SADT activities*

The two simplified meta-models of the example (GRAI and SADT activities) in UML class diagrams are represented in Figure 6.

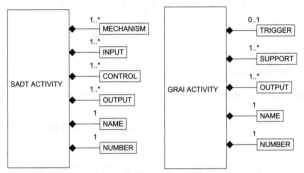

Figure 6. *GRAI and SADT simplified meta-models*

These meta-models are simplified because the links between the constructs of the languages are not represented; it is just a list of constructs. Indeed, in this paper we focus only on the comparison of the constructs themselves. In a first comparison, we can identify three elementary constructs which are the Name, the Number and the Output, because they are common to the two activities. For simplify, these three constructs can be grouped into only one elementary construct, which is called Activity.min [9].

$$\text{Activity.min} = \{\text{Name, Number, Ouput}\} \qquad [9]$$

5.1. Definition of the elementary constructs and the correspondences rules

5.1.1. First step: write the equations

Thus, we have to consider five constructs that are so far unaccounted for. In the general case, we can define 31 elementary constructs, but all of these are not to be considered further. Indeed, it is important to note that it is possible to reduce the number of the elementary constructs by adding some assumptions depending on the context. For instance, our equations do not assume that the intersections of the constructs of the same language are equal to the empty set. Then, if as a first assumption, we consider that these intersections are equals to the empty set, then the number of the elementary constructs is considerably reduced. Indeed, in this case this number is not equals to [3] but to equation [10] below in removing all the elementary constructs resulting from the comparison of two constructs of the same language. Thus, if we use equation [10], we can reduce the number of elementary constructs to be considered to 11.

$$N_{EC} = \left[2^{\sum_{i=1}^{N_L} N_C(L_i)} - 1 \right] - \left[\sum_{i=1}^{N_L} 2^{N_C(L_i)} - 1 \right] \qquad [10]$$

Where:

N_L is the number of the considered languages,

$N_c(L_i)$ is the number of the constructs of the language L_i.

This number will be reduced again in section 5.1.3 in adding another assumption.

5.1.2. Second step: interview the providers of the languages

Concerning the five unaccounted-for constructs of the two activities we can write some equations between the constructs by interpreting the results of the interviews in terms of set-theoretic constraints. Thus, we can write the six relationships below which will be used to define all the elementary constructs with our equations.

1)   Trigger $\subset$ Control with Trigger $\neq$ Control

2)   Trigger $\cap$ Input $= \varnothing$

3)   Trigger $\cap$ Mechanism $= \varnothing$

4)   Support $\cap$ Control $\neq \varnothing$

5)   Input $\subset$ Support with Input $\neq$ Support

6)   Mechanism $\subset$ Support with Mechanism $\neq$ Support

5.1.3. Third step: resolve the equations

Before resolving the equations, for this example, it is possible de reduce again the number of the elementary constructs. Indeed, if we take the case of the control construct we can see that this constructs is decomposed in three elementary constructs[2].

$$EC_9 = C \cap {}^C M \cap {}^C I \cap {}^C T \cap {}^C S$$
$$EC_{10} = C \cap {}^C M \cap {}^C I \cap {}^C T \cap S$$
$$EC_{11} = C \cap {}^C M \cap {}^C I \cap T \cap {}^C S$$

These three elementary constructs could be integrated as core constructs of UEML. The elementary constructs EC_9 represents a control in SADT which is neither a Trigger nor a Support in SADT. In a general case, we can keep these

---

2 Support $\rightarrow$ S; Trigger $\rightarrow$ T; Control $\rightarrow$ C; Mechanism $\rightarrow$ M; Input $\rightarrow$ I;
Not Triggering Control $\rightarrow$ NTC.

construct in order to have a complete generalization relationship. However, for our example and for transformation issue this construct are not needed and we can consider that a control can always be linked to a Trigger or a Support constructs. We can apply the same principle of all the constructs and finally in this case we have:

$$EC_1 = \varnothing, EC_2 = \varnothing, EC_3 = \varnothing, EC_6, = \varnothing \text{ and } EC_9 = \varnothing$$

so reducing the number remaining to be considered to 6.

Equations [10] can be modified in order to take into account this remark, as is illustrated by equation [11] below:

$$N_{EC} = \left[2^{\sum_{i=1}^{N_L} N_C(L_i)} - 1 \right] - \left[\sum_{i=1}^{N_L} 2^{N_C(L_i)} - 1 \right] - \left[\sum_{i=1}^{N_L} N_c(L_i) \right] \qquad [11]$$

In conclusion we have only 6 elementary constructs (Table 2):

$EC_4 = {}^CC \cap {}^CM \cap I \cap {}^CT \cap S = I_{UEML}$	$P(EC_4) = P(I) \cup P(S)$
$EC_5 = {}^CC \cap {}^CM \cap I \cap T \cap {}^CS = \varnothing$	$P(EC_5)$ has no sense because $EC_5 = \varnothing$
$EC_7 = {}^CC \cap M \cap {}^CI \cap {}^CT \cap S = M_{UEML}$	$P(EC_7) = P(M) \cup P(S)$
$EC_8 = {}^CC \cap M \cap {}^CI \cap T \cap {}^CS = \varnothing$	$P(EC_8)$ has no sense because $EC_8 = \varnothing$
$EC_{10} = C \cap {}^CM \cap {}^CI \cap {}^CT \cap S = NTC$	$P(EC_{10}) = P(C) \cup P(S)$
$EC_{11} = C \cap {}^CM \cap {}^CI \cap T \cap {}^CS = T_{UEML}$	$P(EC_{11}) = P(C) \cup P(T)$

Table 2. *Elementary constructs*

5.2. UEML meta-model and correspondences rules

Finally, we can build the UEML meta-model of this example in UML class diagram (Figure 7).

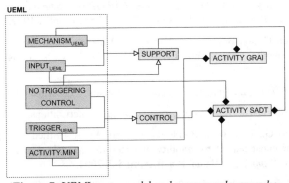

Figure 7. *UEML meta-model and correspondences rules*

This class diagram illustrates the UEML meta-model and the correspondences rules between the UEML constructs and the constructs of the GRAI and the SADT activities. Practically, this rule leads to get elementary constructs belonging to UEML that enable to rebuild constructs of languages (so-called local constructs) by generalization. Since these local constructs are obtained, they can be composed to get the whole language.

6. Conclusion

In this paper, we have wanted to put in evidence some difficulties concerning the comparison of constructs of the enterprise modelling language. We have presented some equations in order to help and simplify the construct comparison in a formal way. We have used these equations with an example (GRAI and SADT activities). Our approach is a systematic approach which provides some help for the determination of the core constructs of the UEML language and the correspondences rules.

7. References

Berio G. *et al.*, *Requirements analysis: initial core constructs and architecture*, UEML Thematic Network - Contract no.: IST – 2001 – 34229, Work Package 3 Deliverable 3.1, May 2003.

Berio G., *UEML 2.0. Deliverable 5.1*. INTEROP project UE-IST-508011 (www.interop-noe.org). 2005

Chen D., Vallespir B., Doumeingts G. Developing an unified enterprise modelling language (UEML) – Roadmap and requirements. – *in Proc. of 3rd IFIP Working conference on infrastructures for virtual enterprise, PROVE*, Sesimbra, Portugal, 1st-3rd May 2002 – Collaborative Business Ecosystems and Virtual Enterprises, Kluwer Academic Publishers.

Doumeingts G., Vallespir B. UEML: *Position du LAP/GRAI. – Seminar of Groupement pour la Recherche en Productique*, GRP, Nancy, France, 25 November 1999.

Knotte T., Busselt C. and Böll D. – *Report on UEML (needs and requirements).* - UEML Thematic Network - Contract no.: IST – 2001 – 34229, Work Package 1 Report, April 2003.

OMG. *Unified Modeling Language Specification. –* Version 1.5, formal/03-03-0, 2003.

Oussalah, 1997, *Ingénierie Objet, Concepts et techniques*, InterEditions, 1997.

Panetto H., Berio G., Benali K., Boudjlida N., Petit M. A Unified Enterprise Modelling Language for enhanced interoperability of Enterprise Models. *Proceedings of the 11th IFAC INCOM Symposium*, Bahia, Brazil, April 5-7, 2004.

Petit M. *et al.*, *Enterprise Modelling State of the Art*, UEML Thematic Network - Contract no.: IST – 2001 – 34229 – Work Package 1 Report, October 2002.

Roque M., Vallespir B. and Doumeingts G. From a models translation case towards identification of some issues about UEML – *in Proc. of the workshop on Entreprise Integration, Interoperability and Networking (EI2N)*, Geneva, Switzerland, February 22, 2005.

Vallespir B., Braesch C., Chapurlat V., Crestani D. L'intégration en modélisation d'entreprise: les chemins d'UEML. – *in Proc. of 4ème conférence francophone de Modélisation et Simulation, Organisation et conduite d'activités dans l'industrie et les services, MOSIM*, Toulouse, France, 23-25 April 2003.

Vallespir B. - *Modélisation d'entreprise et architecture de conduite des systèmes de production.* – Thesis for Habilitation à Diriger des Recherches, University Bordeaux 1, 19 December 2003, in french.

Vallespir B., Doumeingts G., Chen D. *Problem and research orientation on UEML: A point of view.* – IFAC-IFIP interest group on UEML, Vienna, Austria, 19 September 2001.

Vernadat F. UEML: Towards a Unified Enterprise Modelling Language. – *in Proc. of 3rd Conférence Francophone de Modélisation et Simulation, MOSIM*, Troyes, France, 25-27 April 2001.

Vernadat F.B. *Enterprise modelling and integration: principles and applications.* Chapman & Hall, 1996.

Comparison of Goal-oriented Languages using the UEML Approach

Raimundas Matulevičius* — **Patrick Heymans*** — **Andreas L. Opdahl****

*Computer Science Department, University of Namur, Belgium
rma@info.fundp.ac.be
phe@info.fundp.ac.be

**Department of Information Science and Media Studies,
University of Bergen, Norway[†]
Andreas.Opdahl@uib.no

ABSTRACT: *Goal-oriented modelling languages are important during requirements engineering (RE). However, goal-oriented languages differ significantly in both syntax and semantics. The paper analyses and compares the semantics of GRL and KAOS using the UEML approach, which supports fine-grained analysis and comparison of modelling constructs based on the Bunge-Wand-Weber (BWW) representation model and Bunge's ontology. The contribution is threefold. It offers precise semantics of both languages' constructs in relation to the Bunge-Wand-Weber model. It offers a path towards automated transformations between models expressed in GRL and KAOS and towards integrated management of such models. It contributes to a broader understanding of goal-based modelling in general.*

KEY WORDS: *Goal modelling, requirements engineering, GRL, KAOS, UEML, the BWW model.*

1. Introduction

Focusing on stakeholder goals during requirements engineering (RE) results in investigating not only *what* the new system should do but also providing the rationale (*why*) for the new system. RE is closely coupled to the goal-oriented views (Kavakli and Loucopoulos, 2005). In collaborative work situations people are aware of the personal and group goals and act accordingly, not strictly following rules or procedures. The goal-driven view influences design, where unsatisfied goals and needs motivate design activities and suggest criteria for evaluating design solutions.

---

† Currently on leave at CIGIP, Universidad Politécnica de Valencia, Spain.

The literature devises a variety of goal-oriented languages, most notably KAOS (Letier, 2001; van Lamsweerde, 2003), i* (Yu, 1997), GRL (ITU, 2003), Tropos (Bresciani *et al.*, 2004), GBRAM (Anton, 1996), NFR (Chung *et al.*, 2000) and Lightswitch (Regev, 2003). Kavakli and Loucopoulos (2005) show that research on goal-oriented languages is fragmented and that each language addresses different RE activities. Syntax and semantics vary between languages and language semantics often need to be clarified to avoid misunderstandings between stakeholders. Precise semantics is particularly important when stakeholders are technical actors, such as automated software engineering tools or goal-driven agents on the semantic web.

In this paper we compare two goal-oriented languages: Goal-oriented Requirements Language (GRL) and Knowledge Acquisition in autOmated Specification (KAOS). The comparison is based on the Unified Enterprise Modelling Language (UEML) approach, which is currently being applied to develop version 2 of UEML (Berio *et al.*, 2005). The contribution of this work is threefold: firstly, it defines the semantics of both languages' constructs according to the Bunge-Wand-Weber (BWW) model and Bunge's ontology; secondly, the work offers a path towards automated transformations between and integrated management of models expressed in the two languages; and, thirdly, it contributes to a broader understanding of goal-based modelling in general. The analyses of GRL and KAOS also pave the way for including them in UEML 2.

In the following section 2, GRL and KAOS, the BWW model and the UEML approach; section 3 describes the research method; results are presented in section 4 and discussed in section 5; finally, conclusions are presented in section 6.

2. Theory

2.1. *GRL*

The Goal-oriented Requirements Language (GRL) supports goal-oriented modelling and reasoning about requirements (ITU, 2003). It has four main categories of constructs: *intentional elements*, *links*, *actors*, and *non-intentional elements*.

The *intentional elements* tend to answer questions about intents, motivations and rationales: what behaviours, information and structure are chosen for inclusion into the requirements model; what criteria are used to deliberate among alternatives. Intentional elements are *goal*, *softgoal*, *task*, *resource* and *belief*. A *goal* is a condition or state of affairs that the stakeholders would like to achieve. Like a goal, a *softgoal* is a condition that the stakeholder wants to achieve, but there are no clear-cut criteria to determine whether this condition is achieved. A *task* describes a particular way of doing something. A *resource* is an entity for which the main concern is whether it is available. A *belief* is used to express design rationale.

Link categories include *means-ends*, *decomposition*, *contribution*, *correlation* and *dependency*. *Means-ends* links are used to describe how goals are achieved, typically through tasks. A *decomposition* link defines the subcomponents of a task, typically (but not limited to) the subgoals that must be accomplished. A *contribution* link describes the impact that one element has on another by design. *Correlation* links describe side effects of one element to others. *Dependency* links describe the inter-agent dependent relationships.

Actors are holders of intentions and characterise active entities, who want goals to be achieved, tasks to be performed, resources to be available and softgoal to be "satisficed". *Non-intentional element* is a reference to object outside a GRL model.

Unlike *i**, GRL does not separate between strategic dependency model and strategic rationale model. A GRL model could be composed of either a global goal model or serious of goal models distributed amongst actors. If a goal model includes more than one actor, then the dependency relationship is used to relate them.

2.2. KAOS

A KAOS (Knowledge Acquisition in autOmated Specification) model includes a goal model, object model, agent model and operation model (Letier, 2001; van Lamsweerde, 2003). We focus on the goal model; however, agent, object and operation models are not excluded completely, as all those models are interrelated.

A *goal* is a prescriptive assertion that captures an objective which the system-to-be should meet. Goals can be classified according to one of four patterns: *maintain, avoid, achieve* and *cease*. A goal can be refined through *G-refinement*, which relates it to a set of subgoals whose conjunction, possibly together with *domain properties*, contributes to the satisfaction of the goal. A goal can have alternative G-refinements which result in different software designs. A set of goals is *conflicting* if these goals cannot be achieved together. This means that under some *boundary condition* these goals become logically inconsistent in the considered domain.

An *object* is a thing of interest in the system. Its instances can be distinctly identified and may evolve from state to state. Objects have *attributes*. Goals *concern* objects and attributes. An *agent* plays a role towards a goal's satisfaction by controlling object behaviour. Goals are refined until they are *assigned* to individual agents. A goal effectively assigned to a software agent is called a *requirement*. A goal effectively assigned to an environment agent is called an *expectation*. An *operation* is an *input-output* relation over objects. Operations are characterised textually by domain and required *conditions*. Whenever the required conditions hold, performing the operations satisfies the goal. If a goal is *operationalised* and has a *responsible agent*, the latter *performs* the operations.

2.3. The BWW model

The BWW model is grounded on Bunge's (1977, 1979) and Wand and Weber's (1993, 1995) comprehensive ontological model, further ensuring that its concepts are thoroughly chosen, explained and defined. According to the BWW model the world is made of *things* that possess *properties*. Properties can be *intrinsic* or *mutual* to several things. Things can form a *composite* thing that has *emergent* properties, i.e., properties not possessed by the individuals composing it. Intrinsic and mutual properties are perceived by humans in terms of *attributes*, which are represented as functions. The *state* of a thing is a set of values of all its attribute functions. Attribute changes are manifested as *events*. Events happen due to internal transformation in a thing or due to interactions among things. Not all states are possible, and not all events can occur. The rules governing possible states and events are termed *state laws* and *transformation laws*, respectively. States can be classified as being *stable* or *unstable*, where an unstable state is a state that must change by law, and a stable state is a state that can only change as a result of an external action to a thing. A *process* is a sequence of unstable states, transforming by law until a stable state is reached.

2.4. *The UEML approach*

The aim of the Unified Enterprise Modelling Language (UEML) is to be an intermediate language that supports integrated use of enterprise models expressed in different languages. The UEML approach – which is currently used to define version 2 of the UEML – uses the BWW model to describe modelling constructs in a way that facilitates precise language integration. Although it focuses on enterprise modelling, the UEML approach is appropriate for describing IS-modelling languages like GRL and KAOS, because they focus on problem domains and not only on planned software artefacts.

Following Opdahl and Henderson-Sellers (2004, 2005) and Opdahl (2006), the UEML approach extends the BWW model in two ways: Firstly, whereas the BWW model only maps a modelling construct onto an ontological concept in general, such as a class, a property, a state or an event, the UEML approach maps in onto a specific ontological class, property, state or event. Secondly, whereas the BWW model usually maps a modelling construct onto single ontological concept, the UEML approach recognises that a modelling construct may represent a *scene* where multiple classes, properties etc. play parts. To accommodate these extensions, the UEML approach offers a structured approach to construct description, where the description of each construct is separated into descriptions of:

- *Instantiation level*: Is the construct intended to represent individual things and their particular properties, states and events? Or is it intended to represent classes and their characteristic properties, states and events? Or is it intended to represent both levels?
- *Classes*: Which thing or class of things in the problem domain is the construct intended to represent? Even when a construct primarily represents a property, state or event, this field remains relevant, because every property, state or event must be a property in, state of or event in a specific thing or class. A construct definition can have several class entries, because some constructs are even intended to represent more than one thing or class at the same time.
- *Properties*: Which property or properties in the problem domain is the construct intended to represent? Again, even when a construct primarily represents not a

property but, e.g., a state or event, this field is relevant, because every state or event pertains to one or more properties. This entry too can be repeated too.

– *Behaviour*: Even when two modelling constructs are intended to represent the same properties of the same things or classes, they may be intended to represent different behaviours. For example, one modelling construct may be intended to represent just their existence, i.e., a static representation. Other modelling constructs may be intended to represent a state of the classes, things or properties, or an event, or a process, i.e., alternative dynamic representations. This entry distinguishes between these four cases and provides sub-entries to specify the relevant case in detail.

– *Modality*: We are used to think about enterprise and IS models as asserting what is the case. However, not all modelling constructs are intended for making assertions. The modality entry distinguishes constructs that are intended to represent recommendations, obligations, permission etc. instead of assertions.

The various ontological concepts – i.e., the classes, properties, states and events– that are used to describe modelling constructs are maintained in a *common ontology*. The common ontology was initially derived from the BWW model, but grows incrementally and dynamically as additional classes, properties, states and events are introduced in order to describe new modelling constructs. In consequence, when two modelling constructs – from the same or from different languages – have both been described using the UEML approach, the exact relationship between them can be identified in terms of the common ontology, paving the way for comparison, consistency checking, update reflection, view synchronisation and, eventually, model-to-model translation across modelling language boundaries.

A template supporting the UEML approach consists of three parts: a *preamble* to be filled with general information about the construct; a *presentation* devoted to concrete syntax and layout conventions; and a *representation*, which describes mapping of the construct to the BWW model. The first version of the template was developed in November 2004 and distributed to InterOP partners. Initial attempts were made in the first half of 2005 to describe BPMN, coloured Petri nets, GRL, ISO/DIS 19440, UEML 1.0, selected diagram types from UML 2.0, XPDL and YAWL. The template descriptions are currently being extended, negotiated and entered into the prototype tool UEMLBase (Berio *et al.*, 2005).

3. Research method

First, we selected the latest self-contained descriptions of GRL (ITU, 2003) and KAOS (Letier, 2001; van Lamsweerde, 2003). We then created meta-models of GRL[1] and KAOS[2], because up-to-date meta-models were not available. For further analysis, 11 GRL and 25 KAOS constructs were then selected as relevant for representing problem domains. Next, the UEML approach was applied to each GRL and KAOS construct. The *preamble* and *presentation* sections in the template were

---

1 See (Dallons *et al.*, 2005).
2 See http://www.info. fundp.ac.be/~rma/KAOSanalysis/KAOSmetaModel.pdf.

straightforward to complete for each construct, because the information could be extracted directly from the meta-models and language descriptions (for concrete syntax). Section 4 therefore focuses on the less trivial *representation* section, which characterises how the constructs map to the common ontology. Finally, we used the analysis results to examine the correspondences between GRL and KAOS.

4. Results

This section describes the semantics of the central *goal* construct, both in GRL and KAOS. We then present the overall comparison of GRL and KAOS constructs.

4.1. *Meaning of* Goal

GRL.goal and *KAOS.goal* are played by an "ontological scene" called *theGoal* (Table 1) that is mapped to a *complex law property*. The scene consists of a set of *represented classes* and *represented properties*[3] mapped to the *common ontology*. For *theGoal* it consists of three parts: a thing *theGoal* belongs to, *theGoal* as a *complex* property, and *theGoal* as a *law property*.

(1) Thing *theGoal* **belongs to:** Both *GRL.goal* and *KAOS.goal* describe the intentions of some BWW thing that wishes the goal would become true. In GRL this thing is identified as the **actor** who holds *theGoal*[4]. The **actor** can also *hold a task*, which could be seen as a solution describing how *theGoal* is fulfilled (ITU, 2003). *Actor* is mapped to the *active thing* class in the common ontology. A KAOS *goal* has an optional attribute **goal owner** that describes the stakeholder who identified and argued for the *goal*. A **goal owner** is mapped to the *stakeholder thing* class, which describes more specifically a general *human thing* class in the common ontology. *Goal* fulfilment is described through the *assignment* to a responsible *agent* who performs *operation operationalising* this *goal*.

(2) *theGoal* **as a complex property:** *Complex property* is a BWW property that has sub-properties. GRL *goal* and KAOS *goal* are complex properties because they are characterised by different attributes that all are *any regular properties* in the BWW model. Attributes for GRL *goal* include **name**, **description**, and **evaluation**. KAOS *goal* is described by **name**, **def**, **formalSpec**, **priority** and **category**.

(3) *theGoal* **as a law property:** *Law* is a property "that restricts values that other properties can have" (Opdahl and Henderson-Sellers 2004, 2005). *Goal* expresses constraints on the possible states of a thing, which might be either the proposed system, the entire organisation or a particular actor. Therefore it is mapped to *component thing*, the least general BWW concept that matches all three. But in GRL there is no construct that indicates what this thing is. We describe it as the **thingGoalIsAbout**.

---

3 Represented classes and properties are an indirection level in the UEML template to account for the many-to-many relationship between constructs and concepts in the common ontology.
4 In the graphical syntax of GRL, the goal is situated inside the actor boundary.

In KAOS "goals concern objects" (van Lamsweerde, 2003). It means that *theGoal* restricts the possible values for the ***attribute***s of the ***concerned objects***. Consistently, a ***concerned object*** is mapped to *component thing* and ***attribute*** is mapped to *any property*. Explicit and implicit attributes are distinguished. Explicit attributes (***concExplicitObjAttribute***) are known to the analyst and referenced in *KAOS.goal's **def*** attribute. Implicit attributes (***concImplicitObjAttribute***) are not defined in *goal's **def*** and thus left implicit in ***def's*** reference to the ***concerned object***. Both explicit and implicit attributes are *any properties*.

KAOS *goal* subtypes – *maintain goal, achieve goal, avoid goal,* and *cease goal* – refine the ontological grounding of their supertype by indicating which kind of *law theGoal* is. *Maintain goals* (resp. *avoid goals*) are *state laws*, indicating the allowable (resp. forbidden) states that ***concerned objects*** can be in. An *achieve goal* (resp. *cease goal*) indicates that a change is required between a state where the ***concerned objects'*** properties are false (resp. true) and one where both are true (resp. false). In the BWW model this is a *transformation law*.

4.2. Comparing GRL and KAOS

Table 1 lists correspondences between GRL- and KAOS-constructs, showing the primary mapping to the ontology, i.e., the dominant ontological concept in the scene, but restricted to the class and property entry for space reasons. A "+" correspondence indicates that two constructs of different languages map to similar scenes as it is shown in section 4.1 for *goal*. Similar scenes are defined for *GRL.goal* and *KAOS.goal* (and also *KAOS.requirement* and *KAOS.expectation*); *GRL.actor* and *KAOS.agent* (and also *KAOS.environment agent* and *KAOS.software agent*); *GRL.softgoal* and *KAOS.softgoal*; *GRL.task* and *KAOS.operation*; *GRL.belief* and *KAOS.domain property*; and *GRL.means-ends* and *KAOS.operationalisation*.

BWW concept	GRL interpretation		KAOS interpretation	
	Represented class/property	Mapping to the common ontology	Represented class/property	Mapping to the common ontology
theGoal belongs to a thing	***Actor***	*Active thing*	***Goal owner***	*Stakeholder thing*
theGoal as a complex property	*theGoal* attributes are ***Name***, ***Description***, and ***Evaluation***.	*Any regular properties*	*theGoal* attributes are ***Name***, ***Def***, ***Priority***, ***Category***, and ***FormalDef***.	*Any regular properties*
theGoal as a law property	*theGoal* is about ***thingGoalIsAbout***	*Component thing*	*theGoal* concerns ***Concerned object*** through *** concImplicitObjAttribute***	*Component thing,* *Any property*
			theGoal concerns ***attribute*** through *** concExplicitObjAttribute***	*Any property,* *Any property*

Table 1. *Comparison of theGoal for GRL and KAOS*

A "+/-" correspondence indicates some semantic similarities and some differences between two constructs. For example, *GRL.decomposition* is "the ability to define what other elements need to be achieved or available in order for a task to perform" (ITU, 2003). KAOS *domain conditions* (*domPre* and *domPost*) "capture the elementary state transitions defined by operation applications in the domain" and *required conditions* (*reqPre, reqPost,* and *reqTrig*) "capture additional strengthening to ensure that the goals are met" (Letier, 2001; van Lamsweerde, 2003). The definitions are related, but KAOS conditions (1) are much more fine-grained and (2) are not constructs but attributes of *operationalisation* and *operation*. This also applies to *GRL.attribute link* and *KAOS control, monitor, input,* and *output* constructs; *GRL.conflict* and *KAOS.conflict; GRL.dependency* and *KAOS.dependency; actor holds goal* in GRL and *KAOS.assignment; actor holds task* in GRL and *KAOS.performance*.

A "-" correspondence means that a construct in one language has no corresponding construct in the other. Examples are the GRL-constructs *contribution* and *correlation* (between softgoals and tasks) and *non-intentional element*[5] and the KAOS-constructs *boundary condition* and *event* constructs.

As for behaviour, only *KAOS-operation* is described as *process* and *KAOS-event* as *event*. All other KAOS and GRL constructs are described as *existence*. As for instantiation level, all GRL-constructs and most KAOS-constructs cover both levels (type *and* instance). Exceptions are the KAOS-constructs *operation, event, performance, input,* and *output*, which cover the type-level only.

GRL		KAOS		Comparison
Constructs	Primary class/ property	Constructs	Primary class/ property	
		Agent	Active component thing	+
Actor	Active thing	Environment agent	Active component thing	+
		Software agent	Software component thing	+
		Goal	Complex law	+
		Requirement	Complex law	+
		Expectation	Complex law	+
Goal	Complex law	Achieve goal	Transformation law	+/-
		Avoid goal	State law	+/-
		Cease goal	Transformation law	+/-
		Maintain goal	State law	+/-
Softgoal	Complex law	Softgoal	Complex law	+
Goal.evaluation= conflict*	/////////	Conflict	Mutual	+/-
		Boundary condition	State law	-
Task	Transformation law	Operation	Transformation law	+
/////////	/////////	Event	Changing thing	-
Belief	State law	Domain property	State law	+
Resource	Acted on thing	Object model*	-	-
Means-ends	Complex mutual	Operationalisation	Complex mutual	+
Dependency	Complex law	Dependency*	/////////	+/-

5 But we should note that this analysis omits the investigation of the KAOS object model, which is typically used to model static non-intentional information.

Contribution (between softgoals)	Complex mutual	G-refinement	Complex mutual	+/-
				+/-
Correlation (between softgoals)	Complex mutual			
Decomposition** (between goals)				+/-
Contribution (between softgoal and task)	Complex mutual			-
Correlation (between softgoal and task)	Complex mutual			-
Decomposition (between task and other elements)	Law	Domain and required conditions*		+/-
Actor holds task*		Performance	Complex mutual	+/-
Actor holds goal*		Assignment	Complex mutual	+/-
Actor holds softgoal*				-
Actor holds resource*				-
Non-intentional element*		Object model*		-
		Object	Component thing	+/-
Attribute link*		Control	Binding mutual	+/-
		Monitor	Binding mutual	+/-
		Input	Binding mutual	+/-
		Output	Binding mutual	+/-

* – not language construct;

** – *decomposition between goals* is defined only for purpose of convenience in GRL.

Table 2. *Comparing GRL and KAOS constructs*

5. Discussion

This section focuses on comparison and integration of goal-oriented languages. An initial evaluation of the UEML approach is presented elsewhere (Opdahl, 2006).

Kavakli and Loucopoulos (2005) examine 15 goal-oriented languages and classify them along four dimensions: "usage" (what RE activity does goal modelling contribute to?), "subject" (what is the nature of goals?), "representation" (how are goals expressed?) and "development" (how are goal models developed and used?). Taken separately, each language tends to focus only on one "usage". At the "subject" level, approaches use different definitions and categories of goals. At the "representation" level, approaches come with their own specific syntax, semantics and degree of formality. The survey shows that (1) the research area is fragmented; but (2) "contributions from different frameworks seem to complement each other". The authors argue for more integration efforts to "obtain a stronger framework that takes advantage of the many streams of goal-oriented research" (Kavakli and Loucopoulos, 2005). Elsewhere Kavakli (2002) proposes integration at the "usage" level through unifying goal method meta-model. Our work focuses on the "subject" and "representation" levels, supporting integration on the semantic level.

Regev and Wegmann (2005) compared various goal and related concepts found in KAOS, GBRAM and GRL. The authors provide theoretically grounded definitions of the key constructs and interrelations between them, based on the concept of *regulation* borrowed from the system theory. Further, the authors suggest formalisation of constructs using the BWW model. The present work might thus benefit from being aligned with Regev and Wegmann's (2005) definitions.

Integration of goal-oriented languages with other approaches has been addressed by several authors. Anton *et al.* (1994) combine goals with scenarios to improve business process re-engineering. Liu and Yu (2004) use GRL models to guide the design based on scenarios (use case maps). van Lamsweerde and Willemet (1998) describe a process for inferring formal KAOS requirements from scenario descriptions. These works link approaches, but do not integrate them syntactically or semantically. Mylopoulos *et al.* (2001) address GRL models in UML using stereotyped classes, associations and tags. Heaven and Finkelstein (2004) embed KAOS into UML. Goal model definition using UML profiles allows combination of requirements and design models; but first, the problems of the UML semantic consistency should be solved. But none of the approaches to integrate goal-oriented and other languages uses ontological grounding to define explicitly language syntax and semantics. Thus, language integration or combination is performed in ad-hoc or informal way.

6. Conclusions and future work

Two goal-oriented languages – GRL and KAOS – were mapped to the BWW model using the UEML approach and then analysed and compared. The paper shows that it is difficult to compare these languages at the syntactic and semantic levels. Firstly, neither language maintains a meta-model for abstract syntax. They use different concrete syntax presentations, too. Secondly, language semantics is not precisely defined in the source publications. The paper shows how the two languages can be compared using the UEML approach. It also suggests a more precise semantics for language constructs by mapping them onto the common ontology. The results point towards automated translations between GRL and KAOS models based on semantic correspondences between their modelling constructs and, eventually, to integrating the two languages. For example, this could substantially improve the traceability between different RE stages: GRL may be used for early requirements elicitation and KAOS for late requirements specification (Kavakli and Loucopoulos, 2005).

Further work includes analysis of other goal-oriented languages. This could serve as a basis for creating a unique, integrated, expressively complete goal-modelling language and/or to devising semantic-preserving model transformations, consistency rules or view synchronisation mechanisms across language boundaries. Currently a prototype tool, UEMLBase, is under development. It helps automating the UEML approach for defining and for finding common integration points based on the mappings. The tool will also help future negotiation of construct definitions made by different (groups of) researchers in order to reach consensus and include these constructs in UEML version 2.

7. Acknowledgements

The authors would like to thank all the participants involved in the UEML work in the InterOP Network of Excellence, IST-508011.

8. References

Anton A. I., McCracken W. M., Potts C., "Goal Decomposition and Scenario Analysis in Business Process Reengineering", *Proceedings of the 6th International conference on Advanced Information Systems Engineering, CAiSE'94*, Springer-Verlag New York, Inc., 1994, p. 94–104.

Anton A. I., "Goal-based Requirements Analysis", *Proceedings of the 2nd International Conference on Requirements Engineering, ICRE'96*, IEEE Computer Society, 1996, p. 136–144.

Berio G., Opdahl A., Anaya V., Dassisti M., Panetto H., Wohed P., Baïna S. *et al.*, Deliverable DEM1: UEML 2.1. November 2005, www.interop-noe.org.

Bresciani P., Perini A., Giorgini P., Giunchiglia F., Mylopoulos J., "Tropos: An Agent-oriented Software Development Methodology". *Autonomous Agents and Multi-Agent Systems*, 8(3), 2004, p. 203–236.

Bunge M., *Ontology I: The Furniture of the World*, Treatise on Basic Philosophy, vol. 3. Reidel, Boston, 1977.

Bunge M., *Ontology II: A World of Systems*. Treatise on Basic Philosophy, vol. 4. Reidel, Boston, 1979.

Chung K. L., Nixon B., Mylopoulos J., Yu E., *Non-Functional Requirements in Software Engineering*, Kluwer Academic Publishers, Boston, 2000.

Dallons G., Heymans P., Pollet I., "A Template-based Analysis of GRL", *Proceedings of the 10th International Workshop on Exploring Modeling Methods in Systems Analysis and Design*, EMMSAD'05, Porto, 2005. FEUP Edicoes, p. 493–504.

Heaven W., Finkelstein A., "UML Profile to Support Requirements Engineering with KAOS", *IEE Proceedings - Software*, 151(1), 2004, p. 10–27.

ITU. Recommendation Z.151 (GRL) – Version 3.0, September 2003.

Kavakli E., Loucopoulos P., "Goal Modeling in Requirements Engineering: Analysis and Critique of Current Methods", Krogstie J., Halpin T., Siau K. (eds), *Information Modeling Methods and Methodologies (Adv. Topics of Database Research)*, Idea Group Publishing, 2005, p. 102–124.

Kavakli E., "Goal-oriented Requirements Engineering: A Unifying Framework", *Requirements Engineering Journal*, 6(4), 2002, p. 237–251.

van Lamsweerde A., Willemet L., "Inferring Declarative Requirements Specifications from Operational Scenarios", *IEEE Transactions on Software Engineering*, 24(12), 1998, p. 1089–1114.

van Lamsweerde A., The KAOS Meta-model: Ten Years After. Technical report, Universite Catholique de Louvain, 1993.

Letier E., *Reasoning about Agents in Goal-Oriented Requirements Engineering*. PhD thesis, Universite Catholique de Louvain, 2001.

Liu L., Yu E., "Designing Information Systems in Social Context: A Goal and Scenario Modelling Approach". *Journal of Information Systems*, 29(2), 2004, p. 187–203.

Mylopoulos J., Kolp M., Castro J., "UML for Agent-oriented Development: The Tropos Proposal", *Proc. 4th Int. Conf. on The Unified Modeling Language, Modeling Languages, Concepts, and Tools*, Lecture Notes in Computer Science; vol. 2185, 2001, p. 422–441.

Opdahl A. L., Henderson-Sellers B., "A Template for Defining Enterprise Modelling Constructs", *Journal of Database Management (JDM)*, 15(2), 2004, p. 39–73.

Opdahl A. L., Henderson-Sellers B. "A Unified Modelling Language without Referential Redundancy", *Data and Knowledge Engineering (DKE)*, 55(3), 2005, p. 277–300.

Opdahl, A. L., "The UEML Approach to Modelling Construct Definition", *Proc. I-ESA'06*, Bordeaux, France, May 2006.

Regev G., Wegmann A., "Where do Goals Come From: The Underlying Principles of Goal-oriented Requirements Engineering", *Proc. IEEE RE'05*, Paris, France, August 2005.

Regev G., *A Systemic Paradigm for Early IT System Requirements Based on Regulation Principles: The Lightswitch Approach*, PhD thesis, Swiss Federal Institute of Technology (EPFL), August 2003.

Wand Y., Weber R., "On the Ontological Expressiveness of Information Systems Analysis and Design Grammars", *Journal of Information Systems*, 3, 1993, p. 217–237.

Wand Y., Weber R., "On the Deep Structure of Information Systems", *Journal of Information Systems*, 5, 1995, p. 203–223.

Yu E., "Towards Modeling and Reasoning Support for Early-phase Requirements Engineering", *Proceedings of the 3rd IEEE International Symposium on Requirements Engineering, RE'97*, IEEE Computer Society, 1997.

Session 2:
Ontologies for Applications Interoperability

A Multi-Views Business Process Ontology for Flexible Collaboration

Razika Driouche* — **Zizette Boufaïda*** — **Fabrice Kordon****

*Lire Laboratory, Department of Computer Science, Mentouri University of Constantine, 25000, Algeria

driouchera@yahoo.fr

boufaida@hotmail.com

**Lip6 Laboratory, Pierre & Marie Curie University, 4 Place Jussieu, 75252, Paris Cedex 05 France

Fabrice.Kordon@Lip6.fr

ABSTRACT: *New forms of cooperation like collaborative business scenarios require flexible and semantic integration of heterogeneous processes come from various companies. Heterogeneity cross-organisational business processes needs adaptation of existing concepts for business process management. A shared ontology can encapsulate heterogeneity in business process model and offer common concepts to different partners. In this paper, an ontology based approach is proposed that shows how to integrate business processes using service ontologies and Web services composition. It combines both ontologies and Web services in order to address the processes integration problem.*

RÉSUMÉ : *Les nouvelles formes de la coopération comme les scénarios de collaboration commerciale requiert une intégration flexible et sémantique des processus hétérogènes proviennent de différentes compagnies. L'hétérogénéité des processus métiers nécessite une adaptation des concepts existants pour leur gestion. Une ontologie partagée peut encapsuler l'hétérogénéité des processus et offrir des concepts commun aux partenaires. Dans ce papier, une approche basée ontologie est proposée pour montrer l'intégration des processus par les ontologies des services et la composition de Web services. L'approche combine ces technologies pour maîtriser le problème d'intégration des processus métiers.*

KEY WORDS: *EAI, Business Process, Service Ontology, Web Service, Orchestration, Business Collaboration.*

1. Introduction

A new technology called EAI (Enterprise Application Integration) has emerged as a field of enterprise integration. In essence, EAI provides tools to interconnect multiple and heterogeneous enterprise application systems such as CRM (Customer Relationship Management), SCM (Supply Chain Management), ERP (Enterprise Resource Planning) and legacy systems. The most difficulty of this interconnection is due to the fact that the integrated systems were never designed to work together (Linthicum 2003), (Izza *et al.,* 2005).

Collaboration of heterogeneous partners leads to the interoperability issue (Panetto *et al.,* 2004), which represents a major barrier in the business sector. Obstacles to heterogeneity arise from the fact that partners do not share the same semantics for the terminology of their business process models. Moreover, they use various collaboration scenarios with different organizational constraints. In addition, the growing heterogeneity of standards for information interchange implies that no partner has enough power to impose their standard. So, semantic heterogeneity occurs because there is a disagreement about the meaning, i.e. inconsistent interpretation. In the semantic Web, ontologies are often seen as new solutions providing semantically enriched information exchange facilities (Gruber 1993). They provide a common terminology that captures key distinctions in business domain.

The field of investigation is referred to as collaborative business between partners. It describes the internet based interlinked collaboration of all participants in an added value network from the raw material supplier to the end consumer (Scheer *et al.,* 2003). It allows a comprehensive information exchange between employees and even between companies. For instance, in a collaborative fulfilment process different partners cooperate to fulfil a customer order (e.g. for assembling a PC) according to a specified delivery time and other quality constraints. Other examples include treatment of a patient by different physicians and hospitals or a travel-booking process containing several services for booking a flight, hotel, etc. Ensuring that such process is challenging due to the high degree of heterogeneity of the collaboration partners. It implies achieving a business process execution which is affected by various quality characteristics such as response time, cost and constraints on I/O parameters (e.g., price limits, product configuration or delivery deadlines).

This paper is an overview of the proposed approach for building the business process ontology. The latter serves as an interoperable infrastructure for partner business collaboration. The approach combines both ontologies and Web services in order to address the process integration problem. Ontologies offer the semantic aspects to model common business terminology, which save the business context for each partner in its service ontology. Web services composition gives a support to orchestrate the business process execution.

The paper is organised as follows. Section 2 outlines some important related works. Section 3 describes the business process modelling views. Section 4 gives more detail of the approach. The latter focuses on service ontology building and business process integration scenario. Finally, section 5 discusses conclusion and future work.

2. Related works

Web services are defined as an application providing data and services to other applications through the Internet (Alonso *et al.,* 2004) (Dogac 2004). They can be deployed inside (EAI) or outside (B2B) the enterprise. They are published with appropriate URL by their provider over the Internet or intranet. Once published, these Web services are accessible by their consumers via Web standards such as SOAP (Simple Object Access Protocol), WSDL (Web Service Description Language) and UDDI (Universal Description, Discovery and Integration) (Alonso *et al.,* 2004). In addition, Web services can be used for integrating applications and processes via standards such as BPEL (Business Process Execution Language) and WSFL (Web Service Flow Language) (Holfreiter *et al.,* 2003).

In the EAI domain, Web services take the role of an EAI bus to which all applications connect (Linthicum 2003). Today, some new integration products based on Web services such as Cape Clear, XML Global, Colloxa, BPWS4J (BPEL4WS Java Runtime), etc. (Acharya 2003). Even, if Web Services are promising in solving the integration problem, they do not correctly address the semantic aspect supported by UDDI registries with the help of some standards, like NAICS (North American Industrial Classification Scheme) (Dogac 2004) and UNSPSC (UNiversal Standard Products and Services Classification) (Owl 2003). This inconvenient is mainly due to the lack of service ontology in current Web services (Alonso *et al.,* 2004).

Ontologies could be key elements in many applications such as semantic integration, web-services search and composition, and web site management for organization and navigation (Gahleitner *et al.,* 2004). Researchers do also believe that ontologies will contribute to solve the problem of interoperability between software applications across different organisations (Albani *et al.,* 2005), providing a shared understanding of common domains. Ontologies allow applications to agree on the terms that they use when communicating. Thus, ontologies shared among interoperating applications, allow the exchange of data to take place not only at a syntactic level, but also at a semantic level.

In the context of data integration, there are many works using ontology based approaches such as COIN (COntext INterchange) project (Goh 1997), OBSERVER (Ontology Based System Enhanced with Relationships for Vocabulary hEterogeneity Resolution) project (Mena *et al.,* 1996), TSIMMIS (Hammer *et al.,* 1995), Information Manifold (Levy *et al.,* 1996) and so on. These works are not concerned about the Web services flexible support.

Other works that are addressing the Web Services viewpoint such as SODIA from IBHIS project (Turner *et al.,* 2004) that implement federated database systems in the context of Web services. Fujitsu has introduced Web services integration technology for the BPM (Business Process Management) for visualizing, improving and executing new or existing processes in real-time (Nakagawa 2004). These works lack semantic aspect.

In the context of application and process integration, some important initiatives that aim to bridge the gap between Web services and ontologies. OWL-S (Martin *et al.,* 2003) provides an ontology markup language in order to semantically describe capabilities and properties of Web services. BPML (Holfreiter *et al.,* 2003) and BPEL (Alonso *et al.,* 2004) are standards providing languages to model and execute business processes in application integration context. Artemis (Dogac *et al.,* 2004) project provide framework to support the concept of semantic WS in the healthcare domain. The ESSI WSMO working group, part of the ESSI cluster aligns the research and development efforts in semantic Web Services between the SEKT, DIP Knowledge Web and ASG research projects. This group aims at developing a language called WSML (Web Service Modeling Language) that formalizes the WSMO (Web Service Modeling Ontology) (Roman *et al.,* 2004). The proposed approach takes some of the best ideas emerged from these works to apply in business collaboration domain. Our work differs in two aspects. First, it does not concentrate only on flexibility in composition of Web Services, but it evenly considers organizational aspects in process definition. Second, it focuses on services similarities in interface, behaviour and quality.

3. Business process multi-views model

Compared to traditional business processes, the complexity of interorganisational processes has risen considerably as a result of the strategic, structural and cultural differences between the partners (Sven *et al.,* 2004). The allocation of performances and resources of the business partners, the determination of responsibilities for materiel and financial exchange relationships as well as the information and data exchange over interfaces have to be planned and coordinated. Thus, the demands on BPM increase (Linthicum 2003). Finding consensus between the different partners is considerably facilitated by a general approach. It encompasses the common model of a collaborative business process.

On purpose of process modelling, the model takes into account: the process profile description, specifying what the process does and how to invoke its functionalities; and the process requester perspective, associated to a particular partner profile and operating in a business context with special organizational constraints that specifies which collaboration scenario is required. The model considers business collaboration, functional, organizational and technical aspects.

Business collaboration view defines the choreography of the business collaboration and structures the business information exchanged. A business collaboration is performed by two (binary collaboration) or more (multi-party collaboration) partners. It might be complex involving a lot of services between business partners. However, the most basic collaboration is a binary one realized by a request from one side and a response from the other side.

Functional view describes the business process profile. It shows the process structure: the sets of services, I/O parameters, execution order and participated partners.

The fundamental principle of the organisational view is to collect information about partners and organizational constraints in order to specify the business context. For this purpose, the business process must be defined in the exact business context. This means, an enterprise describes a process exactly as it is executed in its organisation and not in any other company.

Technical view monitors the process execution basing on partners goals. The control flow is the most important aspect for describing a business process. The collaborative partners have to continuously compare the results of the execution with their goals and adjust deviations by handling exceptions.

In our approach, functional aspects are used to organize processes into the business process ontology and to permit process discovery on the basis of partner needs. Organisational aspects are exploited to give the appropriate business context and further improve the process execution according to the business collaboration scenario and control aspect in technical view.

4. Overview of the approach

In our approach, each partner considers their part in the inter-enterprises process. A possibility to reduce complexity and to focus on special aspects is the use of different views like business collaboration, functional, organisational and technical.

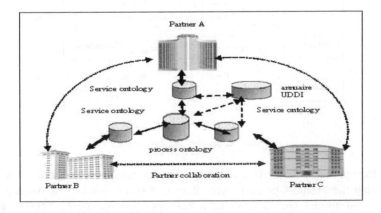

Figure 1. *System architecture*

In the system, several types of legacy, client/server and Web applications are identified. They are developed using different programming languages. They work on different operating system platforms and use various format for the exchange of data. Services (local) ontologies can enhance business collaboration between partners, for the benefit of processes integration. Hence, the integration system aims at offering a support for integrating heterogeneous and distributed systems, accessing multiple ontologies published in the private UDDI registry (Figure 1). It permits an appropriate exchange of information between partners and generates the process (shared) ontology based on dynamic composition of services.

4.1. Service ontology design

A service is mainly described by a set of operations and I/O parameters providing the service interface description. Pre and post-conditions are stated on each single operation and on the whole service. They are logical expressions on I/O entities. They must be verified before the execution of an operation or of the service and that are satisfied after the execution respectively. For example, a selling service may require as a precondition a valid credit card and as input the credit card number and expiration date. As output, it generates a receipt and as post condition the card is charged. Further characterization of service regards the order in which the operations are to be performed. Then, what messages the service reacts and what messages the service produces. Moreover, services maintain relations between them such as semantic one (synonymy, specialization, aggregation...) and conjuncture one (localization, composition, exchange...). For each service, some properties are identified (location,). These aspects are represented in the model by means of UML class diagram (Alonso *et al.,* 2004).

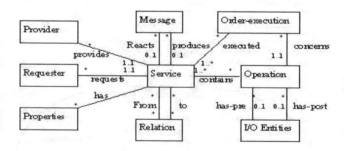

Figure 2. *Service ontology model*

In the approach, the service ontology aims to define the semantic of services composing the business process. According to Gruber, ontology is defined as an explicit and formal specification of a conceptualization (Gruber 1993). In the context of business integration, two fundamental approaches can be selected to achieve semantic integration: shared (global) ontology and non-shared (local) ontology approach (Gahleitner *et al.,* 2004). In our work, we combine the two approaches and generate the shared ontology using mapping process (Gahleitner *et al.,* 2004). In the service ontology, three types of service are introduced.

Atomic service. It is an elementary service directly invocable. That is the description of the service proposed by the provider. It is described in terms of interface (input, output, operations, error parameter and message types), behavior, quality and implementation properties. In our ontology, we study the description of atomic services to establish semantic relations between them and to group them into sets (cluster) of similar services.

Composite service. It represents a cluster of similar atomic services. It is classed based on the service business domain. This is generally appropriate within large and complex enterprises with several different business domains (production, marketing). Three kinds of relation between composite services are considered, the *is-similar* relation that holds when a composite service has the same operations of another one. The *is-equivalent* relation is maintained when the two services have the same preconditions, inputs, operations, outputs and postconditions. The *is-part* relation is viewed when a composite service includes the other.

Domain services. It is a composite service enriched with organizational properties. They are augmented with information about provider/requester partners, time availability, causality constraints, synchronisation and the objects they manipulate: resource, inventory, orders and products. Three kinds of relation between domain services are considered, the *has-same* relation, that holds when a domain service has the same business domain of another one, and *is-complement* that is obtained when the execution of a domain service implies the execution of the other. The *is-independent* relation shows that the two services are disjoint.

According to the presented service model, a methodology is developed to build service ontology, articulated in three phases.

4.1.1. *Service description and comparison*

In this work, WSDL language (Alonso *et al.,* 2004) is used to represent the structure of Web services in terms of interface, behavior and quality properties. In this phase, atomic services are compared on the basis of their properties to evaluate their similarity according to properly defined similarity criteria. Semantic relationships are established among them on the basis of the performed similarity computation. Two atomic services are grouped in the same cluster when the weight of semantic relationships connecting them is greater than a given threshold.

4.1.2. *Service mapping and inferencing*

To perform a semantic analysis of services on the basis of their own properties. A multi-strategy process is adopted, which computes similarities between entities using different algorithms. Using just one approach is unlikely to achieve as many good mapping candidates as one the combination of several approaches. There are:

– Interface similarity. The service interface includes the I/O entities, operations and message types. To perform a semantic analysis of service interface, three types of entities similarity are distinguished. For each type, domain experts affect a value in the interval [0.1].

- *I/O similarity* refers to the evaluation of the input/output information entities names of the two services. Lexical ontologies such as WordNet or domain specific thesauri are used to define terminological relationships (e.g. synonym and the antonym) for acquiring similarity (Gahleitner *et al.,* 2004).
- *Operation similarity* refers to the evaluation of the operations of the two services by comparing their names, their input/output information entities based on WordNet or domain specific thesauri.
- *Message similarity* focuses on the message type to measure similarity. Two services having the same type of received (resp. sent) messages are similar.

Finally, the global interface similarity for each pair of services is evaluated by taking a weighted sum of I/O, operation and message similarities. Only services where similarity is greater than 0.5 are taking into account.

– Behaviour similarity. Concerns the evaluation of sets of operations for services. A service is defined as a vector S with N dimension:

$$S= (O_1, O_2, ..., O_N)$$

$\forall\ i \in \{1, 2, ..., N\}/\ O_i$ is an operation of service S.

The behavior similarity relies on the idea of semantic bridge concept [8], which means for each source operation in the first vector there is a target operation in the second one. Given two services S_i and S_j, operation o_{ik} of service S_i is bridged to operation o_{jh} of service S_j if:

  - o_{ik} and o_{jh} has the same name;
  - o_{ik} and o_{jh} has the same I/O parameters;
  - o_{ik} and o_{jh} has preconditions (resp. postcondition) logically equivalent.
That is mean, the two operations are equivalent.
We can now extend the definition of semantic bridge to service. Two services are bridged if there is a bijective relation between their associated vectors.

– Quality similarity. Each service is characterized by a set of quality parameters provided by available classification standard (for example, ISO 9000 STANDARD). Some services may be very good, reliable and quick to respond; others may be unreliable, sluggish, or even malevolent. Specific application dependent quality parameters are considered (for example, the number of credit cards accepted by an on-line ticket reservation service). Each quality parameter is described by means of a name, a parameter type and a measure unit. The quality similarity is measured based on the domain expert evaluation based on user requirement, to identify if the constraint quality is mandatory or only desirable.

Inference mechanism is used when the service has not a similar service that means the service does not belong in any cluster.

4.1.3. *Service clustering and classifying*

The result of similarity-based description is set of clusters of similar services with defined similarity relationships. A hierarchical clustering algorithm [22] is used to determine clusters based on global similarity established among services. Some problems appear, when the service exists in many clusters. If the intersection of the clusters is not the empty set so, they should be amalgamated.

After the application of the three phases, the effort is concentrated on the suitability of the OWL DL, which is equivalent to the SHOQ(D) to formally describe the obtained ontology (Horrocks *et al.,* 2003). For checking, we need to use the inference services provided by the DL formalism for supporting the building process and improving our ontology quality. Many systems can be exploited such as FACT, DLP (Horrocks *et al.,* 2003) and RACER (Protégé 2005). The use of the RACER system can make possible to read OWL file and to convert it in the form of a DL knowledge bases. It can also provide inference services. To manipulate the application ontology, PROTEGE-OWL (Protégé 2005), version 3.1.1 offers a convivial graphical user interface. It permits to visualize and to edit the ontology hierarchical relations. So, we can exploit the ontology to enhance the service discovery.

4.2. Business process integration scenario

Collaborative processes are defined as the abstraction of complex business process involving different companies. They specify the interaction between Web services and their coordination. In this work, business processes are defined as a composition of domain services. Only, at the execution time for a given domain service, a composite services retrieved and invoked. If the needed service is not available then another similar service in the same cluster is invoked. For this purpose, a composition strategy is defined as follows:

A CS (Composition Strategy) of Web services is formally defined by:
CS= (S, R, C).
S: a set (S1, ..., Sn) of domain services.
R: a client service request.
C: a composition schema that fulfils R by suitably orchestrating (S1, ..., Sn).

For example, in the tourism agency, the reservation process needs several services orchestrated in this order: service for booking a flight, service for hotel reservation, service for car location and service for payment. The tourism agency collaborates with airlines companies, hotels, cars companies and banks to satisfy the customer request. For each service, the provider partner gives their constraints to execute it.

Begin

1- Give set of source services S-S = {S1, ..., Sn}basing on user request R;
2- T-S = ø /* empty target services set */
3- Repeat
    Identify for each target service the appropriate parameters
    T-S$_{i}$ ⟵ (S-S$_{i}$, Partner, data-constraint, input, treatment-constraint, output);
    Remove S-S$_{i}$ from S-S;
    Put T-S$_{i}$-target in T-S;
    Until S-S = ø /* empty source services set */
4- try to sort the services in T-S set in the execution order;
5- execute the set of target services;
6- handle exceptions;

End.

In the following, we present the processes integration scenario.

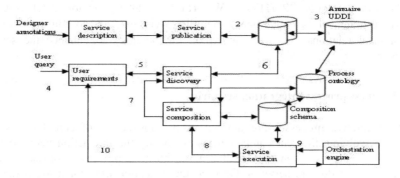

Figure 3. *Business Process Integration Scenario*

While the main component of our approach is enumerated, let's give now the scenario of the process integration. As shown in Figure 3, the integration scenario begins once the Web services have been described using the WSDL language (1). Then, they are published both in the service ontologies registries and in the UDDI registry (2, 3). Next, the user requirement is used to enhance the requested services (4). When the services are identified, they can be identified by service discovery. If a given service is not available at the execution time then another similar service in the same cluster is selected and invoked in the appropriate service ontology (5, 6). Once the needed services are discovered basing on a composition strategy to form business process using composition schema (7). In this approach, trace of each composition schema is kept in the repository to minimize response time. Once the set of desired services have been discovered, they are ordered according to specific strategy and executed under the control of the orchestration engine (8). The latter monitors the service execution and handles possible exceptions (9). Finally, the result is returned to the user (10).

5. Conclusion

This paper has focused on proposing an approach for EAI that exploits both ontology and Web services. This approach aims to build the service ontologies based on domain services, augmented with information about organizational aspects to keep business context for each partner. These ontologies are developed for supporting the design and execution of business processes using Web services composition strategy.

The important benefit of this work is that we provide transparency for the process execution. It bases on a multi-views process model to encircle the most aspects of business context. Moreover, the focus on service similarity can improve the response time where the invoked service is not available.

Future work will focus on the integration of the composition scenario with a collaborative one. The attention is related to the ebXML (Holfreiter *et al.*, 2003) collaboration scenario in order to offer an interoperable infrastructure for business collaboration. For service ontologies, some perspectives are addressed: (i) experimentation to validate the service ontology; (ii) using the framework MAFRA (Gahleitner *et al.*, 2004) to support the service ontologie integration; (iii) improving syntactic services similarities basing on semantic aspects.

6. References

Acharya R., "EAI: A business perspective", *eAI Journal*, www.bijonline.com, 2003.

Albani A., Dietz J., Zaha J., "Identifying business components on the basis of an enterprise ontology", *Interoperability of enterprise software and applications*, Geneva, 2005, Konstantas D., Bourrières J.-P., Léopard M., Boudlida N., edition, p. 335-347.

Alonso G., Casati F., Harumi K., Machiraju V., "Web services-concepts, architectures and applications", Berlin, Springer-Verlag, 2004.

Dogac A.,"Semantic Web Services", *Proceedings of International Conference on Web Engineering,*. 2004, Munich.

Dogac A., Laleci G., Kirbas S., Kabak Y., Sinir S., Yildiz A., Gurcan Y., "Artemis: deploying semantically enriched web services in the healthcare domain", http://www.ing.uinbs.it/~deantone/interdata_tema3/Artemis/artemis.html, 2004.

Gahleitner E., Wob W., "Enabling distribution and reuse of ontology mapping information for semantically enriched communication services", *15th International Workshop on Database and Expert Systems Applications,* IEEE Computer Science, 2004, Zaragoza, Spain.

Gruber R., "A Translation Approach to Portable Ontology Specification", *Knowledge Acquisition*, vol. 5, no. 2, 1993, p.199-220.

Hammer M., Garcia-Molina H., Ireland K., Papakonstantinou Y., Ullman J., Widon J., "Information Translation, Mediation and Mosaic-Based Browsing in the TSIMMIS System", *Proceedings of the ACM SIGMOD International Conference on Management of Data*, 1995, California, p. 483.

Holfreiter B., Huemer C., "Modeling Business Collaborations in Context", *Proceedings of on the Move to Meaningful Internet Systems OTM Workshops*, Springer-Verlag, 2003.

Horrocks I., Patel-Schneider P. F., Harmelen F. V., "From SHIQ and RDF to OWL: The making of a web ontology language", *Journal of Web Semantic*, vol. 1, no. 1, 2003, p. 7-26.

Izza S., Vincent L., Burlat P., "Unified Framework for Application Integration", 7th *International Conference on Enterprise Information Systems'05*, 2005, USA.

Jain A. K., Dubes R. C., *Algorithms for Clustering Data*, Prentice-Hall ,1988.

Levy Y. A., Rajaraman A., Ordille J. J., "Quering Heterogeneous Information Sources Using Descriptions", *Proceedings of Very Large Data Bases*, 1996, Bombay, India, p. 251-262.

Linthicum D., *Enterprise Application Integration*, Boston, Edition Addison-Wesley, 2003.

Martin D., Burstein M., Lassila O., Paolucci M., Payne T., Mcllraith S., "Describing web services using OWL-S and WSDL", http:// www.daml.org/services/owl-s/1.0/, 2003.

Mena E., Kashyap V., Sheth A., Illarramendi A., "OBSERVER: An Approach for Query Processing in Global Information Systems Based on Interoperability across Pre-existing Ontologies", *Proceedings 1st International Conference on Cooperative Information Systems*, 1996, Brussels, p.14-25.

Nakagawa M., "Business Process Management with Web-Service Integration Technology", *Fujitsu Science Technology Journal*, vol. 40, no.1, 2004, p. 17-21.

Panetto H., Scannapieco M., Zelm M., "INTEROP NoE: Interoperability research for networked enterprise application and software", *OTM Workshop*, Lecture Notes in Computer Science, vol. 3292, Springer-Verlag, 2004, Heidelberg R. Meersman *et al.* edition, Berlin, p. 866-882.

Protégé OWL, version 3.1.1. http://protege.stanford.edu/, 2005.

Sven Z., Anja H., Otmar A., "Cross Enterprise Business Process Management Architecture – Methods and Tools for Flexible Collaboration", *OTM Workshop*. Lecture Notes in Computer Science, vol. 3292, Springer-Verlag, 2004, Heidelberg R. Meersman *et al.* edition, Berlin, p. 483-494.

Scheer A.-W., Grieble O., Zang S., "Collaborative Business Management", *E-Collaboration-Prozessoptimierung in der Wertschöpfungskette*, Deutscher Universitäts, Verlag, Wiesbaden Kersten, W., edition, 2003, p. 29-57.

Chauvet J. M., *Web services avec SOAP, WSDL, UDDI, ebXML*, Eyrolles edition, 2002.

Roman D., Lausen H., Keller U., Oren E., Bussler C., Kifer M., Fensel D., "Web service modelling ontology", WSMO working draft, http://www.wsmo.org/2004/d2/v1.0/20040920/, 2004.

Session 3:
Collaborative and Networked
Enterprise Interoperability

1. Introduction

A *design principle* can be intended as an *axiom;* it expresses a fundamental truth which stands for evidence and can only be invalided by counter-examples. A *pattern,* instead, can be interpreted as a proven solution to a problem in a context: as a consequence each pattern is an elementary reference model relating a context, a problem and a solution at a given level of detail of the domain of reasoning. The level of detail considered in this work will correspond to the networked enterprise, which represents a special sub-set (or "chain") of enterprises, where each enterprise is considered as a basic interoperating units. This aggregated level will be addressed according to two fundamental approaches: the GRAI and the SCOR models. Both these approaches allow dealing with supply chain management and then can be used as a starting point for designing interoperability. The SCOR model, acronym of *Supply Chain Operations Reference model*, is a highly scalable standard for Supply chain Management; its aim is modelling supply-chain management systems. Therefore it can be easily extended to networked enterprise that always is comprehensive of the concept of supply chain. The SCOR model is based on five management processes (SCC, 1994): (1) *plan,* (2) *source,* (3) *make,* (4) *deliver* and (5) *return. Plan* category consists of processes allowing balancing aggregate demand and supply in order to efficiently satisfy sourcing, production and delivery requirements. *Source* processes model procure goods and services. *Make* processes allow the identification of all the activities for transforming product to a finished state. *Deliver* category consists of processes providing finished goods and services (i.e. order, transportation and distribution management). *Source, make* and *deliver* processes are modelled to meet planned or actual demand. The last processes (*return*) are associated with returning or receiving returned products for any reason; these processes extend into post-delivery customer support. SCOR model contains three levels of process detail. The first level includes the scope definition of the supply chain and the performance targets set by the analysis of the gaps with the competition performances. In the second level, the company is configuring its "as is" supply chain and the "to be" by implementing its operation strategies. The third level is used to define the process element, the process performance metrics and the best practices. The implementation level is not included in the SCOR model definition. Some approach as have been developed to assure interoperability based on SCOR, such as SPIDER-WIN (IST507 601). A common model template has been developed to support all information and requirements detected. The reference model was derived from SCOR: a unique open modelling template (process structure, interfaces and common naming) allowed to document requirements consistent across the different models. This application is more strictly related to the building of simulation models, and the decisional part was faced using a less structured interview approach (see SPIDER-WIN for detail), with respect to the one proposed here. The *GRAI* model (Vallespir *et al.,* 1993) consists of a grid (GRAI grid) representing a decision sub-system in terms of set of decisions allowing to control the physical sub-system. The two fundamental elements of a GRAI grid are:

a *vertical* axis and a horizontal one. The vertical axis is based on a temporal criterion (strategic, tactical, and operative), while the horizontal one is oriented to a functional decomposition criterion. Each box of the grid identifies a decision centre, defined as a set of decisions made within one function and one temporal level. The relationships among the decision centres are identified by simple information flows and decision links (decision frames containing decision objectives, decision variables, constraints and criteria). A valid model for an interoperable networked enterprise is the reference model called *Global Control Structure* (Ducq *et al.*, 2004). The main goal of this model, developed without considering interoperability issues, is to provide a reference model for an efficient and well-working networked enterprise chain. The challenge, here addressed, is the application of the *global control structure*, for interoperability design. This work has been performed within a subgroup of the INTEROP Network of Excellence named "Design Principles for Interoperability" (Chen *et al.*, 2004). The purpose of the paper is to contribute to the designing of interoperability at the design stage by providing some design principles, as few of the on-going research works are concerned with this topic.

2. Reference context

The design criteria proposed mainly refers to the concept of networked *enterprise*. A networked enterprise can be interpreted (Butera 1990, Micelli 2000) as a system of recognisable and multiple connections and structures among which some *"nodes"* operate, characterised by an high level of *auto-regulation* and *auto-control* (open vital systems) able to cooperate for pursuing common goals and shared results. Examples of networked enterprises, for instance, are sub-contracting organisations in terms of enterprises involved in an identified productive cycle, etc. All the involved actors within a networked enterprise are required to define common plans and/or use a common distribution network, but at the same time they still preserve their *individual autonomy*. This cooperating scenario represents an interesting opportunity for SMEs, since the cooperation allows them to exploit their complementary competences. The contractual strength is great for each actor and, at the same time, they have autonomy for managing their production activities. Autonomous decisions should be taken without being in competition with the plans of the networked enterprise. This organizational form is based on the need of *pooling knowledge and competencies* and joining different activities located in their own most suitable locations. A great degree of interoperability is required in such a context, where interoperability is intended as "the *ability* of *two or more entities (be they systems, units, forces, organizations, systems, processes) to operate effectively together for a common goal, by means of an interface (link). Interfaces (or links) consist of a temporary bilateral relationship characterised by several exchanges of entities having generic contents (data, information, material, services, products, etc.)*". The concept of networked enterprise includes the configuration of "chain" of enterprises, which belongs to the supply chain concept. The design principles presented in the next paragraph will allow deriving design parameters for the basic units of the networked enterprise. These units are here considered to be the *Fundamental interoperability units* (FIoU) (Dassisti *et al.,* 2004), differently from the classical design approaches focused on each single node of the network. The FIoU are made of two interoperating entities, tied using symbiosis channels (Veryard, 1994); these units are here used as basic building blocks of the networked enterprise in defining the reference meta-model (MMBU introduced in the next paragraphs). The main problem in assuring interoperability is that most of the enterprises participating in a networked enterprise operate independently; this fact might prevent enterprises to provide *the right products to the right customers at the right time* (Chidambaram *et al.,* 1999). As a result, even if all these organizations are individually efficient, the system as a whole will not operate as efficiently as possible. In networked enterprise there are many interfaces (links), such as the ones between customer and supplier: these interfaces represent a potential weak point for several reasons (non symmetric relationships; the Bullwhip effect; etc.). As a consequence of this, whenever a chain of enterprise fails, it usually happens due to the weakest links. The idea behind the work is the integration of SCOR and GRAI decisional modelling, presented in the previous paragraph, to identify the design criteria for each basic interoperating unit and their interface, to guarantee a correct functioning as a node of a networked enterprise. The final aim is the definition of a meta-model, general enough to be followed as a guide pattern whenever two organisations need to effectively co-operate. The combination of the SCOR and GRAI model allows the identification of complementary features and then the advantageous utilisation of their own strong features. In other words the SCOR model assures a global view, a standard vocabulary and standard process identification, while the GRAI model defines a more detailed level, the temporal planning and all those aspects not considered in the SCOR. The SCOR model does not include: Sales & Administration processes, Tech development processes, Product & Process design, Post delivery support processes and it indirectly refers to, but does not explicitly address, Training Quality Information Technology (IT) administration (non-SCM) ones. These lacking aspects can be covered by the use of GRAI model.

Let us summarise deeper. The reference design pattern, here developed by the combination of the SCOR model (concerning supply chain aspects), and the GRAI one (decision structure aspect). The general focus of the pattern proposed is the definition of some basic functions; these are identified according to the five SCOR management processes (source, make, plan, deliver, and return) and some additional functions not considered in SCOR. The expected result will be a general and complete model, where the Sales & Marketing, Design, Inventory and Quality functions are considered. At the global level, there are only the strategic and the tactical ones also, because the operational one will be considered at the local level. The grid, designed according to the above specified functions, can be considered as a general framework: the specific production processes (make to stock, make to order, engineering to order, etc) are in fact not included. This needs to be adapted (or instantiated) according to objectives and politics of the specific network considered.

3. Design principles and patterns for interoperability

The reference design pattern consists of a set of design principles here identified. These are based on the following axiom: "in the design process of a system it is possible, starting from the design solution found at a more aggregated level, to devise detailed design specifications of its components consistent with the overall system behaviour". This statement allows the designer to draw decisions at a higher level of abstraction, in a top-down fashion, thus maintaining the internal coherence of the system due to the global vision of the same. The design principles here addressed are mainly rules expressed in an axiomatic form. It is important to underline that the scope of the design patterns and the related meta-model described is to provide reference tools for guiding the designer. The two represent an ordered guide for taking right design decisions to assure interoperability of enterprises. Bearing in mind the premises provided in the reference context about the networked enterprise, the first step to be performed in designing interoperability is to clearly understand the position and the role of the enterprise within the set of enterprises. The first design principle thus descends:

First design principle: *"When designing interoperability for an organisation, evaluate its domain and boundaries of action inside the networked enterprise, identifying the necessary actors and the material and immaterial exchanges to be performed."* To state it better: *the designer should locate the enterprise inside the chain of relations among enterprises in a clear and well defined way, characterising the actors closely related to it and the related boundaries of its field of action.*

A clear identification of the interacting organisations within the networked enterprise is essential to the designer. The designer is thus required to identify the key points of co-operation, the core competencies to be developed, the necessary physical and informative infrastructures, etc. In other words the designer should identify the supplier-customer organisations to identify the FIoU entity. It is evident that this is a strictly decisional process, which greatly benefits from a modelling support form the GRAI scheme adopted. It is always mandatory to refer to a model, even if it is at a global level. The next design principle to be referred by designer is related to this latter point:

Second design principle: *"When designing an interoperable organisation, first of all define the global reference pattern of its networked enterprise. Interoperability descends by taking into account the behaviour of the network."* This principle implies that *the designer should constantly consider a reference pattern for interfaces and links. The model of the organisation descends coherently from the pattern considered.*

An example of global reference pattern for an interoperable networked enterprise is the *global control structure* (Ducq *et al.,* 2004). This pattern has been developed for providing a reference model for an efficient and well-working networked enterprise chain; the interoperability issues are not taken into account. To this aim SCOR features (concerning supply chain aspects) and GRAI ones (concerning decision aspects) have been considered together. The SCOR management processes (SOURCE, MAKE, PLAN, DELIVER, RETURN) are the basic functions of the model. Some additional functions (Sales & Marketing, Design, Inventory, Quality), not considered in the SCOR model, are also introduced for completeness. At the global level, there are only the strategic and the tactical level. To take into account the operational level it is necessary to go down toward a more detailed level. The expected result will be a *local model*, designed starting from the global level. It consists of two tactical levels and an operational one (Ducq *et al.*, 2004). The aim of the first two levels is to synchronise the global model with each node, ensuring the coherence of all decisions. The operational level is more related to operational issues: the function *"to manage resources"*, not present in the global pattern, aims to adapt the capacity (human and technical resources) of the nodes to the requirements of the networked enterprise. All the other functions, identified in the local level, are similar to the ones of the global pattern, but more detailed and concerning local decisional aspects of the member of the Networked enterprise (Ducq *et al.*, 2004). The strong statement made here is the following: if the global pattern aims to provide standard procedures for the global network, then each local entity manages itself with the same language, the same performance indicators and the same procedures of the global grid. All these aspects allow the organisation, participating to a Networked enterprise, to easily co-operate.

Let us recall the basic assumption of this work: "in order to better design interoperability, the reference meta-model must be not a model representing one organisation but a model representing two interoperating entities (the FIoU)". This model will be addressed, in the rest of the paper, as a *Meta-Model Basic Unit* (MMBU), because it can be seen as the elementary link unit of the networked enterprise chain. To provide a complete MMBU, it is necessary to integrate the global pattern into the local one: *the strategic level has been added to the local model* (Figure 1). Generally speaking, the strategic level presents the most theoretical aspects related to planning and definition activities (i.e. design, inventory, quality policies and business plan, etc.), whereas the operational one concerns the operative aspects (general scheduling, synchronisation of processes, scheduling of deliveries, etc.). Let us analyse the MMBU: it consists of *ten functions* (columns) and two other columns always present in the framework of a GRAI grid: the *External and Internal Information*. The External information deal with Benchmarking results, customer expectation and orders; the Internal ones deal with the mission, the vision, the global grid, the performance, etc.

	External information	Sales & Marketing SM	Design Des M	SOURCE SouM	Inventory IM	MAKE MM	PLAN PM	Resources ResM	DELIVER DelM	RETURNS RM	Quality QM	Internal information
Strategic	Benchmarking results, customer expectations, import-export requirements	Market analysis- Marketing strategy	To define design policies and design technologies	To identify partners roles & relationships	to define inventory policies	to define production plan (make or buy)	to define business plan	to define human and technical management strategies	to define deliver strategy and deliver partners	to define customer service plan	to define quality policies	Business rules, Budget objectives, Mission, Vision
Tactical LT	Firm orders, Firm partners, Potential partners	Local consolidated forecast	To plan design and technologies- Prototyping	to define procurements parameters. To negotiate local contract	to manage integrated inventory	To define local MPS	To implement working methodology and communication channels	To define human and technical investiments	to optimise transportations. To negotiate transportation contracts	to define local Customer Service Plan	General management review of quality policies	Global GRAI grid- suppliers performances
Tactical BT	new orders	To mangage form sales	to manage products and processes design	to evaluate critical procurements to manage unforecast situation	to plan stock taking	to define local work load	to optimise products flows	to balance the internal capacity	Monthly deliver planning	To analyse local customer opinions, claims, improvement opportunities	To define quality actions plan	Local performance information status of resources
Operational	new orders	to validate orders, to schedule delivery and customer	to follow up projects	to manage short term or last minute orders	to synchronise raw materials, semi-finished products and finished products	to schedule production	To syncronise all processes	Re-allocation of resources	To adjust delivery load and routing. To manage urgent delivers	to manage returned products and other customer requests	to manage quality actions	To collect performance information- Status of production system

Figure. 1. *Meta-model basic unit (MMBU).*

The ten functions make it possible to take into account the SCOR rules (SOURCE, MAKE, PLAN, DELIVER, RETURNS boxes) and all the implications related to the four temporal levels identified. The SCOR aspects are also detailed, by identifying some additional boxes: sales management, design management, inventory management, resources management, quality management. All these functions are detailed according to the four temporal levels identified. Finally it is possible to represent the informative flows and the decision frames (decision objective + decision variables + criteria +constraints) by arrows: different arrows allow distinguishing the informative flows from the decision frames. Figure 1 represents an example of informative flow (dashed lines) and decision frames (solid lines), even if all the informative flows and decision frames have been analysed in the MMBU. The next design principle results from this rationale:

Third design principle: *"In designing an interoperable organization, apply the meta-model basic unit (MMBU), to build the networked enterprise." The MMBU (figure 1) is a pattern, represented in a GRAI grid form, of two efficiently and effectively interoperating entities.*

At the same time it is necessary to model the organisation (one of the two local entities belonging to MMBU). The next design principle results from this rationale:

Fourth design principle: *"When designing an organization, build its aggregate decision-structure model. A useful tool for this goal is the GRAI grid." When elaborating a GRAI grid model pay attention to make clear and well defined the information and decision flows. Verify the consistency of the model using GRAI rules.*

A valid pattern for this model could be represented by the local control structure provided in (Ducq *et al.,* 2004). At this stage it is necessary to compare the MMBU and the local model and to verify their coherence. This step is a critical one, because the models of the two entities should be integrated within the meta-model provided. The next design principle results from this rationale:

Fifth design principle: *"In designing an organisation, after considering the meta-model basic unit and the organisation model, analyse the coherence between them." The general assumption - the meta-model basic unit is well-designed (according to the best-in-class tools) - implies that each organisation model, representing an instantiation of the meta-model, should assure the expected behaviour of the organisation within the network (coherence).*

It is quite difficult to have a local model strictly corresponding to the MMBU. Furthermore the MMBU should be *continuously* considered as a *guideline* during the design of any organisation model. For instance a local grid incoherent with MMBU is a grid without one of the five SCOR management processes because they are the core of this approach. The absence of the function "To Manage Customer service (RETURNS)", for example, implies a weak attention to customer needs. The next two design principles are also related to GRAI decision models. They are already proposed in (Chen *et al.,* 2005), but an appropriate statement is required for the approach proposed in this paper. The general commitment is to improve the *decisional interoperability* (that is a *"measure of capability to drive a good decision not only for the designer himself but also for his partners closely related*"). A good degree of decisional interoperability means that decision made by one designer does not pass beyond the limit of actions of other designers concerned by his decision).

Sixth design principle: *"When performing a decision activity, make its decisional frame explicit." A decisional frame contains a set of items which limits the freedom of decision-making; these items should be explicitly described.*

Making the decision frames explicit could be very useful in a design phase in order to clarify decision objectives, decision variables, constraints on variables and criteria. This principle aims to clearly define the boundaries of action of each decision and to improve decisional transparency of a decider.

Seventh design principle: *"Implement a mechanism to exchange decisional frames between deciders." Making decisional frame known by your collaborative decision-maker improves decisional interoperability.*

Building and filling a decisional frame is a *necessary condition but not a sufficient one* in order to have a good decisional interoperability, because it is desirable to exchange decision frames among the partners of interoperation. The designer should consider a specific mechanism allowing exchanging decision frames between decision makers. ERP software can be a good aid to this purpose. Another good tool to this goal is the pattern proposed in (Chen *et al.*, 2005), that allows analysing the decisional interoperability. It consists in drawing up a decisional frame pattern containing a decisional frame with some extra information (exactly the decision name and the decision level). For instance, in a manufacturing system it could be necessary to make a production overload decision: the decision frame pattern could be the following:

Decision name	Production overload decision
Decision level	Horizont:3 weeks Period:1 week
Decision objective	Minimise sub-contracting
Decision variable	Extra-hours and sub-contracting
Constraints	Extra-hours: <100h/week; sub-contracting: 200<h<500/week
Criteria	Minimise time

Table 1. *An example of decisional frame pattern*

The same pattern should be drawn up concerning the other interoperating system/s too and here it is the core of this approach: a transparent decision frame patterns among all the interoperating systems can be seen as a promising signal of decisional interoperability. In fact, a decision drawn by a decision maker has a significant *impact* on the decision made by another decision maker and vice-versa. At the same time all the decisions made often imply several decision making *iterations* to reach a satisfactory decision. The mutual knowledge of decision frames makes each decision be within the decisional space of all partners. The degree of freedom of a decision space is the one identified by the constraints on the variables.

The last design principle results from some points about the study of different GRAI interoperating models and from the experience of GRAI modellers. In the GRAI grid, on the vertical axis, there are two different quantities: the *horizon* (the interval of time over which the decision extends) and the *period* (the interval of time after which we reconsider the set of decisions). Let us consider, for instance, two interoperating organizations (A and B) exchanging decision frames concerning their MPS. The periods, considered by the two interoperating organisations, are different and A suddenly changes its MPS: a lot of inconsistencies result because B will check its MPS according to its own period and it could be late because the changes occurred in A could involve B too. A useful consideration for dealing with this particular situation is that the interoperating decision centres adopt the same horizon and in particular the same period. The last design principle to be adopted results from this rationale:

Eighth design principle: *"When designing and re-engineering an organization, pay particular attention to local decisional centres linked to the correspondent decisional centres of the other partners. A good solution could be using for linked decisional centres the same horizon but especially the same period."* It could ensure to avoid inconsistencies deriving from updated decisions of one interoperating partner.

4. Meta-model validation: an industrial case study

In this section an example of use of the meta-model proposed is presented. The case study adopted has allowed the validation of the meta-model at the analysis stage. The case study concerns an enterprise leader in the Murge (Puglia-Italy) sofa district. An interoperability analysis has been performed with and without the meta-model and the correspondent results have been compared. It often happens, especially during particular periods (i.e. Christmas holidays), that the company is required an overproduction which cannot be fulfilled by any of its own plants. This particular situation implies the necessity to turn to sub-contractors for fulfilling the excess demand and the insufficient productive rate. In particular, from eight to twelve weeks (according to the sofa models and clients positioning, production and transport times) before the established delivery date, the company compares available production capacity with the required one (according to information provided by Marketing and Sales domain). External enterprises will be "activated", when the available production capacity is less than the customer request. They are informed only the starting week of their job, than they receive a draft job concerning what they should perform. About two weeks before the production starting, the company planning manager send the production plans and technical schedules; finally, sub-contractor is weekly provided with raw materials. Let us consider the general system consisting of the company (system A) and its generic sub-contractor (system B), which is required to cooperate with Contempo Spa when an excess demand occurs. The application of the MMBU to the interoperability problem previously explained will be illustrated. The first step to be performed consists of a careful analysis of interoperability problem. Then the logical issue performed has been trying to consider and model the global reality (the company + sub-contractor) and representing it in only one model, as proposed in the FIoU and MMBU. The expected result has been the instantiation of MMBU for the case study. The word *instantiation* implies a different point of view on the matter: from the theoretical level to a real situation. In other words it has been necessary to recognise the existence (in this real interoperability problem) of the functions and the decision centres, according to the MMBU and the specific name of each identified decision centre in the case study and finally the functions and decision centres not represented in the MMBU. The result of this step has been two *AS-IS* instantiated models (one for the Contempo and the other one for sub-contractors). The next step performed has been the comparison between each model and the correspondent GRAI grid, resulted from a general analysis of Contempo and its generic sub-contractor considered independently. The two couples of grids represent the same reality even though they have been performed by different designers, so the modelling phase is characterised by a high degree of subjectivity. *On the contrary*, this comparative analysis has allowed deducing that our approach is useful for identifying a lot of decision centres already existing in the reality, even if they are not usually identified by traditional approach to Interoperability. In particular, MMBU manages to detect a lot of decision centres concerning interoperability issues: <Inventory agreements among partners>, <To optimise products flows among partners>, <To synchronise production processes> are only few examples. The main difference between the two models is related to the two different modelling logical bases. The MMBU approach is mainly based on supply chain modelling: the main focus is on collaborative aspects and agreements; while the usual modelling approach performs a visual analysis and considers the two entities separately. Moreover the MMBU approach is based on a standard (SCOR) and on careful studies performed by GRAI experts; consequently it guarantees a much higher level of completeness and detail.

As a conclusion it is possible to state that the MMBU approach can be considered a useful modelling guide, when an interoperability analysis has to be performed, because it allows designer to consider all decisional modelling aspects.

5. Conclusions

The approach, presented in this paper, allows the identification of several design principles for interoperability. A Meta model based on SCOR and GRAI model has been introduced. The focus has been on the high level of abstraction for studying organisation and decision interoperability in the context of networked enterprise. Using design principles to design interoperability, as a desired property at the design stage, is an alternative approach compared to holistic ones. The meta-model presented needs further refinements. An open question remains unsolved: how to evaluate ability to interoperate. In the near future it will be necessary to identify some performance indicators for assessing the proposed approach and the degree of interoperability reached. Further applications on real cases are also needed to induct new concept and design principles for modelling interoperability.

6. References

Chen D. *et al.*, Deliverable D6.2, Design principles/Patterns for Interoperability, Internal Document, November 2004, INTEROP.

Dassisti, M., Scorziello, F., "Enterprise Model Interoperability: A case study of two university laboratories", *Proceedings of the 4th CIRP International Seminar on Intelligent Computation in Manufacturing Engineering*, Sorrento, Napoli, Italy, 30 June-2 July 2004, p. 61-65.

Butera F., *Il castello e la rete*, Milano, Editions F. Angeli, 1990.

Micelli S., *Imprese, reti e comunità virtuali*, Etas libri, 2000.

Chidambaram S., Whitman L., Hossein Cheraghi S., "A Supply Chain Transformation Methodology", *Proceedings of the 4th Annual International Conference on Industrial Engineering Theory, Applications and Practice,* San Antonio, Texas, USA, November 17-20 1999.

Vallespir B., Merle C., Doumeingts G., "GIM: a technico-economic methodology to design manufacturing systems", *Control Eng. Practice*, vol. 1, no. 6, 1993, p. 1031-1038.

Ducq Y., Vallespir B., "Modelling principles and performance indicators definitions for the Supply Chain control", *Proceedings of the International IMS Forum,* Villa Erba, Cernobbio, Italy, 2004.

Chen D., Daclin N., Design principles and pattern for decisional interoperability (slides), INTEROP WP6 workshop, Luxembourg, 2005.

Veryard, Information Coordination- The management of information models, systems and organisations, Prentice Hall, ISBN 0-13-099243-7, 1994.

Supply Chain Council. Model SCOR. Available at http://www.supplychain.org/public/home.asp; 2004.

Spider Win: http:\\www.spider-win.de.

Framework for Enterprise Interoperability[1]

David Chen — Nicolas Daclin

LAPS/GRAI, University Bordeaux 1
351, Cours de la Libération, 33405 Talence cedex, France
david.chen@laps.u-bordeaux1.fr
Nicolas.daclin@laps.u-bordeaux1.fr

ABSTRACT: *The domain of enterprise interoperability is not precisely defined and the concept of interoperability itself is still confusing and interpreted from many different points of view. This paper presents a framework for enterprise interoperability which is developed within the frame of INTEROP NoE. The purpose of the framework is to identify the basic dimensions regarding to enterprise interoperability and to define its domain of research. The paper will also clarify some confusing concepts around the notion of interoperability and discuss the relation between interoperability domain and other relevant ones. Complementary dimensions to this framework are also presented and the use of this framework to capture and structure enterprise interoperability knowledge is discussed. Future work and conclusion will be given at the end of the paper.*

KEY WORDS: *Enterprise interoperability, Interoperability framework, Enterprise integration.*

1 This work is partly funded by the EC within the frame of INTEROP NoE, Network of Excellence – Contract no.: IST-508 011.

1. Introduction

Increasingly, the success of an enterprise depends not only on its internal productivity and performances, but also its ability to seamlessly interoperate with others. Enterprise interoperability is becoming an important issue for both large and SMEs to gain competitiveness in the global market.

Two main initiatives relating to interoperability development are currently carried out: ATHENA Integrated Project (IP) and INTEROP Network of Excellence (NoE). ATHENA (Advanced Technologies for Interoperability of Heterogeneous Enterprise Networks and their Applications) consists of a set of projects and will lead to prototypes, technical specifications, guidelines and best practices for interoperability (ATHENA, 2003). INTEROP (Interoperability Research for Networked Enterprises Applications and Software) aims at integrating expertise in relevant domains for sustainable structuration of European Research on Interoperability of Enterprise applications (INTEROP, 2003).

However, interoperability still means many things to many people and is often interpreted in many different ways with different expectations. Definitions on interoperability abound, but definitions do not allow a clear understanding. This situation is not only true in industry but also in research communities and sometimes even within a working group. Without a clear and shared understanding on the precise meaning of interoperability, research and development efforts cannot be efficiently carried out and coordinated. Consequently, the purpose of this paper[2] is on the one hand to clarify the enterprise interoperability concept, and on the other hand to define the enterprise interoperability domain allowing to capture and structure the knowledge of the domain.

2. Basic concepts and definitions

2.1. *Interoperability*

Definitions on interoperability have been reviewed in (Chen *et al.*, 2002, 2004), (Vernadat, 1996). Generally, interoperability is the ability or the aptitude which two systems have to understand one and the other and to function together. The word "inter-operate" implies that one system performs an operation for another system and vice-versa. From computer technology point of view, it is the faculty for two heterogeneous systems to function jointly and to give access to their resources in a reciprocal way. In the context of networked enterprises (extended, virtual...), interoperability refers to the ability of interactions (exchange of information and services) between enterprise systems. Interoperability is considered as significant if the interactions can take place at least at the three levels: data, services and process, with a semantics defined in a given business context (IDEAS, 2003).

---

2 This paper is based on the work performed in INTEROP NoE, DI: Domain *of* Interoperability.

The enterprise interoperability addressed here deals with the interoperation of information. It is concerned with: (a) ability to exchange information and to understand the information exchanged; (b) ability to use exchanged information to perform a work (adapted from IEEE 1990).

In this paper, interoperability is considered as a problem of compatibility, not only at ICT level, but at all levels of enterprise. Thus developing interoperability means to find solution which removes incompatibilities that may exist between any two heterogeneous enterprise systems (Chen *et al.*, 2006). The term incompatibility is understood as the lack of common characteristics between two entities (be they enterprises, systems, organisations or software). In other words, two entities are considered as incompatible (partly or totally) if an interface is needed to relate them together for the purpose of mapping or translation. Consequently two enterprises are considered interoperable if, when they establish a business relationship, there is no interfacing effort to exchange information and use the information so exchanged.

To define the domain of interoperability, it is not only necessary to define what interoperability is but also what is not. The following tends to clarify some confusion concepts relating to interoperability.

• Interoperability vs. integration

Generally, interoperability has the meaning of coexistence, autonomy and federated environment, whereas integration refers to the concepts of coordination, coherence and uniformatisation. From the point of view of degree of coupling, the "tightly coupled" indicates that the components are interdependent and cannot be separated. This is the case of an integrated system. The loosely coupled means that the components are connected by a communication network; they can exchange services while continuing their own logic of operation. It is the case of interoperability. Thus two integrated systems are inevitably interoperable; but two those interoperable are not necessarily integrated (Chen *et al.*, 2004). The table below gives the summary of the discussion above.

INTEGRATION	INTEROPERABILITY
Consistency of local objectives to global ones	No consistency between local and global objectives
Tightly coupled Components interdependent	Loosely coupled Components independent
Uniformatisation (languages, methods, tools, etc.)	Identity, diversity and autonomy preserved
Intra enterprise fusion, re-structuration, etc.	Inter enterprise (virtual enterprise,...)

Table 1. *Integration vs. interoperability*

Another point of view is given by ISO 14258 (1999). Two systems are considered as Integrated if there is a detailed standard format for all constituent components. Interoperability is more related to Unified approach where there is a common meta-level structure across constituent models, providing a means for establishing semantic equivalence, and Federated one where models must dynamically accommodate rather than having a predetermined meta-model. Most of on-going research on interoperability adopts the unified approach, few is concerned with federated one.

• Interoperability vs. collaboration/cooperation

We consider that the concept of interoperability is also different from the concepts "collaboration" and "cooperation". Interoperability is a property relating to the compatibility (in the broad sense and not only at the hardware/software level) of two systems. It does not have a particular objective of collaboration/cooperation and does not imply a partnership relation. Two interoperable companies do not necessarily collaborate in a joint industrial project; two companies which collaborate together can have serious problems of interoperability.

Clearly cooperation and collaboration refers to the association of a number of persons for their common benefit, collective action in the pursuit of common goal, especially in some industrial or business process. Interoperability has no business objective and mission and does not solve any business problems. In other word, interoperability is about incompatibility engineering. It is a support to business collaboration/cooperation.

2.2. *Interoperability barriers*

Many interoperability issues are specific to particular application domains. These can be things like support for particular attributes, or particular access control regimes. Nevertheless, common barriers to interoperability can be identified and most of them are already largely discussed (EIF, 2004), (ERISA, 2004).

In this paper we focused our attention to the identification of the common barriers to interoperability. By the term "barrier" we mean an "incompatibility" with respect to a particular concern which obstructs the sharing of information and prevent from exchanging services. At current stage of research, three categories of barriers (conceptual, technological and organisational) are defined as follows:

Conceptual barriers: They are concerned with the syntactic and semantic differences of information to be exchanged. These problems concern the modelling at the high level of abstraction (such as for example the enterprise models of a company) as well as the level of the programming (for example low capacity of semantic representation of XML).

• Syntactic difference can be found whenever different people or systems use different structures to represent information and knowledge. For example the UEML initiative (UEML, 2001) aims at providing a neutral model to allow mapping between different enterprise models built using different syntaxes.

• Semantic problem is considered as an important barrier to interoperability as the information and knowledge represented in most of models or software have no clearly defined semantics. At current stage, the most known technique to solve this problem is the semantic annotation and reconciliation using ontology.

Technological barriers: these barriers refer to the incompatibility of information technologies (architecture & platforms, infrastructure...). These problems concern the standards to present, store, exchange, process and communicate the data through the use of computer. Typical barriers are those you may encounter when a Microsoft PC has to interoperate with Macintosh.

Organisational barriers: They relate to the definition of responsibility and authority so that interoperability can take place under good conditions. These can be seen as "human technologies" or "human factors" and are concerned with human and organisation behaviours which can be incompatible to interoperability.

• Responsibility needs to be defined to allow two parties knowing who is responsible for what (process, data, software, computer...). If responsibility in an enterprise is not clearly and explicitly defined, interoperation between two systems is obstructed.

• Authority is an organisational concept which defines who is authorised to do what. For example, it is necessary to define who is authorised to create, modify, maintain data, processes, services, etc.

• Organisation structure refers to the style by which responsibility, authority and decision making are organised. For example we can talk about centralised vs. decentralised organisations, or hierarchical vs. matrix or networked organisation structures.

2.3. Enterprise levels

This section defines the interoperations that can take place at the various levels of the enterprise. Although the definitions are mainly given from a point of view of IT based applications, they apply to non-computerised systems as well. This categorisation is based on the ATHENA Technical framework (ATHENA, 2005).

• The interoperability of **data**: It refers to make work together different data models (hierarchical, relational, etc.) and of the different query languages. Moreover, their contents are organized according to conceptual schemas (i.e. vocabularies and sets of structures of data) which are related to particular applications. The interoperability of data is to find and share information coming from heterogeneous bases relating to these various aspects, and which can moreover reside on different machines with different operating systems and data bases management systems.

• The interoperability of **services**: It is concerned with identifying, of composing and making function together various applications (designed and implemented independently) by solving the syntactic and semantic differences as well as finding the connections to the various heterogeneous data bases. The term "service" is not limited to the computer based applications; but also functions of the company or of the networked enterprises.

• The interoperability of **processes**: it aims to make various processes work together: a process defines the sequence of the services (functions) according to a specific need of the company. Generally in a company, several processes run in interactions (in series or parallel). In the case of the networked enterprise, it is also necessary to study how to connect internal processes of two companies to create a common process.

• The interoperability of **business**: It refers to work in a harmonise way at the levels of organization and company in spite of for example, the different modes of decision-making, methods of work, legislations, culture of the company and commercial approaches etc. so that business can be developed and shared between companies

3. Framework for enterprise interoperability

3.1. *Basic dimensions*

The interoperability framework presented in this paper aims at defining the research domain of enterprise interoperability and identifying knowledge in this domain. The proposed framework has two basic dimensions as shown in Figure 1: (1) Enterprise dimension which consists of enterprise levels, (2) Interoperability dimension representing interoperability barriers as discussed in the previous section. The domain of enterprise interoperability is therefore defined by the scope of this interoperability framework.

barriers / levels	CONCEPTUAL	TECHNOLOGICAL	ORGANISATIONAL
BUSINESS			
PROCESS			
SERVICE			
DATA			

Figure 1. *Simplified representation of the interoperability framework*

The necessity to develop such a framework has been discussed in (Petit *et al.*, 2004). Existing interoperability frameworks (such as for example, IDEAS Interoperability framework, ATHENA interoperability framework, etc.) do not represent explicitly barriers to interoperability; they are not aimed at defining the domain of enterprise interoperability and structuring interoperability knowledge with respect to their contribution to remove various barriers.

As shown in Figure 1 the intersection of a level category (line) and a barrier category (column) constitutes a sub-domain. Thus this Interoperability Framework defines the interoperability research domain by the set of sub-domains which compose. It can be used to categorise interoperability knowledge. A piece of knowledge is considered as relevant to develop interoperability if it contributes to remove at least one barrier at one level.

It is to note that a piece of knowledge may concern more than one barrier and cover more than one level. For example (see Figure 2), the semantic annotation technique using ontology contributes to remove the semantic barrier and covers all the four levels. UEML V1.0 is concerned with syntactic barrier and covers all the four levels, while PSL (Process Specification Language) contributes to remove both syntactic and semantic barriers but limited to process level.

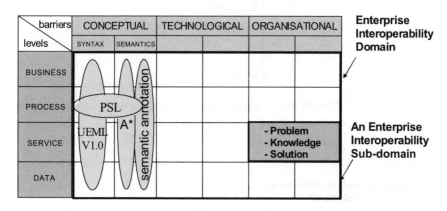

Figure 2. *Mapping knowledge/solutions to enterprise interoperability framework*

The vision held at the current stage of research in the Domain *of* Interoperability of INTEROP is that the development of interoperability must essentially focus on finding knowledge and solutions to remove these barriers to make two enterprises compatible according to the points of view of interoperability. Although the three categories of barriers concern all the four interoperability levels (Data, Service, Process and Business), conceptual and organisational barriers are more important at the higher levels while technological (IT) barriers have more impact on the lower levels.

3.2. Complementary dimensions

The two basic framework dimensions discussed in section 3.1 can be extended with complementary dimensions. In order to allow flexible use of the framework for different purpose, the third dimension is left open i.e. it is defined as a variable dimension that can be replaced by a specific one. At the current stage of research, three complementary dimensions have been identified as: (1) knowledge dimension, (2) Engineering phase dimension, (3) interoperability measurement dimension. In the following sub-sections, we will present briefly these complementary dimensions.

3.2.1. Interoperability knowledge[3] dimension

The term knowledge used here means pieces of knowledge (solutions) which solve interoperability problems by removing at least one barrier to interoperability at one or several enterprise levels.
This dimension is based on ATHENA Interoperability Framework (Athena, 2003) which categorises knowledge (solutions) into three categories: Conceptual, Technological and Applicative as shown in Figure 3.

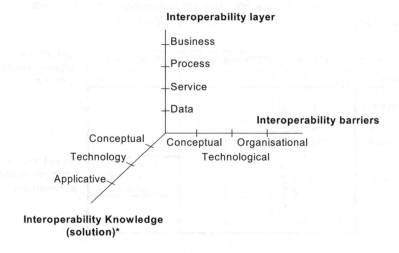

Figure 3. *Interoperability knowledge (solution) dimension*

With this third dimension, it is possible to positioning knowledge (solution) on interoperability in the framework in a more precise way. For example as already mentioned, "semantic annotation" is a method to move semantic barrier at the all four enterprise levels (conceptual knowledge/conceptual barrier/all enterprise levels). A* tool currently developed in the ATHENA project is a technological solution to remove semantic barrier at all enterprise levels (technology knowledge/conceptual barrier/all enterprise levels).

---

3 Knowledge including specific solutions for interoperability.

3.2.2. *Interoperability engineering dimension*

This dimension aims at defining a set of phases (steps) to follow as well as methods, modelling languages and tools to use to help establishing interoperability between two enterprises (or any two business entities). The system life cycle phases defined in ISO 15704 Standard (ISO 15704, 2001) has been adapted and three main phases have been defined as follow: (1) Requirements definition, (2) Design specification, (3) Implementation. Figure 4 shows this dimension in relation to the two basic Interoperability Framework dimensions.

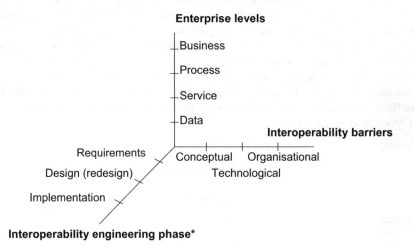

Figure 4. *Interoperability engineering phase dimension*

Using this framework in a particular interoperability project, the Requirements definition phase consists in identifying the types of barriers to interoperability that exist between two particular enterprise and the enterprise levels concerned. Specific problems and requirements to interoperability are also to be defined at this stage. The Design specification phase consists of identifying relevant solution components to interoperability with respect to barriers and requirements and properly combining these solution components so that they can work together. The Implementation phase allows realising and testing the solution and measuring the degree of interoperability achieved.

3.2.3. *Interoperability measurement dimension*

The Interoperability measurement dimension aims at defining metrics to qualify the degree of interoperability. The degree of interoperability is a measure allowing characterising the ability of interoperation between two enterprises (or systems). At the current stage of research, this dimension contains two measurement phases: (1) Compatibility measurement, and (2) Performance measurement. Both measurements are related to the two basic dimensions interoperability framework as shown in Figure 5.

The compatibility measures are to be performed during the engineering stage i.e. when one re-engineers systems in order to establish interoperability. The measures are done with respect to the barriers to interoperability at various enterprise levels. The highest degree of interoperability means that all the three categories of barriers to interoperability at the all four enterprise levels are removed (or do not exist). The inverse situation means the poorest degree of interoperability (interoperability does not exist). Various intermediate degrees between the two extreme cases (best and worst) can be defined as well.

The performance measures are to be performed during the operational phase i.e. run time, to evaluate the quality of interoperation between two cooperating enterprises (or unities). In (Daclin *et al.*, 2006), a basic interoperation cycle has been defined with three phases (exchange information, use information exchanged, exploitation of result). Criteria such as cost, delay and quality can be used to measure the performance with respect to barriers and levels during a basic interoperation cycle. Each characteristic of each phase is valued with local coefficients in order to get a global coefficient ranging from "poor interoperability" to "good interoperability".

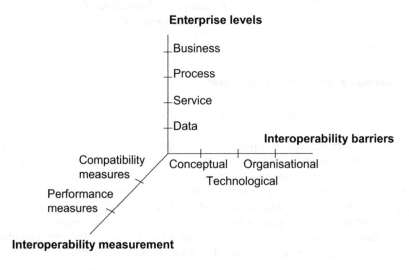

Figure 5. *Interoperability measurement dimension*

4. Concluding summary

This paper made the hypothesis that enterprises are not interoperable because of barriers to interoperability. Barriers are incompatibilities of various kinds and at various levels of an enterprise. Most of them are common to all enterprises. The approach adopted is barrier-driven to define the research domain of enterprise interoperability with the help of an Interoperability Framework.

The Interoperability framework proposed has two basic dimensions (enterprise levels and barriers to interoperability). The enterprise interoperability domain and sub-domains are defined by this framework. The use of the framework to identify and structure interoperability knowledge is illustrated.

The Interoperability framework has taken into account some existing works. The dimension of enterprise levels is based on the technical architecture of ATHENA interoperability framework; the dimension of barriers to interoperability is based on the concepts developed in IDEAS interoperability framework and European Interoperability Framework (EIF).

The two basic framework dimensions are enhanced by a third dimension left open. Three complementary dimensions are identified: (i) *Interoperability knowledge* for precise structuring of knowledge/solutions, (ii) *Interoperability engineering phase* to allow defining a methodology, (iii) *Interoperability measurement* for characterising the degree of interoperability.

Benefits and application of the framework is to allow a better understanding of enterprise interoperability research problems. It will also contribute to the standardisation work in this area and some preliminary discussion has already started in CEN TC310/WG1 in relation to ISO TC184 SC5/WG1. Furthermore knowledge and solutions can be structured in the framework to allow gap analysis so that future research orientation can be defined to close the gaps.

Future works are concerned with: (1) refining the interoperability framework, in particular the barriers to interoperability dimension, (2) identifying knowledge and mapping to the interoperability framework.

Interoperability is not only a matter of removing barriers but also in the way in which these barriers are removed. Another future enrichment of the framework is to add a third basic dimension called: interoperability approaches (integrated, unified, federated) so that interoperability knowledge/solutions can be classified according to the approach (manner) used to remove the barriers.

Acknowledgement

The authors thank the reviewers for their valuable comments and suggestions which allow improving the quality of this paper.

5. References

ATHENA, Advanced Technologies for Interoperability of Heterogeneous Enterprise Networks and their Applications, FP6-2002-IST-1, Integrated Project, April 2003.

ATHENA, "Project A4" (Slide presentation), ATHENA Intermediate Audit 29.-30., C. Guglielmina and A. Berre, September 2005, Athens, Greece.

Chen, D. and Vernadat, D., Enterprise Interoperability: A standardisation View, Enterprise Inter-and-Intra Organisational Integration, Eds. K. Kosanke *et al.*, Kluwer Academic Publishers, ISBN 1-4020-7277-5. October 2002, pp. 273-282.

Chen, D. and Vernandat, F., Standards on enterprise integration and engineering – A state of the art, In *International Journal of Computer Integrated Manufacturing* (IJCIM), Volume 17, no. 3, April-May 2004, pp.235-253.

Chen, D and Doumeingts, G., European Initiatives to develop interoperability of enterprise applications – basic concepts, framework and roadmap, *Journal of Annual reviews in Control*, Volume 27, Issue no. 2, 2003, pp.151-160.

Chen, D. Dassisti, M., Tsalgatidou, A. *et al.*, Interoperability Knowledge Corpus, An intermediate Report, Deliverable DI.1, Workpackage DI (Domain of Interoperability), INTEROP NoE, November 25th 2005.

EIF: European Interoperability Framework, White Paper, Brussels, 18, February 2004, http://www.comptia.org,

ERISA (The European Regional Information Society Association), A guide to Interoperability for Regional Initiatives, Brussels, September 2004.

IEEE, IEEE standard computer dictionary: a compilation of IEEE standard computer glossaries, 1990.

IDEAS Consortium, Thematic Network, IDEAS: Interoperability Development for Enterprise Application and Software – Roadmaps, Annex1 – Description of Work, 13-05-2002.

INTEROP, Interoperability Research for Networked Enterprises Applications and Software, Network of Excellence, Proposal Part B, April 23, 2003.

Petit, *et al.*, Knowledge map of research in interoperability in the INTEROP NoE, WP1, Version 1, August 11th 2004.

UEML Consortium, IST - 2001 - 34229, Unified Enterprise Modelling Language (UEML), Thematic Network, Annex 1, Description of Works, 2001.

ISO 14258, 1999, Industrial Automation Systems – Concepts and Rules for Enterprise Models, ISO TC184/SC5/WG1, 1999-April-14 version.

ISO 15704, 2000, Industrial automation systems – Requirements for enterprise-reference architectures and methodologies, ISO 15704:2000(E).

Daclin, N., Chen, D., Vallespir, B., Design Principles and Pattern for Decisional Interoperability, IFIP 5.7 APMS conference, Washington DC (USA), 2005.

Vernadat, F.B., Enterprise Modelling and Integration: Principles and Applications, Chapman & Hall, London, (1996).

Web Services
and Interoperability

WSI Workshop Chairs' message

The aim of this second edition of *"Web Services and Interoperability"* (WSI'06) workshop was to gather researchers and practitioners from a variety of research areas and industry branches in order to explore the nature of Web Services and problems and challenges facing this new technology. The perspective was both technical and business-oriented.

In response to the WSI'06 call for papers, six regular papers were accepted for presentation and publication. Each paper was reviewed by at least three reviewers. The program committee consisted of experienced reviewers from both academia and industry. This volume contains the revised versions of the selected papers, organized according to the workshop sessions schedule.

Web Services are emerging as the premier technology for implementing service-oriented architectures (SOA) and for conducting enterprise application integration, both in the public sector and in industry. The first session, chaired by Per Backlund, featured three papers: *Rapid Prototyping for Service-Oriented Architectures; Model Driven Architectures for Web Services Platforms*; and *Model-driven design of Interoperable Agents*. The first paper presents a Rapid Prototyping framework for SOAs built around a Model-Driven Development methodology which we use for transforming high-level specifications of an SOA into executable artefacts, both for Web Services and for autonomous agents. The second paper applies the MDA approach to the development of E-applications on Web services platforms and presents a prototype. Paper three presents a model-driven approach to designing interoperable agents in a service-oriented architecture (SOA). The second session, chaired by Eva Söderström, also featured three papers: *Information Security Patterns for Web Services; Detecting similarities between web services interfaces: the WSDL analyzer*; and *Business Process Fusion based on Semantically-enabled Service-Oriented Business Applications*. The first paper illustrates the benefits of using patterns as a means of managing knowledge concerning security in the context of Web Services. The second paper presents the WSDL Analyzer, a tool for detecting similarities between Web service interfaces which supports flexible service invocation in a dynamic environment. Paper three presents the vision and technical architecture of the FUSION IST project, which aims to promote efficient business collaboration and interconnection between enterprises (including SMEs).

First of all, we wish to thank the members of the program committee members for their hard work and dedication towards making this workshop a success. Furthermore, we sincerely thank all the authors for submitting their work, attending the workshop and contributing to the discussions. Finally, we would like to thank the INTEROP Network of Excellence (European FP6 IST-508-011, http://www.interop-noe.org) for its great support.

Per Backlund and Eva Söderström, *University of Skövde, Sweden*
Harald Kuehn, *BOC Information Systems GmbH, Austria*

Session 1:
Model Driven Architectures

Rapid Prototyping for Service-Oriented Architectures

Julien Vayssière* — Gorka Benguria** — Brian Elvesæter*** — Klaus Fischer**** — Ingo Zinnikus****

*SAP Research – Level 12 – 133 Mary Street – Brisbane QLD 4000 – Australia.

Julien.Vayssiere@sap.com

**European Software Institute (ESI) – Corporacion Tecnologica Tecnalia – Parque Tecnológico de Zamudio, # 204 E-48170 Zamudio Bizkaia – Spain.

Gorka.Benguria@esi.es

***SINTEF ICT, P.O. Box 124 Blindern, N-0314 Oslo, Norway.

Brian.Elvesater@sintef.no

****DFKI GmbH, Stuhlsatzenhausweg 3 (Bau 43), D-66123 Saarbruecken, Germany.

Klaus.Fischer@dfki.de

Ingo.Zinnikus@dfki.de

ABSTRACT: *Because Service-Oriented Architectures (SOAs) usually involve different independent stakeholders, producing meaningful prototypes for validating early design ideas is a difficult task. This paper presents a Rapid Prototyping framework for SOAs built around a Model-Driven Development methodology which we use for transforming high-level specifications of an SOA into executable artefacts, both for Web Services and for autonomous agents. The framework was designed to handle a mix of new and existing services and provides facilities for simulating, logging, analysing and debugging.*

Our framework was validated on a real industrial electronic procurement scenario in the furniture manufacturing industry. Once input from business experts had been collected, creating the high-level PIM4SOA (Platform Independent Model for SOA) model, deriving the Web service description and incorporating existing Web services took less than a day for a person already familiar with the techniques and tools involved. We show that rapid prototyping of SOAs is possible without sacrificing the alignment of the prototype with high-level architectural constraints.

KEY WORDS: *Service-Oriented Architecture, Web Services, Agents, Rapid Prototyping.*

1. Introduction and state of the art

Service-Oriented Architectures (SOAs) are an architectural style for distributed systems that has steadily been gaining momentum over the last few years and is now considered as mainstream in enterprise computing. Compared to earlier middleware products, SOAs put a stronger emphasis on *loose coupling* between the participating entities in a distributed system. The four fundamental tenets of Service Orientation (Box 2004) capture the essence of SOAs: *explicit boundaries, autonomy of services, declarative interfaces and data formats* and *policy-based service description*.

Web Services are the technology that is most often used for implementing SOAs. Web Services are a standards-based stack of specifications that enable interoperable interactions between applications that use the Web as a technical foundation (Booth *et al.*, 2004). The emphasis on loose coupling also means that the same degree of independence can be found between the organisations that build the different parts of an SOA. The teams involved only have to agree on service descriptions and policies at the level of abstraction prescribed by the different Web Service standards.

Prototyping SOAs, which we could define as the task of coming up with a working implementation of an SOA that can be used for validating the initial design choices, is therefore a job of a very different nature than prototyping regular software application. The key difference here is that we need to take into account the fact that some of the pieces of the SOA are already existing, developed by organisations over which we have no control, which introduces constraints into the prototyping exercise that do not exist when prototyping standalone applications.

However, the state of the art in tools for prototyping SOAs exclusively assumes that we are starting with a blank page, thereby merely extending the approach of regular software prototyping to the scale of SOAs. When these tools do take existing services into account, they always make the implicit assumption that services will behave as expected, which usually results in very brittle prototypes which are of little value for validating the SOA. This is why we designed an approach that, from the start, takes into account the fact that parts of the SOA needs to be considered as a given and should be treated with a healthy dose of caution.

Our approach relies on a model-based approach to SOA prototyping that allows us to take existing services into account at a fairly high level of abstraction while keeping the development of new components aligned with existing ones at each step of the process, from early modelling all the way down to execution and monitoring.

Section 2 introduces the framework for rapid prototyping for SOA. Section 3 details the model-driven development framework. Section 4 details the service enactment and monitoring platform. Section 5 presents how an autonomous agents framework can be used for performing the tasks of composition, mediation and brokering between Web Services. Section 6 introduces a detailed example based on a real industry scenario. Section 7 concludes and proposes avenues for future work.

2. A framework for rapid prototyping of Service-Oriented Architectures

The framework for Rapid Prototyping of SOAs presented here is composed of three parts: a *modelling* part, a *service* part and an *autonomous agent* part.

The *modelling* part is concerned with applying Model-Driven Development (MDD) techniques and tools to the design of SOAs. It defines models and transformations that are specific to the concepts used for SOAs, such as Web Service descriptions and plans for autonomous agents. The *service* part provides a highly flexible communication platform for Web services. The *autonomous agent* part deals both with designing and enacting service compositions as well as performing mediation, negotiation and brokering in SOAs.

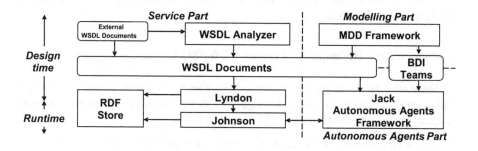

Figure 1. *High-level view of the SOA framework*

Each of these three parts leverages the others in various ways. For example, the service part invokes the autonomous agents framework for starting the execution of a service composition described by a plan. The reverse also applies: autonomous agents may invoke Web Services through the tools from the services part. In turn, a description of a service composition at a platform-independent level can be transformed into a plan for autonomous agents. High-level service models can also be transformed into WSDL (Web Services Description Language) files.

Figure 1 gives a high-level overview of our framework, illustrating the main components as well as the flow of existing and generated artefacts such as WSDL files and BDI (Beliefs, Desires and Intentions) plans. The components involved are:

– The **MDD framework** defines the metamodels used to specify SOAs. It also provides modelling guidelines, model transformation and generation support for execution artefacts such as WSDL files and BDI plans. Importantly, it also supports importing existing WSDL files into the SOA models.

– The **WSDL Analyzer** is a tool for detecting similarities at a structural level between WSDL descriptions of Web services and generating the corresponding mappings. It supports flexible service invocation in a dynamic environment.

– The **Johnson** tool is responsible for invoking Web services and receiving calls issued by Web service clients. The **Lyndon** tool takes WSDL files as input and configures Johnson for playing either the role of service provider, service consumer or service proxy for the service described by the WSDL file analyzed.

– The **Jack** tool is used for specifying plans for autonomous agents which form teams that can invoke or receive calls from Web services. The plans used may be created as the result of an MDD process.

– The **RDF store** stores as RDF (Resource Description Framework) files both design-time information (WSDL files) and runtime information (SOAP messages) for the purpose of monitoring.

3. Model-Driven Development Framework for SOA

Designing SOAs at the enterprise level involves several different stakeholders within the enterprise. In order to support the various views pertinent to these stakeholders, we have defined an MDD framework.

The MDD framework partitions the architecture of a system into several visual models at different abstraction levels subject to the concerns of the stakeholders. This allows important decisions regarding integration and interoperability to be made at the most appropriate level and by the best suited and knowledgeable people. The models are also subject for semi-automatic model transformations and code generation to alleviate the software development and integration processes.

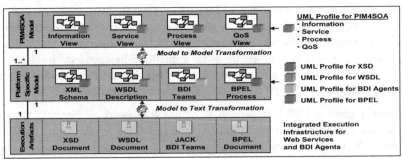

Figure 2. *Model-Driven Development Framework*

Figure 2 details the model-driven development framework. It follows the OMG Model Driven Architecture (MDA) (Soley 2000) approach and defines a Platform Independent Model (PIM) for SOA (PIM4SOA) and Platform Specific Models (PSMs) for describing Web services (XML Schemas and WSDL), Jack BDI agents and BPEL (Business Process Execution Language) (Andrews *et al.* 2003) processes.

PIM4SOA is a visual PIM which specifies services in a technology independent manner. It represents an integrated view of the SOA in which different components can be deployed on different execution platforms. The PIM4SOA model helps us to align relevant aspects of enterprise and technical IT models, such as process, organisation and products models. This model allows us to raise the abstraction level at which we can talk about and reason on the architecture we design.

The PIM4SOA metamodel defines modelling concepts that can be used to model four different aspects or views of a SOA:

1. **Service:** Services are an abstraction and an encapsulation of the functionality provided by an autonomous entity.

2. **Information:** Information is related to the messages or structures exchanged, processed and stored by software systems and components.

3. **Process:** Processes describe sequencing of work in terms of actions, control flows, information flows, interactions, protocols, etc.

4. **Quality of service (QoS):** Extra-functional qualities that can be applied to services, information and processes.

The MDD framework provides model-to-model transformation services which allow us to transform PIM4SOA models into underlying PSMs such as XSD, WSDL, JACK BDI or BPEL. The PSMs depicted in Figure 2 are also visual models which IT developers can further refine by adding platform-specific modelling constructs such as deployment properties. PSMs typically represent a one-to-one mapping to an execution artefact. Dependencies between the various components are modelled at the PIM-level and two-way model transformations help us to ensure interoperability at the technical level and consistency at the PIM-level.

Tool support for the MDD framework has been developed as a set of plugins for Rational Software Modeler (RSM) (IBM Rational Software). RSM is a UML 2.0 compliant modelling tool from IBM based on the Eclipse modelling environment. All models and metamodels were implemented using the EMF Core (Ecore) metamodel. Model transformations have been implemented using the model transformation capabilities of the RSM/Eclipse platform.

4. A Lightweight Web Services Enactment Framework

The part of our SOA Rapid Prototyping framework that deals with the enactment of Web services is composed of three tools which are arranged along a value chain: the WSDL Analyser, the Lyndon tool and the Johnson tool.

4.1. *The WSDL Analyzer*

The WSDL Analyzer is a tool for detecting similarities between Web service descriptions. The tool can be used to find a list of similar services and produces a mapping between messages, thereby enabling brokering and mediation of services.

The algorithm of the WSDL Analyzer improves over an algorithm for finding structural similarities proposed by Wang and Stroulia (Wang *et al.* 2003) by taking into account additional features of the WSDL structure. More specifically, we make use of the *tree-edit distance* measure (Shasha *et al.* 1997) and the concept of a *weak subsumption relation* (Nagano *et al.* 2004).

The idea of the tree-edit distance is that a similarity between two XML structures can be measured by stepwise transforming a tree representation of the first structure into the other. The steps necessary for that transformation provide the measure for their similarity, and, at the same time, induce the mapping between the schemas. Possible steps are basic edit operations such as node inserts, deletes and relabels. The algorithm of Wang and Stroulia considers only node matching without editing, or simple renaming operations such as changing a data type from *string* to *int*. Nagano *et al.* give three different types of weak subsumption: replacing labels, pruning edges and removing intermediate nodes. These operations can be correlated to specific tree-edit operations, namely relabeling and deleting nodes. A possible scenario for using the WSDL Analyzer is that the user already knows a service which provides the correct format. The WSDL of this service can be used as requirement for a similarity search. The WSDL Analyzer allows browsing the original WSDL and the candidate files.

The algorithm detects common structures in port types, operations, messages and data type definitions. WordNet is integrated to improve the matching result. Mappings are assessed with a score which is used to establish a ranking between candidate service descriptions. Based on the similarities, a mapping is generated between two WSDL descriptions which can be used to transform SOAP messages exchanged between similar services at runtime. The result is a ranking of the candidates according to their matching score.

The translation can be done automatically, if there is a one-to-one correspondence between elements. However, if there exist several possible corresponding elements, translation requires intervention from a user in order to unambiguously transform parameters. The latter case shows the limitation of the structural approach. There are possible mismatches which can be *detected* with the help of the WSDL Analyzer, but not automatically *corrected*.

4.3. *The Johnson and Lyndon tools*

Johnson is a runtime tool that enables users to enact most of the roles typically found in an SOA, thereby enacting complex SOA scenarios by sending real SOAP messages between Web services without having to write a single line of code.

Johnson features a Web-based user interface designed to closely resemble Web-based email applications, with the only difference that SOAP messages and Web Services endpoints are used in place of email messages and email addresses. The user can see incoming SOAP messages in the Inbox and create outgoing SOAP messages in the Outbox that will be sent to external Web services. A powerful user-interface generator relieves the user from having to deal with XML documents by generating forms for displaying and editing any XML-based data type.

When playing the role of a Web service consumer, for example, a user would create a message in the Outbox, send that message to a remote Web service, and later see the response message appear in the Inbox. On the reverse, a user enacting a Web service provider would read incoming requests in the Inbox and reply to them by creating response messages in the Outbox.

Central to the architecture of Johnson are the concepts of *endpoint, processing modules* and *processing chains*. An endpoint is an abstraction for the address of a service. To each endpoint is attached a processing chain, which specialises the processing of messages for that endpoint. Each processing chain is composed of a number of processing modules which are called in sequence. Creating new processing modules requires writing code.

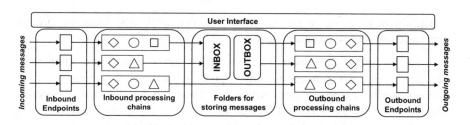

Figure 3. *Architecture of the Johnson tool*

Figure 3 shows a sample instance of Johnson where all the aforementioned concepts are illustrated. The different processing modules are represented as different shapes such as circles, lozenges, squares and triangles. Messages received on the third inbound endpoint from the top do not end up in the inbox but are directly sent out using one of the outbound endpoints. This is possible because this logic is coded in the last processing module of the inbound processing chain.

Being able to specialise message processing for each endpoint basis allows us to play the role of Web services that would implement different subsets of the Web Services stack of specifications, which proved very useful for studying the possible interoperability issues raised by the use of unrelated specifications together.

A processing module was also developed for keeping an audit trail of messages, which forms the basis for troubleshooting and performance measurement. The headers of SOAP messages are turned into RDF and stored in an RDF store.

The Lyndon tool can be seen as the design-time counterpart of the Johnson tool. It analyses WSDL files and automatically configures Johnson for playing either the role of consumer or provider of the service described.

Lyndon parses a WSDL file and determines which endpoints need to be created, and which processing chains need to be assigned to them. Determining which processing modules to include in the processing chain takes into account information extracted from the WSDL file as well as options set by the user. The user may, for example, specify whether Johnson should be configured as a service consumer or a service provider, or whether messages sent to or from the service should be logged. Some configuration information can be extracted from the WSDL file, such as the need for implementing the WS-Addressing specification, which is specified as part of the description of the bindings of a Web service.

Lyndon also generates an RDF representation of WSDL files and stores it into the same RDF store used for logging SOAP messages. Having both design-time and runtime artifacts in the same store is critical to monitoring the SOA and detecting services that do not behave accordingly to the service description they published.

5. An agents-based execution platform

The aim of the extended JACK agent framework for Web Services is to provide a goal-oriented service composition and execution module within an SOA.

Following the Belief Desire Intention (BDI) model, agents are autonomous software components that have explicit goals to achieve or events to handle (desires). Agents are programmed with a set of plans to describe how to go about achieving desires. Each plan describes how to achieve a goal under varying circumstances. Set to work, the agent pursues its given goals (desires), adopting the appropriate plans (intentions) according to its current set of data (beliefs) about the state of the world. The combination of desires and beliefs initiating context-sensitive intended behaviour is part of what characterises a BDI agent.

BDI agents exhibit reasoning behaviour under both pro-active (goal directed) and reactive (event driven) stimuli. Adaptive execution is introduced by flexible plan choice, in which the current situation in the environment is taken into account. A BDI agent has the ability to react flexibly to failure in plan execution. Agents cooperate by forming teams in order to achieve a common goal.

The JACK agent platform is not inherently ready for interaction within a Web service environment. Additional steps are necessary for enabling interactions between the agent platform and Web services, especially when the agents themselves offer services. In this case, some tools are needed for generating the server and client-side code for using JACK inside a Web server.

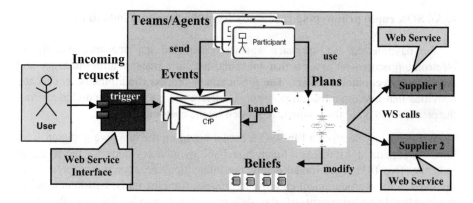

Figure 4. *Extended JACK framework for service composition and execution*

Figure 4 is an overview of the extended JACK architecture for Web service composition and plan execution, with at its core the JACK agent framework with plan library and knowledge base. Following the MDA approach, a modeller specifies at design time a set of plans (PSM level) that constitute the workflow library of the agents. Web service calls are integrated as steps into plans. Workflows are modelled graphically and most of the common workflow patterns are supported.

In order to prepare for a transformation from a PIM4SOA model to the JACK PSM, service providers are mapped to Jack agents/teams. The parts of the PIM which define the processes involved are mapped to agent/team plans and correlated events, whereas the parts which define the interfaces are mapped to the modules which provide the client- and server-side code for the JACK agent platform.

Just like BPEL, our framework supports fixed composition, where the structure and the components of the composition are statically bound, and semi-fixed compositions, where the structure is statically bound but the actual service bindings are performed at runtime. More explorative compositions, where both structure and components are created at runtime, are beyond what BPEL or BDI agents can offer.

However, there are several advantages to BDI agent, especially when it comes to handling failures at runtime. A plan is executed in a context which specifies conditions for plan instances and also other applicable plans. An exception in one plan instance then leads to the execution of another plan instance for the next known service. The BDI agent approach supports this adaptive behaviour in a natural way, whereas a BPEL process specification which attempts to provide the same behaviour would require awkward coding such as nested fault handlers.

Another advantage is that extending the behaviour by adding a new plan for a specific task simply means adding it to the plan library for it to be executed at the next opportunity. Similarly, customizing the composition is facilitated since the different plans clearly structure the alternatives of possible actions. Since the control structure is implicit, changes in a plan do not have impact on the control structure.

6. An SOA rapid prototyping case study from the furniture industry

We have tested our approach against a real industry scenario, namely an electronic procurement process that spans the furniture manufacturing industry and the interior decoration retailers. The procurement process, traditionally, covers the activities that one organization performs to derive the goods to be purchased from the providers to build the products requested by the customer.

We started by creating a PIM4SOA model based on the input we gathered from business experts at AIDIMA, a Spanish technology advisory body for the furniture industry. This PIM4SOA model details the interactions between the different roles involved in the e-procurement end-to-end process, from the initial customer order to the final acknowledgement of the delivery of the goods. To describe these interactions the PIM4SOA model identifies the different roles, the collaborations between those roles, the information exchanged, the internal behaviour of those collaborations and the expected quality that should be provided by the roles.

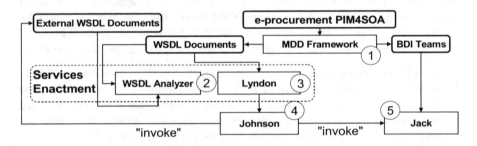

Figure 5. *Approach for the validation of the Rapid Prototyping framework*

The following approach was followed for the validation of the Rapid Prototyping framework (see Figure 5). First we used the MDD framework (1) to derive the WSDL files and BDI models from the e-procurement PIM4SOA model. The next objective was to enact the services identified for the e-procurement scenario using the WSDL Analyser (2) and the Johnson and Lyndon (3) tool. Because some of the pieces of the SOA already existed, we used the WSDL Analyser to locate services similar to those required in the e-procurement scenario. For those that do not exist we have used the Lyndon tool to configure the Johnson platform to simulate them. The next step was to configure Johnson (4) to act as a service proxy; this allowed us to change the final service endpoints without affecting the process execution. Finally the PSM model for Jack (5) was implemented and tested with the enacted services.

– The ***MDD framework*** uses model-to-model transformations to derive the platform specific models for XML schemas, WSDL descriptions, and JACK Model from the PIM4SOA model as stated in section 3. These models are then completed by the platform experts to make them ready for the generation of the execution artefacts through the use of model-to-text transformations.

– The **WSDL Analyzer** compares the types of the parameters of the services required with the available services and returns a ranked set of candidate service. The technical experts then select the services that will be used and the tool provides the appropriate mappings to transform the messages at runtime.

– The **Lyndon tool** configures the Johnson tool for enacting some of the services and for logging all appropriate information in the RDF store for later analysing and debugging of the SOA.

– The **Johnson tool** is also configured to incorporate the endpoints of the mappings services generated by the WSDL Analyzer.

– Finally the **Jack tool** is loaded with the PSM-level model (agents/teams, plans, events, beliefs etc) for the e-procurement scenario.

Once we have implemented the prototype we can execute it together with the client to check that it achieves the stated requirements. If we need to analyse the details of the message exchange we can use the Johnson platform for doing so. Besides, the Johnson platform also allows us to simulate other situations in a flexible and agile way. Situations such as service delays, service shutdown or service errors can be simulated, logged and analysed.

7. Conclusion

This paper presented a rapid prototyping framework for SOAs built around a Model-Driven Development methodology which is used for transforming high-level specifications of an SOA into executable artefacts, both in the realm of Web Services and in that of autonomous agents. The framework can handle a mix of new and existing services and provides facilities for simulating, logging, analysing and debugging.

The framework was validated on a real industrial electronic procurement scenario from the furniture manufacturing industry. Once input from business expert had been collected, creating the high-level PIM4SOA model, deriving the Web service description and incorporating existing Web services took less than a day for a person already familiar with all the tools involved.

After having run a few variants of the SOA, it became clear that the model-based approach we followed delivers significant value in keeping all the pieces of the SOA aligned with high-level business objectives throughout rounds of prototyping.

The work published in this paper is partly funded by the European Commission through the ATHENA IP (Advanced Technologies for interoperability of Heterogeneous Enterprise Networks and their Applications Integrated Project) (IST-

507849). The work does not represent the view of the European Commission or the ATHENA consortium, and the authors are solely responsible for the paper's content.

8. References

Andrews, T., Curbera, F., Dholakia, H., Goland, Y., Klein, J., Leymann, F., Liu, K., Roller, D., Smith, D., Thatte, S., Trickovic, I., and Weerawarana, S. "Business Process Execution Language for Web Services Version 1.1", May 2003. ftp://www6.software.ibm.com/software/developer/library/ws-bpel.pdf

Booth, D., Haas, H., McCabe, F., Newcomer, E., Champion, M., Ferris, C., and Orchard, D. "Web Services Architecture", W3C Working Group, February 2004. http://www.w3.org/TR/2004/NOTE-ws-arch-20040211/

Box, D. "A Guide to Developing and Running Connected Systems with Indigo", MSDN Magazine, January 2004. http://msdn.microsoft.com/msdnmag/issues/04/01/indigo/default.aspx

IBM Rational Software, "Rational Software Modeler". http://www-306.ibm.com/software/awdtools/modeler/swmodeler/

Nagano, S., Hasegawa, T., Ohsuga, A., and Honiden, S. "Dynamic Invocation Model of Web Services Using Subsumption Relations", ICWS 2004, pp. 150.156.

Shasha, D. and Zhang, K. "Approximate Tree Pattern Matching", Pattern Matching Algorithms, A.Apostolico and Z. Galil (eds.) Oxford University Press. 1997, pp. 341-371.

Soley, R. "Model Driven Architecture", OMG, November 2000.

Wang, Y. and Stroulia, E. "Flexible Interface Matching for Web-Service Discovery", Proc. 4th Int'l Conf. on Web Information Systems Engineering (WISE 2003).

Wang, Y. and Stroulia, E. "Semantic Structure Matching for Assessing Web-Service Similarity", Proc. 1st Int'l Conf. on Service Oriented Computing (ICSO 2003), Volume 2910 of Lecture Notes in Computer Science, pp. 197 - 207, Springer-Verlag.

Model Driven Architecture for Web Services Platforms:

Conceptualization and Prototyping

Slimane Hammoudi[*] — Denivaldo Lopes[**]

*ESEO,
4, Rue Merlet de la Boulaye BP 926,
49009 Angers cedex 01
France
slimane.hammoudi@eseo.fr*

**Federal University of Maranhão*
CCET - Department of Electrical Engineering
65080-040 São Luís - MA,

Brazil denivaldo.lopes@gmail.com

ABSTRACT: *Web Services are emerging as a promising technology for the development and deployment of E-applications and for the effective automation of inter-organizational interactions. Several XML standards providing infrastructure to support Web Services description, discovery, interaction and composition have recently emerged including WSDL, UDDI, SOAP and BPEL. An emerging trend in the development of E-Applications on Web services platforms is to separate their technology-independent and technology-specific aspects, by describing them in separate models. The most prominent development in this trend is the model-driven architecture (MDA) approach, which is being fostered by the object management group (OMG). This paper aims to apply the MDA approach to the development of E-applications on Web services platforms and presents a prototype to illustrate this approach. In our previous work we have used UML as a PIM (Platform Independent Model) to experiment with the MDA approach on Web services platforms. In this paper, we use EDOC (Enterprise Distributed Object Computing) language. One of the main lessons learned in this experiment is that EDOC as a DSL (Domain Specific Language) is more suitable than UML for Web services Platforms.*

KEY WORDS: *Web Services, MDA, Platforms, Modelling, EDOC, Mapping and Transformation.*

1. Introduction

Web Services are emerging as a promising technology for the development and deployment of E-applications and for the effective automation of inter-organizational interactions. Several XML standards providing infrastructure to support Web Services description, discovery, interaction and composition have recently emerged including WSDL, UDDI, SOAP and BPEL4WS (W3C 2004) (Andrews *et al.*, 2003). The Widespread adoption of these XML standards has spurred intense activity in industry and academia to address web services research issues. The majority of these researches are based on technological standards and on distributed platforms (e.g., J2EE, JWSDP, dotNet, etc.) for Web Services. However, a global solution clearly separating the technological parts from business logic parts is missing. For example, the problem of services composition is treated under a technical angle in the majority of the existing approaches. To date, enabling composite services has largely been an ad hoc, time-consuming, and error-prone process involving repetitive low-level programming (Hammoudi *et al.*, 2005).

A current trend in the development of E-applications using services is to separate their technology-independent and technology-specific aspects, by describing them in separate models. The most prominent development in this trend is the model-driven architecture (MDA) (Mellor *et al.*, 2004) approach, which is being fostered by the object management group (OMG). In this approach, models become the hub of development, separating platform independent characteristics (i.e. Platform-Independent Model - PIM) from platform dependent characteristics (i.e. Platform-Specific Model - PSM).

In our previous work (Bézivin *et al.*, 2004) (Lopes *et al.*, 2005), we have used UML as a PIM to experiment with the MDA approach on Web services platforms. In this paper, we use EDOC (the Enterprise Distributed Object Computing), an OMG standard, and we will show that EDOC as a DSL (Domain Specific Language) is more suitable than UML for Web services Platforms.

This paper is organized as follows: Section 2 presents an overview of Web Service and MDA. Section 3 presents our approach for mapping specification and transformation definition between two metamodels in the context of MDA. We will present the mappings (from EDOC metamodels) to WSDL. Section 4 illustrates our proposition of a metamodel for the specification of mappings between two metamodels, source plus target. Section 5 shows the implementation of our proposed metamodel for mapping through a plug-in for Eclipse and its application to Web Services platforms. Finally, section 6 concludes this paper.

2. Background

In recent years, Web Service and MDA have been introduced and developed by organisations responsible for standardization, World Wide Web Consortium (W3C) and Object Management Group (OMG), respectively. MDA is a framework based on a set of standards that assist the creation, implementation, evolution and deployment of systems driven by models.

2.1. *Web Services*

The W3C (World Wide Web Consortium) defines a Web Service as: *a software application identified by a URI (Uniform Resource Identifier), whose interfaces and binding are capable of being defined, described and discovered by XML artefacts and supports direct interactions with other software applications using XML based messages via Internet-based protocols.* Various definitions have been proposed in the literature, each one emphasizes some parts of the Web Service characteristics (discovery, invocation, etc.). Actually, the reference model of Web service is based on several XML standards providing infrastructure to support Web services description, discovery and interaction including WSDL, UDDI and SOAP. XML is an extensible markup language that has been used for document and data representation. It is a simple and powerful solution for the problem of Electronic Data Interchange (EDI). SOAP is a protocol to exchange information in decentralized and distributed systems. UDDI is the universal register of Web Services and its core is based on XML files that may store information about a business entity and its services. WSDL is an abstract definition based on XML grammar to describe the syntax and semantics necessary to call up a service. Figure 1 presents the reference model of Web service.

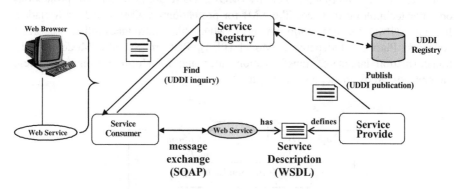

Figure 1. *The Web Service reference model*

Currently, some issues related to Web Services are the subject of intense research such as service composition, security and availability. Web Services composition can be static or dynamic. In a static composition, the services are determined and composed in the design time, while in the dynamic composition; the services are determined and composed at runtime. Some languages were proposed to take into account the service composition such as WSFL, XLANG and, more recently, Business Process Execution Language for Web Services (BPEL4WS) (Andrews *et al.,* 2003). BPEL4WS is a result of the fusion between WSFL and XLANG.

The technology of Web Services is the technology most linked to service-oriented architectures. Service Oriented Architecture (SOA) describes how a system composed of services can be built. Developing applications on SOA requires the adoption of a service-oriented design, which is different from component-oriented design. Service-oriented design is focused on the requirements determined in the strategy and business process levels, while component-oriented design is focused on the program components used to deliver services.

2.2. *MDA*

The OMG's Model Driven Architecture (MDA) is a new approach to develop large software systems in which the initial efforts aim to cover their functionalities and their behaviour. MDA separates the modelling task from the implementation details, without losing the integration of the model and the development on a target platform. The key technologies of MDA are Unified Modeling Language (UML), Meta-Object Facility (MOF), XML Meta-Data Interchange (XMI) and Common Warehouse Metamodel (CWM) (Mellor *et al.*, 2004). Together, they unify and simplify the modelling, the design, the implementation and the integration of systems. One of the main ideas of MDA is that each model is based on a specific meta-model. Each meta-model precisely defines a domain specific language. Finally, all meta-models are based on a meta-metamodel. In the MDA technological space, this is the Meta-Object Facility (MOF). There are also standard projections on other technological spaces like XMI for projection on XML and Java Metadata Interface (JMI) for projection on Java. MDA also introduces other important concepts: Platform Independent Model (PIM), Platform-Specific Model (PSM), transformation language, transformation rules and transformation engine. These elements of MDA are depicted in Figure 2.

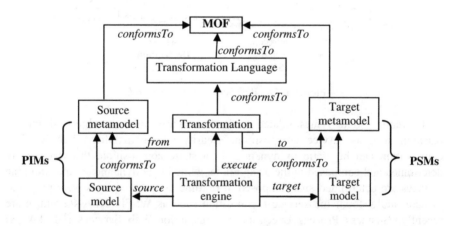

Figure 2. *Transformation in MDA*

Each element presented in Figure 2 plays an important role in MDA. In our approach, MOF is the well-established meta-metamodel used to build meta-models. The PIM reflects the functionalities, the structure and the behaviour of a system.

The PSM is more implementation-oriented and corresponds to first phase of binding a given PIM to a given execution platform. The PSM is not the final implementation, but has enough information to generate interface files, a programming language code, an interface definition language, configuration files and other details of implementation. Mapping (Lopes *et al.,* 2005) from PIM to PSM determines the equivalent elements between two meta-models. Two or more elements of different meta-models are equivalents if they are compatible and they cannot contradict each other. A transformation engine that executes transformation rules carries out model transformation. Transformation rules specify how to generate a target model (i.e. PSM) from a source model (i.e. PIM). In this work, for the prototyping part, we use Ecore (Eclipse Tools Project 2004) as the metamodelling language. Thus, all our metamodels will be defined in Ecore.

3. Modelling and transformation: from PIMs to PSMs

As mentioned in the introduction to this paper, in a previous work, we have used UML as a PIM to experiment the MDA approach on Web services platforms. In this paper, we use EDOC. UML is a general use modelling language, whilst EDOC is a specific modelling language for component based EDOC systems. In fact, the EDOC language is in the same vein as DSL (Domain Specific Language) for distributed enterprise models seen as a set of components. It offers a set of specifications supporting the creation of models for EDOC systems. Amongst these specifications, ECA (Enterprise Collaboration Architecture) (OMG, ECA 2004) is the one, which is of principal interest in this work. ECA provides five metamodels and profiles. Amongst these, the CCA metamodel (Component Collaboration Architecture) is our favoured formalism for the definition of neutral business models. It allows modelling the structure and behaviour of the components, which constitutes a system.

Among Web Services technologies, the most important for our study are UDDI and WSDL. However, to simplify our discussion about Web Services in the context of MDA, we have chosen only to present the WSDL meta-model and the mapping from EDOC metamodel to the WSDL metamodel. Thus, in the application process of the MDA approach using EDOC to the Web service platform J2EE, we proceed as follows: We define the EDOC (CCA) and WSDL metamodels and we illustrate, using our graphical formalism, the mapping followed by the transformations between these two metamodels (section 3.1). We then investigates how the EDOC (CCA) metamodel can be transformed into the JAVA metamodel. To create the final implementation in our approach, it is necessary to define a template and a JWSDP (Java Web Service Development Pack) metamodel to illustrate the use of the JWSDP library and the deployment files. These two last parts of JAVA and JWSDP are presented in (Lopes 2005).

3.1. *From PIM (EDOC) to PSM (WSDL)*

In Figure 2, we have presented the steps of model transformations in the context of MDA. According to this approach, the source and target metamodels must conform to the same meta-metamodel which is Ecore in our approach. The source metamodel chosen is EDOC (CCA), it will be defined using Ecore. As the target platforms are Web Services and J2EE (Java and JWSDP), their Ecore compliant meta-models are required.

According to our approach (Lopes *et al.*, 2005), we use the term mapping as a synonym for correspondence between the elements of two metamodels, while transformation is the activity of transforming a source element into a target element conforming with the transformation definition. Following these two concepts, the mapping specification precedes the transformation definition. Figure 3 illustrates the mapping specification between the two metamodels (EDOC and WSDL) using our graphical formalism:

The EDOC (CCA) metamodel is presented on the left hand side, the mapping in the centre, and the WSDL metamodel on the right. The main elements of the EDOC-CCA meta-model used in our approach are:

- `DataElement` - a generalization for `DataType` or `CompositeData` (a type of data);
- `FlowPort` - extends `Port` and describes the form, which may produce or consume a single `DataElement`;
- `OperationPort` - defines a port, which implements the typical call-return semantics and one-way operation;
- `ProtocolPort` - defines the use of a protocol and can involve the use of two-way interactions between components;
- `ProcessComponent` - a processing component that collaborates with other `ProcessComponents` using Ports within a CCA composition. It externalizes compositional objects as a component.

Our graphical notation for mapping has the following concepts: connection (source and target), association (could be composition) and mapping element. A connection links one or more metamodel elements to a mapping element. The association shows a relationship between mapping element. The composition shows a tight relation between mapping element (i.e. composite mappings). The mapping element associates elements from a source metamodel to elements of a target metamodel. According to Figure 4 the mapping element P2PB maps `ProtocolPort` with the elements `Portype`, `Binding` and `Port` of WSDL. The mapping element O2O maps `OperationPort` into `Operation` and `BindingOperation` of WSDL. The mapping element F2M maps the `FlowPort` element into the element Message of WSDL.

As we will see later, transformation rules are generated from each mapping element. These rules will translate elements from a source metamodel into elements in a target metamodel.

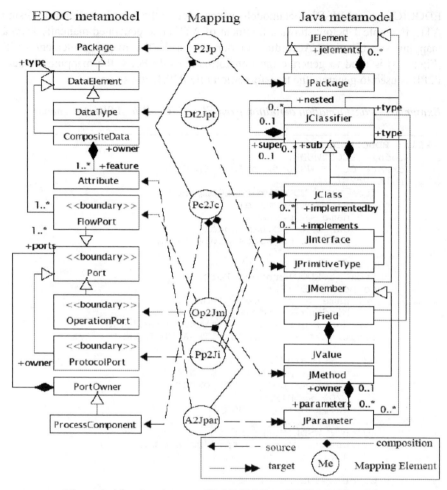

Figure 3. *Mappings between EDOC (CCA) and WSDL metamodels*

In this work, we have used ATL (Bézivin *et al.,* 2003) to create transformation rules, but this can be made using eXtensible Stylesheet Language Transformation (XSLT) logical languages or other transformation languages based on Object Constraint Language (OCL) like ATL. XSLT and logical languages are suitable for the manipulation of XML files (i.e. structured documents) to accomplish the transformation from source to target model. Both are efficient for models based on simple meta-models, but they are limited and error-prone for the transformation of models based on large metamodels. ATL is MDA compliant and uses a repository to store and to manipulate the source and target meta-models in order to perform the transformation following transformation rules defined by the mapping. Despite the use of XSLT and logical languages to make transformation rules, ATL is simpler and allows manipulations to be closer to the elements of metamodels and models. In fact, ATL was designed to make model transformations, whilst XSLT was designed to make general transformations. After identifying the equivalent elements between

EDOC(CCA) and WSDL metamodels, we can define the transformation rules using ATL. Example 1 below shows a fragment of ATL code generated manually from a mapping specification. According to our approach, the mapping element Pc2S (Figure 4) is used to generate the transformation rule Pc2S, the mapping element P2PB is used to generate the transformation rule P2PB, and so on.

Example 1: *transformation definition from EDOC (CCA) to WSDL (fragment)*

```
--File: EDOC2WSDL.atl
2    module EDOC2WSDL;
     create OUT : WSDL from IN : EDOC;
4    rule Pc2S{
         from pc : EDOC!ProcessComponent
6        to sv: WSDL!Service(
             name <- pc.name,
8            owner <- pc.namespace,
             port <- pc.ports >select(......)) )
10 }
     rule P2PB{
12       from pt:EDOC!ProtocolPort
         to port:WSDL!Port(
14           name <- pt.name + 'Port',
             binding <- bd,
16           documentation <- '\t\t<soap:address
         location="'+ 'REPLACE_WITH_ACTUAL_URL' +'"/>\n'
         ),
18       bd : WSDL!Binding(
             name <- pt.name + 'Binding',
20           owner <- port.owner.owner,
             type <- pType,
22           soapBinding <- soapB
         ),
24       soapB : WSDL!SoapBinding(
             transport <- 'http://schemas......',
26           style <- 'rpc'
         ),
28       pType: WSDL!PortType(
             name <- pt.name,
30           owner <- port.owner.owner,
             binding <- bd,
32           operations <- pt.protocol.ports >select()) )
)
}
34 ***
```

4. A metamodel for mapping specification

In this section, we present our proposition for specifying mappings (i.e. correspondences between metamodels). This approach for mapping is based on a metamodel and implemented as a tool in Eclipse. This tool provides support for mapping, which is a preliminary step before the creation of a transformation definition, using ATL. We have applied this tool for the different mappings presented in section 3.

The creation of mapping specifications and transformation definitions is not an easy task. In addition, the manual creation of mapping specifications and transformation definitions is a labour-intensive and error-prone process (Lopes *et al.*, 2005). Thus the creation of an automatic process and tools for enabling is an important issue. Some propositions enabling the mapping specification have been based on heuristics (for identifying structural and naming similarities between models) and on machine learning (for learning mappings).

4.1. *A metamodel for mapping*

In order to define a mapping, we need a metamodel, which enables:

- Identification of what elements have similar structures and semantics to be mapped.
- Explanation of the evolution in time of the choices taken for mapping one element into another element.
- Bidirectional mapping. It is desirable, but is often complex.
- Independence of model transformation language.
- Navigation between the mapped elements.

Figure 4 presents our proposition of a metamodel for mapping specification.

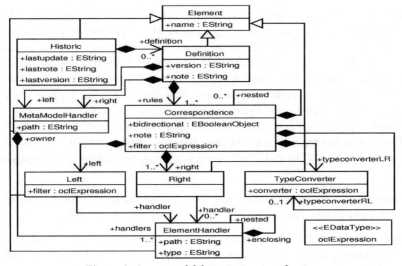

Figure 4. *A metamodel for mapping specification*

A complete definition of this metamodel is presented in (Lopes *et al.*, 2005). In this metamodel, we consider that mapping can be unidirectional or bidirectional. In unidirectional mapping, a metamodel is mapped into another metamodel. In bi-directional mapping, the mapping is specified in both directions. Thus, as presented previously, we prefer to refer to the two metamodels in a mapping as left or right metamodels.

A central element in this metamodel is the element `Correspondence`. This element is used to specify the correspondence between two or more elements, i.e. left and right elements. The correspondence has a filter that is an OCL expression. When bidirectional is false, a mapping is unidirectional (i.e. left to right), and when it is true it is bidirectional (i.e. in both directions). It has two `TypeConverters` identified by `typeconverterRL` and `typeconverterLR`. `typeconverterRL` enables the conversion of the elements from a right metamodel into the elements in a left metamodel. `typeconverterLR` enables the conversion of the elements from a left metamodel into the elements in a right metamodel. Often, only need to specify the `typeconverterLR`.

5. Prototyping: a plug-in for Eclipse

Eclipse Modeling Framework (EMF) is a modelling framework and code generation facility for supporting the creation of tools and applications driven by models (Eclipse Tools Project 2004). EMF represents the efforts of Eclipse Tools Project to take into account the model driven approach. In fact, MDA and EMF are similar approaches for developing software systems, but each one has different technologies. MDA was first designed by OMG using MOF and UML, while EMF is based on Ecore and stimulates the creation of specific metamodels.

Figure 5 shows our plug-in for Eclipse. For the moment, this first prototype supports only the mapping and the generation of transformation definitions. The tool presents as above a first metamodel on the left, a mapping model in the middle, and a second metamodel on the right. The fragments of EDOC (CCA) metamodel and WSDL metamodel are mapped. At the bottom, the property editor of mapping model is shown. A developer can use this property editor to set the properties of a mapping model. Before specifying mappings using our tool, we need to create metamodels based on Ecore. Some tools support the editing of a metamodel based on Ecore such as Omondo or the eCore editor provided with EMF. The use of our tool using EDOC (CCA) and WSDL metamodel can be explained in the following steps:

1. We created a project in eclipse and we imported the EDOC (CCA) and WSDL metamodels into this project.

2. We used a wizard to create a mapping model. In this step, we chose the name for the mapping model, the encoding of the mapping file (e.g. Unicode or UTF- 8), and the metamodels files in the XMI format.

3. The EDOC (CCA) and WSDL metamodels are loaded from the XMI files, and the mapping model is initially created, containing the elements `Historic`, `Definition`, and `left` and `right` `MetamodelHandlers`. For each `MetamodelHandler` there is also created `ElementHandlers` that are references to the elements of the corresponding metamodel.

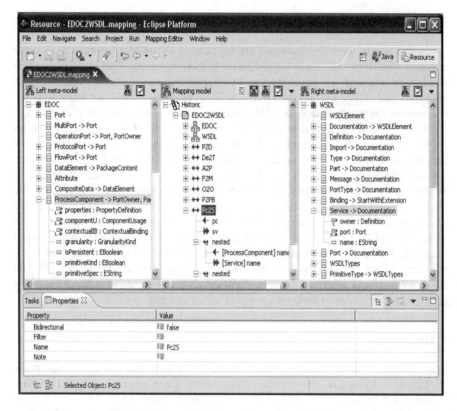

Figure 5. *Mapping specification from EDOC (CCA) to WSDL*

4. We edit the mapping model. First, we define the inter-relationships between the metamodels creating correspondences between their elements. Second, we create for each correspondence the nested correspondences. Third, for each nested correspondence, we create one Left and one or more Right elements. In addition, each Left and Right element has a ElementHandler. If it is necessary, the TypeConverter is created to define the casting between the two mapped elements.

5. The mapping model can be validated according to its metamodel, and it can be used to generate a transformation definition (e.g. using ATL language).

According to Figure 5, the mapping element Pc2S maps the element ProcessComponent from EDOC to the element Service of WSDL. A mapping model defined using our tool can be exported as an XMI file.

The tool can generate a transformation definition from a mapping model. For the moment, we have implemented a generator for ATL.

6. Conclusion

In this paper, we have discussed the application of the MDA approach for Web services platforms. We have used EDOC (CCA) to create Platform-Independent Models (PIM) and we have models two target platforms PSMs: Web services (WSDL) and J2EE (Java and JWSDP). In a previous work, we used a UML metamodel for the definition of PIMs and for an implementation on Web Services Platform. The ATL transformation definitions from UML to WSDL and from EDOC (CCA) to WSDL have produced similar results. However, we have noted that the EDOC (CCA) metamodel is closer to WSDL than the UML metamodel, which could be easily verified by ATL rules: the rules to pass from EDOC (CCA) to WSDL are less complex and shorter than those translating UML to WSDL. We have discussed the MDA transformation process, explicitly distinguishing mapping specification and transformation definition. We have proposed a metamodel for mappings and designed a tool supporting this metamodel allowing the definition of mappings between two metamodels and the generation of ATL transformation rules. We have tested our tool on different PSMs for Web services: J2EE, dotNET and BPEL4WS. In our future research, we will develop techniques of *schema matching* in order to also integrate them into our plug-in for Eclipse.

7. References

Tony Andrews, Francisco Curbera, Hitesh Dholakia, Yaron Goland, Johannes Klein, Frank Leymann, Kevin Liu, Dieter Roller, Doug Smith, Satish Thatte, Ivana Trickovic and Sanjiva Weerawarana, "Business Process Execution Language for Web Services Version 1.1", May 2003. ftp://www6.software.ibm.com/software/developer/library/ws-bpel.pdf.

Jean Bézivin, Slimane Hammoudi, Denivaldo Lopes and Frederic Jouault. Applying MDA Approach for Web Service Platform. *8th IEEE International Enterprise Distributed Object Computing Conference (EDOC 2004)*, September 2004.

Jean Bézivin, G. Dupre, F. Jouault, G. Pitette, and J. E. Rougui. First Experiments with the ATL Model Transformation Language: Transforming XSLT into XQuery. *2nd OOPSLA Workshop on Generative Techniques in the context of MDA*, October 2003.

Eclipse Tools Project. *Eclipse Modeling Framework (EMF) version 2.0*, June 2004. Available at http://www.eclipse.org/emf.

Slimane Hammoudi, Denivaldo Lopes and Jean Bézivin. Approche MDA pour le développement des e-applications sur la plate-forme des services Web. *Revue d'Ingénierie des Systèmes d'Information*, special issue on: Web services, theory and applications, June 2005.

Denivaldo Lopes. Etude et Application de l'approche MDA pour les plates formes des services Web. PhD thesis, Nantes University, July 2005.

Stephen Mellor, Kendall. Scott, Axel Uhl, and Dirk. Weise. *MDA Distilled: Principles of Model-Driven Architecture*. Addison-Wesley, 1st edition, March 2004.

OMG. Enterprise Collaboration Architecture (ECA) Specification, OMG formal/04-02-01, February 2004.

W3C. Web Services Architecture, February 2004. http://www.w3c.org/TR/2004/.

Model-Driven Design of Interoperable Agents

Klaus Fischer* — Brian Elvesæter** — Arne-Jørgen Berre** — Christian Hahn* — Cristián Madrigal-Mora* — Ingo Zinnikus*

*DFKI GmbH, Stuhlsatzenhausweg 3 (Bau 43), D-66123 Saarbrücken, Germany
klaus.fischer@dfki.de
christian.hahn@dfki.de
cristian.madrigal-mora@dfki.de
ingo.zinnikus@dfki.de

**SINTEF ICT, P. O. Box 124 Blindern, N-0314 Oslo, Norway
brian.elvesater@sintef.no
arne.j.berre@sintef.no

ABSTRACT: *This paper presents a model-driven approach to designing interoperable agents in a service-oriented architecture (SOA). The approach provides a foundation for how to incorporate autonomous agents into an SOA using principles of model-driven development (MDD). It presents a metamodel (AgentMM) for an agent architecture for a specific style of agents, i.e. BDI agents, and relates AgentMM to a platform-independent model for SOAs (PIM4SOA). The paper argues that this mapping makes it possible to design interoperable agents in the context of SOAs. In the discussion of the two metamodels strengths and weaknesses of both metamodels are discussed and extensions how each of them might be improved are presented.*

KEY WORDS: *Modelling, Metamodels, Agents, Model-Driven Development, Service-Oriented Architectures.*

1. Introduction

Model-driven development (MDD) is emerging as the state of practice for developing modern enterprise applications and software systems. MDD frameworks define a model-driven approach to software development in which visual modelling languages are used to integrate the huge diversity of technologies used in the development of software systems. As such the MDD paradigm provides us with a better way of addressing and solving interoperability issues compared to earlier non-modelling approaches (D'Souza 2001).

The current state of the art in MDD is much influenced by the ongoing standardisation activities around the OMG Model Driven Architecture (MDA) (OMG 2003). MDA defines three main abstraction levels of a system that supports a business-driven approach to software development. From a top-down perspective it starts with a computation independent model (CIM) describing the business context and business requirements of the software system. The CIM is refined to a platform independent model (PIM) which specifies software services and interfaces required by the business independent of software technology platforms. The PIM is further refined to a set of platform specific models (PSMs) which describes the realisation of the software systems with respect to the chosen software technology platforms[1].

An important aspect of defining a MDD framework is to develop metamodels and model transformations. A metamodel describes the concepts and their relationships for the purpose of building and interpreting models. Metamodels can be developed for describing different business domains (e.g. eProcurement and Telecom) and different software technology platforms (e.g. Web services and agent systems). The OMG MDA specifies two core technologies for developing metamodels and model transformations. The Meta Object Facility (MOF) (OMG 2004) is the common foundation that provides the standard modelling and interchange constructs for defining metamodels. The MOF Query/View/Transformation (QVT) (OMG 2005) provides a standard specification of a language suitable for querying and transforming models which are represented according to a MOF metamodel.

The focus of this paper is on PIM to PSM development. The basic idea is to present a PIM for service-oriented architecture (PIM4SOA) (Benguria et al. 2006) and compare it to a metamodel for a specific agent architecture (AgentMM). If a mapping between the two is feasible, meaning that PIM4SOA models can actually be translated into agent models, it is on the one hand possible to derive interoperable agents when the design is started from PIM4SOA models and, on the other hand, to clearly define under which circumstances given agent models are interoperable according to the PIM4SOA.

---

1 The terms PIM and PSM are relative to the defined software platform.

The paper is structured as follows: In section 2 we present the PIM4SOA metamodel. In section 3 we present the metamodel for a specific agent architecture. In section 4 we compare the two metamodels and discuss in section 5 the application of MDD for designing interoperable agents in an SOA. Conclusions and future work is presented in section 6.

2. Metamodel for service-oriented architectures

The metamodel for service-oriented architectures (SOAs) addresses the conceptual and technological interoperability barrier. It aims to define platform independent modelling language constructs that can be used to design, re-architect and integrate ICT infrastructure technologies supporting SOA. The concept of SOA has growing its importance during these last years. Enterprises typically view SOA as an IT solution and often the focus is on the technologies involved. The PIM4SOA has the following goals:

– The PIM4SOA model should bridge the gap between the business analysts and the IT developers and support mapping and alignment between enterprise and IT models.

– The PIM4SOA model should define a platform independent abstraction that can be used to integrate and define mappings to Web services, agent, peer-to-peer (P2P) and Grid execution platforms.

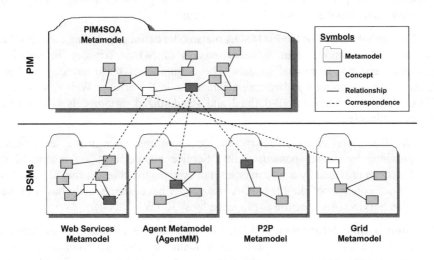

Figure 1. *Mapping metamodel concepts between the PIM and PSMs*

One challenge in defining the PIM4SOA metamodel is to decide which concepts to include and abstract from the target execution platforms (PSMs) that support the architectural style of service-orientation. The current version of the PIM4SOA metamodel has a strong focus on supporting the Web services technology stack, as this is the main enabling technology for implementing SOAs. Benguria *et al.* (Benguria *et al.* 2006) describes the use of the PIM4SOA metamodel for defining model transformations to specific Web service artefacts such as XML Schema Definition (XSD), Web Service Definition Language (WSDL) and Business Process Execution Language (BPEL) documents.

Future revisions of the PIM4SOA metamodel need to incorporate more of the adaptive and dynamic concepts from the agent, P2P and Grid platforms. The benefits of introducing agents, P2P and Grid concepts will enable us to design SOAs that are more adaptable and flexible, and thus better able to cope with changes over time – which is important for supporting interoperability. Figure 1 illustrates the mapping of metamodel concepts between the PIM4SOA and the targets PSMs. Concepts defined in the PIM4SOA metamodel should ideally map to at least two of the target platforms.

In order to support an evolution of the PIM4SOA metamodel in which new concepts from agent, P2P and Grid platforms can be incorporated, the PIM4SOA metamodels is structured around a small core with extensions, each focusing on a specific aspect of an SOA. Grouping modelling concepts in this manner allows for metamodel evolution by adding new modelling concepts by extending existing modelling concepts in the defined aspects, or defining new modelling concepts for describing additional aspects of SOAs (e.g. security).

The current version of the PIM4SOA metamodel defines modelling concepts that can be used to model four different aspects of SOAs; services, information, processes and non-functional aspects. The definition of these aspects has been influenced by ongoing standardization initiatives in the area of Web services and SOAs. Usage of already well-defined and standardized metamodels is promoted where applicable.

1. **Services:** Services are an abstraction and an encapsulation of the functionality provided by an autonomous entity. Service architectures are composed of functions provided by a system or a set of systems to achieve a shared goal. The service concepts of the PIM4SOA metamodel have been heavily based on the Web Services Architecture as proposed by W3C (W3C 2004).

2. **Information:** Information is related to the messages or structures exchanged, processed and stored by software systems or software components. The information concepts of the PIM4SOA metamodel have been based on the structural constructs for class modelling in UML 2.0 (OMG 2003).

3. **Processes:** Processes describe sequencing of work in terms of actions, control flows, information flows, interactions, protocols, etc. The process concepts of

the PIM4SOA metamodel have been founded on ongoing standardization work for the Business Process Definition Metamodel (BPDM) (IBM *et al.* 2004).

4. **Non-functional aspects:** Extra-functional qualities that can be applied to services, information and processes. Concepts for describing non-functional aspects of SOAs have been based on the UML Profile for Modeling Quality of Service and Fault Tolerance Characteristics and Mechanisms (OMG 2004).

In addition to the standards mentioned above, the work on defining the PIM4SOA metamodel has also been influenced by the UML Profile for Enterprise Distributed Object Computing (OMG 2002).

In this paper we will focus on the service concepts of the PIM4SOA metamodel. Figure 2 shows a partial subset of the PIM4SOA metamodel describing how services are modelled as collaborations. They specify a pattern of interaction between participating roles. It specifies the involved roles and their responsibilities within the collaboration. A collaboration use specifies the application of a collaboration in a specific context and includes the binding of roles to entities in that context. Collaborations are composable and a composite collaboration specifies the use of collaborations. The responsibilities of roles in a composite collaboration are defined through the bindings to roles of its used collaborations. Binary collaborations have two roles – a requester and a provider. The requester provides the input parameters and the provider the output parameters.

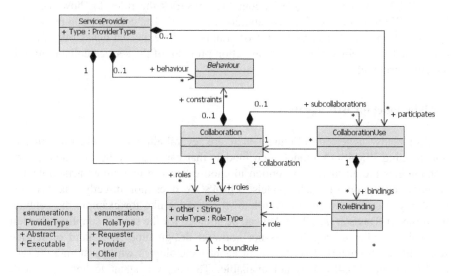

Figure 2. *Service concepts of the PIM4SOA metamodel*

In the PIM4SOA metamodel a service is viewed as a collaboration of a set of roles (ATHENA A6 2006). Therefore, when referring to a *service* in the following it should be understood as a *service collaboration*. Non-composite binary collaborations are the basic building blocks for composite collaborations. Composite services are specified by composite service collaborations. Thus composition of service collaborations is used to specify more sophisticated service definitions. Note that a service is a service definition, not the realisation or an actual instantiation.

Roles represent how a partner participates in the collaboration by providing services and parameters and using services provided by other partners in its service collaboration. Asymmetry may be introduced in service collaborations through defining the role types of the requester and provider.

We constrain that only roles in service collaborations may provide parameters. It needs further evaluation of lifting this restriction.

For comparison BPEL (Andrews *et al.* 2003) has introduced the concept of a partner link type (PLT) between two roles which are typed through WSDL port types (W3C 2001). PLTs introduce the symmetry on top of the basic asymmetrical concept. It was also partially, because it allowed "degenerated" PLTs with a single role. It does not support the nested composition of PLTs. However, when used in partner links, a process may define a set of partner links grouped into a partner.

Service collaborations are elementary symmetrical and composable and asymmetry is introduced optionally. Composite services and composite collaborations are defined using the exactly same mechanism – composition of collaborations.

Collaboration can have a behaviour that specifies the rules for how the roles interact. We refer to this as the collaboration protocol. The collaboration protocol is specified from a global view point. Constraints on the expected behaviour of a role can be deduced. Obviously the collaboration protocol of the service collaboration is a service protocol.

3. Metamodel for BDI agents

As already suggested in Figure 1 there are several alternatives when it comes to transforming PIM4SOA models into models that can actually be executed. Agent technologies are an interesting option to choose because they allow a flexible and adaptive execution of such models. PIM4SOA does not directly ask for this flexibility. However, there are well-known examples like for example the contract net protocol (Davis *et al.* 1983) that can be adopted for the service supplier selection when the number of suppliers is not know at design time. This kind of service selection can be nicely described with agent technologies while a straightforward model for the PIM4SOA is not available. To integrate agent technologies with PIM4SOA is therefore a worthwhile enterprise.

For the design of agents with rational and flexible problem solving behaviour, the BDI agent architecture has been proven successful during the last decade (Rao *et al.* 1991, Rao *et al.* 1995). Three mental attitudes (beliefs, desires, and intentions) allow an agent to act in and to reason about its environment in an effective manner.

It is therefore of no surprise that a vast number of tools and methodologies have been developed to foster the software-based development of BDI agents and multi-agent systems. Rather than inventing our own agent metamodel, we took a bottom-up approach in which we extracted the metamodel (AgentMM) from one of the most sophisticated tools for the design of BDI agents (i.e. JACK™ Intelligent Agents (AOS)). **Error! Reference source not found.** presents the most interesting part of this metamodel for the discussion that we want to do in this paper.

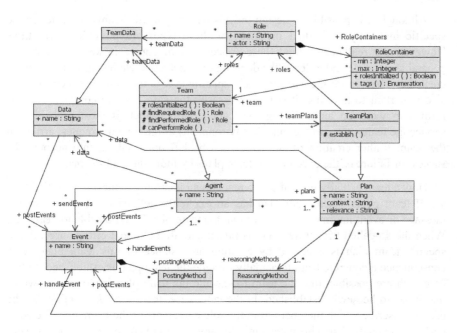

Figure 3. *Partial metamodel for BDI agents*

We start with a neural description of the concepts that are included in AgentMM and discuss the relation between PIM4SOA and AgentMM in the next section.

The most important concept in AgentMM is the concept of a team. Teams are either atomic, in which case we can refer to them as agents, or consist of a set of roles that all together form the team. It is important to note that even in the most simple case where all roles of a team are meant to be filled by an individual atomic agent it is not the case that all members of the teams need to be involved in all the tasks the team is able to work on. Rather for each individual task a set of individuals (we do not want to call them agents because they can be teams, too) from the team members are selected to actually work on the task. Tasks a team is able to work on, are defined by the roles the team is able to perform. The roles a team requires to be filled by individuals are role containers where the team definition specifies how many individuals are needed at minimum as a role filler and how many individuals are allowed at maximum where both numbers can be set to 0 or any (which of course means any finite number).

Role definitions are the second important concept for the definition of teams. A role defines which messages (in Jack these messages are rather events that teams send to each other, however, we do not want to go into the details of the discussion of these concepts) the role fillers are able to react to and which messages they are likely to send.

Although it is possible to design models where types for teams and roles are so specific that only individual instances of these types are possible at run-time. However, the real idea behind these concepts is of course to keep the types as general as possible and to leave the decision of which concrete instances are actually created or selected for the execution of a specific task to the runtime execution. It is also important to note that it is not necessarily the case that the complete team is formed to work on an incoming top-level request (which is most probably the service the team offers to the outside environment) at the time the request arrives at the team. Rather creation of sub-teams can be left open, taking into account the success or failure of the execution of team plans by individual sub-teams.

How a team actually goes about to react on an incoming request is specified by a set of team plans. Each team plan has an explicitly defined objective (incoming message or event internal to the team) that the team plan is responsible to deal with. When the so-called triggering event is raised and all additional criteria are valid, a specific team plan is executed by creating an instance of this team plan. As a consequence a concrete team to actually execute the team plan is established. In this case both are possible, that the team to execute the team plan is already known or that it has to be newly established. In the latter case, the *establish()* method can be used to describe which members from the role containers of the team are selected to perform the team plan. This means that for any specific task to work on a new sub-team can be dynamically formed from the set of team members that actually work on the task. The separation of the team members into different role containers that correspond to different role types helps with respect to selecting adequate agents.

Although message events can be posted to teams, it is in the current version of AgentMM rather difficult to describe the interaction among teams. This is due to the fact that there seems to be no straightforward way to specify the reaction of the sender to replies from individual team members of a sub-team when a message event is sent to a role container that holds more than one member. It is probably possible to map the replies to the synthesis of belief sets but, on the one hand, this means that in the protocol description the answers will not be visible as messages but rather as changes to belief sets. On the other hand, it seems to be not possible to react to these belief set changes in the team plan that actually sends the message (at least not in a straightforward manner). This disadvantage is not a general problem of agent technologies but rather is a result from the decision to derive AgentMM from the Jack BDI development environment. However, the best way to describe interactions from a centralised point of view for the whole interaction is far from obvious.

4. Comparison of the metamodels for PIM4SOA and BDI agents

Although the concepts PIM4SOA and AgentMM differ quite significantly a mapping of PIM4SOA models to AgentMM model seems to be feasible because AgentMM is more expressive. Therefore, a transformation of PIM4SAO models to AgentMM is our main aim.

The first element we inspect is the *ServiceProvider*. At first glance an agent seems to be the best match, but since a *ServiceProvider* references roles, it is recommended to assign it to a team. The name of the *ServiceProvider* coincides with the name of the team and its roles are the roles the team performs.

While a *ServiceProvider* is supposed to represent an atomic team, i.e. a team that consists of an individual agent, a *Collaboration* is mapped onto a team that may consist of any number of agents. However, because collaborations do not specify any cardinalities for roles, we assume that a collaboration asks for exactly one filler for each of the required roles. Therefore we suggest to map collaborations to a team structure where the required roles have a min-max requirement of exactly one role filler. Additionally a generic team plan is created that represents the collaborations behaviour as a body and requires all roles that are specified in the collaboration. Each collaboration use then is an additional team plan where the generic team plan of the collaboration is used and extended by a renaming of roles (in AgentMM this is done by a "uses role1 as role2" specification).

The most severe difference between PIM4SOA and AgentMM is the manner in which the interaction protocol among the members of a *Collaboration* (team) is described. In PIM4SOA this interaction protocol is specified from a centralised point of view for both parties involved. Such a description is in AgentMM in its current form not directly available. When one wants to transform the PIM4SOA interaction protocol into AgentMM models it is necessary to extract from the centralized description of the PIM4SOA model the projections of the behaviour for the individual parties of the interaction. Because it is clear who initiates the interaction it is clear that for the initiator it is possible to provide a team plan that reflects its behaviour of the initiator and to provide a set of plans that describe the reaction to the incoming messages on the server's side. It needs to be investigated in how far the protocol descriptions in the PIM4SOA models can be automatically transformed into the models that need to be executed by the individual parties in AgentMM.

5. Discussion

There are quite a number of similarities between PIM4SOA and AgentMM. The concepts *ServiceProvider*, *Collaboration*, and *CollaborationUse* on the one hand and team, role, and team plan on the other hand correspond quite nicely as we could see in the last section. The difference in actually describing interactions on the one hand is a challenge when one wants to transform the models from PIM4SOA to AgentMM. On the other hand, it also provides chances to actually improve the AgentMM with additional models that are possibly more compact and easier to read.

The idea of allowing more than one role filler for specific roles in a team in AgentMM is more general than the idea of roles in collaborations of PIM4SOA models. However, it also complicates the description of the interaction among these roles. Even if we restrict ourselves to the case of two roles interacting with each other we need to have quite powerful concepts available to express how messages should be exchanged among these groups. Let us assume that we have two role containers of type *role1* and *role2*, respectively, and that each of these containers has more than one role fillers. If we allowed writing "role1 → role2" meaning that a message is sent from *role1* to *role2*, what should this actually mean? That every member of the role container *role1* would send this message to every member of role container *role2*? It would be possible to constrain the selection of senders and receivers but it is open how an elegant way of describing these constraints could look like. Additionally, one should realise that sending messages is one thing but it is also necessary that it should be possible to describe the handling of replies in an intuitive manner.

However, even if we restrict ourselves to the situation where messages have to be exchanged between individuals (teams or agents), AgentMM already provides advantages over PIM4SOA because it allows the intuitive description of more complex protocols. The contract net protocol (where a manager selects the best offer from a set of bidders (Davis *et al.* 1983)) is a good example for such a situation. In the contract net protocol the number of bidders that will be approached is not known at the design time of the protocol. Still the contract net protocol has a clear initiator for each of the interactions (the manager) and all other parties involved (bidders) need only to reply to incoming messages. The restriction that applies to the models that can be easily described in AgentMM is as follows: The protocol needs an individual initiator that can interact with any number of roles where for each of these roles any number of role fillers can be dynamically assigned at run-time where the interaction between the initiator and the participating roles are pure request-response patterns. We do not say that it is impossible to design more complicated protocols in AgentMM, However, in its current version there is at least no straightforward design pattern available to describe such protocols.

PIM4SOA, however, provides in the end at least a concrete proposal for how to describe the message interchange between two interacting parties from a centralised point of view and therefore could be included in AgentMM to at least deal with describing the interaction between two parties in specific cases.

6. Conclusions and Future Work

The paper presented a metamodel for SOAs (PIM4SOA) and a metamodel for a specific class of agents (AgentMM). The similarities between the two metamodels are high enough to allow a mapping of PIM4SOA to AgentMM to a large degree. Therefore the idea of designing interoperable agents by using PIM4SOA models and transforming them into AgentMM models seems to be feasible. The extension that AgentMM provides on the one hand gives the chance to introduce greater flexibility and adaptiveness into SOAs. For concepts that prove to be particularly useful in this context there is even the chance that they might be included into the PIM4SOA in the long run. The major part of future work that needs to be done is in the comparison of the process models of the two metamodels.

The work published in this paper is partly funded by the European Commission through the ATHENA IP (Advanced Technologies for interoperability of Heterogeneous Enterprise Networks and their Applications Integrated Project) (IST-507849). The work does not represent the view of the European Commission or the ATHENA consortium, and the authors are solely responsible for the paper's content.

7. References

AOS, "JACK Intelligent Agents", The Agent Oriented Software Group (AOS). http://www.agent-software.com/shared/home/.

Andrews, T., Curbera, F., Dholakia, H., Goland, Y., Klein, J., Leymann, F., Liu, K., Roller, D., Smith, D., Thatte, S., Trickovic, I., and Weerawarana, S. "Business Process Execution Language for Web Services Version 1.1", May 2003. ftp://www6.software.ibm.com/software/developer/library/ws-bpel.pdf.

Benguria, G., Larrucea, X., Elvesæter, B., Neple, T., Beardsmore, A., Friess, M. "A Platform Independent Model for Service Oriented Architectures", paper presented at the I-ESA'2006 conference, Bordeaux, France, March 2006.

Davis, R. and Smith, R.G. "Negotiation as a metaphor for distributed problem solving", Artificial Intelligence, vol. 20, 1983, pp. 63–109.

D'Souza D., "Model-Driven Architecture and Integration - Opportunities and Challenges, Version 1.1", Kineticum, 2001. http://www.catalysis.org/publications/papers/2001-mda-reqs-desmond-6.pdf.

IBM, Adaptive, Borland, Data Access Technologies, EDS, and 88 Solutions, "Business Process Definition Metamodel – Revised Submission to BEI RFP bei/2003-01-06", Object Management Group (OMG), Document bei/04-08-03, August 2004. http://www.omg.org/docs/bei/04-08-03.pdf.

OMG, "UML Profile for Enterprise Distributed Object Computing Specification", Object Management Group (OMG), Document ptc/02-02-05, 2002. http://www.omg.org/ technology/documents/formal/edoc.htm.

OMG, "MDA Guide Version 1.0.1", Object Management Group (OMG), Document omg/03-06-01, June 2003. http://www.omg.org/docs/omg/03-06-01.pdf.

OMG, "UML 2.0 Superstructure Specification", Object Management Group (OMG), Document ptc/03-08-02, August 2003. http://www.omg.org/docs/ptc/03-08-02.pdf.

OMG, "UML Profile for Modeling Quality of Service and Fault Tolerance Characteristics and Mechanisms", Object Management Group (OMG), Document ptc/04-09-01, September 2004. http://www.omg.org/docs/ptc/04-09-01.pdf.

OMG, "Meta Object Facility (MOF) 2.0 Core Specification", Object Management Group (OMG), Document ptc/04-10-15, October 2004. http://www.omg.org/docs/ptc/04-10-15.pdf.

OMG, "Meta Object Facility (MOF) 2.0 Query/View/Transformation Specification", Object Management Group (OMG), Document ptc/05-11-01, November 2005. http://www.omg.org/docs/ptc/05-11-01.pdf.

Rao A. S. and Georgeff M. P., "Modeling Agents within a BDI-Architecture", R. Fikes and E. Sandewall (Eds.), Proc. of the 2rd International Conference on Principles of Knowledge Representation and Reasoning (KR'91), Morgan Kaufmann, Cambridge, Mass. April, 1991, pp. 473-484.

Rao A. S. and Georgeff M. P., "BDI-Agents: from theory to practice", Victor Lesser (Ed.), Proceedings of the First Intl. Conference on Multiagent Systems, San Francisco, AAAI Press/The MIT Press, 1995.

W3C, "Web Services Description Language (WSDL) 1.1", World Wide Web Consortium (W3C), W3C Note, 15 March 2001. http://www.w3.org/TR/2001/NOTE-wsdl-20010315.

W3C, "Web Services Architecture", World Wide Web Consortium (W3C), W3C Working Group Note, 11 February 2004. http://www.w3.org/TR/2004/NOTE-ws-arch-20040211/.

Session 2:
Web Services for Interoperability

Information Security Patterns for Web Services

Jesper Holgersson — Eva Söderström — Per Backlund

*School of Humanities and Informatics, University of Skövde, Box 408, 541 28
Sweden*
jesper.holgersson@his.se
eva.soderstrom@his.se
Per Backlund@his.se

ABSTRACT: *Web Services (WS), a currently popular subject among application developers, IT
architects, and researchers, can be defined as a technology for publishing, identifying and
calling services in a network of interacting computer nodes. The purpose of this paper is to
illustrate the benefits of using patterns as a means of managing knowledge concerning
security in the context of Web Services. We draw upon experiences from an industrial project
in which a pattern catalogue for Web Services was created. The pattern catalogue consists of
29 patterns, which are generic solutions for service-based development and service-oriented
architectures. In particular, Web Services are in focus as the enabling technique.*

KEY WORDS: *web services, information security, patterns.*

1. Introduction

Web Services (WS), a currently popular subject among application developers, IT architects, and researchers, can be defined as a technology for publishing, identifying and calling services in a network of interacting computer nodes (Henkel and Wiktorin, 2005). Most large organisations have some form of attitude or position towards this phenomenon (Azzara, 2002), and there will be a basic change in how applications are created and disseminated (Wong, 2002). However, there are still aspects to be resolved: security, transactions, process flows, user interaction etc. (Dunn, 2003; Wong, 2002; Smolnicki, 2004; Estrem, 2003). This paper is focused on the security issues, since Web Services by their very nature, bring new challenges in this area. Examples are: Maintaining security while routing between multiple Web Services; Unauthorised access; Parameter manipulation/malicious input; Network eavesdropping and message replay; and Denial of Service (DoS).

The purpose of this paper is to illustrate the benefits of using patterns as a means of managing knowledge concerning security in the context of Web Services. We draw upon experiences from an industrial project in which a pattern catalogue for Web Services was created. The pattern catalogue consists of 29 patterns, which are generic solutions for service-based development and service-oriented architectures. In particular, Web Services are in focus as the enabling technique. The paper is structured as follows: background information is provided in Chapter 2, before the pattern catalogue is introduced with four example patterns in Chapter 3. The paper is concluded by a discussion of future work in Chapter 4.

2. Background

This chapter will introduce the concepts of patterns and Web Services, in order to set the scene for explaining the pattern catalogue in more detail in Chapter 3.

2.1. *Patterns*

Patterns have been proposed as a means for managing knowledge in various contexts (Gamma *et al.*, 1995; Coplien and Schmidt, 1995 ELEKTRA, 1998). A pattern can be defined as description of a problem, which occurs over and over again in our environment paired with a core solution to that problem. It is a core solution in the sense that it can be used a number of times without doing things in the exactly same way twice. There are different styles for writing patterns but the core of a pattern should always include the problem, the context in which the problem occurs and the proposed solution to the problem. The pattern is described in plain text (e.g. organisational patterns from Coplien and Schmidt, 1995) or in the form of models and diagrams (e.g. design patterns from Gamma *et al.*, 1995). In this paper we adopt a style as illustrated in Table 1.

Name and source	The name and origin of the pattern.
Also known as	Other names of the pattern as well as references to where they can be found.
Type	Refers to the classification of the pattern in the pattern catalogue.
Purpose	Describes the purpose of the pattern.
Forces	Describes the context affecting the problem and its solution.
Problem	Describes the problem which the pattern is dealing with.
Solution	Gives the core solution to the problem. The solution should also indicate in what way the patter solves the problem.
Consequences	Describes any side effect that the application of the pattern may have. There may be situations in which the proposed solution may have a negative effect on the resulting context.
Related patterns	Describes the relation to other patterns in order to allow for an internal structure of the catalogue.

Table 1. *Pattern style for the Web Services pattern catalogue*

We have chosen patterns as the means of codification of the knowledge contributions identified since they constitute a way of giving the results a concrete form. Furthermore, patterns may be organised in a pattern repository for better overview and access.

2.2. Web Services introduction

Web Services is a technology for publishing, identifying and calling services in a network of interacting computer nodes (Henkel and Wiktorin, 2005). A number of different actors may be involved in providing and using Web Services, depending on how they are rolled out (e.g. if published for public access or not). There must be at least one provider and one consumer. In addition, there may also be a registry displaying the Web Services and providing information about them to potential consumers. Figure 1 shows a basic WS model and the interaction between the actors involved in the WS consumption along with the communication standard used.

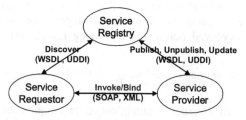

Figure 1. *Web Service actors and operations*
(from Tsalgatidou & Pilioura, 2002)

As illustrated in Figure 1, the service provider, here the holder of the WS implementation publishes a WS in a WS registry, using WSDL and UDDI. A WS requestor, i.e. the node that wants to use the WS, searches the registry also using WSDL and UDDI. If a suitable WS is found, the requestor binds to it, using SOAP and XML. The actors (Provider and Requestor) in the WS model should be considered as logical constructs, meaning that a WS can exhibit characteristics of both (Kreger, 2001).

By using a set of basic standards, i.e. XML, SOAP, WSDL and UDDI, Web Services enable information exchange along with service-based development and are thereby part of a more general strive for information exchange and software development based on well defined service interfaces.

2.3. *Information security for WS*

Information security can be defined as:

"...the concepts, techniques, technical measures, and administrative measures used to protect information assets from deliberate or inadvertent unauthorized acquisition, damage, disclosure, manipulation, modification, loss or use." (McDaniel, 1994)

This means that there have to be mechanisms that protect information during transit as well as in storage. In this context, the following requirements have to be considered in order to achieve information security (Boncella, 2004; Åhlfeldt *et al.*, 2005):

- *Confidentiality* which means that information during transit can not be read by unauthorised entities.
- *Integrity* which means that information can not be changed or tampered with during transit by unauthorised entities.
- *Availability* which means that a WS have to be accessible for its authenticated and authorized users.
- *Traceability* which means that all activities performed between sender and receiver shall be possible to record in order to prevent that sender or receiver can deny their interference in a, for instance, SOAP-message transaction.

By fulfilling these requirements, information security can be obtained, hence protecting information both in transit as well as when stored on a server. For Web Services, information security is of particular importance, since organizations' source systems are deployed publicly. Or as King (2003, p8) puts it, when you deploy a WS

"...you are by default allowing access through port 80 (...) directly in to the heart of your infrastructure."

However, as for all Internet communication techniques, Web Services have security weaknesses that have to be highlighted and managed. It is essential for organisations to be aware of these potential problems when using Web Services. The main security problem differentiating Web Services from other Internet communication techniques is to maintain security while routing between multiple Web Services (O'Neil, 2003; Boncella, 2004). When a SOAP message path involves intermediaries, i.e. other Web Services residing between the original sender and receiver, traditional security techniques for data in transit (such as SSL and VPN), handling any other type of Internet communication technique, do not work. Traditional security techniques operate on the lower OSI stack levels, encrypting the entire communication session without the possibility to selectively encrypt or digitally sign a specific part of the message. This means that the intermediary needs to decrypt the whole message upon arrival in order to extract information about where to forward the message etc. When a message is decrypted and thus written in clear text, it is vulnerable to unauthorised access, which may result in that the requirements of confidentiality and integrity are hence not fulfilled. The pattern catalogue covers several security aspects such as preventing unauthorised access, avoiding replaying of messages etc.

3. Pattern repository for Web Services information security

In the following subsections we will briefly introduce the pattern catalogue and thereafter we present four security patterns in more detail.

3.1. *Introducing the catalogue*

The catalogue (see Figure 2) was developed as a collection of generic solutions, so called patterns, for service-based development and service-based architectures. The patterns present core solutions to common problems that may arise when companies want to implement and use Web Services. The problem situations are thus in focus, and not the solutions per se. Instead, the solutions are generally on a relatively high level of abstraction. This means that implementation specific details, when applicable, are only stated as references to the specifications in question.

In general, all patterns affect one another, and the solution to one problem may also solve another one. Similarly, one solution may require a complementary solution in order to completely solve a problem.

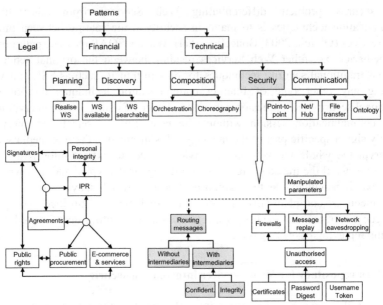

Figure 2. *Overview of the pattern catalogue*

Figure 2 illustrates what patterns are included in the catalogue (29 in all). This paper is focused on security aspects, the highlighted part of the figure. Each pattern is expressed using the style presented in section 2.1.

3.2. *Four example patterns*

As mentioned, this paper is focused on patterns related to maintaining security while routing between multiple Web Services. The motivations are: SOAP-routing is a key problem; the practical relevance of the patterns is expected to be high; and most importantly, this problem is unique to Web Services compared to other Internet technologies.

Name and source	To preserve message security in a point to point connection. From SERVIAM-LIT-05, SERVIAM-SUF-02.
Also known as	-
Type	Technical patterns; Security patterns
Purpose	To preserve the integrity and confidentiality of a message (from point to point) in a Web Service interaction.
Forces	Hostile actors may try to get unauthorised access to information, e.g. by monitoring HTTP routers, which can damage both the consumer and the service provider.

Problem	There are ample possibilities to pick up SOAP-messages. If the message is sent in plain text the information can be picked up and used for unintended purposes.
Solution	Utilise a cryptogram so that no unauthorised person can read the message. SSL and TSL are two security mechanisms which can handle cryptograms and signatures for messages sent using HTTPS.
Consequences	Point-to-point technologies do not ensure security between the leaf nodes. Neither do point-to-point technologies provide the possibility to filter SOAP messages at firewalls. Furthermore, point-to-point technologies do not provide persistent security since the message is not encoded at the respective nodes. Hence, the message is still vulnerable to unauthorised access at storage.
Related patterns	Achieving message security with intermediaries. Avoiding bypassing of firewalls. Hinder unauthorised access. Hindering eavesdropping. Prevent resending of messages. Protecting a Web Service from manipulated input parameters. Achieving message confidentiality with and without intermediaries.

Pattern 1: Achieving message security – without intermediaries

Name and source	To preserve message security while using intermediaries. From SERVIAM-LIT-05, SERVIAM-SUF-02, WSSa
Also known as	-
Type	Technical patterns; Security patterns
Purpose	To preserve end to end message integrity and confidentiality in a Web Service interaction.
Forces	Unreliable or poorly implemented intermediaries used by hackers or other malicious persons aiming for information that can be used for exploiting both consumers and requestors.
Problem	When a SOAP intermediary is residing between the end nodes in a WS-Interaction, existing Internet security techniques, such as SSL and TLS, cannot handle message confidentiality and integrity since these techniques only provide security between two points (see figure, security context 1). In order to guarantee message security between the end nodes in the WS-interaction (see figure, security context 2) new ways of handling security have to be established.

	One example of this problematic situation might be an e-commerce business which acts like a portal, sending messages to different WS handling payment, deliveries and so on. The point of using WS is that the portal sends one message aimed for different receivers and each receiver should only have access to "his" part of the message. The rest of the message, aimed for other receivers, should be unreadable, i.e. encrypted, for an unauthorised receiver.
Solution	Use XML-Encryption and XML-Signature, via HTTP, according to the specification for WS-Security. XML-encryption guarantees confidentiality for messages sent via intermediaries by providing mechanisms to encrypt certain portions of a message with a specific key, aimed for one single receiver. The same can be used for other parts of the message aimed for other receivers. This means that a receiver can only access its own part of the message, the rest is hidden. An XML-Signature is used in basically the same way, enabling selective signing of certain portions of a message aimed for a specific receiver. The XML-signature guarantees the integrity of the message. If the content of the message has been manipulated during transit, this will be detected by the signature since it will not match the new content of the message.
Consequences	Lowered performance is a negative effect of XML-Encryption since, compared to SSL, a greater number of keys have to be created. Moreover, the usage of XML-Encryption and XML-Signatures are quite complex compared to existing Internet security techniques, such as SSL and TLS. If there are no intermediaries, i.e. point to point interaction, SSL and TLS works fine.
Related patterns	Hinder unauthorised access. Hindering eavesdropping. Prevent resending of messages. Protecting a Web Service from manipulated input parameters. Achieving message confidentiality with and without intermediaries.

Pattern 2: Achieving message security – with intermediaries

Name and source	To preserve message confidentiality while using intermediaries. From SERVIAM-LIT-05, SERVIAM-SUF-02, WSSa.
Also known as	-
Type	Technical patterns; Security patterns
Purpose	To preserve end to end message confidentiality in a Web Service interaction.
Forces	Existing Internet security techniques that not are designed to work in a public Web Service environment might be used by attacking entities in order to get access to sensitive information that can be used to gain unauthorised access or for other malicious purposes.
Problem	When a SOAP intermediary is residing between the end nodes in a WS-Interaction existing Internet security techniques, such as SSL and TLS, cannot handle message confidentiality. The reason for this is that SOAP and SSL works at different layers, resulting in a situation

	where an intermediary, working at the SOAP-level, has to decrypt any encrypted message in order to obtain information in the message. This means that confidentiality of the message cannot be guaranteed.
Solution	Use XML-Encryption via HTTP, to enable selective encryption of certain portions of a message. The distribution of keys can be managed in different ways. One alternative is to use a symmetric key directly. The other alternative, most commonly used, is to generate a symmetric key which is exchanged via an asymmetric key, i.e. key wrapping. XML-Encryption supports several PKI algorithms, such as 3DES and AES. All information about the encryption is included in the SOAP-message header, pointing out references to other parts of the message where the actual encryption takes place. See WSS SOAP Message Security 1.0 for more information.
Consequences	One possible shortcoming is that XML-Encryption, compared to more mature Internet security technologies, such as SSL, is that there is not so much experience using XML-Encryption in order to provide message security for Web Services. Point to point techniques, such as SSL, are much more mature and are thus recommended if there are no intermediaries involved in the WS-interaction. However, XML-Encryption is a much more scalable approach for the usage of public Web Services.
Related patterns	Hinder unauthorised access. Hindering eavesdropping. Prevent resending of messages. Protecting a Web Service from manipulated input parameters. Achieving message confidentiality with and without intermediaries.

Pattern 3: Achieving message security - confidentiality

Name and source	To preserve message integrity while using intermediaries. From SERVIAM-LIT-05, SERVIAM-SUF-02, WSSa.
Also known as	-
Type	Technical patterns; Security patterns
Purpose	To preserve end to end message confidentiality in a Web Service interaction.
Forces	Existing Internet security techniques that are not designed to work in a public Web Service environment might be used by attacking entities in order to obtain sensitive information that can be manipulated for different malicious purposes.
Problem	When a SOAP intermediary is residing between the end nodes in a WS-Interaction, existing Internet security techniques, such as SSL and TLS, cannot handle message confidentiality. The reason is that SOAP and SSL works at different layers, resulting in a situation where an intermediary, working at the SOAP-level, have to decrypt any encrypted message in order to obtain information in the message. This means that confidentiality as well as integrity of the message cannot be guaranteed since if there is a possibility to read the

	message, it is also possible to alter the content of the message.
Solution	Use XML-Signature via HTTP, enabling selective signing of certain portions of a message. The signature of a specific part of the message guarantees that any attempts to manipulate the signed content of this specific part of the message will be discovered by the receiver. Signatures in XML can be used in different ways by using direct or indirect references from the header of the message to the signed parts of the message. For further information, see WSS SOAP Message Security 1.0.
Consequences	One possible negative effect of using XML-Signature is that it might be relative complex to implement mechanisms handling messages with multiple signatures. A positive side effect of using XML-Signature is that mechanisms for authentication are strengthened.
Related patterns	Hinder unauthorised access. Hindering eavesdropping. Prevent resending of messages. Protecting a Web Service from manipulated input parameters. Achieving message confidentiality with and without intermediaries.

Pattern 4: Achieving message security - integrity

4. Future work

In this paper, patterns are proposed as a means to manage knowledge about WS security. We have shown a subset of a pattern repository, and the patterns were identified and validated in an industry-focused project. In order to make the pattern catalogue a useful and trustworthy body of knowledge, it has to be more thoroughly evaluated. Such an evaluation has to comprise both an evaluation of the actual content as well as an evaluation of the usefulness of a pattern repository for Web Services patterns. In this process, it is important to draw upon existing knowledge and good practice of pattern usage in general. One situation illustrating the industry relevance of the patterns is during set-up and enhancement of Web Services and Service-Oriented Architectures. The patterns show potential security problems that must be catered and prepared for before launching and using the architecture in live business situations. Hence, the patterns may help organisations to avoid problems before they actually occur.

The actual usage situation must be clearly understood and the patterns used must fit into that situation or be possible to adapt. Below we point out some properties that we find critical the evaluation of a pattern repository:

- *Tool support and guidelines for creating and managing patterns in systematic way*: This includes the identification of using WS security patterns in practice.

- *Pattern contribution to security practice in Web Services*: How can the patterns contribute to current practice? Are they useful at all? To what extent are they useful?
- *Tool support for reuse and/or customisation*: This is the core of the patterns philosophy and must be developed and facilitated.
- *Traceability:* Traceability is necessary for efficient updating and maintenance. This is a critical question of quality and reliability.
- *Content and validity*: The specific solutions presented have to be validated to guarantee functionality and correctness. What other security patterns are there regarding security for Web Services? What improvements should be made to the catalogue and to the existing patterns? On what level of detail should Web Services patterns be described?
- *Completeness*: The repository has to be evaluated and extended with respect to its relevance to the industry. This work includes both the existing patterns as well as identification of new ones. It may also be feasible to extend the content beyond WS security. It is critical that the evaluation takes place in close collaboration with industry.

Finally we want to point out that quality assessment criteria must be met if patterns are to become a contribution to web services engineering. A strategy for the *elicitation and evaluation* of patterns must be formed (Rolland *et al.* 2000). A strategy for *using* patterns must also be defined in order to make them an integral part of the process of developing web services.

5. References

Azzara, C. *Web Services: The Next Frontier: A Primary Research Opportunity Study*, Topical report: Enterprise Findings, Hurwitz Group, Inc. (2002).

Boncella, R. J. Web Services and Web Service Security. *Proceedings of the Americas Conference in Information Systems*. N.Y., August 2004.

Bragg, R. *et al. Network Security: The Complete Reference*. Emeryville, California: McGraw-Hill/Osborne. 2003. ISBN: 0-07-222697-8.

Coplien, J. and Schmidt, D. Pattern Languages of Program Design, *Reading, Massachussets*: Adison-Wesley Publishing Company, 1995.

Dunn, B. A Manager's Guide to Web Services, *EAI Journal*, January 2003, pp.14-17.

ELEKTRA, *"The Patterns Model"*, UP1, UMIST, Manchester, Paris ESPRIT 7.1 project No. 22927, 1998.

Estrem, W. An evaluation framework for deploying Web Services in the next generation manufacturing enterprise, *Robotics and Computer Integrated Manufacturing*, 19 (2003), pp.509-519.

Gamma, E., Helm, R., Johnson, R. and Vlissides, J. Design Patterns Elements of Reusable Object-Oriented Software, *Reading Massachusets*: Addison-Wesley Publishing Company, 1995.

Henkel, M. and Wiktorin, L. *Architectures and processes* (in Swedish), Serviamprojektet, Project report (part II), February 17, 2005, pp.27-47.

King, S. Threats and Solutions to Web Services Security. *Network Security*, Volume 2003, September 2003.

Kreger, H. *Web Services Conceptual Architecture (WSCA 1.0)*. IBM Software Group, 2001. Available on the Internet (040121): http://www.306.ibm.com/software/solutions/ webservices/pdf/WSCA.pdf.

McDaniel, G. ed. *IBM Dictionary of Computing*. New York, NY: McGraw-Hill, Inc., 1994. ISBN: 0070314896.

Newcomer, E. *Understanding Web Services: XML, WSDL, SOAP and UDDI*. UK, 2002. Addison-Wesley. ISBN: 0-201-75081-3.

Rolland, C., Stirna, J., Prekas, N., Loucopoulos, P., Persson, A. and Grosz, G. Evaluating a Pattern Approach as an Aid for the Development of Organisational Knowledge: An Empirical Study In *CAiSE 2000*, Vol. 1789 (Eds, Wangler, B. and Bergman, L.) Springer, Stockholm, pp. 176-191.

Smolnicki, J. *How XML and web services will change your business*, PriceWaterhouseCoopers, 2003, as is: 2004-01-08, available at: http://www.pwcglobal.com/Extweb/ncinthenews.nsf/ docid/ 2C9CB295270D752DCA256DD5006D122D.

Tsalgatidou, A and Pilioura, T. An overview of Standards and Related Technology in Web Services. 2002. *Distributed and Parallel Databases*. pp.135-162.

Wong, S. Success with Web Services, *EAI Journal*, February 2002, pp.27-29.

Åhlfeldt, R.-M., Backlund, P., Wangler, B. and Söderström, E. Security Issues in Health Care Process Integration: Research-in-Progress Report, In *Proceedings of INTEROP-EMOI 05, 2nd INTEROP-EMOI Open Workshop on Enterprise Models and Ontologies for Interoperability*, Porto, Portugal, June 13-14, 2005, pp.363-366.

Detecting Similarities between Web Service Interfaces: the WSDL Analyzer

Ingo Zinnikus — Hans-Jörg Rupp — Klaus Fischer

DFKI GmbH, Stuhlsatzenhausweg 3 (Bau 43), D-66123 Saarbruecken, Germany
Ingo.Zinnikus@dfki.de
hjrupp@dfki.de
Klaus.Fischer@dfki.de

ABSTRACT: *Current trends in IT development such as the evolving service-oriented architectures encounter substantial interoperability problems. The Web service stack (SOAP, WSDL, UDDI) is the de-facto standard for service-oriented architectures. We present the WSDL Analyzer, a tool for detecting similarities between Web service interfaces which supports flexible service invocation in a dynamic environment.*

KEY WORDS: *Service-Oriented Architecture, Web Services, Mediation, Dynamic Invocation.*

1. Introduction

In present days, there is a growing tendency towards collaborative enterprises. Customer relationship management, e-procurement, supply chain management, and enterprise resource planning are practice in modern enterprises. Current trends in IT development will support e-commerce and e-business even stronger. However, today's enterprises operate in a dynamic environment of accelerated global outsourcing, ever-shrinking product life-cycles, and fickle demand. A major business trend in this environment is the need for increased information-sharing and collaboration among enterprises during the entire product life cycle. While organizations are gradually transforming into "networked organizations", interoperability becomes the main challenge to be tackled to realize the vision of seamless business interaction across organizational boundaries. Therefore, enterprises are looking for ways to make their current business competencies easily available to the market and to achieve higher automation in their own internal processes. The ability to share these competencies as services is a critical step towards the development of the Business-to-Business (B2B) e-commerce.

Service-oriented architectures have the potential to increase interoperability of ITC applications significantly. However, business applications ask for planned and customizable services, which basically come down to the requirement for a methodology to do service invocation and composition in a flexible and efficient manner. The flexible combination and usage of services in such a service-oriented environment is a key feature.

Control of the actual services invoked and the concrete processes performed is crucial. A partner service is selected at design-time and appropriate steps for invocation are implemented using e.g. standard tools such as Apache Axis (Axis). However, almost every change to a system which adopts such an approach is likely to end-up in painstaking programming sessions.

Data exchange per se within an SOA environment is unproblematic, if partners comply with the same data structure. However, basic interoperability problems occur when one of the partners uses a slightly different or even heterogeneous data structure in its interface. In this case, parameter passing requires an additional mapping or mediation step which transforms data from one schema to the other. This step can be prepared manually at design time by formulating reconciliation rules or by applying schema matching algorithms which help to create mappings between schemas automatically.

Web-based applications in service-oriented architectures are currently based on the Web service standards such as SOAP (Christensen *et al.* 2001), WSDL (Gudgin *et al.* 2003) and UDDI. Web services offer easy and standardized internet-based communication for loosely coupled and dynamically discovered components. Partners in a collaboration exchange descriptions of protocols and interfaces, e.g. WSDL descriptions. A crucial task in the context of enterprise application integration is to adapt a process to the partner service and change invocation and processing of the response. For supporting this process, we developed the WSDL Analyzer.

The WSDL Analyzer is first and foremost a tool for detecting similarities and differences between WSDL files. The tool can be used to find a list of similar services (matchmaking, service discovery). Since the similarity algorithm produces a mapping between WSDL files, the tool can also be used for supporting mediation between services. Possible use cases are the management of interface changes or the integration of a new supplier into a supply network. If we assume that the new supplier already provides interfaces, we can compare these with the required interfaces in the supply network. The WSDL Analyzer detects similarities and differences and generates a mapping between similar interfaces. It thus supports the rapid and flexible integration of new partners in collaboration and helps to tackle interoperability problems.

A WSDL specification is the description of a Web service including a description of its interface and a description of where the actual implementation exists and how it can be used. The basic idea and assumption underlying the WSDL Analyzer is that, if two services are conceptually similar they are more likely to also be structurally similar than otherwise. In a WSDL description of a service, data is encoded in XML, i.e. structured trees. The algorithm assumes that the two trees being compared are WSDL specifications and relies on the structure of the WSDL schema to simplify the tree comparison.

WSDL specifications are hierarchical. At the lowest level of the hierarchy, the data types are defined, which themselves are defined in XML and are hierarchical; one layer above the messages are defined, whose structures depend on the defined data types; the next layer specifies the service operations, which are composed of messages. Finally, the whole service is defined as the composition of its data types and operations.

The paper is structured in the following manner. Section 2 provides an overview of the approach with reference to related work. Section 3 presents the theoretical foundations for the WSDL Analyzer. Section 4 describes the algorithm and section 5 the transformation of messages for flexible Web service invocation. In section 6, we discuss features and problems. Finally, in section 7 we conclude and outline areas that would require further research.

2. Analysing WSDL descriptions

Two papers by Wang *et al.* (Wang *et al.* 2003a, Wang *et al.* 2003b, see also Wu *et al.* 2005) build the foundation for the WSDL Analyzer. There, the structure matching approach is combined with methods stemming from Information Retrieval (IR) research. For the WSDL Analyzer, we concentrated on finding structure similarities and omitted the IR part. The reason is that while IR methods help to find similar services, they do not help in generating a mapping from one WSDL file to another, since the vector-space approach commonly used in IR neglects information about the structure of documents. For the WSDL Analyzer, the algorithm proposed by Wang *et al.* for finding structural similarities is improved by taking into account additional features of the XML-based WSDL structure.

The structure-matching algorithm is inspired by traditional signature-matching methods for component retrieval (Zaremski *et al.* 1995). Another related research area is schema matching (Rahm *et al.* 2001) which aims at identifying semantic correspondences between two schemas, e.g. database schemas, ontologies, XML message formats, etc. The advent of XML as common data representation format lead to a revival of matching algorithms already investigated in the database and pattern matching research (e.g. Shasha *et al.* 1997). Since WSDL is based on XML, the results from this research can be applied in a modified way to finding similarities in WSDL descriptions of services.

The approach proposed here, following Wang *et al.*, exploits various types of schema information (e.g. element names, data types and structural properties), characteristics of data instances, as well as background knowledge from dictionaries and thesauri (e.g. WordNet). The algorithm calculates the similarity between the structure of a required service and the structures of a set of candidate services. The algorithm respects the structural information of data types and is flexible enough to allow relaxed matching and matching between parameters that come in different orders in parameter lists.

The comparison of two WSDL files (see Figure 1 for the WSDL structure) is a multi-step process: it involves the comparison of the operations' set offered by the services, which is based on the comparison of the structures of the operations' input and output messages, which, in turn, is based on the comparison of the data types of the objects communicated by these messages.

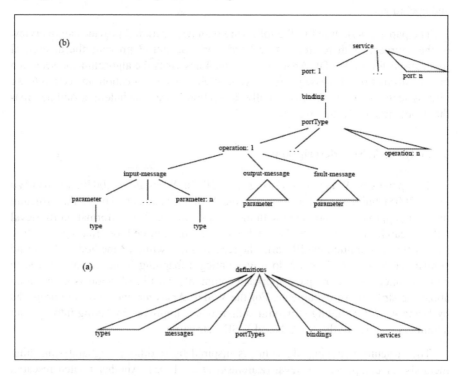

Figure 1. *WSDL structure (a) vs. Web service structure (b)*

The *tree-edit distance* measure (Apostolico *et al.* 1997) and the concept of a *weak subsumption* relation (Nagano *et al.* 2004) can be seen as a theoretical foundation of this approach. The more recent concept of weak subsumption is not considered by Wang *et al.* and the tree-edit distance is only mentioned, but not related to their algorithm, hence the rather arbitrary character of their algorithm.

The idea of the tree-edit distance is that a similarity between two XML structures *A* and *B* can be measured by stepwise transforming a tree representation of *A* into the tree representing *B*. The steps necessary for that transformation provide the measure for their similarity, and, at the same time, induce the mapping between the schemas. Possible steps are basic edit operations such as node inserts, deletes and re-labels. The algorithm proposed by Wang *et al.* considers only node matching without editing, or simple renaming operations such as changing a data type from string to int. (Nagano *et al.* 2004) introduce the concept of a weak subsumption. They give three different types of weak subsumption, replacing labels, pruning edges and removing intermediate nodes. These operations can be correlated to specific tree-edit operations, namely re-labelling and deleting nodes. Weak subsumption restricts the allowed editing steps.

3. Theoretical foundations

In this section, we present the background for the WSDL Analyzer, namely the notions of a *tree-edit distance* (Shasha *et al.* 1997) and *weak subsumption* w.r.t. XML schemes as defined in (Kuper *et al.* 2001) and (Nagano *et al.* 2004).

Definition 1 (Metric) *Let M be a set. A function $d : M \times M \to R_0^+$ is a metric on M, iff*

1. *identity: $d(x, y) = 0 \Leftrightarrow x = y$*
2. *symmetry: $d(x, y) = d(y, x)$ for all $x, y \varepsilon M$*
3. *triangle inequality: $d(x, y) \leq d(x, z) + d(z, y)$ for all $x, y, z \varepsilon M$*

The cost function which assigns a non-negative value to an edit operation, is defined as metric:

1. $\gamma(a \to b) \geq 0, \gamma(a \to a) = 0.$
2. $\gamma(a \to b) = \gamma(b \to a).$
3. $\gamma(a \to c) \leq \gamma(a \to b) + \gamma(b \to c).$

Definition 2 *The **tree-edit distance** is defined as:*

$$D_e(T_1, T_2) = \min_S \{\gamma(S) \mid S \text{ is a sequence of edit-operations which transforms } T_1 \text{ in } T_2 \}$$

are the minimal costs of a sequence of operations which is needed for a transformation.

An XML-Dokument is represented as an ordered labeled tree with:

- $\mathcal{O}$: set of node IDs;
- $\mathcal{L}$: set of labels;
- Δ: root node.

Definition 3 *A **data model** is a structure $D = (O_D, label_D, children_D)$, where*

1. $O_D \subset \mathcal{O}$;
2. *$label_D$ is a mapping from O_D to L;*
3. *$children_D$ is a mapping from $O_D \cup \{\Delta\}$ to $\cup_{i \geq 0} O_D^i$ (immediate children of a node);*
4. *The structure that we obtain by considering only children of non-reference nodes is a tree.*

Furthermore:

T: fixed set of type names;

τ: elements of T;

$L(r)$: language, defined by the regular expression r.

Definition 4 *A scheme is a structure* $S = (T_S; \text{pred}_S, \text{regexp}_S)$, *where*

1. T_S *is a finite set of* T;
2. pred_S *is a mapping from* T_S *to* $\mathcal{P}(\mathcal{L})$ *(i.e. the label of a type name);*
3. regexp_S *is a mapping from* $T_S \cup \{\Delta\}$ *to regular expressions over* T_S *(the type names of all children of a node).*

Definition 5 *Let D be a data model and S a scheme. We say D is of type S under the* **type assignment** ρ *and write* $D:_\rho S$ *iff* ρ *is a function from* $O_D \cup \{\Delta\}$ *to* $T_S \cup \{\Delta\}$ *such that:*

1. $\rho(\Delta) = \Delta$;
2. *For each* $o \in O_D$, $\text{label}_D(o) \in \text{pred}_S(\rho(o))$ *(the label of each node with ID o must be contained in the set of labels of type name* $\rho(o)$);
3. *For each* $o \in O_D \cup \{\Delta\}$, $\text{children}_D(o) = [o_1,...,o_n]$, $\rho(o_1)...\rho(o_n) \in L(\text{regexp}_S(\rho(o)))$ *(the type names of all children of a node with ID o must be contained in the set of type names of the children of* $\rho(o)$).

Definition 6 *Let S und S' be two schemes. We say that scheme S* **subsumes** *scheme S' under the* **subsumption mapping** θ *and write* $S \preceq_\theta S'$ *iff* θ *is a function from* $T_S \cup \{\Delta\}$ *to* $T_{S'} \cup \{\Delta\}$ *such that*

1. $\theta(\tau) = \Delta$ g.d.w. $\tau = \Delta$;
2. *For all* $\tau \in T_S$, $\text{pred}_S(\tau) \subseteq \text{pred}_{S'}(\theta(\tau))$ *(the label of type* τ *in* T_S *is contained in the set of labels of type* $\theta(\tau)$ *in* $T_{S'}$);
3. *For all* $\tau \in T_S \cup \{\Delta\}$, $\theta(L(\text{regexp}_S(\tau))) \subseteq L(\text{regexp}_{S'}(\theta(\tau)))$ *(the type names of the children of type* τ *are a subset of the type names of the children of type* $\theta(\tau)$).

If $S \preceq S'$ holds, then each data model D of type S ρ has type S' under a certain type assignment.

With the help of the subsumption relation defined in Definition 6, it is possible to decide whether two Web services are equal, i.e. whether they have the same signature. However, this is a restriction which is too strong for our purposes. In order to detect weaker similarities, the conditions for the subsumption relation have to be relaxed. Nagano *et al.* consider three kinds of structural similarities and give definitions for the respective weak subsumption relations. Intuitively, if scheme A weakly subsumes scheme B, a call to a service which uses A contains at least the information required to call a service using B.

Definition 7 (Weak subsumption w.r.t. relabeling of nodes) *Let S and S' be two schemes. We say that S* **weakly subsumes** *S' under the* **subsumption mapping** (θ_1, ϕ_1) *and write* $S \preceq^\omega_{(\theta_1, \phi_1)} S'$ *iff* θ_1 *is a function from* $T_S \cup \{\Delta\}$ *to* $T_{S'} \cup \{\Delta\}$ *and* ϕ_1 *a function* $\mathcal{L}$ *to* $\mathcal{L}$ *such that*

1. $\theta_1(\tau) = \Delta$ iff $\tau = \Delta$;
2. For all $\tau \in T_S$, if $\theta_1(\tau) \neq \epsilon$ then $\phi_1(pred_S(\tau)) \subseteq pred_{S'}(\theta_1(\tau))$;
3. For all $\tau \in T_S \cup \{\Delta\}$, $\theta_1(L\ (regexp_S(\tau))) \subseteq L(regexp_{S'}(\theta_1(\tau)))$.

Example 1 *Figure 2 shows an example for "'typecasting"' by relabeling.*
With:

$\theta_1(\tau_i') := \tau_i$, *for each i (identity)*
$\phi_1(\{ \tau_{131}' \}) := int$
$\phi_1(pred_S(\tau_i')) := pred_S(\tau_i)$ *for i $\neq$ 131*
then: $S' \preceq^{\omega}_{(\theta_1, \phi_1)} S$,
i.e. each data model D, which is of type S' under a certain type assignment, is also of type S.

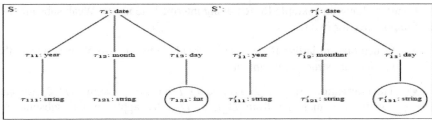

Figure 2. *"Typecast" by relabelling of nodes*

Definition 8 (Weak subsumption w.r.t. pruning edges) *Let S und S' be two schemes.*
*We say that S **weakly subsumes** S' under the **subsumption mapping** θ_r and write $S \preceq^{\omega}_{\theta_r}$*
S' iff θ_r is a funktion from $T_S \cup \{\Delta\}$ to $T_{S'} \cup \{\Delta\} \cup \{\epsilon\}$ such that

1. $\theta_r(\tau) = \Delta$ iff $\tau = \Delta$;
2. For all $\tau \in T_S$, if $\theta_r(\tau) \neq \epsilon$ then $pred_S(\tau) \subseteq pred_{S'}(\theta_r(\tau))$;
3. For all $\tau \in T_S \cup \{\Delta\}$, $\theta_r(L\ (regexp_S(\tau))) \subseteq L(regexp_{S'}(\theta_r(\tau)))$.

Example 2 *Figure 3 shows an example for pruning edges. With:*
$\theta_r(\tau_{14}') := \epsilon$
$\theta_r(\tau_{141}') := \epsilon$
$\theta_r(\tau_i') := \tau_i$ *for i $\neq$ 16,161*
then: $S' \preceq^{\omega}_{\theta_r} S$,
i.e. each data model D, which is of type S' under a certain type assignment, is also of type S.

Definition 9 (Weak subsumption w.r.t. removing intermediate nodes) *Let S and S'*
*be two schemes. We say S **weakly subsumes** S' under the **subsumption mapping** θ_s and*
write $S \preceq^{\omega}_{\theta_s} S'$ iff θ_s is a function from $T_S \cup \{\Delta\}$ to $T_{S'} \cup \{\Delta\} \cup \{\epsilon\}$ such that

1. $\theta_s(\tau) = \Delta$ iff $\tau = \Delta$;
2. For all $\tau \in T_S$, if $\theta_s(\tau) \neq \epsilon$ then $pred_S(\tau) \subseteq pred_{S'}(\theta_s(\tau))$;
3. For all $\tau \in T_S \cup \{\Delta\}$, $regexp_S(\tau)[\tau'/regexp_S(\tau')]$ *(obtained by replacing τ' with*
   $regexp_S(\tau')$ *in $regexp_S(\tau)$), such that*
   $\theta_s(L(regexp_S(\tau)[\tau'/regexp_S(\tau')])) \subseteq L(regexp_{S'}(\theta_s(\tau)))$.

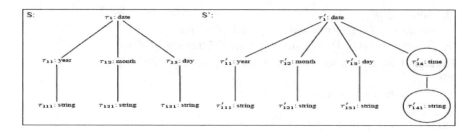

Figure 3. *Pruning edges*

Figure 4 shows an example for removing intermediate nodes. Weak subsumption is of importance for two reasons:

- Structural similarity: If the relation holds between two Web services, the services are structurally similar.

- Transformation: If a Web service *D_1* weakly subsumes *D_2*, we can transform a message from *D_1* to *D_2* by applying the subsumption mapping and transform the reply message.

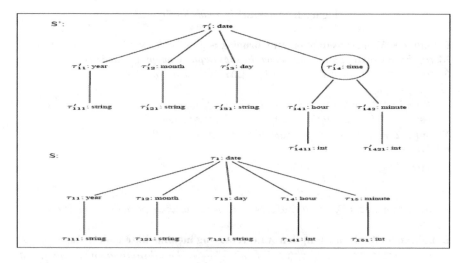

Figure 4. *Removing intermediate nodes*

4. Comparing WSDL descriptions

The overall process starts by constructing a logical tree representation of the WSDL files which are compared. The root node is the service itself; the bindings, the port types, operations and messages are added. The data type section is inserted as node below the message level. It is interesting to note here that the data types of web services specified in WSDL are XML elements (to be precise, XML schema definitions, XSDs); as such, they can potentially be highly complex structures. Leaf nodes of the logical tree are the primitive XSD data types.

Comparing two WSDL trees comes up to finding corresponding paths in the trees. The overall score of how well the two services match is computed by identifying the pair-wise correspondence of their corresponding nodes (service, bindings, port types, operations, messages, data types) that maximizes the total sum of the matching scores of the individual pairs. The result of this comparison is a matrix assessing the matching scores, i.e., the degree of similarity, of pair-wise combinations of source and target nodes.

The algorithm of Wang *et al.*: does not add up editing costs, but rewards identity. They reward identical nodes, and ignore different nodes. Since XSD definitions contain (primitive) data types as leaf nodes (e.g. *string* or *int*), they compare these data types and reward identical data types by a maximal score *max*. Since some data types are convertible (e.g. *int* into *string*), convertible data types obtain a lower score, e.g. 4/5 *max*). Conversion of data types is a restricted form of re-labelling.

Wang *et al.* ignore the name of labels (e.g. element names) for structural matching and consider only primitive and complex XSD data types. On the one hand, this is reasonable, since element names might be different in service descriptions of different providers. However, we found out that comparing node labels improves the matching result. In a first step, node labels are checked for substring inclusion to detect corresponding labels. In a second step, WordNet was used to detect semantic relations between node labels. The user of the WSDL Analyzer can choose whether she wants to map only the structure (data types) or consider also names (substring) and semantic relationships between terms (WordNet).

The approach by Wang *et al.* can be reformulated in terms of the tree-edit distance. A direct match (no re-labelling or deleting) is assessed best; a re-labelling gets a lower score. Deleting and adding nodes obtain the lowest score (= 0 in Wang *et al.*).

Definition 10 (Bonus function) *Let a,b be nodes in two service trees. The bonus B for an operation is defined as*

1. *Relabeling u:*

$$B(u(a,b)) = \begin{cases} max, & \textit{if a and b leaf nodes, a and b of the same type} \\ \frac{4}{5}max, & \textit{if a and b leaf nodes, a without loss of information} \\ & \textit{convertable into b} \\ \frac{2}{5}max, & \textit{if a and b leaf nodes, a with loss of information} \\ & \textit{convertable to b} \\ 0, & \textit{if a and b leaf nodes, a not convertable to b} \\ 0, & \textit{else} \end{cases}$$

2. *Pruning s: B(s(a)) = -1*
3. *Removing e: B(e(a)) = 0*
4. *Inserting f: B(f(a)) = $arbitrary$*

Pruning is assessed as a more significant structural difference than deleting intermediate nodes. The boni are added up over the compared trees. A higher value indicates a higher similarity. The cost function γ is based on the bonus function.

Definition 11 (Cost function) *Let o be an edit operation. Then*

$$\gamma(o) = max - B(o).$$

Note that this cost function is not a metric since the symmetry condition is violated (see Definition 1)

5. Transformation of messages

If the weak subsumption relation holds between service A and service B, a mapping from a WSDL describing service A to a WSDL describing service B is generated. A translation of a SOAP message instance destined for A in a message for service B can be supported. Based on the mapping, the values sent to A can be extracted and inserted into the corresponding tags in the message for B. The translation can be done automatically, if there is a one-to-one correspondence between elements. However, if there exist several possible corresponding elements, translation requires intervention from a user in order to unambiguously transform parameters. The latter case shows the limitation of the structural approach. There are possible mismatches which can be detected with the help of the WSDL Analyzer, but not automatically corrected.

6. Discussion

The WSDL Analyzer detects similarities between WSDL descriptions of Web services. Our first evaluations show that in areas where standardizations already exist the results are clearly better than in areas with no common standards. In areas with standardization, precision and recall reach values higher than 90%. The WSDL

Analyzer supports adapting service calls between partners in a collaborative setting where common schemes already exist and fine-tuning is required.

Strict data type matching as in Wang *et al.* leads to moderate results. In order to improve the mapping results, we used substring matching and WordNet which can be enabled in the WSDL Analyzer GUI (Figure 5). The experiments show that, especially in rather standardized areas the results are better than with pure data type mapping.

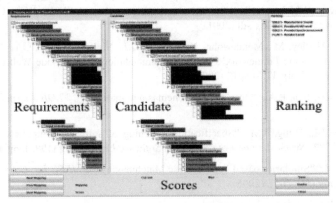

Figure 5. *WSDL Analyzer GUI*

7. Conclusion and future work

In this paper, we presented the WSDL Analyzer, a tool for detecting similarities between Web service interfaces. The tool compares WSDL descriptions of Web services and provides a mapping between descriptions. The mapping is based on a subsumption relation between XML structures and can be used to transform SOAP messages.

Since some mismatches can only be detected, but not solved, the automatic generation of a complete mapping is not always possible. We plan to export a partial mapping into formats which can be imported by available (commercial) tools. The mapping can then be further refined in order to reconcile even more complex mismatches.

A further extension covers the related problem of Web service composition. In this case, a mapping from the output of service *A* to the input of service *B* has to be generated. Obviously, this is analogous to the similarities detected by the WSDL Analyzer.

The work published in this paper is partly funded by the European Commission through the ATHENA IP (Advanced Technologies for interoperability of Heterogeneous Enterprise Networks and their Applications Integrated Project) (IST-

507849). The work does not represent the view of the European Commission or the ATHENA consortium, and the authors are solely responsible for the paper's content.

8. References

Apache Axis: http://ws.apache.org/axis/.

Christensen, E., Curbera, F., Meredith, G., Weerawarana, S., "Web Services Description Language (WSDL) 1.1" W3C Recommendation, World Wide Web Consortium, http://www.w3.org/TR/wsdl (2001).

Gudgin, M., Hadley, M., Mendelsohn, N., Moreau, J.J., Nielsen, H.F., "SOAP Version 1.2 Part 1: Messaging Framework", W3C Recommendation, World Wide Web Consortium, http://www.w3.org/TR/soap12 (2003).

Rahm, E., Bernstein, P.A., "On matching schemas automatically", *VLDB Journal* 10 (2001), pp. 334–350.

Zaremski, A.M., Wing, J.M., "Specification matching of software components" in: *ACM SIGSOFT'95 Symposium on Foundations of Software Engineering* (1995), pp. 6–17.

Wu, J.,Wu, Z., "Similarity-based Web Service Matchmaking" in: *IEEE Int. Conf on Services Computing* (SCC'05). (2005).

WordNet: http://wordnet.princeton.edu/.

Nagano, S., Hasegawa, T., Ohsuga, A. and Honiden, S. "Dynamic Invocation Model of Web Services Using Subsumption Relations", ICWS 2004, pp. 150–156.

Shasha, D., Zhang, K. "Approximate Tree Pattern Matching", Pattern Matching Algorithms, A. Apostolico and Z. Galil (eds.) Oxford University Press (1997), pp. 341–371.

Kuper, G.M., Simeon, J., "Subsumption for XML Types". in: *8th Int'l Conf Database Theory- ICDT 2001* (LNCS 1973) pp. 331–345.

Apostolico, A., Galil, Z., eds., *Pattern matching algorithms*, Oxford University Press, Oxford (1997).

Wang, Y., Stroulia, E. "Flexible Interface Matching for Web-Service Discovery", *Proc. 4th Int'l Conf. on Web Information Systems Engineering* (2003a).

Wang, Y., Stroulia, E. "Semantic Structure Matching for Assessing Web-Service Similarity", *Proc. 1st Int'l Conf. on Service Oriented Computing* (ICSOC 2003), Volume 2910 of Lecture Notes in Computer Science, (2003b), pp. 197–207.

Business Process Fusion based on Semantically-enabled Service-Oriented Business Applications

Athanasios Bouras[*] — **Panagiotis Gouvas**[*] — **Andreas Friesen**[**]
Stelios Pantelopoulos[***] — **Spiros Alexakis**[****] —
Gregoris Mentzas[*]

[*]*Information Management Unit, Institute of Communications and Computer Systems
of the National Technical University of Athens
9, Iroon Polytechniou str., 157 80 Zografou, Athens, Greece*

{bouras, pgouv, gmentzas}@mail.ntua.gr,

[**]*SAP Research, CEC Karlsruhe
Vincenz-Prießnitz-Str. 1, D-76131 Karlsruhe, Germany*

andreas.friesen@sap.com

[***]*Singular Software SA
Al.Panagouli & Siniosoglou, 142 34, N.Ionia, Attica – Greece*

spantel@singular.gr

[****]*CAS Software AG
Wilhelm-Schickard-Str. 10-12, D-76131 Karlsruhe*

spiros.alexakis@cas.de

ABSTRACT: *European enterprises, which contain several heterogeneous systems, create fuzzy networks of interconnected applications, services and data sources, and cooperate with international partners in the enlarged Europe, need holistic Enterprise Applications Integration (EAI) solutions in order to operate their e-business effectively. The FUSION project aims to promote efficient business collaboration and interconnection between enterprises (including SMEs) by developing innovative technologies for the semantic fusion of heterogeneous service-oriented business applications. Such applications may exist either within an enterprise or in several collaborating companies within the enlarged Europe. This paper presents the vision and technical architecture of the FUSION IST project.*

KEY WORDS: *Enterprise Application Integration, Service-Oriented Architecture, Semantic Web Services, Semantic-enriched Service-oriented Business Applications, Business Process Fusion.*

1. Introduction: background and rationale

In today's fiercely competitive global economy, companies are realizing that new initiatives such as e-business, customer relationship management and business intelligence go hand-in-hand with the proven organization-wide enterprise application integration (EAI) strategy. The goal of EAI is to integrate and streamline heterogeneous business processes across different applications and business units while allowing employees, decision makers and business partners to readily access corporate and customer data no matter where it resides.

Business process fusion is the transformation of business activities that is achieved by integrating the interfaces of previously autonomous business processes by pipelining different middleware technologies and enabling the effective (semi-) automated exchange of information between various systems within a company or between enterprises. The development of Service Oriented Business Applications (SOBA, which constitutes a set of independently running services communicating with each other in a loosely coupled message-based manner – Haller *et al.* 2005) and the publishing of Web Services may implement the vision of business process fusion, by providing an abstraction layer for the involved interfaces through the Web Service Description Language (WSDL). This architecture will also play a significant role in streamlining mergers and acquisitions, by linking previously incompatible systems (IBM, 2004).

However, semantics and ontologies are important to application integration solutions because they provide a shared and common understanding of data, services and processes that exist within an application integration problem domain, and how to facilitate communication between people and information systems. By leveraging this concept we can organize and share enterprise information, as well as manage content and knowledge, which allows better interoperability and integration of inter- and intra-enterprise information systems.

We claim that recent innovations in the development of Semantically-enriched Service-Oriented Business Applications (SE-SOBA) – which enlarge the notion of SOA by applying Semantic Web Service technology and using ontologies and semantic web mark up languages to describe data structures and messages passed through web service interfaces – combined with the rule-based formalization of Business Scenarios and Processes will provide a dynamically reconfigurable architecture that will enable enterprises to respond quickly and flexibly to market changes, thereby supporting innovation and business growth, increasing the potential for an improved return on IT investments and a more robust bottom line.

This paper aims at the announcement and presentation of the EC co-funded IST project entitled "Business Process Fusion based on Semantically-enabled Service-Oriented Business Applications" (FUSION). FUSION project, a 30-month project officially started at February 1st, 2006, addresses both enterprise application and business processes heterogeneity problem by proposing a Semantic Web Services –

based innovative framework and holistic solution for both intra- and inter- EAI. Led by SAP AG, FUSION consortium consists of 14 partners from five European countries (Germany, Greece, Poland, Hungary, and Bulgaria), including Research Institutes, Technology Developers, Innovation Transfer bodies as well as end users.

The structure of this paper is as follows: in the following section, we present the innovation challenges addressed by FUSION project. The proposed conceptual framework and technical architecture referring to the innovative business-driven semantic-enriched service-oriented architecture are defined in section 3, while, in section 4, we present the proposed business-oriented FUSION ontology. Moreover, the state-of-the-art survey and comparative analysis regarding semantic web services frameworks are performed in section 5. Finally, section 6 presents further work and concluding remarks.

2. FUSION Innovative Challenges

SMEs cooperating with international partners in the enlarged Europe need holistic Enterprise Applications Integration (EAI) solutions in order to operate their e-business effectively. At the same time they are facing intercultural barriers, since current interoperability and integration efforts are more focused on "data" of the systems rather than on "processes".

Our vision is that the FUSION solution will enable business collaboration and interconnection between SMEs by developing a framework for the semantic integration of service-oriented business applications that exist within an enterprise or in several collaborating companies, taking into consideration the intercultural, regulatory and legacy aspects of the enlarged Europe countries.

The 30-month FUSION project will, finally, result (see Figure 1), through the FUSION deliverables (both reports and prototypes), in:

– an innovative FUSION approach for Semantic Service-oriented Business Application integration (i.e. CRM and ERP) covering essential business processes of and between collaborative organizations, especially SMEs, based on increasingly familiar and stable standards that are designed to facilitate agility, loose coupling and easy interaction, like WSDL, UDDI and SOAP,

– the FUSION Methodology for Semantic Service-oriented Business Application Integration that will facilitate the integration of business software applications that exist in the same or different organizations,

– the FUSION Ontology constituting the corner stone of SE-SOBA Integration and serving as a common reference for the association with the business application repositories and the semantic description of Web Services Instances,

– the FUSION Integrated System allowing the interconnection of heterogeneous information systems, resource sharing and services provision. The mechanism will enable the implementation of service-oriented business applications based on Web Services standards (like UDDI, WSDL and SOAP) and Semantic Web technology standards (OWL-S), and

– three trans-national FUSION cases that will prove the concepts and tools of the solution, concerning three different "Enlarged Europe" use cases will be deployed and executed.

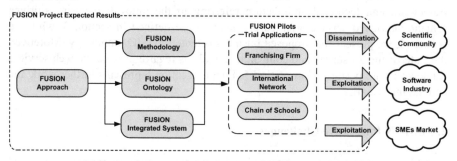

Figure 1. *Graphical representation of FUSION expected results*

All three use cases, regarding a franchising firm, an international Network of independent international career managers and a chain of schools of foreign languages and computing, are operating in the "old" and the "new" European part and would like to facilitate the globalization of their business by supporting the collaboration between the different legal entities and the interoperability of their business applications.

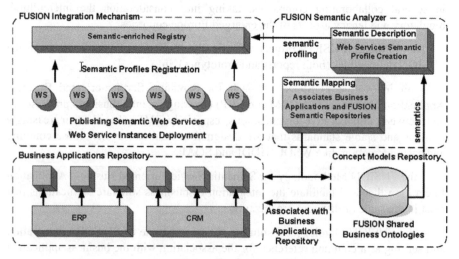

Figure 2. *Intra-organizational Enterprise Application Integration*

Finally, FUSION consortium aims at wide-scale dissemination of knowledge obtained and exploitation of the project results to the software industry as well as to the SMEs market in general. All project partners will collaborate in the dissemination of the results among the academic community, the IST community and the software market. Commercial exploitation aims at the fulfilment of the long term IST and e-Europe strategic objective for the growth and competitiveness of the European economy across the enlarged Europe.

3. FUSION approach and technical architecture

The FUSION solution is a holistic framework that facilitates the integration of heterogeneous enterprise applications that exist in the same organization (Figure 2) or in different organizations (Figure 3).

The FUSION solution will invoke the creation, administration and deployment of Web Services Instances of the pre-selected features of the enterprise applications and their semantic description (Semantic Profile) based on a business concept model, called FUSION ontology, which serves as a common reference allowing the semantic integration of the business applications. The deployed Web Services Instances will be published at a semantic-enriched UDDI service registry, while the created Semantic Profiles of Web Services Instances will be registered in the FUSION semantically-enriched registry, which is part of the FUSION Semantic Repository, powering the system-integrated categorization and discovery services.

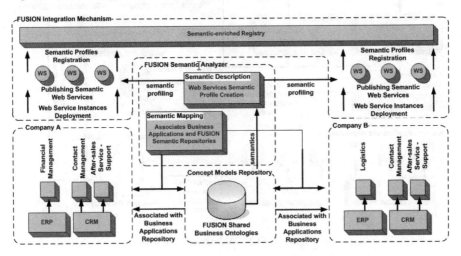

Figure 3. *Inter-organizational Enterprise Application Integration*

The way we envision business analysts to work with the FUSION solution is that they:

– define the concepts that exist inside the business application (e.g. product, contact, order, etc) and use well-defined business ontologies / concept models that are independent from the technical architecture of the business application,

– associate the concepts and services with the business application repository / resources,

– create and administrate Web Services Instances, create semantic profiles of Web Services Instances and publish the profiles on the FUSION semantically-enriched registry, and

– orchestrate aggregate compositions of semantic web services based on FUSION-enabled descriptions of various business applications.

As mentioned above, the FUSION solution may be applied on either Intra-Organizational Enterprise Application Integration or Inter-Organizational Enterprise Application Integration to support semantic workflows and added-value supply chains. FUSION system constitutes of two main components: a) the Semantic Services Analyzer and b) the Integration Mechanism (see Figure 4).

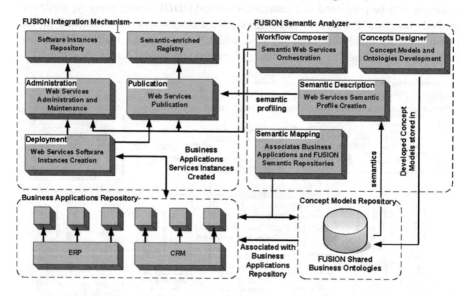

Figure 4. *FUSION Integrated System*

The Semantic Services Analyzer is a graphical environment that facilitates the semantic conceptualization of Service-Oriented Business Applications regardless their technical infrastructure. The Semantic Services Analyzer enables the utilization of the produced business conceptualization for the automatic creation of Web Services. The graphical environment enables system analysts to associate the theoretical concepts to the business application resources providing a connection between the system semantics and their technical realization.

The Integration Mechanism is the component of the FUSION Solution responsible for the administration of the Semantic Repository (containing the Concept Models and Services Repository, the Web Services Software Instances Repository and the Semantic-enriched Service Registry), for the creation, administration and the maintenance of the Web Services and the publication of Web Services in the semantic-enriched UDDI Registry. The Integration Mechanism does not offer any graphical interface but it communicates via SOAP with the Semantic Services Analyzer. This enables the remote creation and deployment of Web Services Software Instances by a group of users, potentially from multiple legal entities, that have the proper rights to connect to the Integration Mechanism, and the administration of the Mechanism by authenticated personnel (e.g., in case of inter-organizational EAI, the authenticated personnel comes from the "core partner" of the inter-organizational supply chain that potentially owns the FUSION System).

4. Business-driven FUSION ontology

The FUSION ontology constitutes the corner stone for the semantic modelling of FUSION-enabled services, workflows and supply chains. The FUSION ontology will enable efficient business collaboration and interconnection between SMEs supporting the semantic fusion of service-oriented businesses applications that exist within an enterprise or in several collaborating companies.

The FUSION ontology will conceptualize the identified attributes, concepts and their relationships of the service-oriented businesses applications and will be developed in three layers: upper, middle, and lower. This multi-layer architecture of FUSION ontology development provides a rich representation of service-oriented business applications, captures the significant requirements of both services and workflows, supports efficient representation of services, workflows and supply chains in intra- and inter- organizational level and provides a flexible structure that could be easily refined and updated.

The upper layer of the FUSION ontology will capture the semantic modelling – including a vocabulary of terms and their specification and structure – of workflows and supply chains covering the following aspects of workflow modelling:

– Data/Information Semantics: capturing the (semi-) formal definition of data in input and output messages of a Web Service, supporting discovery and interoperability by annotating input and output data of Web Services using ontologies,

– Functional Semantics: capturing the (semi-) formal representation of the capabilities of Web Services in order to support discovery and composition of Web

Services annotating operations of Web Services as well as provide preconditions and effects,

– Execution Semantics: capturing the (semi-) formal representation of the execution or flow of services in a workflow or supply chain or of the operations in a service, in order to support analysis (verification), validation (simulation) and execution (exception handling) of the workflow models using State Machines, Petri nets, activity diagrams etc.

In order to enhance the discovery, composition, and orchestration of Web services, it is necessary to increase the semantic description of their interfaces. The FUSION middle-layer ontology will incorporate several data, functional and quality aspects encountered in provided web services in general. This ontology specifies domain-independent web services concepts – concerning input and output parameters, quality criteria and functional description – and is typically completed by the (domain-) business application- specific lower-layer FUSION ontology.

5. State-of-the-art Semantic Web Services

As it has already been stated, FUSION project will specify and develop an innovative framework, based on Service-Oriented Architecture and Semantic Web Technologies, realizing semantic-enabled service-oriented applications applied to EAI scenarios. The Semantic Web initiative's purpose is similar to that of the Web Services (Preece & Decker, 2002): to make the Web machine-processable rather than merely "human-processable". Thus, Web Services are considered as an essential ingredient of the semantic web and benefit from the semantic web technologies. The emerging semantic web technologies and standards provide an abstraction layer, using well defined semantics, contained in formal domain ontologies, to annotate Web Services and Processes in a machine-processable way. Key components of the Semantic Web technology are a) a unified data model such as RDF (Resource Definition Framework), b) languages with well defined, formal semantics, built on RDF, such as the Web Ontology Language – OWL (DAML+OIL, DARPA Mark-up Language and Ontology Inference Layer), and c) ontologies of standardized terminology for marking up web resources, used by semantically enriched service level descriptions, such as OWL-S (former DAML-S, DAML-based Web Service Ontology).

Enriching Web Services descriptions with formal defined semantics by introducing the notion of semantic mark-up, leading towards the Semantic Web Services, enables machine-interpretable profiles of services and applications, realizing the vision of dynamic and seamless integration. As this semantic mark-up is machine –processable and –interpretable, the developed semantic profiles of web services can be exploited to automate the tasks of discovering web services, executing them, composing them and interoperating with them (McIlraith *et al.*,

2001), moving a step forward towards the implementation of intelligent, semantic web services.

The combination of Web Services and Semantic Web technologies, resulting in the deployment of machine-processable and, therefore, usable for automation semantic web services, supports and allows a set of essential automated services regarding the use of deployed web services (McIlraith *et al.*, 2001; McIlraith *et al.*, 2001-b):

– automatic Web Service discovery, involving automatic location Web Services that provide a particular functionality and that adhere to requested properties expressed as a user goal,

– automatic Web Service composition, involving dynamic combination and aggregation of several web services to provide a given functionality,

– automatic Web Service invocation, involving automatic execution of an identified Web Service by an agent, and

– automatic Web Service interoperation within and across organizational boundaries.

These semantically enriched web services oriented features can constitute the ideal solution to integration problems, as they enable dynamic, scalable and reusable cooperation between different systems and organizations. Currently four different standards for semantic web services are emerging: OWL-S, METEOR-S, SWSF and WSMO. In the following these standards will be explained and compared:

– OWL-S: OWL-S (Martin *et al.*, 2004), formerly DAML-S (DAML, 2003), is a service model (a service ontology written is OWL) that tends to become a standard regarding Semantic Web Services. OWL-S is an upper ontology for services, already developed and presented to the Semantic Web Services project of the DAML program. OWL-S upper service ontology provides three essential types of knowledge about a service, each characterized by the question it answers: a) What does the service provide for prospective clients? The answer to this question is given in the "profile", which is used to advertise the service, b) How is it used? The answer to this question is given in the "process model", and c) How does one interact with it? The answer to this question is given in the "grounding". Grounding provides the needed details about transport protocols. Moreover, a variety of third party software components for OWL and OWL-S have been already developed and can be utilized in potential OWL-S based solutions.

– METEOR-S: Another proposal for a semantic web service standard is METEOR-S that is developed in LSDIS laboratory of the University of Georgia, aiming to extend Web Services standards with Semantic Web technologies to achieve greater dynamism and scalability (METEOR-S). Specifically, METEOR-S focuses on adding semantics to WSDL and UDDI (this work termed WSDL-S is being provided as input for next version of WSDL that will support semantic representation), and to BPEL4WS, while METEOR-S discusses a semi-automatic approach for annotating Web services described using WSDL. METEOR-S provides specific tools per each phase regarding the Semantic Web Services lifecycle: a) Semantic Annotation of web-services, b) Semantic Publication of web-services, c) Semantic Discovery of web Services, and d) Orchestration & Composition of Web Services.

– SWSF: Another Semantic Web Services project of the DAML program is the Semantic Web Services Framework (SWSF) (Battle *et al.*, 2005) which represents an attempt to extend the work of OWL-S and consists of two major parts: a) the language SWSL as an underlying basis, containing two sublanguages: SWSL-FOL which is based on first-order logic and primarily used to express the formal characterization of web service concepts and SWSL-Rules that is similarly to WSML-Rule based on logic programming; and b) the Semantic Web Service Ontology (SWSO) that presents a conceptual model by which web services can be described.

– WSMO: Based on the Web Service Modelling Framework (WSMF) (Fensel & Bussler, 2002), the Web Service Modelling Ontology (WSMO) (Lausen *et al.*, 2005), developed – mainly – in DERI (Galway, Ireland), is a formal ontology and language that consists of four different main elements for describing semantic web services: a) Web Services representing the functional and behavioural aspects which must be semantically described, b) Ontologies (formal semantics provision), c) Goals constituting objectives that the client might have when consulting a web service, and d) Mediators that are used as connectors (interoperability). Furthermore, WSMO comes along with a web services modelling language (WSML) (deBrujin & Lausen, 2005) and an integrated environment for execution (WSMX).

In comparison, METEOR-S and OWL-S semantic web services frameworks are rather complementary in a way, as OWL-S can provide the conceptual high-level model, while METEOR-S can provide implemented and fine-tuned tools and algorithms. Moreover, SWSF extends the OWL-S standard by enabling rule languages and extends the description-logic framework used in OWL-S to first-order logic making easier the description of concepts and their relationships. On the contrary, WSMO and OWL-S are rather contradictive semantic web services approaches, as they provide incompatible tools and languages (WSML vs. OWL/OWL-S).

METEOR-S and OWL-S approaches fully respect the industrial Web Services Standards (i.e. WSDL, UDDI, BPEL and BPEL4WS), while WSMO promotes WSML that is an alternative to OWL – that is an official W3C standard. However, the compatibility among WSML and OWL is supported through custom parsers WSML2OWL and vice versa – that could not be considered, both conceptually and technically a best practice. In addition, existing OWL-oriented tools, e.g. editors, validators, inference tools, matchmaking algorithms are fully compatible and could be used to enrich the OWL-S approach.

Summarizing the above mentioned trends and comparative results regarding Semantic Web Services standards, FUSION project will adopt the OWL-S approach for deploying its own semantic web services-based solution for both intra- and inter-EAI.

6. Future work

In this paper, we have given a short overview of FUSION, a newly started IST project. The FUSION objectives and research interests do not focus on basic research in the field of semantic web services (SWS); hence the FUSION project does not aim to deliver a new semantic web services development framework. The consortium will examine and use the current state-of-the-art SWS frameworks and apply them to e-business processes and transactions, focusing its research activities towards the semantic enrichment of business processes within the concepts of service-oriented enterprise architecture.

Therefore, the main contribution of the FUSION project will be an approach, methodology and a multi-layer FUSION Ontology for conceptualizing the modelling of FUSION-enabled services as building blocks for business processes and for establishing shared concept models enabling different applications to define semantically same information using a common reference.

The combination of Web Services, Semantic Web technologies and SOA results in the deployment of Semantic SOA architectural framework, which is based on machine-processable and, therefore, usable for automation semantic web services, supporting a set of essential automated services regarding the use of the deployed semantic-enriched service-oriented business applications (SE-SOBAs). The proposed Semantic SOA framework, FUSION, enables the formalization and the documentation of the semantics related to the interfaces and the data structures of the deployed web services, a capability that could not be supported by the current web services enabled SOA and technologies.

Currently, we work towards the in-detail functional and technical specification of the FUSION architecture and the basic technical, structural components. However, a lot of work is still to be done towards the development and the finalization of the integrated FUSION technical solution, its deployment in real enterprise scenarios, and the evaluation of the proposed semantic service-oriented architecture.

7. References

Battle, S. *et al. Semantic Web Services Framework (SWSF) Overview*, 2005.

deBrujin, J., & Lausen, H. *Web Service Modeling Language (WSML)*. W3C Submission, June 2005.

Fensel, D., & Bussler, C. The Web Service Modeling Framework WSMF. In: *Electronic Commerce: Research and Applications*, 2002.

The DAML Services Coalition, *DAML-S: Semantic Markup for Web Services*, 2003.

Haller, A., Gomez, J., & Bussler, C. Exposing Semantic Web Service principles in SOA to solve EAI scenarios. In *Proceedings of the Workshop on Web Service Semantics: Towards Dynamic Business Integration*, International Conference on the World Wide Web (WWW2005).

IBM. Service-Oriented Architecture and Web Services: Creating Flexible Enterprises for a Changing World. *Ziff Davis Media Custom Publishing*, 2004.

Lausen, H., Polleres, A., & Roman, D. *Web Service Modeling Ontology (WSMO)*, 2005.

Martin, D. *et al.* OWL-S: Semantic Markup for Web Services, 2004.

McIlraith, S., Son, T., & Zeng, H. Semantic web services. *IEEE Intelligent Systems*, 16(2): 46-53, 2001

McIlraith, S., Son, T., & Zeng H. (b). Mobilizing the Web with DAML-Enabled Web Service. In *Proceedings of the 2nd International Workshop on the Semantic Web,* Hong Kong, China (pp. 82-93), 2001.

LSDIS, University of Georgia. *METEOR-S: Semantic Web Services and Processes.* Homepage: http://lsdis.cs.uga.edu/projects/meteor-s/

Preece, A., & Decker, S. Intelligent Web Services. *IEEE Intelligent Systems Journal*, 17(1):15-17, 2002.

Interoperability Solutions
to Trust, Security, Policies and QoS
for Enhanced Enterprise Systems

IS-TSPQ Workshop Chairs' message

The aim of the *International Workshop on Interoperability Solutions to Trust, Security, Policies and QoS for Enhanced Enterprise Systems* (IS-TSPQ) is to explore architectures, models, systems, and utilization of non-functional aspects, especially addressing the new requirements on interoperability. The IS-TSPQ'06 was the first international workshop on the topic. The theme will be continued in a workshop in 2007.

The final workshop program was composed of six papers drawn from the submissions. Each paper underwent a careful and thorough review process involving three reviews. This volume contains the revised versions of these papers organized according to the workshop session schedule.

The workshop program presented two technical paper sessions, and two discussion sessions. In the *Business and Requirements view* session, the technical papers addressed issues of semantic interoperability, negotiation methods, and risk assessment on both system design and usage times. In the *Infrastructure Provision* session, the technical papers addressed issues about mechanisms for QoS, security and trust.

The discussion sessions addressed themes of *current interoperability issues* and *the longer term issues*. To summarise the outcome of the discussion, we can state the following.

There is a strong interplay between social, environmental issues and the foreseen technical solutions. Before the technical issues can be closed, the social and regulatory frameworks need to develop further. However, we need to make visible to these framework developers the potential that new technology provides. For example, in the healthcare sector, there is a lack of guidance that should stem from regulatory frameworks, public policies, etc. Also, for collaborative systems, there is a need to clarify the organisational issues that determine the methods for defining responsibilities, gains and consequences of organisational decisions. As a sign of good ongoing development, eGovernment projects provide business processes for their area, even management solutions. Research focus areas in eGovernment solutions include privacy, democracy, and regulation.

In the current technology development, MDD solutions are one of the main trends that address the gap between social needs and technical solutions. The persisting issues in MDD include identification of the right target software architecture, the right kind of metadata for managing the target software elements and interoperability between them, and identification of the recurring, common protocols for interoperability and management needs.

The technical development of managing non-functional aspects requires support from the existing distribution platforms. The main development areas raised here include: identity management, monitoring solutions and adaptation mechanisms.

In the longer term discussion it was agreed that collaboration solutions would reach maturity when a) software agents become legal entities; b) models become a management level thinking tool (instead of reflecting that); and c) agents become able to self adapt and coordinate their roles within a changing environment, following a society level of coordination, as autonomous systems.

Finally, we wish to thank the international program committee for their thorough and prompt work on reviewing the submitted papers, and especially the authors for their contribution. The workshop was organised with support of the INTEROP Network of Excellence (European FP6 IST-508-011, http://www.interop-noe.org/).

Lea Kutvonen, *University of Helsinki, Finland*
Peter Linington, *University of Kent, UK*
Jean-Henry Morin, *University of Geneva, Switzerland*

Session 1:
A Business and Requirements View

Constraint-Driven Negotiation Based on Semantic Interoperability in BTO Production Networks

Alexander Smirnov — Nikolay Shilov — Alexey Kashevnik

39, 14 Line
199178 St.Petersburg
Russia
smir@iias.spb.su
nick@iias.spb.su
alexey@iias.spb.su

ABSTRACT: Business interoperability is one of the keys to establishing partnerships and alliances acting in global markets. Thereby in knowledge-driven economy interoperability on the level of semantics assuming knowledge/competences exchange and sharing is currently of high importance. The paper describes an approach to building a knowledge management platform for enabling negotiation within a BTO production network. The platform is based on an ontological knowledge representation that provides for knowledge sharing and reuse. Based on the proposed platform a negotiation protocol is described. Negotiating units use the same knowledge representation formalism and the same shared ontology what makes it possible to avoid unnecessary translations and facilitate the negotiation process. The advantage of the proposed protocol is illustrated via an example.

KEY WORDS: semantic interoperability, knowledge management platform, negotiation.

1. Introduction

Increasing global competition and toughening requirements from customers cause major changes in the world economy. One of the outcomes of these changes is growing rate of collaboration between manufacturers. This can be explained by the fact that network-like organizations consisting of a large amount of nodes are usually more flexible and robust when compared with hierarchically organized large-scale companies. This flexibility is essential for the build-to-order (BTO) strategy. The BTO concept, unlike BTS (build-to-stock), assumes reduced inventory levels and production on demand in response to an order and in accordance with the order's requirements.

Together with advantages, networked structures raise number of problems. The most important problem is coordination of the large amount of independent members of the large network. One of the arising challenges for them is to understand each other at different levels (technological, semantic, etc.). Business interoperability is one of the keys to establishing partnerships and alliances acting on a global scale. Such production systems will be more dynamic and responsive to changes in the environment and customer needs. Therefore, interoperability on the level of semantics assuming knowledge/competences exchange and sharing is currently of high importance.

When dealing with multiple organizations and multiple processes within a complicated production network, trying to identify and locate a member that has responsibility and/or competence in a particular part of the network can be a laborious, time-consuming process. Developing and maintaining a competence directory of all the relevant parties associated with troubleshooting and solving potential problems can significantly reduce the time. Further, linking this directory to key decision points and frequent problems can further enhance its effectiveness (Lesser *et al.,* 2005). Hence, companies investing more than their competitors into connecting to more people/companies and into sharing knowledge faster and further gain competitive advantage.

In BTO production networks it is important to derive and process knowledge from various sources including:

– customer needs, perceptions, and motivations, etc.;

– expertise within and across the supply chain;

– best practices, technology intelligence, forecasting, systemic innovation, etc.;

– products in the marketplace, who is buying them and why, what prices they are selling at;

– what competitors are selling now and what they are planning to sell.

The FP6 project "Intelligent Logistics for Innovative Product Technologies" (ILIPT) is aimed to development of new methods and technologies to facilitate the implementation of a new manufacturing paradigm (Stone *et al.,* 2005). The ILIPT project will address the conceptual and practical aspects of delivering cars to customers only within several days after placing the order, the automotive industry's exciting and radical new business model (ILIPT, 2005). One of the tasks of the ILIPT project is development of a common knowledge management platform to support interoperability within the "5-day car" supply chain. This will make it possible to accumulate, share, reuse and process knowledge across the "5-day car" supply chain that in turn can significantly help in increasing the supply chain effectiveness and in decreasing the lead time.

The paper proposes principles of the knowledge platform to be built as a part of the ILIPT project and presents a negotiation protocol based on these principles. Though the presented protocol originates from the area of intelligent agents its application not limited to this area. It, for example, can be equally applied to information systems for knowledge sharing and exchange based on technology of Web-services.

2. Ontology-based semantic interoperability

Proposed here approach to the problem of semantic interoperability is based on the four-level architecture of information representation (Gradwell, 1987; Gradwell, 1990). The topmost level represents real-world abstractions (concept categories), the second level represents facilities for schema design (constructs), the third level describes the schema itself; and the fourth level describes instances/data. Within the presented approach this model is combined with the classification of knowledge according to the abstraction and types (Neches *et al.,* 1991) that distinguishes *universal, shared, specific,* and *individual* knowledge abstraction levels.

In the resulting knowledge sharing architecture (figure 1) the universal level is considered as the common knowledge representation paradigm based on the formalism of object-oriented constraint networks. The abstractions provided at this level are shared by the ontologies. The universal level corresponds to the knowledge representation level that provides the common notation for knowledge description and enables compatibility of different formats (e.g., KIF, OWL, etc.).

The shared abstraction level and specific abstraction level (knowledge sharing levels) are considered sharable and reusable since ontologies of these levels share common representation paradigm and common vocabulary. They focus on ontological knowledge common for the particular area. Knowledge represented by these levels suits well for sharing and reuse, since, on the one hand, they do not concentrate on any specific properties, and on the other hand, knowledge of these levels is not a universal abstraction rarely taken into account for practical knowledge sharing and reuse.

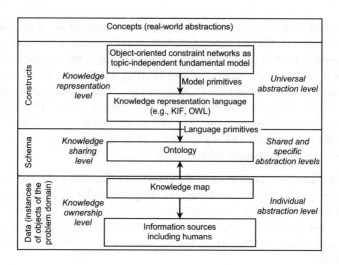

Figure 1. *Knowledge sharing levels based on information representation and knowledge abstraction architectures*

The knowledge ownership level increases scalability of the system with due regard to number of knowledge sources that can be attached to the system and users that can be served.

The conceptual model of the proposed ontology-driven interoperability support (Figure 2) is based on the developed earlier idea of knowledge logistics (Smirnov *et al.*, 2004). It correlates with the conceptual integration developed within the Athena project (Ruggaber, 2005). The common ontology describes common entities of the enterprise systems described by their local ontologies and relationships between them. As a result it is possible to treat all available knowledge and competencies as one distributed knowledge base.

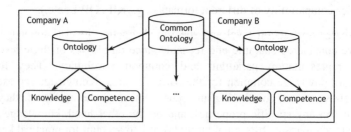

Figure 2. *Conceptual model of ontology-driven interoperability support*

Real-world problems in the areas of management, engineering, manufacturing, etc. are usually presented as constraint satisfaction problems (e.g., Baumgaertel, 2000). Thereby, to simplify the formulation and interpretation of the problems, in the presented approach they are described via object-oriented constraint networks. This formalism supports declarative representation, efficiency of dynamic constraint solving, as well as problem modelling capability, maintainability, reusability, and extensibility of the object-oriented technology. The semantics is provided for by using ontologies to enable knowledge sharing and exchange in a BTO network. The technological base for the approach is provided by the technology of open services (Web or GRID services).

3. Knowledge management platform for BTO supply chain

3.1. *State of the art*

Carried out analysis of existing knowledge management platform implementations showed that some of the technologies put into the basis of the KMP (e.g., ontology management and distributed architecture) are de facto a standard for this class of systems. Figure 3 represents some of the analysed systems and some of criteria. Since the information was collected from public sources not everything is known. However the main trend can be seen. Though the interoperability at the technological level (e.g., XML support) is very well developed, the interoperability at the semantic level (e.g., support of ontology description formats such as RDF or OWL) is not sufficiently addressed. The trend to building service-oriented architecture (SOA) that is a step to enterprise application integration (EAI) is also at an early stage in this area (a weak or no support of SOAP can be seen).

● - supported ◖ - not known or weakly supported ○ - not supported	Ontology-Based	Distributed Architecture	XML Support	RDF/OWL Support	SOAP Support
Inria KmP (http://www-sop.inria.fr/acacia/soft/kmp.html)	●	●	◖	◖	○
Unicorn Workbench (http://unicorn.com/)	●	●	●	◖	◖
ICONS (http://www.icons.rodan.pl/)	●	●	●	●	○
h-TechSight (http://www.etse.urv.es/~drianyo/hTechSight/projecte.html)	●	●	●	○	○
CORMA (http://www.corma.net/)	●	◖	◖	◖	○
kBOS (http://www.kbos.net/)	◖	●	●	◖	○
KIM Platform (http://www.ontotext.com/kim/index.html)	●	○	●	●	○

Figure 3. *Comparison of existing knowledge management platforms*

3.2. Proposed knowledge management platform concept

The proposed knowledge management platform performs a supporting function for the system communication bus and is accessed via a certain interface corresponding to existing standards (e.g., Web-service standards including SOAP and WSDL). At the moment it is planned to have a Web-based graphical user interface for users and Web-service interface for information systems.

Semantic interoperability is achieved via using an ontology providing for common notation and terminology (Figure 4). To provide for semantic interoperability the usage of ontologies as one of the most advanced approach to knowledge mark-up and description is proposed. Ontologies establish the common terminology between members of a community of interest (SemanticWeb, 2005). This enables organisation of semantic interoperability between various subtasks of BTO system configuration and management. Besides, ontology model is a means to overcome the problem of semantic heterogeneity. Ontologies provide reusable domain knowledge. Knowledge represented by ontologies is sharable and understandable for both humans and computers.

The approach orients to availability of domain knowledge. The knowledge has to be collected before it can be used. Knowledge collecting includes phases of knowledge representation and integration. Due to the ontology model the heterogeneous knowledge being collected is represented in a uniform way.

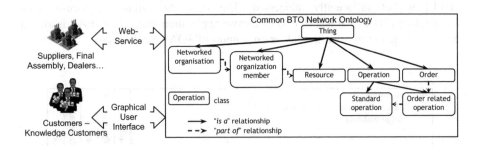

Figure 4. *Access to the common ontology (a fragment is presented) within the knowledge management platform*

4. Modification of the Contract Net protocol for negotiation in BTO networks

4.1. Negotiation protocol choice

Making feasible decisions fast is very important in BTO production. Since time limits often do not allow performing optimization to find optimal solutions for problems it is reasonable to speak about feasible solutions. Below a negotiation protocol is presented that is based on the described above principles for building a knowledge management platform for a BTO production network.

In order to choose a protocol the main specifics to the approach were be formulated as follows:

1. *Contribution*: the units have to cooperate with each other to make the best contribution into the overall system's benefit – not into the units' own benefits;

2. *Task performance*: the main goal is to complete the task performance – not to get profit out of it;

3. *Mediating*: the units operate in a decentralized community, however in all the negotiation processes there is a unit (e.g., final assembly) managing the negotiation process and making a final decision;

4. *Common terms*: since the units work in the same system they use common terms for communication. This is achieved via usage of the common shared ontology.

The protocols analyzed in order to choose one most suitable for the approach include protocols for agent-based negotiation, namely: voting, bargaining, auctions, general equilibrium market mechanisms, coalition games, and constraint networks (Weiss, 2000). Based on the analysis of these protocols and the above requirements to them, the contract net protocol (CNP) was chosen as a basis for the negotiation model in the approach. A performed experimentation with CNP showed that to operate efficiently utilizing the conventional CNP is not enough. It was necessary to provide mechanisms of units' knowledge representation, deals analysis and negotiation which would ensure task performance. Below, the improvements made in order to fulfill these lacks are presented. Made improvements concern the formalism of knowledge representation and a scenario of the interaction.

4.2. Conventional CNP

CNP is one of basic coordination strategies between agents in multi-agent systems. It was originally introduced in Davis *et al.,* 1983. The main scenario of this protocol is as follows: (i) *managers* (*initiators* in FIPA) divide tasks, (ii) *contractors* (*participants* in FIPA) bid, (iii) manager makes contract for lowest bid, (iv) there is no negotiation of bids. The UML sequence diagram of the FIPA-based contract net protocol is presented in figure 5. Since CNP is a basic protocol any particular system requires some modifications for CNP to be implemented (Payne *et al.*, 2002; Sandholm *et al.*, 1995; Zhang *et al.*, 2002).

4.3. Modified CNP

Since the approach assumes object-oriented constraint networks for knowledge representation this formalism has been also chosen for representation of knowledge and for communications between units. Two types of constraints were defined: "local" and "global". Each contractor deals with the local constraints describing its limitations, e.g. time of the task execution cannot be less than some value (time $\geq$ time $_{lower\ bound}$). Manager also deals with the local constraints and the main purpose of these constraints is definition of requirements for the task execution, e.g. the task execution cannot last longer than some time (time $\leq$ time $_{upper\ bound}$). Manager can also have objectives such as minimization of the task execution costs (costs $\rightarrow$ min). Global constraints describe constraints defined by the community, e.g. resource limitations such as time or costs. For constraints processing the technologies of constraint satisfaction and propagation are used.

Thus, a generic call for proposals from a manager to contractors has the following form: <Objective; Constraints; Content>.

Objective is optional and used for meeting manager's constraints such as minimization of costs for a task processing. Constraints are also optional and used for a similar purpose, namely to meet requirements for the task execution. Content is a message itself including functions to be performed by contractors and other parameters. As it can be seen the units exchange constraints instead of data.

Contractors' proposals besides the content part contain constraints corresponding to manager's objective and constraints. This will be illustrated in the example given at the end of the paper. If in case of conflicting interests contractors cannot meet the requirements of the manager they still can propose the closest possible parameters and it is up to the manager to decide whether to accept the proposal or not.

Modifications of the CNP-based negotiation model include:

– *iterative negotiation*: the negotiation process can be repeated several times until acceptable solution is achieved (Figure 5);

– *proposal conformation*: concurrent conformation of constraint-based proposals between manager and contractors;

– *flexible set of messages*: new messages corresponding to FIPA *Request* and *Confirm* communicative acts, and message *Clone* not corresponding to any FIPA communicative act are included (specific message types depend on a particular scenario and are not discussed in the paper);

– *roles*: manager and two types of contractors: (i) "classic" contractors negotiating proposals, and (ii) auxiliary service providers not negotiating but performing required operations (e.g., ontology modification, user interfacing, etc.);

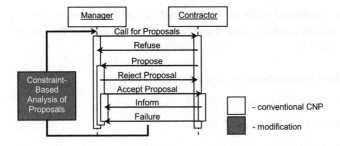

Figure 5. *UML sequence diagram of FIPA-based contract net protocol and its modification*

– *role changing*: agents/units can change their roles and adjust autonomy during a scenario (this possibility depends on a particular scenario);

4.4. *Experimentation with the modified constraint-based CNP*

To compare the results of the conventional CNP and constraint-based CNP the following illustrative example is considered. The experimentation is done using multi-agent environment MAS DK (Gorodetski *et al.,* 2001). The environment has been chosen for illustrative purposes; the protocol can be applied for interaction between Web-services as well.

The example scenario is as follows. A manager (configuration agent or CA) is supposed to obtain knowledge from three contractors (W1, W2 and W3) with the time of knowledge acquisition being minimal. These criteria (time and costs) have been chosen because they are widely used. It is also preferable for the Configuration agent to choose a cheaper deal among the deals with the same time: CA: time → min, costs → min.

The contractors can make different offers such that the costs inversely depend on the time of knowledge delivery the higher the costs. This dependency is described by a table function given below:

```
W1: 30min/$15
W2: 15min/$20; 25min/$10; 45min/$5; …
W3: 50min/$25; 60min/$15; 70min/$10; …
```

The resulting time and costs are calculated as follows:

```
time = max(time_W1, time_W2, time_W3)
costs = sum(costs_W1, costs_W2, costs_W3)
```

The first scenario (Figure 6, left) is done in accordance with the conventional CNP. The configuration agent sends calls for proposals to all the contractors concurrently. Besides description of the task to be performed each call contains additional constraints. In this case these constraints will contain the following:

```
time → min.
```

The offers from contractors will contain the following:

```
W1: 30min/$15; W2: 15min/$20; W3: 50min/$25.
```

The result will be 50 min and $60.

The second scenario is done according to the presented in the paper modified CNP. It contains concurrent conformation and iterative negotiation (figure 8 right). At the first iteration the Configuration agent sends calls for proposals to all the contractors concurrently as in the first scenario, and the offers from the contractors are the same:

```
time → min.
W1: 30min/$15; W2: 15min/$20; W3: 50min/$25
```

After this the Configurator analyses the results and sends new calls to the contractors 1 and 2:

```
time ≤ 50 AND costs → min
```

The contractors reply as follows:

```
W1: 30min/$15; W2: 45min/$5
```

The result is 50 min and $45:

```
W1: 30min/$15; W2: 45min/$5; W3: 50min/$25.
```

5. Conclusions

The paper proposes an approach to building a knowledge management platform for BTO production network and based on it modified contract net negotiation protocol. Interoperability at technological level is achieved via usage of open service standards and interoperability on semantic level is achieved via usage of a common shared BTO ontology. Modifications of the presented negotiation protocol include an introduction of the constraint-based negotiation, iterative negotiation, concurrent conformation, extended set of available messages, and adjustable roles of the negotiating units. Experiments show that the proposed protocol has some advantages and allows obtaining more efficient negotiation results than the conventional CNP.

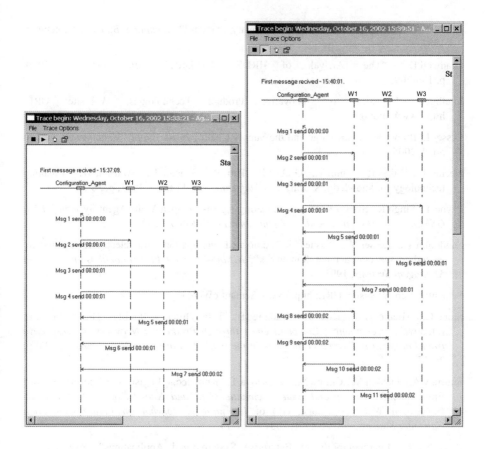

Figure 6. *Experimentation with the conventional (left) and modified (right) CNP*

The paper is due to the research carried out as a part of Integrated Project FP6-IST-NMP 507592-2 "Intelligent Logistics for Innovative Product Technologies" sponsored by European Commission, projects # 16.2.35 of the research program "Mathematical Modelling and Intelligent Systems" and # 1.9 of the research program "Fundamental Basics of Information Technologies and Computer Systems" of the Russian Academy of Sciences, and grant # 05-01-00151 of the Russian Foundation for Basic Research.

6. References

Baumgaertel H. "Distributed constraint processing for production logistics", *IEEE Intelligent Systems*, vol. 15 no. 1, 2000, p. 40-48.

Davis R., Smith R. "Negotiation as a metaphor for distributed problem solving", *Artificial Intelligence*, vol. 20 no. 1, 1983, p. 63-109.

Gradwell D. "Developments in Data Dictionary Standard", *Computer Bulletin*, September, 1987.

Gradwell D. "The Arrival of IRDS Standards", *8th BNCOD*, 1990, p. 196-209.

Intelligent Logistics for Innovative Product Technologies. Web-site. URL: http://www.ilipt.org.

Lesser I., Butner K. "Knowledge and the Supply Chain", *Inside Supply Management*, vol. 16 no. 4, 2005.

Neches R., Fikes R., Finin T., Gruber T., Patil R., Senator T., Swartout W. "Enabling technology for knowledge sharing", *AI Magazine*, vol. 12 no. 3, 1991, p. 36-56.

Payne T., Singh R., Sycara K. "Communicating Agents in Open Multi-Agent Systems", *First GSFC/JPL Workshop on Radical Agent Concepts (WRAC), 2002.*

Sandholm T., Lesser V., "Issues in automated negotiation and electronic commerce: extending the contract net framework", *ICMAS-95 First International Conference on Multiagent Systems*, 1995.

Semantic Web. Web site. URL: http://www.SemanticWeb.org.

Stone G., Miemczyk J., Esser R. "Making Build to Order a Reality: The 5-Day Car Initiative", *Strengthening Competitiveness through Production Networks. A prospective from European ICT research projects in the field of "Enterprise Networking"*, 2005, p. 26-37.

Smirnov A., Pashkin M., Chilov N., Levashova T. "Knowledge Logistics in Information Grid Environment", *The special issue "Semantic Grid and Knowledge Grid: The Next-Generation* Web" (H. Zhuge, ed.) of *International Journal on Future Generation Computer Systems*, vol. 20 no. 1, 2004, p. 61-79.

Ruggaber R. "Interoperability of Enterprise Systems and Applications", *Strengthening Competitiveness through Production Networks. A perspective from European ICT research projects in the field of "Enterprise Networking"*, 2005, p. 58-70.

Weiss G. (ed.) *Multiagent systems: a modern approach to distributed artificial intelligence*, The MIT Press, Cambridge, Massachusetts, London, 2000.

Zhang H., Wu B., Dong M., Shi Z. "Dynamic contract net protocol", *ICIIT'2002 International Conference on Intelligent Information Technology*, 2002, p. 564-572.

Gorodetski V., Karsayev O., Kotenko I., Khabalov A. "Software development kit for multi-agent systems design and implementation", *CEEMAS'01 Second International Workshop of Central and Eastern Europe on Multi-agent Systems* (eds. B. Dunin-Keplicz and E. Nawarecki), 2001, p. 99-108.

Risk Assessment of Business Contracts

Vandana Kabilan* — Hans Weigand**

*Department of Computer and Systems Sciences
Royal Institute of Technology and Stockholm University
FORUM 100, SE 164 40
Sweden
vandana@dsv.su.se

**Infolab, Tilburg University
PO Box 90153, 5000 LE Tilburg
The Netherlands
H.Weigand@uvt.nl

ABSTRACT: Enterprises conduct business transactions with other enterprises for a number of economic, business and strategic motivations. These business relationships are often governed through legal business contracts. Contracts are instruments in not only establishing the legality of the business relationships but also (1) to spell out the expected behaviour from all parties concerned, (2) to make explicit all the obligations and responsibilities that each party undertakes to fulfil and (3) to divide the potential risks and costs involved in the proposed business transaction so as to be a mutually satisfactory arrangement. In this paper, we focus on the risk assessment and evaluation of proposed business contracts. By analyzing the obligations and their fulfilment criteria as stipulated in the business contract and thereafter applying risk models, we propose a methodology for evaluating the suitability of a proposed contractual terms and conditions for a particular business organization.

KEY WORDS: e-contracting, risk assessment, interoperability.

1. Introduction

Business organizations conducted business transactions for centuries. With the electronic revolution the mechanism for establishing these business and trade relationships have changed drastically. Interoperable systems have become indispensable for supporting transaction execution. In the near future, they are expected to play increasingly a supporting role in the establishment of the relationship as well. One of the supporting roles could be the establishment of trust. There are many factors that govern the formation of business relationships – like business compatibility, value or service profitability, and business policies, and amongst these also trust. The question of trust arises when a business enterprise decides to enter in a trading relationship with other business enterprises, especially in cases when the proposed partner is as yet an unknown candidate. The purpose of establishing legal contracts is manifold: to comply to the governing judiciary and regulatory frameworks, to make explicit all obligations and expected fulfilling activities, to formulate mechanisms for dispute resolution and remedial options in case of non fulfilment of promised activities and to divide the costs, liabilities for damages and risks involved in a pro-active manner. E-contracting facilitates business entities to offer and negotiate these business contracts electronically without even having physically seen each other. Hence, the need for assessing and evaluating the pros and cons of a contract offer from different perspectives is paramount. As put forward by Grossman (2002) an enterprise cannot benefit from its negotiated contract terms, if it is not aware of what terms (obligations, milestones and risks) lie buried in the contract.

This paper proposes a systematic method of identifying the risks involved in a business transaction based on a combination of existing risk modelling techniques. The proposed method is intended as a decision support system that shall enable the contract designer or the business manager to take informed decisions and choices in the contract negotiation process. Although the techniques are not original, as far as we know their combination and application to the e-contracting problem is new. In section 2 we discuss some of the relevant previous research. In section 3 we describe the methodology and in section 4 we extensively demonstrate its use on a case study. Section 5 is the conclusion.

2. Previous research

Useful research has been performed in the area of contract monitoring (Xu & Jeusfeld, 2003), contract negotiation (Schoop *et al.*, 2003), contract logics (Daskalopulu *et al.*, 1997; Tan *et al.*, 1998) and e-contracting frameworks (Angelov *et al.*, 2003; Radha Krishna *et al.*, 2003). In most cases, the focus is on modelling and guaranteeing the "success scenario" and not on the handling of failures.. One useful article that we have found is by Tan and Thoen (2003) that describes a structured, model-driven approach to contracting that each party can use to assess the personal risks and trust it entails. Following Williamson (1985), they define uncertainty as "doubt about our ability to predict the future outcome of current actions" and risk as "the potential variation in outcomes". What is needed is that parties involved in a negotiation can select mechanisms that reduce the perceived risk and uncertainty to the point where they have enough confidence to be willing to engage in the transaction. The generic trust model of Tan and Thoen makes the fundamental assumption that a party will engage in a transaction if the potential gain outweighs the uncertainty associated with the transaction. In case of doubt, it makes sense to either increase the potential gain or reduce the uncertainty. Potential gain is broken down into three elements: perceived direct benefit, perceived relationship benefit, and perceived strategic benefit. These perceptions depend to a certain extent on the trust, which can be broken down into trust in the other party and trust in control mechanisms. Both trust sources have an objective and subjective aspect.

The method proposed by Tan and Thoen prompts the user to estimate the three components of the potential gain, as well as the costs for controls, and on this basis, the total potential gain can be calculated. Furthermore, for each identified risk, the system asks the user to indicate (by means of scrollbars) the probability that this could happen ("can do"), the probability that the other party will use the opportunity ("will do"), the control effectiveness, and the trust in the control. In this way, the utility loss and behavioural risk can be calculated.

The set of parameters defined in the model of Tan and Thoen is useful and will be taken into account in the method proposed below. However, they do not explain how to *identify* the possible risks. Furthermore, they seem to consider each risk in isolation (no combinations); by consequence, they do not sort out the effect of a certain control mechanism for different scenarios, and do not distinguish between individual risks and total risk.

3. Proposed methodology

There are numerous risk assessment methods and models available in the areas of auditing, investment analysis, and critical mission design, among others. The methodology that we propose here is a combination of existing methods tuned to the contract drafting and contract assessment. Like the CORAS project[1], our approach is model-based, but we focus on e-commerce transactions and contracts rather than IT–critical systems.

The method contains the following main steps:
1. *Assumed Inputs:* The contract draft proposed, business model or value model for the enterprise carrying out the contract assessment, reference contract, business and risk ontology wherever available and risk mitigation and control patterns like that proposed by (Karteseva *et al.*, 2004) etc.
2. *Identification of primary obligations.* The underlying assumption for starting here is that we regard non-fulfilment of obligations (by either party) to be the main risk in interoperable systems.
3. *Scenario modelling.* From the primary obligations, the *risk events* can be derived as being the non-performance of an obligation. The risk events usually do have a temporal sequence. With scenario modelling, these partial orderings are presented.
4. *Global risk assessment.* Using the *Event Tree* method, identify the risks for each possible scenario (combination of risk events). The risk is expressed in

---

1 CORAS Project (IST-2000-25031), project details publications and tools available online at http://coras.sourceforge.net/index.html.

the form of a *probability* estimate and a *utility loss* estimate. An aggregate risk can be computed over all the possible scenarios.

5. *Detailed risk analysis.* The risk of a scenario may be broken down using a *Fault Tree* Analysis that analyzes the causes of non-fulfilment. These will be different for different situations, but some general analysis format can be used as a heuristic. In addition to this backward looking analysis method, a forward-looking Event Tree method can be applied.

6. *Risk mitigation.* The risk assessment is typically followed by risk mitigation. In this phase, preventive and compensating risk measures are considered. The effects of these measures should be assessed again by extending the Event Tree and then repeating steps 3-5. Examples of risk measures are down payments, a letter of credit procedure, trust dependencies and sanctions. In a rational decision process, multiple alternatives are generated and compared before the best one is chosen.

4. Contract case scenario

We consider a typical purchase and sale of commercial goods scenario between trading partners situated at different geographical locations. We assume that the trust between these two partners is not very high, so that they both employ sufficient control mechanisms to check and evaluate the performance of each other, either by themselves or through a trusted third party.

We consider a situation where the seller and the buyer are negotiating the terms of an agreement for trade, based on the INCOTERMS C Patterns[2]. These patterns allocate the obligations, costs and risks and liabilities almost equally between the two.

We consider the simplest case in this paper, where the seller always makes or assembles the goods once the buyer places an order. The primary obligation of a seller is to deliver goods made to specification that is usually included in the contract terms and conditions. The buyer's primary obligation is to pay for the goods he has ordered. In addition there are other nested or secondary obligations like the seller's obligation to package the goods suitable for transportation by the transport medium stipulated.

The C terms stipulate that the seller shall arrange for the carrier, though the costs and liability is to be borne by the buyer. This means that on part of the seller, he has to search and instruct a carrier, giving the carrier the mandatory minimum lead time for notification. The carrier is obliged to accept the goods and transfer the goods to destination.

The buyer has authorized a third party Inspection agency to inspect the goods for quality and quantity as stated in the underlying contract. The Inspection agency

---

2 INCOTERMS is developed, maintained and promoted by the ICC Commission on Commercial Law and Practice, see http://www.iccwbo.org/incoterms/.

(inspector) has to carry out the checks on arrival of the goods at destination and provide proof/info to the buyer about the goods.

The buyer then is obliged to send delivery acceptance notification to the seller. For simplicity sake, we model that the seller sends the invoice after he receives the delivery acceptance notification. Thereafter the buyer has to fulfil his obligation to pay, by instructing his bank accordingly.

4.1. *Identification of primary risks*

Based on the Obligations types and obligation states proposed by Kabilan *et al.*, (2003), we analyze the main obligations and the party responsible for performing the identified obligations (risk owner). We assume that the obligation for both export and import clearance rests with just one party and not divided between the two. All these obligations are common obligations from the INCOTERMS and thus the following analysis is applicable to all such contracts based on the INCOTERMS.

If a framework like INCOTERMS is not available, the primary obligations are to be derived from the business model (not worked out in this paper). For the contract scenario described above, we list the main obligations, performers as in Table 1 below:

S.No	Obligation	Role Responsible	Fulfilled When	Unfulfilled When (Risk Events)
1	Obligation to Deliver	Seller	Seller hands over goods to carrier	Goods are not ready on time. Goods are not handed over to Carrier. Goods delivered are not to specification. Goods are of unacceptable quality/damaged.
2	Obligation to Pay	Buyer	Buyer transfers the money to the seller. May involve a third party, the buyer's bank who is actually responsible for the money transfer. Nevertheless the obligation responsibility rests with the buyer.	Payment is delayed. Payment is not made. Bank transfer failed (this case is analysed for transfer of risks and rights).
3	Obligation to Package	Seller	Goods are packed as per the standards specified.	Goods are not packed. Goods are packed but not appropriate to the mode of transport and specified terms.
4	Obligation to Insure	Seller/Buyer	An insurer has been contracted and notified when the delivery is to commence.	Insurer has not been arranged. Insurer has not been notified and all activities needed to activate the insurance have not been done (reference to documentary evidence may be given).

5	Obligation for arranging Carriage	Seller/Buyer	A transport/carrier has to be contracted.	Carrier is not arranged. Carrier is not notified.
6	Obligation to Inspect	Buyer	Inspection on delivery Buyer authorizes an inspector to perform the inspection within the stipulated time period in the contract.	Buyer fails to inspect. Buyer fails to inspect within stipulated time. Inspector has not been arranged Inspector fails to inspect the goods.
7	Obligation for export and import clearance	Seller/Buyer	All documents procedures, fees for export and import has been successfully completed.	Export and import clearance has not been done Export duties have not been paid

Table 1. *Primary obligations, roles and risk events*

4.2. *Scenario modelling*

After the analysis of the different obligations included in the contract terms we use a method based on a Probabilistic Risk Assessment technique called Event Sequence Modelling. We model the different obligation, their activation and their fulfilment states in a similar pattern as event sequence modelling (following the guidelines presented in (Kabilan *et al.,* 2005). The non-fulfilments are not included, as the goal is to clarify the partial ordering between the obligations. We do not address the question here where this partial ordering is derived from.

In this paper, we use Event Process Chain diagram to model the obligation and their corresponding fulfilling business actions as depicted in Figure 1.

The figure depicts mainly the *seller* side of the business transaction for sake of simplicity. We have also simplified the diagram due to space constrictions and thus depict only the normal "fulfilment" path for the identified obligations. We have used Event-Driven Process Chain notations for the illustration but we could use any other notation like UML sequence diagram, UML activity Diagram, BPMN etc. The identified abstract processes are modelled in oblong rectangles as *Events* and the decision points, checks, or dependencies have been collapsed into *functions* shown as the pink hexagons in Figure 1. The objective of the figure is to illustrate graphically the time-ordered sequence and dependencies of different risk events. The *events* are colour-coded to represent different obligation states, for example, red for *inactive*, green for *active*. The scope of each identified obligation is indicated by the scope of the parenthesis on the side of the obligation model.

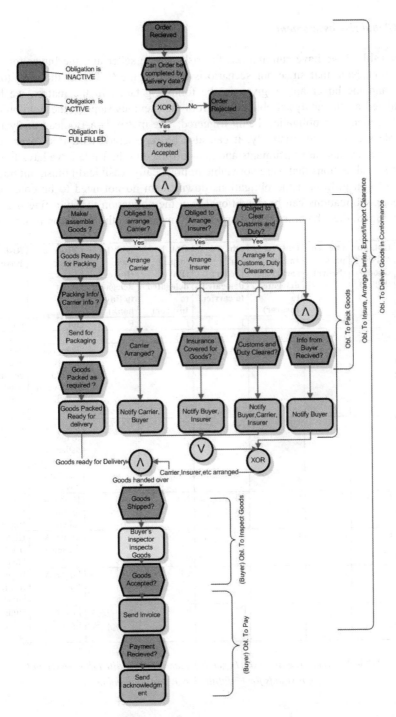

Figure 1. *Scenario model using EPC*

4.3. *Global risk assessment*

In Table 2 we have summarized the risks to the seller and the buyer for each obligation. Note that since our scenario is based on the C Terms, the risks to the seller and the buyer are as given in the following table. In the matrix, we have considered all the analysed obligations from the previous steps in the time-ordered linear sequence of obligation being triggered. The matrix is a Boolean analysis of possible scenarios; alternatively, it can also be represented as a tree (event tree, where the "events" are fulfilments and non-fulfilments). In Table 2 we have left out several combinations that were not viable or practically feasible. In most, but not all, cases of non-fulfilment the obligations downstream do not need to be considered anymore. Obligations can be conditional, e.g. the obligation to pay a fine if goods are damaged; then the branch "non-applicable" means that the condition is not met.

S no	Obl. To Make Goods (Seller)	Obl. To pack (Seller)	Obl. To Insure (Seller: delegated to Insurer)	Obl. To carry (Seller: delegated to carrier)	Obl. To inspect (Buyer: delegated to Insurer)	Obl. To Pay (Buyer: delegated to Buyer bank)	Risks to Seller	Risks to Buyer
1	F	F	F	F	F	F	nil	nil
2	UF	NA	NA	NA	NA	NA	NA	NA
3	F	UF	NA	NA	NA	NA	High costs involved. Due to damage in transit.	Buyer does not get his goods. High risk.
4	F	F	UF	NA	NA	NA	High risk to the seller as seller bears damages cost	Low risk to buyer.
5	F	F	F	UF	NA	NA	High risk for the seller,	Low risk for Buyer.
6	F	F	F	F	UF	F	Low risk for seller	High risk for buyer.
7	F	F	F	F	UF	UF	Low risk for seller	High risk for buyer.
8	F	F	F	F	F	UF	Low risk for seller	High risk for buyer.

Table 2: *Event Tree Analysis. Legend: F stands for Fulfilled (Success)) and UF stands for Unfulfilled. NA: Not Applicable*

The last two columns apportion the risk to the seller and the buyer as being either "high" or "low". In a first quick assessment, this may be sufficient. After more detailed risk assessment (see below), the risk could be expressed more precisely as the product of a *probability* estimate P and a *utility loss* (impact) L estimate, where the P is the probability that *in that scenario*, the loss L will be realized (this is not the same as the probability that this scenario will happen – this one will be used later). The utility loss is to be calculated as the difference between the potential gains and potential losses (for the case at hand, the assumption that utility equates value is reasonable). For example, if we consider the simple scenario that Buyer does not pay and Sender delivers, the gain is 0 and the loss is the costs that Seller has made (not the amount of the invoice, but his production costs) – or, more precisely, the product of these costs and the probability that indeed he has lost these items and they will not be recaptured. In the scenario that Buyer does pay after delivery, the gain is the amount of the payment and the loss is the production costs, so there is a negative profit loss amounting to the profit margin of the Seller.

Risks can be assessed in two ways: individual and total. The individual assessment looks at one scenario at a time. If the risk in that scenario is unacceptable, it should be addressed by some risk mitigation instrument. Note that for this level of analysis, in principle we need not know the probability of the risk event (the scenario).

It is quite well possible that even with additional control measures, not all scenarios are without risk. But this is also not necessary. According to the *expected utility hypothesis* in economics (Arrow, 1963), the utility of an agent facing uncertainty is calculated by considering utility in each possible state and constructing a weighted average. The weights are the agent's estimate of the probability of each state. The total risk assessment calculates the aggregate of all the individual risks; this total risk should be less then zero.

Individual and total risk assessment should be used together. If the total risk is less then zero (the expected utility is positive), but there are some situations with a very high risk, a risk aversive person will not engage himself in the contract. On the other hand, the individual risks may all be low, but if the expected utility is negative or very low, it would not be rational to engage either.

4.4. Detailed risk assessment

In some cases, it is not easy to make a risk estimate of a certain scenario, and some detailed risk assessment is needed. There are two main techniques that can be of help: inductive and deductive. Fault Tree Analysis (FTA) is an example of a deductive or reverse method where the objective is to identify and assess the causes of a certain consequence (Vesely *et al.*, 1981). The Event Tree Analysis (ETA) is an example of an inductive or forward-looking method where the objective is to identify and assess the consequences of a certain cause. We will give an example of each.

To illustrate the Fault Tree Analysis, we refer to Figure 2. It provides a generic pattern that should be filled in for each particular situation. For example, applied to the failure of the payment obligation, it shows that the payment cannot be done at all, or arrives too late, or not properly (e.g. based on a wrong exchange rate). A technical reason could be a short failure of the bank network. Note that at this level of analysis, not only non-fulfilments are considered, but other risk events as well. The various risk categories identified by (Schmitt *et al.*, 2005) could also be employed as generic patterns.

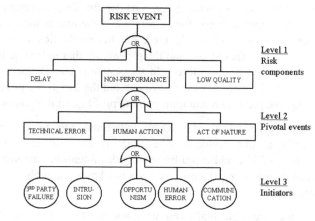

Figure 2. *Fault Tree Analysis (generic pattern)*

As an example of ETA, we present in Figure 3 a scenario for a seller's obligation to deliver. In this type of analysis, we first have to identify the "trigger" event (could be a business event, monetary event or legal event), which activates the obligation being investigated, and then we analyze subsequent contingencies and their outcomes in terms of the state of the obligation. The possible state values are:

- *InActive*: obligations come into existence when contract is signed but they are not activated yet for execution.
- *Active:* each time an order comes in and is accepted, the seller's obligation to deliver becomes active.
- *Fulfilled:* each obligation is linked to a "performance-event" on successful completion of which, the obligation is completed satisfactorily.
- *Unfullfilled:* whenever, the expected performance event does not take place, or is unsatisfactory, and then the obligation is violated or unfulfilled.
- *Pending*: when the performance is partially completed, that is, the obligation may still be "fulfilled" following some "remedial actions" being invoked. For example, in case of damaged or sub-standard goods, the buyer may choose to accept part of the consignment, provided that the seller redelivers the damaged goods or makes some penalty payment etc. An obligation also is said to be in "pending" state while a "reconciliatory"

obligation is "active". The original obligation is restored to "fulfilled" state once the "reconciliatory obligation" is fulfilled. For more details, see (Kabilan *et al.*, 2003).

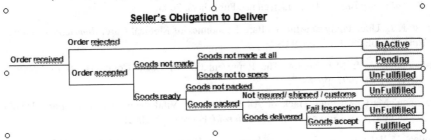

Figure 3. *Event Tree Analysis example*

In Figure 3, we see that a delay or non-occurrence of insurance or shipment can cause the Seller's obligation to deliver to be "unfulfilled". Though, it was the Buyer's responsibility to arrange for carrier, insurance and export/import duty clearance (see Table 1). This poses a potential risk to the Seller. Similarly, we see that if the goods are not packed as required, the Seller is open to risks. This is dependent on the Seller having received proper information regarding the mode of carriage etc.

5. Conclusion

The background of this paper is the perceived need for effective contract management and negotiation to reduce business risks associated with contractual violations. Once the decision makers are aware of the embedded obligations, liabilities and risks, they can make qualified judgement regarding the best alternatives as well as other risk mitigating actions that they would include in the contract. The stepwise method that we propose guides a user in analysing the contract and identifying the obligations, their fulfilment requirements, and their temporal dependencies. This analysis helps in computing the possible risks and violations that could occur and for each of them, possible outcomes, and suggestions for their avoidance. For reasons of space, we have not worked out the risk mitigation step. Although useful work has been done in that area (e.g. Kartseva *et al.*, 2004), we also consider it a topic for future research, in particular the potential use of risk mitigation patterns. Also more attention is needed for the handling of indirect, less tangible risks, such as those having to do with the partnership and strategic benefits.

Another interesting research question is on the relationship between the primary obligations and a business or value model (see Schmitt *et al.*, 2005), and more in general, on the place of risk analysis in process design. There is a need for risk assessment at an early stage, when only high-level models are available, in order to guide the design process. However, sometimes process details can have a large impact on the risk calculation.

6. References

Angelov S, Grefen P., The 4W Framework for B2B E-Contracting. *Int. J. Networking and Virtual Organisation,* 1(3).Inderscience Publishers, 2003.

Arrow, K.J., Uncertainty and the Welfare Economics of Medical Care, *American Economic Review,* Vol. 53, 1963, pp. 941-73.

Daskalopulu, A & M.J. Sergot, The Representation of Legal Contracts, *AI and Society* 11(Nos. 1-2), 1997, pp. 6-17.

Grossman, Mark. Keeping Track of All Contracts is Vital Operation, The Miami Herald Technology Law Column. *The Miami Herald.* February 2, 2002.

Kabilan, V. Johannesson, P. Rugaimukammu, D. Business Contract Obligation Monitoring through use of Multi-Tier Contract Ontology. *Proceedings of Workshop on Regulatory Ontologies (Worm CoRe 2003),* November 2003, Italy. Springer-Verlag LNCS, 2003.

Kabilan V, Dzdrakovic J, Johannesson P. Use of Multi-Tier Contract Ontology to deduce Contract Workflow Models for Enterprise Interoperability. *Proceedings of 2nd INTEROP-EMOI Workshop on Enterprise Models and Interoperability collocated with CAISE 2005,* Porto, 2005.

Kartseva, V,Y-H. Tan, and J. Gordijn, Developing a Modelling Tool for Designing Control Mechanisms in Network Organisations, *Proceedings of the 17th Bled International e-Commerce Conference,* 2004.

Radha Krishna, P.K. Karlapalem, D, Chiu, An EREC framework for e-contract modelling, enactment and monitoring. *Data and Knowledge Engineering* 51 (1), 2004, pp. 31-58.

Schmitt M, Grégoire B, Dubois E. A risk based guide to business process design in inter-organizational business collaboration. *International Workshop on Requirements Engineering for Business Need and IT Alignment (REBNITA 2005),* Paris, August 2005

Schoop, M., A. Jertila, T. List, Negoisst: A Negotiation Support System for Electronic Business-to-Business Negotiations in E-Commerce, *Data and Knowledge Engineering,* 47(3), 2003, pp. 371-401.

Tan, Yao-Hua, Thoen, W., Modeling Directed Obligations and permission in Trade Contracts.*31st Annual Hawaii International Conference on System Sciences,* vol 5, 1998

Tan, Yao-Hua, Thoen, W. Electronic Contract Drafting Based on Risk and Trust Assessment. *Int. J. on Electronic Commerce* 7(4), 2003, pp.55-72

Vesely, W.E. *et al. Fault Tree Handbook* (NUREG-0492), US Nuclear Regulatory Commission, Washington D.C., 1981. Available at http://www.nrc.gov/reading-rm/doc-collections/nuregs/staff/sr0492/sr0492.pdf

Williamson, O.E. *The Economic Institutions of Capitalism.* New York, Free Press, 1985.

Xu, Lai, Manfred A. Jeusfeld, Pro-active Monitoring of Electronic Contracts, *Proc. CAiSE '03,* LNCS, Springer-Verlag, 2003.

Exploring the Interoperability of Web Services using MOQARE

Andrea Herrmann — Jürgen Rückert — Barbara Paech

Institute of Computer Science
University of Heidelberg
69120 Heidelberg, Germany
{herrmann, rueckert, paech}@informatik.uni-heidelberg.de

ABSTRACT: *Interoperability is one important quality attribute of Web Services. In this work, we analyse what threatens the technical interoperability of Web Services and which factors contribute to their interoperability. We use the method MOQARE (Misuse-oriented Quality Requirements Engineering) – a method for elicitation and documentation of non-functional requirements. Our objectives are to justify the quality attribute interoperability by business goals and to elicit and structure threats of interoperability and countermeasures supporting interoperability in a new graphical, easily extensible manner.*

KEY WORDS: *interoperability, Web Services, requirements engineering, quality, non-functional requirements.*

1. Introduction

In this work we analyse the interoperability of Web Services using the MOQARE method. As a result we obtain factors that contribute to interoperability as well as threats that prevent it. An objective is to justify the quality attribute interoperability by business goals. This enables business analysts to detect low-level quality influences on high-level business goals. Another objective is to elicit and structure threats of interoperability and countermeasures supporting interoperability in a new graphical, easily extensible manner. This objective enables quality managers to formulate engineering recommendations, which help architects, developers and testers to ensure technical interoperability and which help Web Service consumers using the Web Service accurately. We concentrate on the technical aspects of the interoperability between web services, not discussing communication or legal aspects of the interoperability between enterprises. Our overall motivation is to create an information structure that allows grouping the huge amount of available technical information about interoperability.

This publication is structured as follows: section 2 introduces fundamental terms in the area of Web Services, section 3 shortly describes MOQARE. In section 4, the results of our analysis of Web Services, using MOQARE, are presented. Section 5 is the summary and discussion of this paper.

2. Web Services

The **Service Oriented Architecture** and the **Web Service Technology** as its most popular realization enable service consumers to dynamically select and compose services offered by service providers. The most frequent kind of application is a use-on-demand of services in combination with an ad-hoc purchase of services. Services are distributed in the World Wide Web, either inside an enterprise or across different enterprises.

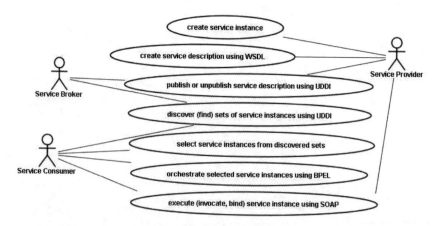

Figure 1. *Widely accepted actors and use cases around Web Service usage*

The Service Oriented Architecture supports the widely accepted **use cases** (Zimmermann *et al.*, 2003) presented in Figure 1. A service provider *describes* the web services which it produced and now offers to the market, using the interface description language WSDL (WSDL 2001) and *publishes* these descriptions in an UDDI (UDDI 2004) business registry maintained by a service broker. A service consumer *discovers* web services from the distributed UDDI business registries and *selects* the one that satisfies its business goals best. The service consumer *executes* the web service by sending a SOAP (SOAP 2003) message to the web service. The business goals can rarely be fulfilled by calling a single service; therefore, the service consumer repeats the process and finally executes a sequence of web services – the service consumer *orchestrates* Web Services e.g. by using a business process modelling language like WS-BPEL (BPEL 2003).

Interoperability plays a major role for systems that are distributed on the Web. The Web Service definition by W3C (WSG) contains interoperability as a central criterion: "A Web Service is a software system designed to support interoperable machine-to-machine interaction over a network."

Web Service interoperability concerns several areas: communication interoperability (HTTP and other transport protocols), message interoperability (SOAP), syntactical (WSDL) and semantical interoperability and process interoperability (BPEL etc.). (Ponnekanti 2004) decomposes the syntactical interoperability into structural, value and encoding misfits. (Ardissono 2003) adds the message flow incompatibility.

The WS-I open industry consortium (www.ws-i.org) promotes Web services interoperability across platforms, operating systems and programming languages. Its major deliverables "Basic Profile" and "Basic Security Profile" (ongoing) focus on communication and syntactical interoperability by integrating the standards SOAP, WSDL, UDDI, XML, XML Schema and HTTP resulting in interoperability recommendations, sample applications and test suites.

3. MOQARE

The basic idea when developing MOQARE (Misuse-oriented Quality Requirements Engineering) was to apply misuse cases for deriving realizable requirements out of business goals and quality goals, covering all quality attributes of ISO 9126 (ISO 9126) – functionality (including the subfactors security and interoperability), reliability, usability, maintainability, portability, and efficiency. The misuse cases originally were invented and applied for defining security requirements (McDermott *et al.*, 1999), (Sindre *et al.*, 2000), (Sindre *et al.*, 2001). MOQARE adopts the general idea to identify misuses with respect to a quality attribute and thereof further requirements that prevent misuse, i.e. support that the system realizes the wanted quality attribute. This approach helps to complement the requirements. MOQARE is a systematic methodology and notation for elicitation and documentation of all kinds of non-functional requirements. It integrates the idea of the misuse cases with concepts and terminologies from other methods of the security (van Lamsweerde *et al.*, 1998), (CSRC 1999), (Moore *et al.*, 2001), (Firesmith 2004), non-functional requirements (Sutcliffe *et al.*, 1998) or architecture analysis (Kazman *et al.*, 1998), (Kazman *et al.*, 2000) context to build the most complete set of concepts. The different concepts are often not clearly defined and even mixed because of lack of differentiation. Most of the sources do not offer a systematic methodology, often only ways of drawing drafts or templates.

The full description of the method and its comparison to other methods so far is documented in a working paper, and the concepts are published (Herrmann *et al.*, 2005). An overview and comparison of the literature sources we considered are described in a technical report which will be available soon. Figure 2 depicts the most important concepts. Different icons serve for a fast recognition of types and are applied later on in the "MOQARE analysis of Web Services" graphs; the grey rectangle highlights quality goals.

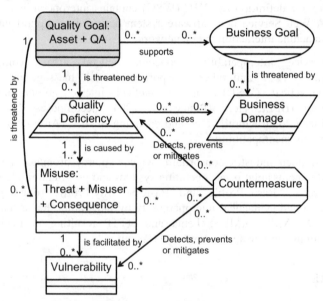

Figure 2. *The MOQARE concepts*

A system is developed and used because it supports important *business goals*. These business goals might be threatened by *business damages* that are caused by *quality deficiencies* of the system.

The *quality goal* describes more specifically which part and property of the system supports the business goals. A quality goal is the combination of an asset plus a quality attribute (QA). Both have to be protected. An *asset* is any part of the system. By "system" we do not only include the software, hardware, network, but also the physical building, the company, the administrators, maintainers and users of the system. Assets can be data, communications, services, hardware components, and personnel (Firesmith 2003).

A *quality deficiency* means that the asset does not comply with the QA. It is not necessarily the exact opposite of the QA. For example, if the quality goal is "availability of data", the quality deficiency can consist in temporary inaccessibility for all users or for certain users, irreversible destruction of the data, manipulation of the data, and many more. A *threat* is an action which would actively threaten the quality goal and cause the quality deficiency. The threat is usually performed by a *misuser*, who can be a person (hacker, users, administrators, etc.), other systems or forces of nature like fire and thunderstorm. Security is a special case, where the *misuser* can be an intruder or a user who executes a use case he/she is not supposed to use, following a harmful goal. All other ISO 9126 QAs are threatened by regular system personnel (e.g. an end user) who try to use the system as intended, but fail for some reason. Not only end-users are relevant, but also administrators and maintainers, and developers. To identify assets, misusers and threats, not only normal use is relevant, but also growth, attacks and other extreme situations.

Often, the threat is facilitated, made possible or even provoked by a *vulnerability*. A vulnerability is a property of the system and might be a code flaw or a design flaw or a flaw in the software development process, in operation or management, but also any – even wanted – property of the system, if it can be misused with respect to the quality goal. A *misuse* describes the whole misuse scenario, including misuser, threat and its consequences (quality deficiency and business damage). The misuse is documented in the form and granularity of a misuse case which is similar to a use case. This means they are more elaborated than threats, which usually are described by a few key words.

To handle threats and misuses and to support the quality goal, we need *countermeasures*. Countermeasures can either detect or prevent or mitigate a misuse. The countermeasures can be new functional requirements (e.g. use cases), constraints on functional requirements (including metrics), architectural or other constraints. Countermeasures can counteract against the threat, against the system vulnerability or against the misuse having the predicted consequences.

MOQARE starts with a functional description or draft of a planned or existing system. The requirements elicitation is guided by a four steps process and supported by checklists. The procedure identifies the concepts in the following order, which is not to be understood as an obligatory order but rather a guideline. As requirements elicitation is a creative activity, the steps can also be performed iteratively, and they even must be repeated if a countermeasure is a new quality goal.

1. find the quality goals (based on business goals, quality deficiencies, and business damages)

2. describe misuses (including threat, misuser, vulnerabilities, consequences)

3. define countermeasures

4. for those countermeasures which are new quality goals, re-start at step 2

The results of this analysis are presented in a misuse tree, an example of which will be developed in the following section.

4. Analysis of Web Services with MOQARE

Our analysis of Web Services here is focused on the aspect of interoperability. According to ISO 9126 (ISO 9126), interoperability is defined as: "Attributes of software that bear on its ability to interact with specified systems."

Usually MOQARE starts with the question how a system can support business goals. In this paper, MOQARE in a first phase analyses the rationales behind the quality goal "Interoperable Web Services", and in a second phase detects threats and proposes countermeasures for supporting this quality goal. In the first phase, the rationales are identified in the form of business goals by performing a business goal analysis. We based our work on knowledge gathered during hands-on experience with Web Service Technology. Our elicited quality goals and countermeasures allow detailing technical information about quality on a higher abstraction level, especially security, given in (Berre et al., 2004).

As the resulting misuse tree is too big for displaying as a whole the parts are presented in Figures 3 to 12. Figure 3 shows the business goals, business damages and their relationships. Figures 4 to 12 show the derivation of quality goals from the quality deficiencies and business damages (see quality goal "Web Service interoperability" in Figure 6). Figures 8 to 12 focus on quality goals availability, reliability and interoperability.

Concerning Web Services, the three stakeholders Service Consumer (SC), Service Provider (SP) and Service Broker (SB) all have their own business goals. These **business goals** are related to each other, as can be seen in Figure 3. For instance, when the Web Service is useful for the SC, this supports the SP business goal of a high market share and also the SB business goal of a good reputation. A fourth business goal is the SB goal of placing many Web Services on the market, which also supports the SB reputation. Parting from these four business goals, seven **business damages** have been identified through brainstorming using MOQARE concepts (Figure 3):

1. restricting the number of potential customers (SC) (due to Web Service itself);
2. unauthorized / unregistered use of Web Service
3. use of Web Service produces more cost than benefit
4. Web Service is not useful (for SC)
5. spying of (request and response) messages
6. Web Service code is stolen
7. Web Service offerings (interfaces) are copied by another SP

Apart from interoperability, some more QA have been identified through brainstorming which support the business goals and work against the quality deficiencies. These are: suitability, maintainability, availability, reliability, safety, immunity and access control of the Web Service and the security of the code (see Figures 4 to 7). We do not analyse other QA than interoperability, except for the discussion of three major threats to the quality goal "Web Service availability" to show how further QA enter the analysis as countermeasures (Figure 8). This serves as another example that QA are linked to each other, influence each other (Chung *et al.*, 1999) and that interoperability is not the only important QA for a Web Service.

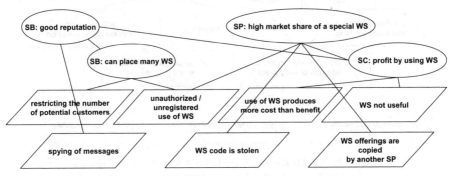

Figure 3. *MOQARE analysis of Web Services: business goals and business damages*

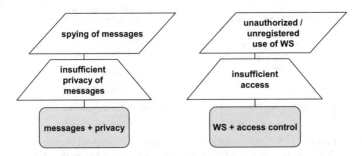

Figure 4. *MOQARE analysis of Web Services: business damages "spying of messages" and "unauthorized/unregistered use of WS"*

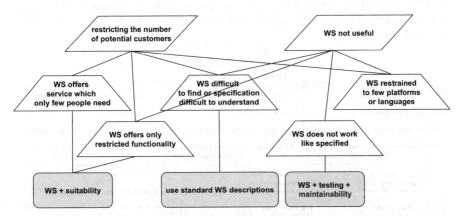

Figure 5. *MOQARE analysis of Web Services: business damages "restricting the number of potential customers" and "WS not useful"*

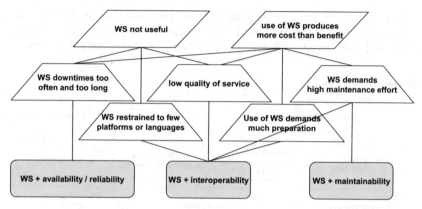

Figure 6. *MOQARE analysis of Web Services: business damages*
"WS not useful" and "use of WS produces more cost than benefit"

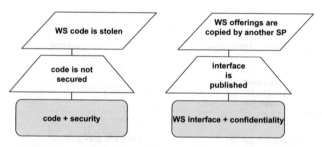

Figure 7. *MOQARE analysis of Web Services: business damages*
"WS code is stolen" and "WS offerings are copied by another SP"

In a second step, MOQARE was used to analyse the threats menacing the quality goal "interoperability of Web Service", and then to find the countermeasures which are the requirements which support or provide interoperability. The results can be seen in Figures 8 to 12.

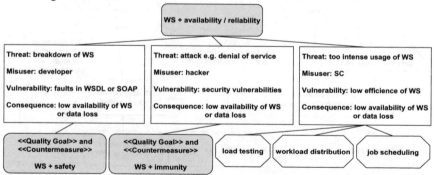

Figure 8. *MOQARE analysis of Web Services and their quality goal*
"Web Service + availability/reliability"

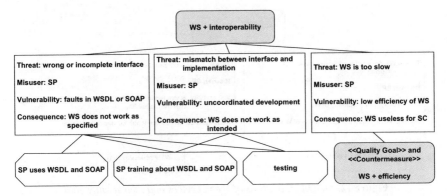

Figure 9. *MOQARE analysis of Web Services and their quality goal*
"Web Service + interoperability", Part 1

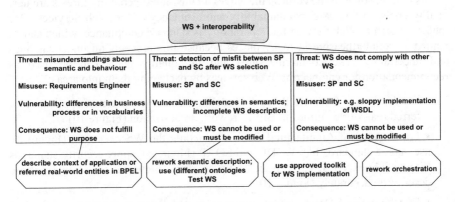

Figure 10. *MOQARE analysis of Web Services and their quality goal*
"Web Service + interoperability", Part 2

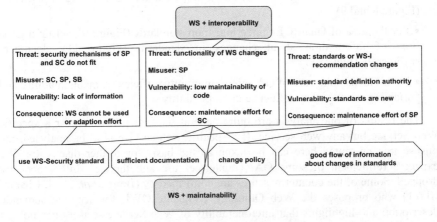

Figure 11. *MOQARE analysis of Web Services and their quality goal*
"Web Service interoperability", Part 3

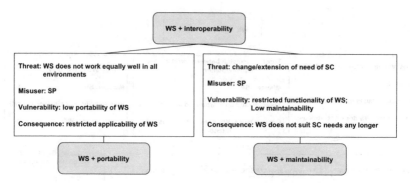

Figure 12. *MOQARE analysis of Web Services and their quality goal*
"Web Service + interoperability", Part 4

As before, some of the **countermeasures** against interoperability threats are new quality goals, in this case maintainability and efficiency of the Web Services. One major concern in Web Service Interoperability is standard compliance, which can be named as countermeasure in many places because this prevents misunderstandings and uncertainty. The countermeasures and the quality goals can be used as recommendation for engineering Web services by packaging them into areas:

• For the area of Business Process Modelling: describe context of application or referred real-world entities in BPEL, rework orchestration (Figure 10)

• For the area of Architectural Design: schedule the WS execution (Figure 8), use agreed standards like WSDL and SOAP (Figure 5), apply security standards (Figure 11), keep security policies up to date (Figure 11), define semantic description accurately (Figure 10)

• For the area of Development: use correct development environment for WS implementation, consider version of standards (Figure 10)

• For the area of Testing: do WS testing in general and load testing in particular (Figure 8 and 9)

• For the area of Quality Engineering: train standards (Figure 9), set up a good flow of information about changes in standards (Figure 11), document sufficiently (Figure 11)

• For all areas: take care of QA safety, immunity, efficiency, maintainability and portability because they influence interoperability.

The results of our analysis are quite general, i.e. not performed for a specific Web Service but any web service. If a specific web service is to be analysed, the misuse tree presented here can be taken as the basis for further discussion. We expect a refinement of some QA, countermeasure and threats while others are dropped. Some of the countermeasures are confirmed by (Berre *et al.* 2004, Chapter III.6.1) who proposes the Web Ontology Language OWL for accurate semantic description and highlights that interoperability of Web Service security has not yet been achieved.

Clearly, to use the misuse tree as requirements documentation, it must be incorporated into a requirements tool. Therefore, as part of our rationale-based CASE-tool SYSIPHUS (Sysiphus 2006) we are developing a web-based application, which allows to graphically represent the whole misuse tree as well as a selected sub-tree, a single level, or to list all concepts of one type, e.g. all countermeasures.

5. Summary and discussion

This paper presented the MOQARE method to analyse the technical interoperability of Web Services and thereby requirements on Web Services, their development, operation and maintenance. We explored the quality goal "Web Service interoperability" in two ways: We justified the quality attribute interoperability by business goals, and we elicited and structured threats of interoperability and countermeasures supporting interoperability in a new graphical, easily extensible manner. This helps business analysts to understand the lower level effects and dependencies of interoperability. Furthermore it supports development, training and operation personnel in ensuring interoperability through the whole Web Service lifecycle. We do not claim our results to be complete because the completeness of a set of threats and requirements is always difficult to define and to check. Our analysis can serve as starting point for further refinement and structuring of threats and countermeasures for special Web Service instances and thereby could help to elicit, refine and structure the existing knowledge about the quality of Web Services. As we found various possibilities to avoid threats to interoperability, our analysis not only justifies the use of existing standards – it detected a concrete need for research on Web Service portability and maintainability. Therefore it might help standardisation organisations and developers of infrastructures in finding interoperability gaps.

Acknowledgements

This work is a result of the research project SIKOSA which is funded by the Ministry for Science, Research and Art of Baden-Württemberg, Germany (Ministerium für Wissenschaft, Forschung und Kunst Baden-Württemberg).

6. References

Ardissono L., Goy A., Petrone G., *Enabling conversations with web services*, 2. International Conference on Autonomous Agents & Multiagent Systems 2003, 819-826.

Berre, A.-J. *et al.*, *State-of-the art for Interoperability architecture approaches, Deliverable D9.1*, Technical report, November 19, 2004, Network of Excellence - Contract no.: IST-508 011, www.interop-noe.org.

BPEL *Business Process Execution Language for Web Services version 1.1* (WS-BPEL), 5 May 2003, http://www-128.ibm.com/developerworks/library/specification/ws-bpel/, last visited 11/2005, Technical report, IBM, BEA Systems, Microsoft, SAP AG, Siebel Systems.

Chung L., Nixon B.A., Yu E. and Mylopoulus J. (2000), *Non-Functional Requirements in Software Engineering*, Kluwer Academic Publishers.

CSRC = Computer Security Resource Center, "Common Criteria, Version 2.1", http://csrc.nist.gov/cc/.

Firesmith D.G., "Analyzing and Specifying Reusable Security Requirements", *Requirements for High Assurance Systems (RHAS) Workshop*, Monterey, California, September 2003.

Firesmith D.G., "Specifying Reusable Security Requirements", *Journal of Object Technology*, vol. 3 no. 1, 2004, p. 61-75.

Herrmann A., Paech B., „Quality Misuse", *REFSQ - Workshop on Requirements Engineering for Software Quality*, 2005.

ISO 9126: International Standard ISO/IEC 9126. Information technology – Software product evaluation – Quality characteristics and guidelines for their use.

Kazman R., Klein M., Barbacci M., Longstaff T., Lipson H., Carriere S.J., The Architecture Tradeoff Analysis Method, Technical Report CMU/SEI-98-TR-008, 1998, Software Engineering Institute, Carnegie Mellon University.

Kazman R., Klein M., Clements P., ATAM: Method for Architecture Evaluation, Technical Report CMU/SEI-2000-TR-004, 2000, Software Engineering Institute, Carnegie Mellon University.

McDermott J., Fox C., "Using Abuse Case Models for Security Requirements Analysis", *15th Annual Computer Security Applications Conference*, 1999, p. 55-6.

Moore A.P., Ellison R.J., Linger R.C., Attack Modeling for Information Security and Survivability. Technical Note CMU/SEI-2001-TN-001, 2001, Software Engineering Institute, Carnegie Mellon University.

Ponnekanti S., Fox, A., "Interoperability Among Independently Evolving Web Services", *5. Middleare 2004*, 311-330.

Sindre G., Opdahl A.L., "Eliciting Security Requirements by Misuse Cases", *TOOLS Pacific 2000*, 2000, p. 120-131.

Sindre G., Opdahl A.L., "Templates for Misuse Case Description", *REFSQ - International Workshop on Requirements Engineering for Software Quality*, 2001, p. 125-136.

SOAP 1.2, http://www.w3.org/TR/SOAP, last visited 11/2005, Technical report, W3C.

Sutcliffe A., Minocha S., "Scenario-based Analysis of Non-Functional Requirements", *REFSQ – International Workshop on Requirements Engineering for Software Quality*, 1998, p. 219-234.

Sysiphus http://wwwbruegge.in.tum.de/Sysiphus, 21.02.2006.

UDDI: Universal Description, Discovery and Integration Specification (UDDI), http://www.uddi.org/specification.html, last visited 12/2005, Technical report, Organization for the Advancement of Structured Information Standards (OASIS).

van Lamsweerde A., Willemet L., "Inferring Declarative Requirements Specifications from Operational Scenarios", *IEEE Transactions on Software Engineering*, Special Issue on Scenario Management (December), 1998, p. 1089-1114.

WSDL: Web Services Description Language (WSDL) 1.1, http://www.w3.org/TR/wsdl, last visited 12/2005, Technical report, W3C.

WSG: Web Services Glossary, W3C Working Group Note, 11 February 2004, http://www.w3.org/TR/2004/NOTE-ws-gloss-20040211/, last visited 12/2005, Technical report, W3C.

Zimmermann O., Tomlinson M., Peuser S., *Perspectives on web services*, Springer, 2003.

Session 2:
Infrastructure Provision

Quality of Service Evaluation in Virtual Organizations Using SLAs

Gustav Boström — Pablo Giambiagi — Tomas Olsson

Swedish Institute of Computer Science
Box 1263, SE-16429 Kista
Sweden
gusbo@sics.se
pablo@sics.se
tol@sics.se

ABSTRACT: Cooperating in Virtual organizations requires trust between the constituting organizations. SLA contracts are put in place in order to specify the quality of service of services offered. For these contracts to be effective they also need to be monitored effectively. In a Service Oriented Architecture this often means monitoring Web Service invocations and evaluating if the service fulfils the obligations in its SLA. In this paper we present an implementation of a rule engine based SLA Evaluator specifically designed for the needs of a virtual organization. The evaluator fits in the context of a virtual organization through the use of open XML-based standards and a loosely coupled, event-driven architecture.

KEY WORDS: Service Level Agreement, Virtual Organization, WSLA, Rule Engine.

1. Introduction

The services in a Service-Oriented Architecture (SOA) usually belong to different organizational domains and therefore there is no single line of authority regulating their interactions. This is especially true for *Virtual Organizations*. In principle a consumer must trust the provider to deliver the expected service, or establish a contract with it. For our purpose, a contract is a generic term for the specification of a service which is negotiable and either statically enforceable or monitorable. In other words, a contract describes an agreement between distinct services that determines rights and obligations on its signatories, and for which there exists a programmatic way of identifying contract violations. As a service specification, a contract may describe many different aspects of a service, including functional properties (i.e. behaviour) and also non-functional properties like security (e.g. access control), quality of service (QoS), information flow and reputation. In order to programmatically monitor compliance with contracts it is necessary to describe it in a machine-readable form.

In this paper we present an implementation of an *Evaluator Service* used for monitoring compliance of service level agreements (SLAs) in virtual organizations. The evaluator is specifically designed for heterogeneous virtual organizations (VOs) with high interoperability requirements and high demands for dynamic configurability. The interoperability requirements come from the fact that services in VOs might have been developed with different technologies and without a central organization to mandate a common IT-infrastructure. At the same time, in order to become efficient a high degree of integration is necessary. The different partners in a VO have to be able to dynamically connect their systems without the need of custom integration solutions. These issues are addressed by the EU-funded TrustCoM project that has adopted a web services based Service Oriented Architecture. This is however just the first step. It is necessary to refine this into a specification of the message formats that will be used for communicating. It is of vital interest that as far as possible these formats are based on standards. It is also necessary to specify how these standards are actually used, that is to define standards' profiles. Furthermore it is not feasible to integrate systems in a tightly coupled, synchronous, manner. The different partners of the VO need to be independent, as far as possible, of the other partners' systems. To fulfil these requirements we propose a web services based solution using the WSLA specification and an event-driven architecture. We also separate the SLA compliance evaluation component from the service instrumentation component providing the metrics since this instrumentation will differ according to which platform the service is built on. Internally we use the Drools rule-engine (Drools, 2005) as a means of achieving high configurability to different SLAs. This means that different Quality of Service metrics can be evaluated without the need for re-programming. The paper starts with an overview of contract languages for service level agreements. This is followed by an architecture description of the evaluator. To conclude we discuss related work.

2. Languages for service level agreements

There exist a number of contract models for web services. The business process standard ebXML describes a Collaboration Protocol Agreement (CPPA, 2002) as a contract between business partners that specifies the behaviour of each service (by simply stating its role) and how information exchanges are to be encoded. IBM's Web Service Level Agreement (WSLA) is an XML specification of performance constraints associated with the provision of a web service (WSLA, 2003). It defines the sources of monitoring data, a set of metrics (i.e. functions) to be evaluated on the data, and obligations on the signatories to maintain the metric values within certain ranges. The set of predefined metrics and the structure of WSLA contracts were initially designed for services involving job submissions in a grid-computing environment. However, the language is rich enough to match the needs of SLAs within the TrustCoM framework, naturally accommodating the distribution of tasks and responsibilities in the SLA Management subsystem (see section 3).

WS-Agreement is a more recent Global Grid Forum recommendation that has not reached the standard status yet (WS-Ag, 2004). It is based on WSLA but has been adapted to more recent web-services standards, e.g. WS-Addressing and WS-Resource Framework. Furthermore, WS-Agreement recognizes that the metric language is domain-specific and consequently leaves it unspecified. It is however because of this underspecification that we chose to base this work on WSLA.

2.1. *WSLA particulars*

The WSLA language (WSLA, 2003, Keller *et al.*, 2003, Dan *et al.*, 2004) provides means of specifying (binary) SLAs between services in a standardized way. It furthermore considers third parties to take over the responsibility to measure, evaluate and manage various parameters in the specification.

Besides identifying the parties, a WSLA document lists the service definitions that the signatory parties agreed upon, i.e. the operations offered by the service provider, as well as which and how service parameters and metrics are to be monitored. WSLA also supports the definition of complex aggregation functions in order to derive parameters from a set of metrics. Notably, parameters of both the Provider and the Consumer can be specified. These parameters are called *SLA parameters* in the standard and it is the duty of simple or aggregating monitors to compute them.

Finally, a WSLA document collects the obligations of the parties with respect to the SLA parameters specified in the service definitions. On the one hand, these cover maintaining a specific state, such as the size of storage reserved for the Consumer or the (maximum) response time to a request. On the other hand, actions may be specified that are to be performed under certain circumstances by any of the involved parties, e.g. in reaction to external events and to the violation of other obligations. The former are called *Service Level Objectives* (SLO) and the latter *Action Guarantees*. Every obligation is related to a specific party, its *obligee*.

3. Architecture

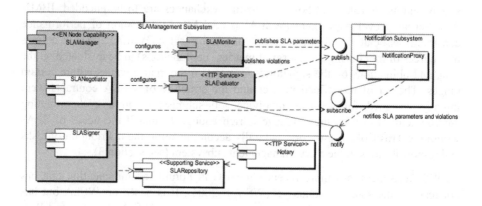

Figure 1. *The SLA Management subsystem.*
Core components are marked with grey

The SLA Evaluator service is part of the SLA Management subsystem (Figure 1) that also includes an SLA Manager and a number of SLA Monitors. In order to be highly interoperable, the monitor and evaluator communicate using a notification subsystem (WSN, 2004).

The SLA Manager is responsible to set up the monitor and evaluator configuration. Thus the manager is the management interface to the subsystem. The Monitor measures the service performance and sends the data to the SLA Evaluator. A Monitor instance can be situated locally at the service provider or at a trusted third party. The SLA Evaluator in turn is normally situated at a trusted third party. The evaluator checks whether the performance data comply with the obligations in the SLA, and sends notifications of either violations or fulfilments. Notice that an evaluator can be connected to more than one monitor.

3.1. *Example scenario*

As an example we will use a scenario taken from (Henkel *et al.*, 2005): Let us imagine a financial service provider of services such as mortgages and loans for cars. One essential web service of such a company could be to assess customers' credit worthiness using variables such as the customer's credit history and income. To make this web service available to external usage, the provider and a user need to agree on a service level agreement (SLA).

One important metric, for which an external user would like to have an SLA, is the average response time. For instance, the average response time, from the time receiving a call till the time sending an answer, could be guaranteed to be less than 0.1 sec. The SLO for such an SLA using the WSLA language is shown below. The SLO is evaluated when the value is updated (that is, on *new values*).

```
...<Obligations>
    <ServiceLevelObjective name="g1">
        <Obliged>financial provider</Obliged>
        <Validity> ... </Validity>
        <Expression>
            <Predicate xsi:type="Less">
                <SLAParameter>AverageResponseTime</SLAParameter>
                <Value>0.1</Value>
            </Predicate>
        </Expression>
        <EvaluationEvent>NewValue</EvaluationEvent>
    </ServiceLevelObjective>...
</Obligations>...
```

3.2. SLA Manager

Assuming that the service provider and the service consumer agree on a service level according to the SLA above, then the SLA Manager performs the following actions:

1.   It sets up and configures the monitoring and evaluation of the service provider's compliance to the SLA:

- Instantiates and configures an SLA Evaluator accordingly
- Configures a trusted third party SLA Monitor as well
- Connects monitors and the SLA Evaluator using WS-Notification

2.   When the SLA expires or upon a request to the SLA Manager, it disconnects the Monitor and SLA Evaluator and releases the previously assigned resources.

3.3. SLA Evaluator

The SLA Evaluator was implemented as a web service using the WS-Resource Framework (WSRF, 2005) as implemented within the Globus Toolkit (GT4, 2005). Thus we have used the factory pattern in order to instantiate an evaluator service, called a resource in WSRF terms (Figure 2). The evaluator component of the SLA Evaluator resource can be seen in more detail in Figure 3.

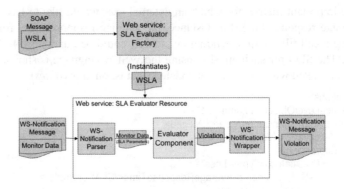

Figure 2. *The SLA Evaluator Web Services*

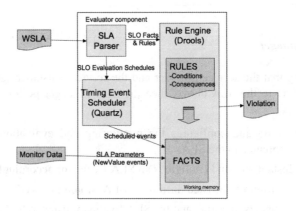

Figure 3. *The SLA Evaluator component*

The Evaluator component contains the core functionality of the SLA Evaluator resource. It has three major subcomponents: an SLA Parser, a Scheduler and a Rule Engine.

SLA Parser The SLA Parser extracts configuration information from the WSLA document given at instantiation time. The configuration information is translated into *evaluation schedules* sent to the scheduler, and into *facts & rules* sent to the rule engine. The evaluation schedules are used to program the scheduler to activate the rule engine using scheduled events. Facts & rules are used directly to program the rule engine both to check for violations and fulfilments as well as to handle NewValue events (used to update SLA parameters).

For the scenario in section 3.1, there is no evaluation schedule since the SLA has an EvaluationCondition element with value NewValue. Thus the SLA Parser sends to the rule engine facts and rules to handle NewValue events and to determine whether the SLA parameter *AverageResponseTime* is less than 0.1 sec.

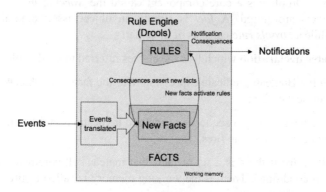

Figure 4. *SLA Evaluator: Event – Rule Activation – Consequence execution loop*

Rule Engine Figure 4 presents the rule engine in more detail. In our implementation we have used the open source engine Drools (Drools, 2005). Drools is a forward-chaining rule engine with a simple API for creating domain-specific rule languages. In our case the SLA Parser translates the WSLA document into Drools rules and facts using this API. Drools uses a variant of the Rete algorithm (Forgy, 1982) modified in order to handle typed objects.

The two types of events, scheduled events and NewValue events, are input values to the rule engine. The events modify the facts in the rule engine's working memory. These new facts activate and fire rules, which in turn update the facts in the working memory (with possible further rule activations and firings) or send notifications of violations and fulfilments. As seen in Figure 2, these notifications are then wrapped into WS-Notification messages and sent to a notification broker for further forwarding.

Scheduler We used the open source scheduler Quartz (Quartz, 2005) to implement the Scheduler component. In order to send an event to the rule engine, Quartz needs a job description specifying how it should update the facts of the working memory of the rule engine as well as how to fire all activated rules. As well, it needs a simple trigger that executes the job at the scheduled evaluation times.

3.3.1. Transformation of WSLA into executable rules for Drools

In a first attempt at translating WSLA documents into Drools XML-formatted rules, we tried to use XSL transformations (XSLT, 1999). This however proved to be awkward given the interdependencies of the elements in the WSLA-document. Instead we used Java code, which directly invokes the Drools' Java API. This turned to be much easier since all the WSLA-elements were readily accessible and references to them could be resolved more simply.

DROOLS – Drools has a core component called the *working memory* where its rules and facts are stored. A *fact* is simply an object asserted in the working memory, while a *Drools rule* consists of three parts:

Parameter declaration which lists the classes referred to by the rule;

Condition a Boolean predicate expression over the facts (i.e. objects) that match the parameter declaration;

Consequence typically a sequence of method invocations and fact modifications that is executed when the rule fires.

A rule is *active* if there is a set of facts that matches all parameter declarations and fulfils all conditions. Then, if the working memory is called to fire all rules, all consequences of the active rules are executed.

ECA MODEL – The execution of the Evaluator component follows the event-condition-action (ECA) rule model (see Figure 4). In the ECA model incoming events are matched against the event part of each rule. Then the conditions of matching rules are tested, and if true, the corresponding actions are triggered. Though not explicitly supported, the Drools engine can fairly easily be adopted for this sort of model. Both rule parameter declarations and conditions in a Drools rule can be used to model the conditions in an ECA rule. The action part in an ECA rule is equally simple to model using the *consequence* of a Drools rule. An event can be encoded as a fact added to the working memory with every event occurrence. An ECA rule matching this event can be represented in Drools using a rule whose parameter declaration matches the fact and whose condition checks that the event is *new*. This means that only rules referring to the event fact will be executed when the event fact is added to the working memory.

TRANSLATION CODE – Below is the pseudo code for how a WSLA is translated into Drools rules, where RuleTriggerEvent, RuleActivation and Obligation are Java classes. An instance of RuleTriggerEvent is used to indicate what rules can be activated by an event. An instance of RuleActivation is used to control that a rule is not fired more than once. An instance of Obligation holds the validity period of the SLO and keeps track of what SLA parameters have violated the SLO. The rules that follow are listed in execution order.

1: **for all** SLO in the WSLA **do**
2:        Transform the negation (for violation) of the Boolean Expression element into disjunctive normal form, DNF.[1]
3:        **for all** AND-nodes in the DNF **do**
4:                Create a rule with
5:                **Parameter Declarations**
6:                        - Named RuleTriggerEvent instance[2] (name = unique to the SLO)
7:                        - Named RuleActivation instance (name = unique to the rule)
8:                        - Named Obligation instance (name = unique to the SLO)
9:                        - All named SLA parameters in the AND-node[3]
10:              **Conditions**
11:                      - Has the RuleTriggerEvent been triggered?
12:                      - Has the rule not been fired yet? (the RuleActivation instance)
13:                      - Is the Obligation valid at this time?
14:                      - A Boolean test for each SLA parameter in the AND-node
15:              **Consequence**
16:                      - Add all parameters of the AND-node as violators of Obligation.
17:                      - The rule is set to have been fired (the RuleActivation instance)
18:        **end for**
19: **end for**

Below is the pseudo code that issues a notification when an SLO is violated.

1: **for all** SLO in the WSLA **do**
2:        Create a rule with
3:        **Parameter Declarations**
4:                - Named RuleTriggerEvent instance (name = unique to the rule)
5:                - Named Obligation instance (name = unique to the SLO)
6:        **Conditions**
7:                - Has the RuleTriggerEvent been triggered?
8:                - Is the Obligation violated by any SLA parameter?
9:        **Rule Consequence**
10:              - A message is sent announcing that the Obligation is violated.
11: **end for**

Finally, there is a rule similar to the violation rule responsible to send a *notification of fulfilment* when the RuleTriggerEvent is triggered and the SLO is not violated. The pseudo code for this rule is omitted for brevity.

In order for the evaluator to manage NewValue events, all events are removed when the rules have stopped firing. Since events occur asynchronously, the working memory is synchronized, letting only one event at a time activate and fire rules.

SCENARIO – Consider again the scenario of section 3.1. It has only one SLO referring to only one SLA parameter. We therefore get the two rules that follow for sending notification of violations.

---

1 DNF (Disjunctive Normal Form) is a set of ORed AND-statements, for instance, the DNF of "((A OR B) AND C) OR D" is "(A AND C) OR (B AND C) OR D" where A, B, C and D are Boolean expressions including Boolean predicates over SLA parameters.

2 A named class instance has a name field that is used to identify its instances when declared. No extra condition for testing the identity is then needed.

3 Name identifier unique for each SLA parameter.

```
1: {Rule 1: Test of violation}
2: Parameter Declarations
3:      - Named RuleTriggerEvent instance (name = "Rule Trigger Event of g1")
4:      - Named RuleActivation instance (name = "rule 1 of g1")
5:      - Named Obligation instance (name = "g1")
6:      - Named SLAParameter instance (name = "AverageResponseTime")
7: Conditions
8:      - Has the RuleTriggerEvent occurred?
9:      - Has the rule not been fired yet? (using the RuleActivation instance)
10:     - Is the Obligation valid now?
11:     - Is AverageResponseTime.getValue() < 0.1?
12: Rule Consequence
13:     - AverageResponseTime added as violator of Obligation instance.
14:     - The rule is set to have been fired (using the RuleActivation instance)
15:
16: {Rule 2: Notification of violation}
17: Parameter Declarations
18:     - Named RuleTriggerEvent instance (name = "Rule Trigger Event of g1")
19:     - Named Obligation instance (name = "g1")
20: Conditions
21:     - Has the RuleTriggerEvent occurred?
22:     - Does parameter AverageResponseTime violate the Obligation?
23: Rule Consequence
24:     - A message is sent indicating that the Obligation g1 has been violated.
```

In this case, it was not necessary to have two rules, but when there is more than one SLA parameter in the SLO, the second rule gathers all violating SLA parameters into one violation message.

3.4. *Message protocol between Monitors and Evaluators*

Neither WSLA nor WS-Agreement specifies how monitors and evaluators should communicate. To fill this gap, we defined an XML Schema type for the metric messages in the Evaluator WSDL file and used it to format the content of notifications sent from the monitor to the evaluator. The format is loosely based on WSLA's specification of SLA parameters and includes the identifier of the service provider so that, if needed, the Evaluator can pass on to VO Management the information on which partner has violated which agreement.

4. Related work

Several other examples of SLA evaluation systems exist. WSOL is a language for describing SLAs (Tosic *et al.*, 2002) for which there exists an implementation of an SLA Management system based on Apache Axis Web Services handlers (Ma *et al.*, 2005). This system seems not to separate between the monitoring instrumentation of a service (what we refer to as a monitor) and the evaluator part (which uses the data from the monitor and evaluates its compliance). IBM has implemented a prototype of a WSLA-monitoring system (Keller *et al.*, 2003). Their

Condition Evaluation service component is very similar to our evaluator. This component is however not described in such detail. We provide a more exhaustive description on how such a component can be developed using a rule engine. Our use of WS-Notification for transmitting SLA metric data between monitors and evaluators also makes our component more suitable for situations were the monitors and evaluators are situated in different organizations. Paschke et al. also present an evaluator based on rules (Paschke *et al.*, 2005). However this approach is more complex than ours since it mixes different forms of logic and uses Prolog. Their approach is also not based on a standard format for describing the SLA.

5. Conclusions

In this paper we presented the architecture of a component for evaluating a service compliance with an SLA. The use of the Drools rule engine has proved to be quite effective for making an SLA executable. The support for temporal rules however proved to be quite weak. The addition of the Quartz scheduler was therefore necessary. The performance of the SLA rules also seems to be satisfactory. By using WS-Notification and a specified format for SLA metric and violation messages we also achieve a high level of interoperability between monitor components and evaluators. In fact, in the TrustCoM project the monitor components are developed by other organizations using .Net instead of Java. This however comes at a price. Even though the SLA-rule evaluation is fast, WS-Notification implies a Web Service invocation for every metric-message sent. This incurs a significant overhead in XML processing and it is doubtful whether Web Services are a good solution for production use today. Faster mechanisms for communicating will probably be needed. The modular nature of our evaluator should make using another protocol easy. The use of threading for sending violation notifications should also mitigate the problem somewhat for outgoing messages.

Acknowledgements

The developments presented in this paper were partly funded by the European Commission through the IST programme under Framework 6 grant 001945 to the TrustCoM Integrated Project. The authors wish to thank Lutz Schubert from HLRS for useful discussions and the implementation of the notification subsystem.

6. References

CPPA, *Collaboration-Protocol Profile and Agreement Specification*, Version 2.0, www.ebxml.org, 2002.

Dan, A., Davis, D., Kearney, R., Keller, A., King, R., Kübler, D., Ludwig, H., Polan, M., Spreitzer, M., and Youssef, A., Web services on demand: WSLA-driven automated management, *IBM Systems Journal*, 43(1), 2004.

Drools, *The Drools Rule engine*, v. 2.1, http://www.drools.org/, 2005.

Forgy, C., Rete: A Fast Algorithm for the Many Pattern/Many Object Pattern Match Problem. *Artificial Intelligence*, 19:17–37, 1982.

GT4, *The Globus Toolkit v4*, http://www.globus.org/toolkit/, 2005.

Henkel, M., Boström, G., and Wäyrynen, J., Moving from internal to external services using aspects, In *Interoperability of Enterprise Software and Applications*, Springer-Verlag, 2005.

Keller, A. and Ludwig, H., The WSLA framework: Specifying and monitoring service level agreements for web services, *Journal of Network and Systems Management*, 11(1):57–81, 2003.

Ma, W., Tosic, V., Esfandiari, B., and Pagurek, B., Extending apache axis for monitoring of web service offerings, In *Proceedings of the IEEE EEE05 international workshop on Business services networks BSN '05*. IEEE Press WSLA, 2005.

Paschke, A. and Bichler, M., Sla representation, management and enforcement, In *EEE*, 2005, pages 158–163.

Quartz, *Quartz enterprise job scheduler*, http://www.opensymphony.com/quartz/, 2005.

Tosic, V., Patel, K., and Pagurek, B., Wsol – web service offerings language, In *WES, 2002*, pages 57–67.

WS-Ag, *Web Services Agreement Specification* (WS-Agreement), https://forge.gridforum.org/projects/graap-wg/document/WS-AgreementSpecification/, 2004.

WSLA, *Web Service Level Agreements*, www.research.ibm.com/wsla/, 2003.

WSN, *WS-Notification 1.0*, http://www.ibm.com/developerworks/library/ws-resource/ws-notification.pdf, 2004.

WSRF, *WS-Resource Framework 1.2*. http://docs.oasis-open.org/wsrf/wsrf-ws_resource-1.2-spec-pr-02.pdf, 2005.

XSLT, *Xsl transformations 1.0*, http://www.w3.org/TR/xslt, 1999.

Improving Interoperation Security through Instrumentation and Analysis

A framework and case study

David Llewellyn-Jones — Madjid Merabti — Qi Shi — Bob Askwith — Denis Reilly

School of Computing and Mathematical Sciences
Liverpool John Moores University
James Parsons Building
Byrom Street
Liverpool, L3 3AF
UK

{D.Llewellyn-Jones, M.Merabti, Q.Shi, B.Askwith, D.Reilly}@ljmu.ac.uk

ABSTRACT: Interoperation between heterogeneous services results in a variety of serious security concerns, from privacy through to authentication and policy enforcement. We look at composition analysis techniques, enabled using instrumentation, as a means of improving security in interoperating systems. The techniques described harness the system of systems nature inherent in all interoperating system configurations. We present the ongoing development of a framework for combining instrumentation and composition analysis capabilities in a novel manner and discuss a case study involving the prevention of data leakage through access control analysis.

KEY WORDS: Interoperation, Security, Component composition, Instrumentation, Access Control, middleware.

1. Introduction

The implications for security of interoperation between systems are both broad and potentially serious. The interfacing of heterogeneous systems can cause particular difficulties, especially where individual services are used that were not designed with security in mind.

A number of theories and architectures exist concerned with the security of data and services between systems. For example, CORBASec offers a framework intended for use with CORBA (Lang, *et al.* 2002). This provides a very practical solution to some of the security difficulties involved in interoperation between systems. A number of theoretical composition results may also apply where interoperability plays a role, such as Non-interference (Focardi, *et al.* 1997) and Composable Assurance (Shi, *et al.* 1998), however to our knowledge no system exists that draws on both practical instrumentation techniques and theoretical composition results to provide an applicable analysis framework. The novelty of our approach therefore derives from this use of instrumentation techniques to allow the practical application of security composition analysis, and has particular application where interoperability is concerned. A framework for such analysis is presented using instrumentation to provide the input parameters needed for analysis. An example scenario will be considered, and we will derive the functionality needed of a service for the instrumentation to perform effectively, thus allowing such security techniques to be used.

In general, there are a range of security issues that affect or are affected by interoperation – such as policy reconciliation and access control – and a number of solutions have been proposed to tackle them (for example, Dawson et al. (Dawson, *et al.* 2000) and Kokolakis and Kiountouzis (Kokolakis, *et al.* 2000)). There are numerous others for which specific solutions often exist, including buffer overruns, authorisation issues and insecure protocols. Rather than concentrate on a framework or methodology to tackle particular issues, we present a novel approach that relies on dynamic analysis of an interoperating federation, and which is extensible so that future security concerns may be addressed if they are amenable to the method of analysis employed. To demonstrate the use of the framework we have concentrated primarily on access control difficulties in this paper. The leakage of data through unenforced access mechanisms is a serious concern, since it opens the potential for private data to be read or amended by unauthorised people or services. In a distributed environment this difficulty is exacerbated by the fact that having control in one part of the system does not provide any guarantee as to the effectiveness of the access control mechanisms in another part of the system. The result is a real potential for data being passed to unauthorised services.

The structure of this paper is as follows. In the next section we discuss an overview of the framework for analysis of security properties in system of systems. This is broken down into its two major parts: section 3 considers instrumentation and section 4 considers composition analysis. Both are essential elements in the overall framework. Whilst the framework we present is extensible, it is instructive to consider a specific example of its use in greater detail. We do this in section 5, where the case of access control and data leakage is investigated. Finally we conclude and discuss future work in section 6.

2. A Framework for system of system analysis

The crucial feature that we harness for the application of our security framework is the componentised nature of interoperable systems. Such systems will by definition be comprised of more than one smaller systems or services working together to form a larger application, or federation, potentially with additional interface components used to allow successful interoperation.

For example, services accessed via a website may be based on multiple lower-level services distributed across a variety of systems and organisations. Figure 1 shows an example scenario where a web service provider offers a service based on data provided by a number of organisations (e.g. it could be map data and traffic data from two separate organisations).

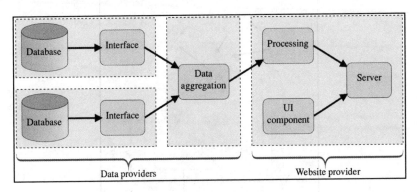

Figure 1. *Example web service interoperation*

Composition analysis provides a method for establishing security properties based on information concerning the properties of the individual components and the topological configuration of the network or interfaces between those components.

A variety of properties relevant to security can be established in this way. For example, our previous work has looked at buffer overrun vulnerabilities where composition analysis can be used to establish whether such vulnerabilities are likely to be triggered, or can be circumvented using carefully chosen intermediary components (Llewellyn-Jones *et al.*, 2005a).

We present the ongoing development of our framework based on instrumentation and composition analysis below. An implementation of the framework using Jini (Jini 2001) and the MATTS composition analysis engine (Llewellyn-Jones *et al.*, 2005b) will be discussed, followed by an example application enforcing access control policies to prevent data leakage across interoperating systems.

The framework incorporates two phases, as shown in Figure 2. The first establishes dynamic dependencies between application services from a federation using instrumentation services at run time. The second undertakes a composition analysis based on these dependencies. For this second stage, during the analysis process, additional information regarding individual components is generally required for an accurate result to be obtained. For example, in the access control case study, information concerning the access rights of individual components may be needed, along with information concerning the internal dependencies that exist between interface hooks (e.g. input and output channels). Such information depends on the property being tested and the dependencies established during the first phase.

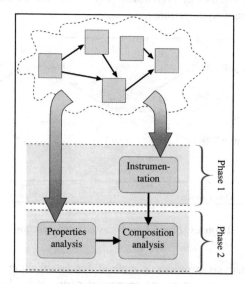

Figure 2. *Analysis process*

We have deliberately chosen to separate instrumentation from the composition engine so as to improve flexibility and allow either to be re-implemented or swapped if an alternative method is desired.

Composition analysis and property analysis are both undertaken in parallel during the second phase. The reason for this is that the properties required are liable to change throughout the analysis process, based on information already obtained. For example, properties of interface hooks that are not bound to may not be needed for the analysis to be performed, but the fact that the property will not be needed cannot be established before we know the dependencies. In the case of access control, we can avoid the need to check access rights for components that are found not to access any external data.

We will now consider the two phases in more detail, along with details about the current implementation.

3. Instrumentation phase

Instrumentation works in conjunction with middleware technologies (e.g. CORBA, Jini, etc.) to unobtrusively provide dynamic information about the behaviour and performance of distributed application services. Although in its generic form instrumentation is intended to refer to the class of instruments that may be capable of detecting various properties, for our current purposes we are interested only in using them to establish *dependencies* between services. For a more complete exposition, see Reilly (Reilly, *et al.* 2003).

Our current implementation is based on Jini Middleware Technology, a Java middleware developed by Sun Microsystems (Arnold, *et al.* 1999). In theory any middleware solution satisfying the minimal requirements set out below could have been used.

For the purposes of instrumenting a service, we utilise a design pattern. This allows us to create services that can be interposed between communicating services with interfaces implemented at run-time to relay calls between the communicating services. In addition to relaying calls, the instrumentation is also able to record and forward properties and details about the services and their communications. Interface creation relies on reflection for its dynamic capability. However, in the case that reflection is not available for a particular middleware solution (e.g. in the case of CORBA services) or for time critical applications where the delay caused by reflection is unacceptable, a static interface may also be used, although such interfaces would need explicit generation for each distinct service being monitored.

The approach used to represent dependencies is based on extensions to the work conducted by Hasselmeyer (Hasselmeyer 2001) and makes use of Jini's Administrable interface (Jini 2001). The approach does impose one condition in order to access service bindings, namely that the services are required to implement the Administrable interface. Any service that implements the Administrable interface must define the getAdmin method, which itself returns an object that implements the Dependable interface. Through this the bindings associated with an application-level service can be discovered by accessing the getBindings method, as follows:

```
public interface Dependable {
        public Class getDeclaringClass ();
        public Object[] getBindings ();
}
```

Through querying this method, the instrumentation is able to establish service dependencies. Details of all dependencies within a federation are accumulated by the instrumentation, for the dynamic generation of a digraph that can then be passed on to the composition analysis engine in the second phase. Figure 3 shows a graphical representation of the dependencies between a selection of Jini services, as established through this method of instrumentation.

Of course it will be apparent that services not implementing the Administrable interface cannot be queried in this way. In the future we aim to explore alternative instrumentation methods that do not impose this requirement.

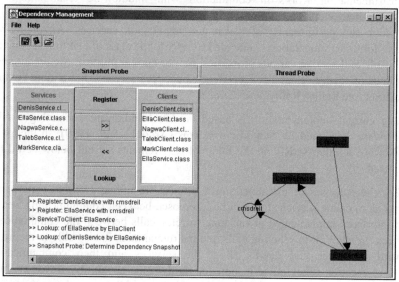

Figure 3. *Graphical representation of dependencies between services*

4. Composition analysis phase

The second phase makes use of the MATTS composition analysis engine. The engine is still being developed, but in essence, it provides a means of analysing systems of systems based on their dependencies. The analysis is directed by a script file in a simple XML format. The script file describes a process that should be followed for each property that is to be tested for. MATTS is able to interpret this script and follow the processes, ultimately resulting in a verification or refutation of the property as it applies to the configuration of the services.

Assuming a suitable script file is being adhered to, the most important information needed by MATTS to undertake its analysis is an overview of the dependencies or links between the components of a system. As has already been explained in the previous section, this information is provided by instrumentation that dynamically reads it during the life span of a federation. As dependencies change, so the federation is re-evaluated based on its new configuration.

During the analysis, it often transpires that additional information is needed to complete the analysis and provide an accurate result. This is because composition results invariably depend on both the composition structure and the specific properties of individual services. These latter properties may be queried at any time during the analysis.

The result of the composition analysis stage yields whether the security property being tested for is satisfied or not. As previously mentioned, this may be whether a particular configuration is liable to trigger a buffer overrun vulnerability, or as we will see later, if it is liable to cause an access violation. Further properties may be tested for through the application of additional scripts.

Such results are important for interoperability security, since they can tell us whether a particular configuration of services will be safe to deploy and use.

At present, the system can be used as a 'warning' indicator, to tell whether a potential security vulnerability is present in a system. In future development we hope to produce a 'pro-active' version that not only establishes possible problems, but also provides dynamic solutions, e.g. through the generation of intermediary services that marshal data safely between otherwise potentially vulnerable services.

The process can be understood most clearly by considering an example.

5. Case study: access control

Access control provides an important security mechanism for preventing unauthorised access to data and retaining data privacy. It can, however, present problems for interoperating systems, since access control mechanisms may not be available for all services and even when available, may not provide uniform access control methods to support interoperation. An access control mechanism that can be layered on top of existing services may therefore provide an effective way to impose access control without the need to significantly modify underlying systems.

Moreover, access control mechanisms often fail to account for potential data leakage that can occur as information is passed between distributed, interoperating systems. If an authorised service passes private data to a second receiving service on a different platform, how can the sending service be certain that the receiving service will not pass the data onwards to a further unauthorised actor, even if the receiving service is itself authorised to have access to the data? Using the framework described in the preceding sections we can easily enforce access control whilst simultaneously preventing data leakage of the nature just described.

Each file in a file system is stored with access control data associated with it determining the situations in which the file may or may not be accessed. For example, Unix-like systems store UIDs, file permissions and related meta-data in a file's inode. Similar data is held by the operating system about the access rights of processes.

The aim of the case study is to ensure read access to data from a file is granted only to those services with sufficient access rights, and similarly for write access.

The benefit provided by the dependency information is that data flow across services can be determined, and a model constructed of the data flow throughout the federation of services. This model can be established at run time and re-analysis can take place whenever dependencies change.

A simple MATTS script, a fragment of which is shown below, describes the requirement that data may only flow into or out of a component if that service has sufficient access rights to read from or write to the originating or destination file respectively.

```
1.  <sandbox id="s2" config="c1">Read access control check</sandbox>
2.  <property id="idAuth">Level component is authorised to</property>
3.  <configuration id="c1" init="1">
4.    <component id="c2">
5.     <input format=""/>
6.     <input id="in1" init="0" format="*"/>
7.     <process config="check" action="check=@n"/>
8.     <process id="auth1" init="1" action="@a[@n][0][idAuth]"/>
9.     <process cond="result &lt; auth1" action="c1=0"/>
10.    <output format="*" cond="c1==1"/>
11.    <component>
12.     <process config="check" action="check=@n"/>
13.     <process id="auth2" init="1" action="@a[@n][0][idAuth]"/>
14.     <process cond="result &lt; auth2" action="c1=0"/>
15.     <input id="in2" init="0" format="*"/>
16.     <output format="*" config="c2" follow="fresh" cond="c1==1"/>
17.     <output format="" cond="c1==1"/>
18.    </component>
19.   </component>
20. </configuration>
```

The MATTS parser works by maintaining both a current position in the script and a current position in the component structure. Each element in the script determines how both of these positions should be updated at each step.

The script above tells the parser to follow the dependencies between components (lines 6, 10, 15 and 16). At each component a process is undertaken (indicated by the **action** attributes in lines 8 and 13, but not actually shown in full) to test the lowest read access required by the data flowing through the system and into that component. A test is then performed to establish if the component has sufficient access rights to read this data (lines 9 and 14). The script continues only if access is granted (lines 10 and 16). The script results in a true result only if it successfully completes, hence will return false if access would not be granted at any of the components in the system.

The script can be augmented by considering slicing properties of components that allow internal dependencies between inputs and outputs to be established in addition to the dependencies between interoperating services. Slicing is an established method of code analysis that determines all subsets of a piece of code that are, for example, affected by a given variable (Weiser 1981). The process can therefore be used to establish if the data received on a particular input has an effect on the data sent on any given output. By introducing this into the script above we can refine the analysis with the consequence that access restrictions that would otherwise be imposed on interoperating systems may on a number of occasions be safely relaxed without affecting the overall security of the system. At present, however, it has only been possible to apply such techniques to a simple virtual machine and bytecode implementation. There is no theoretical reason why the same techniques could not be applied to Java bytecode and this is something we hope to look at in future work.

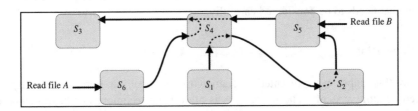

Figure 4. *Service interactions*

As a particular case, consider a number of services $S_1, \ldots, S_6$ that interoperate via distributed middleware as shown in Figure 4. The dependencies (shown as solid arrows) between services can be established through instrumentation. We assume that different access rights are required in order to access the data contained in files A and B. The result of the analysis will tell us that service S_6 must have sufficient rights to access file A; service S_5 must have sufficient rights for access to file B; services S_3 and S_4 must have right to access *both* files A and B; whilst the read access rights of services S_1 and S_2 do not matter, since no data is read into the service. Note the internal dependencies are marked with dotted arrows in the figure.

The framework described here is able to automatically establish these results and, based on the access rights information supplied about each component and file, establish whether any access violations or data leakage is likely to occur after deployment.

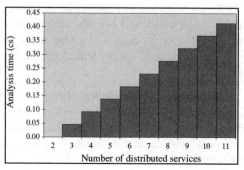

Figure 5. *Distributed service analysis timings*

We applied this technique to a linear configuration of minimal services designed to send small sequences of data to each other across a network. Timing results for this are in Figure 5. In this case, with simple dependencies between services, we can see that analysis time is linear in the number of components. These timings represent times for pure analysis. They do not take into account delays during instrumentation readings or caused by network overheads. Although the times shown are relatively small, the question of delays introduced in larger systems is an issue that needs to be considered carefully.

6. Conclusion

In this paper we presented a framework intended to improve security for interoperating systems. The framework is built using techniques of instrumentation – to establish dependencies between services – and composition analysis – to assess the security implications of using services in conjunction with each other – in a two phase process.

We explained how the framework can be applied as a layer on top of existing services. Our current implementation – based around Jini middleware technology – requires services to implement the Administrable interface in order for the instrumentation to work effectively. This presents an obstacle to applying the technique to legacy systems; however we hope to overcome this limitation in future work by looking at alternative methods to instrument dependencies.

At present the framework is in an early phase of implementation and whilst both instrumentation and analysis parts have been implemented separately using Jini and MATTS respectively, there is still work to be completed in integrating the two effectively. As one aspect of this, the direct analysis engine used to establish service properties through direct inspection of bytecode currently applies only to a simple virtual machine bytecode and we hope that this might ultimately be extended to work with Java bytecode and other low level code.

Looking beyond this, a significant improvement would be to design a more pro-active architecture, not only capable of detecting security breaches, but also of mitigating the problem by interposing additional services into the framework.

As with any security mechanism, we make no claims about providing a panacea for security issues. Nevertheless we do believe the combination of instrumentation and composition analysis is likely to prove a useful tool, especially in the field of interoperation, since it has the potential to provide a sophisticated means of establishing security properties in an automated manner, even in heterogeneous environments where the framework can be overlayed onto existing and legacy systems. The earlier study of an access control mechanism highlighted a case in point, and the extensible nature of the system using scripting allows for future advances to be incorporated into the system easily. Whilst scripts apply to any component configuration, a particular script is however specific to a particular problem scenario (such as access control in the case here).

Besides the general improvement of the framework to make it more integrated and universally applicable, the largest challenge for a system such as this is the establishment of new security scripts. We believe that the practical establishment of such composition analysis techniques provides the prospect of exciting potential in the area of security in solutions for composition and interoperability.

7. References

Arnold K., Osullivan B., Scheifler R. W., Waldo J., Wollrath A., O'Sullivan B., Scheifler R., *The Jini Specification,* Second Edition: Addison-Wesley, 1999.

Dawson S., Qian S., Samarati P., Providing security and interoperation of heterogeneous systems, *Distributed and Parallel Databases*, vol. 8, pp. 119-145, 2000.

Focardi R., Gorrieri R., Non Interference: Past, Present and Future, *DARPA Workshop on Foundations for Secure Mobile Code*, Monterey, California, USA, 1997.

Hasselmeyer P., Managing Dynamic Service Dependencies, *12th International Workshop on Distributed Systems: Operations & Management*, Nancy, France, 2001.

Jini, Architecture Specification 1.2, Sun Microsystems, 2001.

Kokolakis S. A., Kiountouzis E. A., Achieving interoperability in a multiple-security policies environment, *Computers & Security*, vol. 19, pp. 267-81, 2000.

Lang U., Schreiner R., *Developing secure distributed systems with CORBA.* Norwood, MA, USA: Artech House, 2002.

Llewellyn-Jones D., Merabti M., Shi Q., Askwith B., Buffer Overrun Prevention Through Component Composition Analysis, *COMPSAC 2005*, 2005a.

Llewellyn-Jones D., Merabti M., Shi Q., Askwith B., MATTS Technical Manual, Liverpool John Moores University, Liverpool, 2005b.

Reilly D., Taleb-Bendiab A., Dynamic instrumentation for Jini applications, *Software Engineering and Middleware. Third International Workshop, SEM. Revised Papers*, Orlando, FL, USA, 2003.

Shi Q., Zhang N., An effective model for composition of secure systems, *Journal-of-Systems-and-Software*, vol. 43, pp. 233-44, 1998.

Weiser M., Program Slicing, *5th International Conference on Software Engineering*, 1981.

Guarding Enterprise Collaborations with Trust Decisions – the TuBE approach

Sini Ruohomaa – Lea Viljanen – Lea Kutvonen

Department of Computer Science
P.O. box 68
00014 University of Helsinki
Finland
{Sini.Ruohomaa, Lea.Viljanen, Lea.Kutvonen}@cs.helsinki.fi

ABSTRACT: *Enterprise computing is currently moving towards more open, collaborative systems. It becomes essential for enterprise success that joining a business network is made efficient, despite the technical and semantic interoperability challenges involved in connecting different information and communication systems. Trust management is an important factor in the collaboration, as traditional trust-building over months of negotiations has become too slow a method in routine cases. As no business network is feasible without mutual trust between partners, the supporting technology should provide mechanisms for forming trust relationships, making automatic trust-based decisions on routine business transactions, and observing the business peers for malicious or incorrect behaviour on interactions. This paper describes a trust model to fulfil these needs, and gives a strategically overview of the system implementing this model.*

KEY WORDS: *trust management, B2B collaboration.*

1. Introduction

Enterprise computing is moving from internal application integration towards more open, collaborative systems, enabling enterprise solutions to work together across organisational borders. This trend is supported by technical development around the SOA and Web-Services technology: They enable autonomously supported, application-level business services to be combined into collaborative business networks.

We view inter-enterprise collaborations as business networks that are governed by eContracts. For these contracts, the collaboration structure and semantics are modelled in terms of roles of the participating business services and interactions between them, and policy constraints to govern the roles and interactions. For an open collaboration, the partner to fill a particular role can be chosen freely from the open market, as long as it is able to fulfil the requirements for the role. These requirements describe the role's business responsibilities as well as more technical interoperability aspects, such as communication and data representation constraints. Functional interoperability requirements are accompanied by non-functional aspects, such as timeliness, availability, security and trustworthiness.

To support this kind of B2B middleware services, the CINCO group has developed partner selection and negotiation, interoperability tests for technical and business aspects of services, collaboration lifecycle management with partner changes, and breach management (Kutvonen *et al.*, 2005).

The fundamental metainformation element and active agent in the architecture is the eContract, which is created for each business network and which governs the collaboration with a combination of aspects rising from business strategies, legal and other regulatory systems, and technical interoperability needs such as sharing a business process model, and information representation and messaging techniques. The eContract defines not only the successful collaboration cases, but also defines what can be considered a breach, and what partners may or should run as a joint recovery process after a breach case.

To complement this work, trust management concepts, models and middleware facilities are needed. Breaches affecting trust or caused by lost trust become part of the overall behaviour governed by the eContract. The TuBE project aims to address these issues by providing the following:

– Definitions for trust-related concepts, such as trust decision and the context for it, and trustee reputation;

– A general architecture to create and distribute trust-related information;

– Middleware facilities for trust management; and

– Facilities for monitoring and reacting to misbehaviour and anomalies.

We focus on understanding and supporting trust between the partners, i.e. business services. A basic communication and security infrastructure is assumed to be in place, including e.g. identity management, as enterprises will need to identify each other in order to enter into legally binding contracts. Cryptography services deal with message integrity and eavesdropping, and the SOAP messages sent and received are assumed to follow format agreements and arrive in order.

The trust management system has two major tasks: first, it should act as a guard for the service application, applying trust decisions to protect the enterprise from taking too high risks. Second, it should upkeep reputation information on other peers, to allow the system to adjust to how the peers have been behaving in the past.

Trust decisions are needed in two very different situations. When a business network is already running, routine decisions determine whether a particular action should be allowed in the context of the network. Trust decisions are also made when deciding on joining a network or choosing the best partners for it, and whether to remove a peer or leave the network altogether, if it cannot function any longer due to insufficient trust. Both are addressed by the TuBE trust management system.

Trust decisions are built on a combination of situational risk analysis and a strategic viewpoint. Estimating the partner's future actions is key, but some limitations must be considered. For example, if the business network contract defines compensation clauses if some things are not done, the risk analysis should adjust to the strategic situation. Trust decisions should also be able to manage frequent temporary changes in the valuations of the enterprise. The guarded service application acts within the context of a business network, its host enterprise and a technical infrastructure, which should be considered in decision-making. The phase a business network is in can make some actions more important than usual, the enterprise may decide to weigh some risks more as a response to a particular market situation or the underlying system may be low on resources, and we need a means to communicate changes in the situation to the trust management system.

In order to meet these needs, a trust model represents the information to be made available for trust decisions. The representation of risk and the strategic viewpoint to compliment the tactical evaluation will guide the design of a decision-making algorithm. Facilities for describing, accumulating and evaluating experience information will provide a basis for dynamic risk analysis.

This paper provides an overview of the TuBE trust management system and the trust model behind it. Section 2 describes the trust model to fulfil the needs presented in this section, and section 3 gives an overview of the TuBE trust management system to implement the model. Section 5 discusses implementation issues, and section 6 concludes.

2. Trust model

The TuBE trust model defines trust as *the extent to which one party is willing to participate in a given action with a given partner in a given situation, considering the risks and incentives involved.* Similar viewpoints are referred to as trusting intentions by McKnight and Chervany (2003) and situational trust by Josang *et al.* (2004). Our trust management system produces context-dependent and dynamic trust decisions, supported by estimations of the actual trustworthiness of a peer.

For the business network establishment phase, the web-Pilarcos platform provides a populator service (Vähäaho *et al.*, 2003). It uses a business network model for determining the collaboration structure and roles for participants, and a service offer repository for retrieving metainformation about potential partners. Based on these, the populator makes sufficient interoperability tests and suggests an eContract. The suggestion is then negotiated between the future partners. Both the populator and the partners are able to use trust information for decision-making.

During the operation of the network, the partners make local trust decisions on getting involved in interactions, based on a combination of local and shared information. The decision system realized as a guard in the communication channel lies on the organizational border at both sides between actors. A trust decision is triggered by in- or outbound messages that mark a risk-relevant commitment in an action. In cases where obliged interactions are missed because of insufficient trust, recovery processes encoded into the eContract are triggered.

A trust decision is a function of 7 parameters: *trustor, trustee, action, reputation, risk, importance* and *context*. It produces a decision with three possible values: *allow, deny* or *unsure*. In the latter case, the decision must be passed to a higher level for further processing, ultimately to a human. The trustor denotes the party making the subjective trust decision. The trustee is the source or target of the triggering message bound in or out, respectively. The action represents an ordered set of messages with content, and has a decision point determined in that set by when a risk-relevant commitment is being made.

The TuBE trust model elaborates the traditional factor basis of trustor, trustee and action by reputation, risk, importance and context factors. From these, a situational risk estimate and a representation of the risk tolerance for the particular situation are generated dynamically. A decision is produced from comparing the two. The choices for factors beyond the basic triple differ from one model to another, and terminology is mixed (Viljanen, 2005b).

Reputation, as used in the TuBE model, is the measure of a peer's trustworthiness. Every trustor has its own view of what the reputation of a particular trustee is, so the measure is not bound to a global agreement and there is no need to build a representation of a global trust network. To build its subjective view, a trustor combines its own experiences with experiences reported by other peers, considering the credibility and information content of all statements. Such a combination is considered for example by Abdul-Rahman and Hailes (2000).

The risk parameter contains a tactical risk estimate of the action. It consists of a set of identified risks and potential benefits to different assets, such as money, security, customer satisfaction and intellectual property. These risk and benefit estimates are speculations of the effect of a positive decision. Some trust and risk models only consider two possible actions by the trustee: cooperation and defection. However, we find this view too simplified in business collaboration. There are different ways and degrees of defecting, such as slightly delayed delivery compared to no delivery at all, or varying quality of the product. The severity ranges of each risk and the weight ranges of each benefit are considered and stored per asset.

The risk parameter depends on the action to be performed. However, the subjective probability that each risk manifests depends on the trustee's reputation. The risk analysis is completed by combining the structure of the risks and benefits with a set of probability distributions for them, derived from the trustee's reputation. The resulting estimate is a set of cost-benefit probability distributions, one for each asset. Cost-benefit estimates have long been a part of trust models; e.g. Marsh considered several business value concepts in his work (1994). SECURE has applied continuous cost-benefit probability density functions for risk analysis, which squeezes all assets into one result function (Cahill, *et al.*, 2003).

The importance parameter brings a strategic counterpart to the tactical evaluation contained in the risk parameter. While the risk analysis depends on what the trustee may do, the importance parameter directs what should be done independently of the trustee's possible behaviour in the future. This factor guides the tolerance of risk, with considerations such as the cost of denying an action, or the benefit of giving great service even when it is rather risky. For example, if denying service violates a contract, compensation is needed and the trustor's own reputation may suffer. Poblano (Chen, *et al.*, 2001) uses importance as a strategic tool as well.

The context parameter represents a set of temporary adjustments to make to other factors. These adjustments either apply to risk or its tolerance, and their scope may be limited to a particular group of trustees, actions or their parameters. Context changes come from three sources: the internal state of the peer's system, the state of the peer's business and the state of the business network the peer is involved with. Context-aware systems in this sense seem rare (Viljanen, 2005b). On the other hand, items such as the *reciprocity* of trust, as discussed by Marsh (1994), can be expressed as a contextual adjustment to the importance factor.

A system state context change may be needed when a denial of service attack has been detected: the perceived risk to service availability should be increased temporarily. Second, a business state context change is in order when storage space or funds are low: the importance of a "sell item" action is increased, which results in higher tolerated risk for that action. Third, should a business network go into a renegotiation state due to problems with one peer, the risk of some actions strongly dependant on other peers may be increased.

3. The TuBE trust management system

In this section we describe two central subsystems of the TuBE trust management system, which implement the two tasks identified in the introduction: trust decision making and the management of reputation information. In the trust decision subsystem, the guard combines local and global trust information from the data processing component into a local trust decision whenever it is called for. The reputation management subsystem upkeeps reputation estimates used by the trust decision subsystem. It does this by combining experience information from local monitors and reports received from the global reputation network. An overview of the TuBE trust management system infrastructure is given in Figure 1.

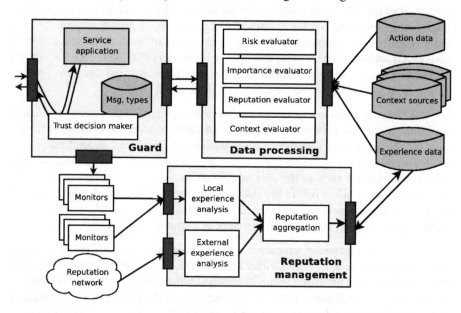

Figure 1. *Overview of the TuBE trust management framework. Connections to external systems are made through the guard and the reputation network*

3.1. *Making trust decisions*

The process to produce a trust decision begins when the guard intercepts a SOAP message on its way to invoke a service method. Each message type is part of a specific action, and the guard stores message types that should trigger the trust decision for the action they represent. As noted in section 2, the triggering message may also originate from the local application. The web-Pilarcos middleware makes sure that inbound messages form well-defined interaction patterns that conform to the eContract.

The guard examines its message type database to determine which parameters in the SOAP message are relevant to the decision. It then extracts these parameters and sends to the trust decision maker the set {*trustee, action, parameters*}. The trust decision maker passes this input to the data-processing component. It receives in return a risk analysis and a constraint set.

The risk analysis represents the calculated risk for the action, expressed as a set of cost-benefit probability distributions, one for each identified asset. For many assets, there are more than two categories of outcomes for different levels of costs and benefits. Others, such as money, can even have continuous ranges of possible cost or benefit, although a human user will probably find categories more intuitive in these cases as well. The constraint set represents the acceptable risk for this action in the current situation, with accepted probability ranges for different benefits and costs. Some aggregating constraints can also be provided in the set, such as the combined probability for either "minor" or "considerable" loss of security. The trust decision is made by comparing whether the risk estimate fits within the constraints. "Unsure" decisions are supported by their own constraint set.

The data-processing component includes four subcomponents: risk, importance and reputation evaluators, which are connected to a context evaluator. The component uses information from the action data storage, experience data storage and different context sources to respond to the guard's queries.

Ontological information about the action and its parameters is held in the action data storage. This information may e.g. identify that a "sell a movie" action is strongly related to the more general "sell" action. The action data storage also contains a set of formulae for estimated default risk for *action*, and when action *parameters* are applied to it by the risk evaluator, a default risk estimate is created. The set of defaults provides parameter-dependent probability distributions for the possible cost or benefit to different assets possibly affected by the action. Experience information concerning the *trustee, action* and relevant other actions is held in the experience data storage, and the defaults given by the default probability distributions are adjusted based on experience information as well as context policies. To respond to a risk request, the data processing component uses the input triple, {*trustee, action, parameters*}, to gather relevant information for the three evaluators and to apply the relevant contextual adjustments to produce a completed risk estimate.

To generate the constraints to represent acceptable risk, a constraint policy set is retrieved from the action data storage for the *action* at hand. The importance evaluator then applies relevant action *parameters* and the *trustee*, following the applicable context policies for this operation, to produce the constraints for acceptable risk. As there is a considerable number of different outcomes and possible risks to represent, they must all be combined to a single set of probability distributions beforehand for efficiency purposes. This can be done as risks are evaluated in the enterprise. SECURE combines the cost-benefit probability density functions for every possible outcome on the fly when performing risk analysis (Cahill, *et al.*, 2003).

3.2. Reputation management

The aggregated experience information used in trust decisions is upkept by the reputation subsystem. A local reputation view is produced by combining experience from a local monitoring system with information gained from the reputation network. Experience captures the effects of past actions to identified assets.

The local monitoring system observes SOAP messages forwarded by the guard, but can also receive information from other data sources. An application-level monitor can detect anomalies in SOAP message exchanges, such as an unusually large quantity of ordered goods, and divergence from contractual specifications, such as requests for payment without a valid order. However, monitoring SOAP message exchanges alone does not capture many out-of-band events that can be considerably more important in the overall experience, e.g. delivering poor-quality goods behind schedule, leaving invoices unpaid or handling reclamations poorly. Many of these events do leave traces in information systems which are not directly connected to the service application. This information about violations can be captured by monitors connected to each of these separate systems. It can then be reported on to the local reputation system.

Some events do not leave traces in information systems at all. For example, poor reclamation handling by a partner can cause customers to take their money elsewhere. This kind of problem can result in a need to break the partnership, but the need is observed by people in the enterprise and dealt with by human interactions. It is essential that the monitoring system also accepts input from human "monitors", which can capture certain kinds of violations much more efficiently than any analysis machinery could.

Most monitors used to gather local experience are far from infallible, and the information they search for may be of different value in determining an actor's reputation. Especially anomaly detection is prone to false alarms (Viljanen, 2005a), as a change in behaviour is not always for the worse. The experience produced by local observation therefore also contains a measure of confidence in the report, on a percentage scale. This confidence is determined by the local reputation system in accordance with the monitor type and the kind of event it reports. The measure is used in determining the impact that the new item of experience has on the current local reputation; the higher the confidence measure, the greater the impact can be.

The amount of information accumulated thus far plays a role here as well: minor problems have more influence on a young business relationship than one that has gone on successfully for years.

The reputation system combines specialized event information from the monitors into experiences. It must consider the relationships between the events to build a larger view: an unusual message exchange for a purchase order is problematic only if payment does not follow, and the human user may provide overriding information. The monitors also provide active responses to threatening events e.g. through context management, but such adjustments are outside the scope of this paper.

The global reputation system combines the experiences of other peers. Sharing experiences with other actors helps businesses avoid making partner selection mistakes that someone else has already made. While the impact of word of mouth can be considerable, this "second-hand" experience brings problems of its own: it is difficult or impossible to check what a statement of experience is based on. Instead of an honest report, it could be a product of collusion or an attempt to make a competitor look bad.

The TuBE reputation subsystem accepts experience information from third parties, and before storing them attaches a percentage measure of credibility to each item of information. The process for deducing this credibility measure lies at the heart of successful use of the global reputation system.

A drop in reputation and its negative impact on trust can have serious effects on the partnership, such as partner removal. Partner removals, as well as locating a replacement partner and renegotiating the contract, are handled by a web-Pilarcos middleware service.

4. Implementation issues

Issues in the realization of the TuBE trust management system include: a) the representation and interpretation of trust information, b) the management of information sources in an effective way, c) performance penalties caused by the guards, and d) the cost of introducing the generic TuBE facilities into enterprise systems.

In the TuBE system, automated measurement of trusting belief alone is not sufficient, but it must be used for decision-making. The trust belief information, such as local reputation views, is seen in form of probabilities; trust is interpreted as a probability measure for success. Using a single probability as a trust belief measure would force an assumption that the outcomes of any action can be divided into two groups, cooperation and defection, in accordance with a game-theoretic world view. We consider this too broad a simplification for business applications. In the field of business interactions, there are clearly several levels of cooperation and defection, such as late delivery or no delivery at all. Our approach to consider each asset separately allows more specific policy in one sense, and in return allows free choice of the specificity of cost and benefit categories according to the enterprise needs. Our aim is that a user enterprise could utilize risk analysis information gathered using separate tools in the configuration of its trust management system.

In each enterprise system, trust decisions are supported by evidence on the behaviour of known or potential trustees. The evidence includes both first-hand and second-hand experience. It is upkept through feedback loops from the local monitoring system and from external reputation systems. The challenges related to these sources are quite different: experience received from the global reputation network requires not only credibility analysis, but also analysis on how experience from very different activities relates to those relevant in the local system.

The monitoring system may cause major overhead in the system, even if the service monitor studies sent and received SOAP messages only. There are also intrusion detection and prevention approaches that hook into the operating system or platform the service application is running on, such as the Java VM, or build sensors inside the application (Viljanen, 2005a).

We must trigger trust decisions at relevant points of the exchange only, carefully adjust the width and focus of any anomaly and breach detection to actual enterprise needs, and limit the amount of information to transfer to the decision point. For example, experience information can be aggregated into compound items in different levels (English, *et al.*, 2003; Liu, *et al.*, 2004), which can alleviate both storage and transfer limitations.

The set of actions and the set of trustees are both large and dynamic, but at any time a single guard needs only a fraction of this information. Caching the data most relevant to the current interaction near the guard is a beneficial trade-off between transfer load and information freshness. The selection of the relevant information can be based on partnership information and business network activities information available from the web-Pilarcos facilities. The TuBE trust management system is strongly based on the concept of *action*, and information on action types and ontology is needed. Here we can utilize service typing information used in describing and matching Web Services in web-Pilarcos (Ruokolainen *et al.*, 2005b). The available information provides for both the action ontology needed for generalizing experiences, and the message typing used in the guard.

We require a reputation network to provide information classified by actions and trustees. In addition, in our model a trustee is a business service, as opposed to e.g. a human user, a computer or an entire enterprise. Current reputation systems are highly varied and incompatible, and there is nothing resembling a standard solution available. We have specified what kind of experience information we wish to receive from the network and the interface through which it is accessed. Studying the interoperability of different reputation systems is an item of future work.

5. Conclusion

This paper proposes a partner-to-partner trust model that is based on a global reputation flow and local trust decisions guarding inter-enterprise collaborations. The trust-aware guards influence actions taken at two levels: the establishment and negotiation of collaboration relationships, and significant inter-enterprise interactions. This kind of trust model is essential for federated architectures for inter-enterprise collaboration management, such as web-Pilarcos (Kutvonen *et al.*, 2005).

Significant features of the TuBE trust model include dynamic, multi-source accumulation of reputation information, and timely interception of business interactions. The solution compliments traditional security services by trust-based soft security, which is more applicable in open collaboration networks (Rasmusson *et al.*, 1996).

Although the field of trust management is still somewhat diverse (INTEROP-NoE, 2005; Viljanen, 2005b; Ruohomaa *et al.*, 2005), the TuBE trust model conforms to the commonly required main elements and furthermore elaborates the trust decision information to aspects relevant for inter-enterprise collaboration and business process management. The TuBE system combines the information collecting tasks traditionally most visible in reputation systems research (Liu, *et al.*, 2004; Obreiter, 2004), and the automated decision making which the first trust management systems (Blaze *et al.*, 1998) have focused on.

Further work on the TuBE systems will bring the design into the existing web-Pilarcos prototype platform, and allow us to compare the effects of various trust decision algorithms to strategic business goals. Furthermore, trust and reputation information ontologies and reputation system interoperability are relevant areas of research.

This article is based on work in the web-Pilarcos and the TuBE projects (Trust based on evidence) at the Department of Computer Science at the University of Helsinki. The web-Pilarcos project is run in collaboration with VTT, Elisa, SysOpen, and in addition funded by the National Technology Agency TEKES in Finland, and Tellabs. The TuBE project is funded by TEKES, Nixu, and StoneSoft.

6. References

Abdul-Rahman, A., Hailes S., "Supporting Trust in Virtual Communities", *Hawaii International Conference on System Sciences, HICSS,* January 2000.

Blaze M., Feigenbaum J., Keromytis A. D., "KeyNote: Trust management for public-key infrastructures (Position Paper)", *Proceedings of Security Protocols: 6th International Workshop*, Springer-Verlag, *LNCS* 1550, April 1998, p. 59–63.

Cahill V. *et al.*, "Using trust for secure collaboration in uncertain environments", *Pervasive Computing*, vol. 2, no. 3, 2003, p. 52–61, IEEE.

Chen R., Yeager W., "Poblano – a distributed trust model for peer-to-peer networks", report, 2001, Sun Microsystems.

English C., Wagealla W., Nixon P., Terzis S., McGettrick A., Lowe H., "Trusting collaboration in global computing systems", *First International Conference on Trust Management}*, LNCS 2692, Springer-Verlag, May 2003, p. 136–149.

Gambetta D., "Can We Trust Trust?", *Trust: Making and Breaking Cooperative Relations*, University of Oxford, Department of Sociology, 2000, . 213-237, Electronic edition.

INTEROP-NoE Task Group 7, "Roadmap for TG7: Interoperability Challenges of Trust, Confidence, Security and Policies", 2005, In preparation.

Jensen C., Poslad S., Dimitrakos T., Eds. *Proceedings of Trust Management: Second International Conference, LNCS 2995*, Springer-Verlag, March 2004.

Josang A., Presti S. L., "Analysing the Relationship between Risk and Trust", Jensen *et al.* (2004), p.135–145.

Kutvonen L., Metso J., Ruokolainen T., "Inter-enterprise collaboration management in dynamic business networks", *OTM Confederated International Conferences, CoopIS, DOA, and ODBASE, LNCS 3760*, Springer-Verlag, Nov 2005, p. 593–611.

Liu J., Issarny V., "Enhanced Reputation Mechanism for Mobile Ad Hoc Networks", Jensen *et al.* (2004), p. 48–62.

Marsh S., "Formalising Trust as a Computational Concept", PhD thesis, University of Stirling, Dept. of Computer Science and Mathematics, 1994.

McKnight D. H., Chervany N. L., "Trust and Distrust Definitions: One Bite at a Time", *Trust in Cyber-societies: Integrating the human and artificial perspectives, LNCS 2246*, Springer-Verlag, 2001, p. 27–54.

Obreiter P., "A Case for Evidence-Aware Distributed Reputation Systems Overcoming the Limitations of Plausibility Considerations", Jensen *et al.* (2004), p. 33–47.

Rasmusson L., Jansson S., "Simulated Social Control for Secure Internet Commerce", *Proc. of the 1996 workshop on New Security Paradigms*, ACM Press, 1996, p. 18–25.

Ruohomaa S., Kutvonen L., "Trust management survey", *Proceedings of Trust Management: Third International Conference, LNCS 3477*, Springer-Verlag, April 2005, p. 77–92.

Ruokolainen T., Kutvonen L., "Service Typing in Collaborative Systems", accepted for publication in the proceedings of I-ESA 2006.

Viljanen L., "A Survey of Application Level Intrusion Detection", report, 2005, University of Helsinki, Dept. of Computer Science.

Viljanen L., "Towards an Ontology of Trust", *Proceedings of the 2nd International Conference on Trust, Privacy and Security in Digital Business (TrustBus'05)*, 2005.

Vähäaho, M., Kutvonen L., "Enhanced trading service in middleware for inter-organisational applications" report C-2003-15, University of Helsinki, Dept. of Computer Science, 2003.

I-ESA'2006
Doctoral Symposium

Doctoral Symposium Chairs' message

The aim of the Doctoral Symposium held in conjunction with the second International Conference I-ESA 2006 was to provide an opportunity for students involved in the preparation of their PhD in any area of Interoperability for Enterprise Software and Applications to interactively discuss their research issues and ideas with senior researchers, and receive constructive feedback from members of the research community and other Doctoral Symposium participants.

Submissions to the Doctoral Symposium came from 10 European countries. After the review process, 15 papers (8 regular and 6 extended abstracts) were accepted and presented during the workshop. This chapter contains the revised versions of the papers classified in four themes according to the doctoral session's scheduler. The papers present students' thesis topics, the work they have performed and the results that they have obtained so far.

The first four papers deal with *Model Driven Development*. In the paper *"Manage QoS in MDD using an aspect-oriented model driven framework"* A.Solberg discusses some challenges of including Quality of Service (QoS) as an integrated part of the MDD approach. C. S. Hahn proposes *"A Model-Driven Approach for Service Composition Using Agent Technology"*. The paper *"Models simulation and interoperability using MDA and HLA"* by H. El Haouzi advocates for an approach combining MDA (model driven architecture) and HLA (High Level Architecture) for ensuring interoperability between business and manufacturing models. *"A Study of Aspect-Driven Transformations to Facilitate Model Driven Development"* is proposed by P. Liyanagama.

The second theme deals with *Business Process Modelling*. Mining techniques allowing to discover workflow models and to improve their transactional behaviour are discussed by W. Gaaloul in *"Workflow Reengineering trough Log Event-based Analysis"*. Two papers, *"Dependency Based Approach for Process Design"* by A. Edirisuriya and *"Declarative Approach of Process Models"* by T. Ilayperuma, introduce complementary works towards a method that helps to transform a business model into a business process model in a systematic way. S. Sandron proposes a process for *"Improving Alignment of Business Models and Business Process Models for Ensuring Strategic Fit of Business Processes"*.

The *Software Development and Interoperability* theme includes three works. The paper *"An Interactive Multi-Agent Based TV Game Show Implementation"* of B. Gâteau focuses on the implementation of Moise[Inst], a model for specifying rights and duties of agents within an organisation. The paper *"Plug and Play Business Software"* by A. Jacobsson proposes an integrated framework of ICT-tools intended to assist enterprises in realizing innovations and conducting business across organizational boundaries. In the paper *"Formalising Problem Frames with Ontology"* G. Saval proposes to relate Problem Frames and other modelling languages by using a common ontology.

The last theme deals with **Enterprise Modelling and Knowledge Management**. Knowledge management in virtual enterprises is discussed in two papers: *"A Proposal for Modelling Enterprise Knowledge in Virtual Enterprises"* by R. Grangel and *"Methodology for the Development of a Tacit Knowledge Management System for Virtual Enterprises"* by V. Fernandez Pallares. N. Zougar proposes an approach for *"Semantic Enrichment of Enterprise Modelling"*. The last paper *"Capability Representation on Increases ALN"* by D. Cheng proposes an approach to represent and query capability in the description logic ALN.

We express our thanks to the Doctoral Symposium committee. The Doctoral Symposium exists thanks to their generous contribution of time and effort in the review process, sessions chairing and providing valuable comments and ideas during the doctoral symposium.

Jolita Ralyté, *University of Geneva, Switzerland*
Giovanna Di Marzo Serugendo, *Birkbeck College, University of London, UK*

Session 1:
Model Driven Development

Manage QoS in MDD using an aspect-oriented model driven framework

Arnor Solberg

SINTEF ICT, Forksningsveien 1, 0314 Oslo, Norway
Arnor.Solberg@sintef.no

ABSTRACT: In model driven development (MDD), specifying system models as well as the transformations between models at various levels of abstraction can be a complex task. Embracing Quality of Service (QoS) in MDD is particularly difficult because: 1) existing tools and methods for specification of QoS as part of the system models are immature, 2) management of QoS specifications at different levels of abstraction and traceability of QoS is not clearly understood, and 3) the QoS elements to be transformed tend to be distributed across a model and tangled with other system features. This paper presents an approach for QoS-aware MDD. Modelling of QoS are discussed, a conceptual framework for understanding traces and appearances of QoS specifications at different abstraction levels are presented, and the aspect oriented model driven framework (AOMDF) are introduced. AOMDF facilitates separation of pervasive features and supports their transformation across different levels of abstraction.

KEY WORDS: Model driven environment, Quality of Service.

1. Introduction

Model driven development (MDD) shifts software development from a code-centric activity to a model-centric activity. Accomplishing this shift entails developing support for modelling concepts at different levels of abstraction and transforming abstract models to more concrete descriptions of software. MDD aims to reduce complexity in software development through modularization and abstraction.

Models are specifications of the system and are recommended to be developed iteratively in synchrony with the coding of the system. Current practices focus on modelling the functional aspects of the system. However, a system has additional properties that characterize the system. These extra-functional properties, also called quality of service (QoS) properties, address how well the primary functionality is (or should be) performed if it is realized. In other words, if an observable effect of a system action can be quantified (implying that there is more than "done"/"not-done" effect of the behaviour), the quality of that behaviour can be described. The quality requirements should be specified, and these should be taken into consideration during the system development process to ensure that the produced artefacts meet extra-functional as well as functional requirements.

Understanding the implications of integrating the QoS aspect in MDD and development of mechanisms and framework for handling QoS in tasks such as system modelling, transformation specification and traceability are needed While there are a set of proposed ways to specify QoS requirements in system models (e.g., (Aagedal, 2001)), the implications of these specifications and how to react properly, for example during model transformations, is still an issue that needs to be resolved. Also, there is a shortage of methodologies for model-based development that cover complete and precise specification of QoS-requirements. However, in many kinds of systems, the consequences of QoS-failures are severe. For example, it might be extremely important to make sure that availability requirements is met in system domains such as health, traffic control and banking.

In MDD a main mechanism to handle complexity is abstraction. OMG's MDD initiative, the Model Driven Architecture (MDA) (OMG, 2003), proposes a separation of concern mechanism consisting of three different levels of abstraction. These levels are denoted the Computation Independent Model (CIM), the Platform Independent Model (PIM) and the Platform Specific Model (PSM). For example, separation of platform independent and platform specific concerns occurs when a middleware independent model (a PIM) and a corresponding middleware specific model (a PSM) are defined for a particular application. However, an MDD framework should provide mechanisms supporting both vertical and horizontal separation of concerns in order to gain proper management of QoS in MDD. An example of vertical separation of concern is CIM, PIM and PSM abstraction levels. Horizontal separation of concerns is traditionally realized by modelling a system using views (e.g., the ISO RM-ODP framework (ISO, 1995a)). A system view describes a certain facet of the system (e.g., structure, behaviour or distribution). The use of diagram types provided by a modelling language is normative for specifying view mechanisms. However, diagram types (e.g., UML activity, class and state diagrams) only provide separation of structure and behaviour and do not inherently provide separation of user defined views. Aspect Oriented Software Development (AOSD) (Kiczales *et al.* 1997, Ossher *et al.* 2001, Ray *et al.* 2004) supports horizontal separation of concerns by providing mechanisms for encapsulating crosscutting features such as QoS, using aspects.

This paper presents mechanisms for managing QoS in MDD and is based on earlier published results in particular (Simmonds *et al.* 2005, Solberg *et al.* 2005, Solberg *et al.* 2003). Section 2 discusses QoS specification, section 3 present a classification scheme for how to handle QoS in model transformation. Section 4 presents an aspect oriented model driven framework that combines traditional MDD abstraction mechanisms with aspect oriented mechanisms for separating crosscutting features to facilitate management of QoS in MDD.

2. Specification of QoS

In order to guarantee some level of QoS, the appropriate QoS characteristics must be identified and specified. The QoS offered by a component should be specified in such manner that the QoS requirements can easily be distinguished from the specification of its functional properties. This is appropriate since: (i) the QoS of a component is dependent on its environment, (ii) there may be multiple QoS specifications for the component, and (iii) the functional specifications of the component are independent of the particular QoS specification that will be enforced at any point in time. This is an orthogonal separation of concerns between behaviour (functional properties) and constraints (the QoS it offers).

Models of system functionality typically represent service offers that system components can provide, e.g., abstractions of component interfaces and component interactions. For functional specifications, this is sufficient since component behaviour can be objectively defined. An architectural model combines services to a complete functional system specification, and the consistency is typically verified by type matching. For QoS, however, one cannot merely specify the QoS offered by a component, one needs also a way to specify client satisfaction. Specifications of client satisfaction are often done by worth functions that evaluate a QoS offer relative to benefit of a given client and return a worth value. A QoS-aware service configuration then involves both traditional type matching and QoS-optimization.

QoS characteristic might be seen as the most fundamental term required to specify QoS. A QoS characteristic represents some aspect of the QoS of a system service or resource that can be identified and quantified, for instance time delay or availability. In the ISO QoS Framework (ISO, 1995b), a number of QoS characteristics are defined such as delay, throughput, etc. ISO/IEC 9126 (ISO, 1999) provides a consistent terminology of different aspects of quality and identifies six quality characteristics that are further subdivided. The six main characteristics are functionality, reliability, usability, efficiency, maintainability and portability. Despite the lists of QoS characteristics in standards, there is no agreed upon and exhaustive list of QoS characteristics. In the UML profile for QoS standard (OMG, 2004), a QoS catalogue is defined based on ISO/IEC 9126, but it is made clear that this should not be considered as the final and exhaustive list of QoS characteristics. Indeed, the individual modellers are free to define their own QoS characteristics, tailored to their application, but they should then be aware the problems of interoperability with using self-defined characteristics.

QoS requirements should in many cases preferably be associated to instances rather than to classes or types. With the introduction of UML 2.0, new language constructs are available for representing instances of types (e.g., parts, ports) and links between them (connectors). Thus, using UML 2.0 the QoS requirements can be more easily specified for instances within their residing environments. New UML profiles for QoS specifications that are based on UML 2.0 will benefit from having these new instance constructs.

3. Modes of handling QoS in model transformation

To make model transformations QoS-aware, QoS-properties need to be specified and integrated into the models. Assume a model-based system specification (including QoS-specifications) to be used as the source in a model-transformation. How should the QoS-specifications be managed? In the following, two modes for QoS transformations are suggested:

Mode 1, denoted *QoS-mapping* consists of three subcategories: i) One-to-one, ii) Refinement and iii) Abstraction. **Mode 2,** denoted *QoS-resolution,* also consist of three subcategories: i) Functional, ii) Resources, and iii) Combination.

Mode 1 QoS-mapping, complies with the traditional way of handling functionality during model transformations, where three kinds of mappings are performed: One-to-one mapping, refinement and abstraction. In *one-to-one-mapping,* the abstraction level is kept throughout the transformation. Thus, the level of detail of a QoS-specification of the source remains the same in the derived target. If the source and target is according to the same metamodel the QoS-specifications in the source and target will be identical. If the source and target metamodels differ, the syntax of the specification will typically differ, while precision and semantics are preserved. In a *refinement mapping* more details of the source specification appears in the target. The transformation engine thereby needs to recognize the specific QoS-specification and add more information to it according to specified rules and/or through processing and computations. For refinement mappings, the source model specification is at a higher level of abstraction than the target. *Abstraction mapping* is the reverse of a refinement-mapping.

QoS-specifications might be resolved during a model-transformation process (*Mode 2*). The baseline for resolving a QoS specification is the assumption that QoS requirements are resolved either by provision of sufficient resources or by functional means, or a combination of these two. Resolution by functional means implies that QoS-requirements at one abstraction level are transformed to a functional requirement/solution at a lower abstraction level. An example of this principle is the delay in a distributed system. Required delay-threshold could be resolved by means of compression to reduce the amount of data transported over the connection links. Delay is in fact an example of a QoS-characteristic that may be resolved using either functional means (e.g., compression/decompression components) or by means of providing adequate resources (e.g., through high-bandwidth connections). The solution may obviously be a combination of these.

4. The aspect oriented model driven framework

This section describes the aspect oriented model driven framework (AOMDF) and some important technologies on which it is based.

4.1. *Model transformation*

A model transformation can be viewed as a transformation between two model spaces defined by their respective metamodels. A source model to target model transformation specification, describes how elements in the source model space should appear in the target model space by relating metamodel elements in the source and target metamodels. The relationships among transformation concepts are illustrated in Figure 1.

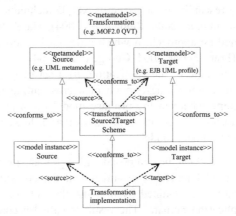

Figure 1. *Model Transformation conceptual model*

The source model instance conforms to the source metamodel (for instance the UML metamodel). The transformation implementation transforms a source model instance to the corresponding target model instance. The target model instance conforms to the target metamodel (for instance the UML profile for CORBA (OMG, 2002)). The specific transformation implementation for a specific source and target model is generated using the *Source2Target* Schema. This schema is the transformation specification, which maps source metamodel concepts to target metamodel concepts. The *Source2Target* Schema must conform to a transformation metamodel (for instance the MOF 2.0 QVT (OMG, 2005)).

Before a transformation can be executed, the transformation must be specified as a mapping. Each mapping identifies the source model that is input to the mapping and the target model that results when the mapping is executed. Many transformation approaches are based on specifying mappings from source meta-model concepts to target meta-model concepts (Czarnecki *et al.* 2003). However, it may not be desirable to map all in-stances of a specific meta-model element at the source level in the same way. For example, middleware platforms such as CORBA, J2EE, Net and Web Services typically have specific protocols for pervasive middleware services such as security, persistence, and transactions. These protocols may differ from one middleware to another, and different services may require different protocols even for the same middleware. Thus, the mapping specifications of these aspects tend to be rigid and proprietary. CORBA, for example, provides the CORBA security service, the CORBA transaction service and the CORBA persistent object service, each of which require a specific protocol. Pervasive middleware services need to be treated explicitly in model transformation to obtain the correct target model. The AOMDF facilitates source to target mappings in which provided platform specific protocols are used.

4.2. *Aspect oriented modelling*

There is ongoing research on the usage of AOSD techniques at the model level (Ray *et al.* 2004, Silaghi *et al.* 2004, Reina *et al.* 2004). The AOMDF is based on an aspect oriented modelling approach in which a design is expressed in terms of the following artefacts (France *et al.* 2004, George *et al.* 2004): i) A primary model that describes the business logic of the application, ii) a set of generic aspect models, where each model is a generic description of a crosscutting feature, iii) a set of bindings that determine where in the primary model the aspect models are to be composed, and iv) a set of composition directives that influence how aspect models are composed with the primary model.

Before an aspect model can be composed with a primary model in an application domain, the aspect model must be instantiated in the context of the application domain. An instantiation is obtained by binding elements in the aspect model to elements in the application domain. The result is called a context-specific aspect model. Context specific aspect models and the primary model are composed to obtain an integrated design view (France *et al.* 2004, Song *et al.* 2005).

4.3. *The framework*

Figure 2 shows the major activities and artefacts supported in the AOMDF. The primary focus of the framework is the transformation of aspect oriented models from more abstract forms to more concrete forms. The major activities are partitioned into four categories: source level, mappings, target level and model composition.

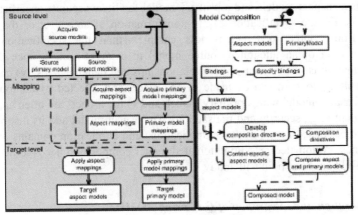

Figure 2. *Aspect oriented model driven framework*

The *source level* includes activities for acquiring or developing abstract aspect and primary models. The aspect models are acquired from an aspect repository if one is available or they are developed by the system architect. The primary model is developed by the system architect. The system architect decides which services will be included in the primary model and which will be treated as aspects. The decisions are based on the distinction of functional and QoS requirements. QoS requirements, such as security and transaction management, are often pervasive. AOSD techniques are used to separate services that address these requirements from the primary business functionality.

The *mappings* category includes activities for developing or acquiring the corresponding target mappings. The transformations between the source and the target levels are defined by separate mappings for each aspect and the primary model. The source and target levels have a recursive nature. Thus, the source level in one context may appear as the target level in another context.

The target level includes activities for applying the mappings to the source level primary and aspect models. The target detailed design models are obtained by applying the source to target transformations that are specified in the mappings.

The model composition part includes activities for instantiating and composing the aspect and primary models using bindings and composition directives (France *et al.* 2004, Straw *et al.* 2004). Aspect models need to be instantiated before they can be composed. Instantiation is performed by binding the aspect model elements to the application specific model elements. Once the instantiation is done, model composition is performed using the composition directives, basic name matching procedures (France *et al.* 2004) and signature matching (Reddy *et al.* 2005). The perceived benefits of the proposed framework includes: i) The framework allows developers to conceptualize, describe, and communicate crosscutting concerns as conceptual units at various levels of abstraction, ii) the horizontal separation of concerns as aspect models and a primary model facilitate separate specifications of mappings, iii) the specification of the transformation of an aspect or the primary model from source to target is less complex than the specification of the transformation of an integrated source model to a target model, since the latter transformation is likely to have more relationships and dependencies, iv) changes to a crosscutting concern can be made in one place, and effected by composing the changed aspect model with a primary model, and v) the aspects are often application independent (e.g., security and transaction). The aspect model and its mappings can therefore be reused across multiple applications and application domains once they are defined. Automated or semi-automated model composition needs to be in place to gain full benefit of points iii and iv.

4.4. Separation and integration of QoS using AOMDF

Managing QoS in MDD using AOMDF, the QoS features will be treated as aspects while the basic system services are modelled in the primary model. For example, for a money transfer service, entities such as account as well as money transfer behaviour such as withdraw and deposit of money will be modelled in the primary model. This is illustrated in Figure 3.

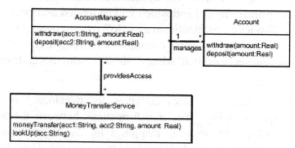

Figure 3. *Simple money transfer primary model*

QoS aspects such as security, transaction control and performance will be modelled as aspects. A transaction control aspect is shown in Figure 4.

Integration of aspects with the primary model is performed by means of model composition. Aspects are modelled as templates/role models and need to be bound to the actual context. Composition directives and rules govern the composition. Techniques for Model composition are discussed in (Song *et al.* 2005, Reddy *et al.* 2005).

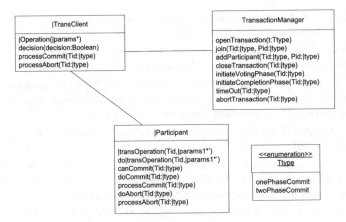

Figure 4. *Transaction control aspect model*

5. Conclusion

This paper discusses some challenges of including QoS as an integrated part of the MDD approach. QoS is an important aspect of software engineering. In some system domain like health, real-time systems, and banking QoS aspects are crucial. Thus MDD frameworks and tools need to incorporate support for QoS management in tasks such as modelling and transformation specification.

Modern systems are complex. Separation of concerns is recognized as a key principle to cope with complexity in software development. In this extended abstract, we have reasoned that both vertical and horizontal separation of concerns should be provided for managing complexity in an MDD framework.

Aspect-oriented technologies can be used to support horizontal separation of cross-cutting concerns from other functionality. The AOM approach emphasizes the separation and modularization of crosscutting concerns in design units (aspects). The AOMDF provides additional support for specifying transformations. The AOMDF allows us to separate out the model and mapping specification for pervasive services from the model and mapping specification of the primary model. The aspect mapping specification then becomes reusable and the mapping specification of the primary model becomes simpler.

6. References

Aagedal, J. Ø. *Quality of Service Support in Development of Distributed Systems*, PhD thesis at University of Oslo, Unipub forlag ISSN 1501-7710, 2001.

ISO/IEC 10746. (a) Basic reference model for open distributed processing, 1995.

Kiczales G. *et al.* Aspect Oriented Programming. *In Proc. of the European Conference on Object-Oriented Programming* (ECOOP), 1997. Springer Verlag LNCS 1241.

Ossher H., Tarr P. Using multidimensional separation of concerns to (re)shape evolving software. *Communications of ACM*, 44(10):43-50, 2001.

Ray I., France R., Li N., Georg G. An Aspect-Based Approach to Modelling Access Control Concerns, *Journal of Information and Software Technology*, 46(9), 2004.

Simmonds D., Solberg A., Reddy R., France F., Ghosh S. An Aspect Oriented Model Driven Framework. *In proceedings of the EDOC (Enterprise Distributed Object Computing) 2005 conference*, 19-23 September, Enschede, The Netherlands.

Solberg A., Aageda J.Ø. Managing the QoS-Aspect in Model-transformations. *In proceedings of the IRMA 2005 conference*, 15-18 May 2005, San Diego, California USA.

Solberg A., Husa K.E., Aagedal J.Ø., Abrahamsen E. QoS aware MDA, *Presented at The SIVOES-MDA workshop,* at the UML conference San Francisco USA. http://www-verimag.imag.fr/EVENTS/2003/SIVOES-MDA/Programme.html.

ISO/IEC JTC1/SC21, *QoS - Basic Framework*, Report: JTC1/SC 21 N9309, 1995.

ISO/IEC JTC1/SC7, *Information Technology – Software product quality – Part 1: Quality model*, ISO/IEC, Report: 9126-1, pp. 25, 1999.

OMG UML™ *Profile for Modeling Quality of Service and Fault Tolerance Characteristics and Mechanisms*, OMG Adopted Specification ptc/2004-06-01, 2004.

Czarnecki, K., Helsen, S. (2003), "Classification of Model Transformation Approaches". *In Proc. of Generative Techniques in the Context of Model-Driven Architecture workshop, OOPSLA 2003.*

Silaghi R., Fondement F., Strohmeier A. Towards an MDA-Oriented UML Profile for Distribution. *In Proceedings of the 8th IEEE International Enterprise Distributed Object Computing Conference, EDOC,* Monterey, CA, USA, September 2004.

Reina A. M., Toress J., Toro M. Towards developing generic solutions with aspects. *In proc. of Aspect Oriented Modelling workshop,* at UML 2004 conference.

France R. B., Ray I., Georg G., Ghosh S. An aspect-oriented approach to design modelling". *IEE Proceedings - Software, Special Issue on Early Aspects: Aspect-Oriented Requirements Engineering and Architecture Design,* 151(4), 2004.

Georg G., Reddy R., France R. Specifying cross-cutting requirements concerns. *In Proceedings of the International Conference on the UML,* Springer, 2004.

Song E., Reddy R., France R., Ray I., Georg G., Alexander R. Verifying Access Control Properties using Aspect Oriented Modeling. *The 10th ACM Symposium on Ac-cess Control Models and Technologies (SACMAT),* Scandic Hasselbacken, Stockholm, 2005.

Straw, G., Georg, G., Song, E., Ghosh, S., France, R. and Bieman, J. Model Com-position Directives. *In Proc. of the 7th UML Conference,* Lisbon, Portugal, 2004.

Reddy, R., France, F., Ghosh, S., Fleurey, F. Baudry, B. Model Composition - A Signature-Based Approach. *The Aspect Oriented Modelling Workshop @ the MoDELS 2005 conference,* Montego Bay, Jamaica.

OMG *UML™ Profile for CORBA™ version 1.0*, formal/02-04-01, 2002.

OMG *MOF QVT Final adopted specification* OMG document ptc/05-11-01, 2005.

OMG *MDA™ Guide v1.0.1*, OMG, 2002. http://www.omg.org/docs/omg/03-06-01.pdf.

A Model-Driven Approach for Service Composition Using Agent Technology

Christian S. Hahn

DFKI GmbH, Stuhlsatzenhausweg 3 (Bau 43), D-66123 Saarbrücken, Germany
christian.hahn@dfki.de

ABSTRACT: *Services provide a universal basis for the integration of business processes that are distributed among the most disparate entities, both within an organization and across organizational borders. One of the major challenges is the automated composition of distributed business processes, i.e., the development of techniques and tools supporting an effective, reliable, low-cost, and time-efficient composition of distributed business processes. This proposal presents an agent-oriented approach to automatically perform the time consuming and error prone task of analyzing business processes, selecting and composing suitable services, detecting problems in the interactions, monitoring execution step by step by proposing a generic model that gives the mappings of terminology between services and holons (i.e. organizational-oriented agents) and describes a comprehensive framework to design interoperable agents able to transfer the functionalities of services on agent platforms to execute them in a flexible manner.*

KEY WORDS: *Agents, Holons, Modelling, Metamodels, Model-Driven Development, Service-Oriented Architectures.*

1. Introduction

Although service-oriented architectures (SOA) have become a very active research area, several fundamental problems have to be addressed. An interesting and demanding challenge is to generate composed services by assembling existing atomic or complex services. New design methodologies and robust development tools for the *service composition* are needed. Additionally, the complexity of the composition task is further aggravated by the heterogeneous nature of the participating services, as those can be described in different ways, uses different interfaces, and most likely deployed by different providers. Thus, the second challenge is to develop modelling techniques to implement flexible, reliable, inter-operating services.

For several reasons, approaches basing on agent technologies are an interesting opportunity when executing services: Firstly, agents are self-aware and through the possibility of learning they acquire the awareness of other agents and their attitudes. Secondly, they are communicative, whereas services are passive until invoked. Thirdly, in contrast to services, agents act in an autonomous manner that is required by many Internet applications. Lastly, agents are cooperative, and by forming organizations they can provide higher-level and more comprehensive services. Current standards in the domain of services do not provide any of those functionalities (Singh *et al.*, 2005).

The paper is structured as follows: In section 2 the basic concepts of our approach are discussed. Section 3 presents a link between concepts of SOA and agent technologies and shows how to design interoperable holonic agents. In section 4 the most important research hypotheses are stated, followed by section 5 illustrating the major research challenges and problems. Conclusions and future work is presented in section 6.

2. Related work

In this section, the main characteristics of service-oriented architectures and intelligent agents are discussed that provide the base for further discussions.

2.1. *Service-oriented architectures*

Services are loosely coupled, dynamically locatable software pieces, which provide a common platform-independent framework that simplifies heterogeneous application integration. Services base on a service-oriented architecture (SOA) and communicate by exchanging messages. Some function-oriented approaches like WSLD (Web Services Description Language) and BPEL4WS (Business Process Execution Language for Web Services) have provided guidelines for planning of service compositions see (Koehler *et al.*, 2003, Casati *et al.*, 2001). However, the technology to compose services has not kept pace with the rapid growth and volatility of available opportunities (Sheng *et al.*, 2004). While the composition of services requires considerable efforts, its benefits can be short-lived and may only support short-term partnerships that are formed during execution and disbanded on completion (Sheng *et al.*, 2004).

Service composition can be conceived as two-phase procedure, involving planning and execution (McIlraith *et al.*, 2002). The planning phase includes determining series of operations that are needed for accomplishing the desired goals from a user query, customizing services, scheduling execution of composed services and constructing a concrete and unambiguously defined composition of services ready to be executed. The execution phase involves processes of collaborating with other services to attain desirable goals of the composed services. In general, two dimensions of service composition can be distinguished: static and dynamic composition. Compared to the static approach, dynamic compositions can better exploit the present state of services, provide run-time optimisations. On the other hand, the dynamic composition of services is a particularly difficult problem due to the continued need to provide high availability, reliability, and scalability in the face of high degrees of autonomy and heterogeneity with which services are deployed and managed on the web (Pires *et al.*, 2003). The use and application of intelligent agents has been suggested to handle these challenges. This link has also been emphasized by the W3C who sees software agents as the running programs that drive web services – both to implement them and to access them as computational resources that act on behalf of a person or organization.

2.2. Intelligent agents

The necessity to explore flexible agent-based mechanisms for service composition is currently discussed as *specific challenge* in the AgentLink RoadMap: While web Service technologies define conventions for describing service interfaces and workflows, we need more powerful techniques for dynamically describing, discovering, composing, monitoring, managing, and adapting multiple services [...] (Luck *et al.*, 2005). Agents are persistent computational entities (e.g., a software program or robot) capable of perceiving and acting upon their environment, in an autonomous manner, in order to meet their design objectives. They interact and communicate with other agents and incorporate reasoning techniques (e.g., planning, decision making, and learning) together with sophisticated interaction to achieve flexible rational behaviour (Wooldridge 2001).

To design of agents with rational and flexible problem solving behaviour, the BDI agent architecture has been proven successful during the last decade (Rao *et al.*, 1995). Three mental attitudes (beliefs, desires, and intentions) allow an agent to act in and to reason about its environment in an effective manner. Team-based agents are a special kind of intelligent agents with distributed expertise (knowledge) and emphasize on cooperativeness and proactiveness in pursuing their common goals.

Several computational models for describing an agent-based teamwork have been proposed including for instance STEAM (Tambe 1997). These models allow multiple agents to solve (e.g., planning, task execution) complex problems collaboratively. In the domain of service composition, team-based agents can facilitate a distributed approach to dynamic composition that can be scalable, facilitate learning about specific types of services across multiple compositions and allow proactive failure handling. In this paper, I will concentrate on a specific organizational-based approach that is called *Holonic Multiagent Systems (HMS)* (see section 3.2).

3. Designing interoperable holonic agents

Model-driven development (MDD) is emerging as the state of practice for developing modern enterprise applications and software systems by solving interoperability issues compared to earlier non-modelling approaches. The ultimate goal of MDD is to improve the quality of software products and the development process, by allowing the reuse of models and mappings between models. Basically, the model-driven approach (MDA) to software development bases on modelling and on the automated mapping of source models to target models, textual code defines the target model. From a top-down perspective it starts with a computation independent model (CIM) describing the business context and business requirements of the software system. The CIM is refined to a platform independent model (PIM) that specifies software services and interfaces required in the business context. The PIM is further refined to a set of platform specific models (PSMs) which describe the realization of the software systems with respect to the specific software technology. A lot of effort in MDA to develop model interoperability standards, as well as model-to-model transformation concepts and techniques for their automation has already been done. The MDA initiative refers mainly to Object Oriented software development and proved to be effective in relevant application domain, such as services (business process integration) (Koehler *et al.*, 2005). Recently, a few proposals to exploit MDA ideas and techniques in agent-oriented software engineering have been maded (Perini *et al.*, 2004, Jayatilleke *et al.*, 2004, Depke *et al.*, 2001). The MDA standards and technological infrastructure are relevant to make agent-oriented methodologies usable by practitioners. In particular, adapting MDA standards for model interoperability and for automatic model-to-model transformation could, on the one hand, support a flexible and customisable software development process and on the other hand, offer a complementary approach to the definition of a common metamodel. One opportunity to build interoperable agents is illustrated in Figure 1. The major aim is to specify a PIM for SOA (PIM4SOA) and transfer included concepts to the Metamodel specifying holons on the PIM-level1 for agent architectures. In a second step, the concepts of this holon metamodel can

---

1 At this point it is necessary to mention that the terms PIM and PSM are relative to the application domain.

then be mapped to various tools for designing agents on the PSM-level. If a mapping from the PIM-SOA to some particular agent development tool is feasible, (i) interoperable agents could be derived and (ii) circumstances could be defined under which given agent models are interoperable according to the PIM4SOA. In the further parts of this section, the single platform levels are discussed in more detail.

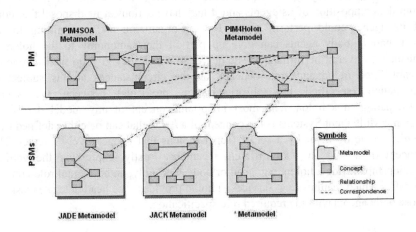

Figure 1. *Mapping metamodel concepts between the PIM-SOA, PIM-Holon and PSM-Holon*

3.1. *The PIM-SOA*

In general, a service is seen as a collaboration of a set of interaction roles. A collaboration use defines the application of a collaboration in a particular context and includes the binding of roles to entities. Collaborations are composable and a composite collaboration specifies the use of collaborations. The responsibilities in a composite collaboration are defined by roles, where binary collaborations have two roles (requester and provider). For detailed information regarding the PIM-SOA I would like to refer to Fischer *et al.* (2006).

3.2 *The PIM-Holon*

Agents acting in an organizational structure can (i) encapsulate complexity of the subsystems by simplifying representation and design and (ii) modularise functionalities providing the basis for rapid development and incremental deployment. To model organizational aspects, we use the concept of a holonic agent or holon as introduced in (Fischer *et al.*, 2003 and Hahn 2004). These concepts are inspired by the idea of recursive or self-similar structures in biological systems (Koestler 1967). In this domain, a superholon consists of parts called subholons, which in turn may be superholons themselves and thus introduce recursion as a modelling technique. Any holon that is part of a whole is thought to contribute to achieving the goals of this superior whole. To the outside, each holon is represented by a distinguished head (an atomic agent) which coordinates the activities of the holon. Apart from the head, each holon consist of a (possibly empty) set of team members, called body agents. The holonic agent may have capabilities that emerge from the composition of its agents and it may have actions at its disposal that none of its agents could perform alone. By self-organizing and committing to the participation, body agents can give up part of their autonomy to the holon to enhance it's overall performance. The degree to which they give up their autonomy is not fixed in advance but depends on the circumstances and is subject to negotiation (specified by self-organization protocols) between the agents participating in a holon. The most important concept of any model describing Holonic Multiagent Systems is the concept of a *holon* that can be either defined by a single atomic *agent* or by a set of (super-)holons that cooperatively interact. The concept of a *role* has two different meanings: Firstly, expressing the vertical relationships inside a holon, e.g. head or body. Secondly, an horizontal role concept specifies which features (e.g. services) a holon provides. The head delegates tasks to those body agents with the required role specification.

3.3 *The PSM-Holon*

Several tools already exist to implement agents and MAS, respectively (e.g. JADE (Bellifemine *et al.*, 2001)) that can be called platform specific. In a first step, we concentrate on JACK Intelligent Agents[2] that is an extension of the Java designed to provide additional programming constructs and concepts for developing complex applications. It is based on the Beliefs, Desires and Intentions model (Bratman 1997) and previous practical implementations of such systems (Huber 1999). The BDI agent model is an event-driven execution model providing both reactive and proactive behaviour. In this model, an agent has certain beliefs about the environment, desires to achieve, and plans describing how to achieve certain activated goals. The BDI architecture is recognized as one of more successfully implemented architecture for developing complex systems in dynamic and error-prone environments (Georgeff *et al.*, 1999). A JACK agent has a library of plans, where a plan is an explanation of how to achieve a particular goal (how to handle an event in JACK). Each agent could have several plans specifying how to reach the same goal using different strategies. This is one of the key characteristics of the BDI architecture that enables an agent to select alternative approaches in the case a particular strategy (plan) fails. JACK also provides support for team-oriented programming which provides a unique collaboration model that is particularly powerful for large scale applications with hierarchical structures. The core part of the team-oriented programming approach is the concepts of a *team* that can be either

---

2 http://www.agentsoftware.com.au/

an atomic agent or illustrated by a set of (sub-)teams. The concept *role* in a team specifies which actions and plans the team is able to perform. Detailed information regarding the JACK metamodel is given in (Fischer *et al.*, 2006).

4. Research hypotheses

The long term goal is to achieve the development of a holon-oriented mechanism to automate the process and the execution of service compositions and thus an approach to organize and orchestrate MAS on a generic basis as discussed in the AgentLink Roadmap (Luck *et al.* 2005). In detail, we concentrate on the following research hypotheses and goals, respectively:

Service Composition in HMS: The process of self-organization in HMS allows to dynamically couple service in an effectively and efficiently manner. The horizontal and recursive structure of holons allow an effective process management, where a head agent can decompose a process with respect to the knowledge and capabilities of its body holons (agents). Consequently, a process has not to be choreographed between independent holons, reducing (minimizing) the risk of interaction failures and thus increasing the performance of dynamic service composition.

Improving the Quality of Service (QoS): Mechanisms to improve QoS are explored as well as for service composition in several research projects. A key benefit of a holon-oriented approach could be a proactive handling of failures that may be encountered at run-time when composing services. Such a failure handling approach improves the quality of combined services. Besides monitoring the execution process, applying social structures and mechanisms (for instance reputation as discussed in (Hahn *et al.*, to appear) can enhance to dynamically discover competent service providers. Aspects of quality of service compositions relate to drop-out safety, performance and reliability.

Model-driven Development of Holonic MAS: The specification of an adequate mechanism to generically develop social structures on the MAS macro-level (see (Fischer and Florian 2005) for a detailed discussion) as already discussed in (Cohen and Levesque 1991) is one research challenge in Distributed Artificial Intelligence. Applying MDD to the development of executable agent platforms could be an interesting solution to this problem as the development process on the one hand, could be enriched by concepts and views of SOA and on the other hand, could be simplified by concentrating on modelling instead of the implementation process of agent systems. Additionally, the use of MDD techniques allows developing interoperable agents.

5. Research challenges

Composing Services in HMS: The composition of atomic services in agent-based environments requires three steps: Firstly, the order in which atomic services are executed has to be defined. Secondly, the atomic services have to be executed in that specified order and thirdly, the execution process has to be monitored to prevent failures. By transferring service-oriented architectures to HMS, the question how to self-organize has additionally to be answered.

Planning Process: A complex service that has to be provided by a holon must be analysed to detect dependencies between single services. In each iteration, (i) the composite service is decomposed into finer services (which again could be a complex service) and (ii) a set of competent body agents is identified (according to their horizontal role) that are able to provide this service. If a potential set of providers is found, the iteration stops for this service. If a particular service cannot be (i) assigned to some body agent and (ii) further decomposed (i.e. the service is atomic), the required service is outsourced, i.e., delegated to an agent outside the holon. After identifying a set of adequate service provider, the holon head delegates the service to the best provider that owns the necessary role (reputation and trust represents one selection criteria). The aim of the delegation/selection process is to minimize service dependencies on a high-level of the holon, in order to minimize interaction failures and to optimise the execution order as independent services can be executed in parallel. The holon head plans the execution order with respect to actual dependencies.

Execution Process: After planning the workflow, the execution starts according to the planned order sequence. The output of the service execution (e.g. information) is sent to the next service provider using interaction/communication patterns.

Monitoring Process: During the execution process, a controlling instance (e.g. holon head) monitors the workflow. If failures (like the drop-out of particular service providers) are detected, new service providers offering same qualities have to be discovered. On the basis of particular selection criteria, the head delegates failing services to competent provider agents and (re-)start the execution order on the basis of not yet executed services. The produced plan may differ from the original as (i) new provider agents are engaged and (ii) the input from already executed services may allow re-arranging and optimising the execution sequence. Finally, the services are executed according to the arranged order.

Self-organization in HMS: The process of self-organizing has already been investigates in (Hahn 2004) and need to be adapted to SOA. Adapting means that autonomous agents should have the possibility to firstly, proactively initiate the creation of a holon if a complex service is requested and secondly, to (re-)structure in order to optimise the orchestration process if the current structure does not seem to be appropriate for actual service requests. In both cases, self-organization protocols have to be specified that allow negotiating between the entities as those may possible loose parts of their autonomy.

Model-Driven Development of HMS: The challenges in an MDD process are in general to map the concepts of one metamodel to the concepts of another. Although a mapping between the concepts of service-oriented architectures and agent technologies seems to be feasible as already pointed out in (Fischer *et al.*, 2006), the transfer of the dynamic process model has to be investigated in detail. For instance, interactions in SOA are specified from a centralistic point of view (e.g. interaction protocols). In contrast, in JACK, the interaction between agents is event-driven and thus specified from the perspective of an atomic agent. In a first step, the MDD process should be considered as static, further investigations should evaluate the impacts of dynamic MDD on agent technologies.

6. Discussion

As business processes, specified as workflows and executed with services, need to be adaptive and flexible, approaches are needed to facilitate this evolution. The methodology of this paper has outlined this concern by designing interoperable holonic agents able to adapt on the functionalities and requirements of services in a flexible manner. Agent technology and in particular the holonic approach allows to establish a loose coupling between agents, the implementation is neutral and does not depend on particular technologies as requested by Singh and Huhns (2005). Additionally, holons are flexible to configure and further the interaction and cooperation between agents. Our main hypothesis is that efficient and effective (web) service composition can be achieved by better understanding how distributed and partial knowledge about the availability and capabilities of services and the environment in which they are expected to operate, can be shared among interacting and cooperating agents that perform the composed service. Self-organizing holons can adapt on the most adequate structure that potentially reduces the risk of failures during interaction to optimise the orchestration process and thus QoS. Social mechanisms like reputation may enhance the service discovery in the holon and improve the quality of service as the risk of delegating tasks to incompetent service providers decreases. Basing on the MDD framework, the development of generic social structures is feasible that (i) automatically adapts on changing descriptions of an SOA and (ii) can be executed on various agent development tools.

7. References

Bellifemine, F., Poggi, A., Rimassa, G., JADE: A FIPA2000 compliant agent development environment. *Agents.* (2001) 216-217

Bratman, M.E., *Intentions, Plans, and Practical Reason,* Cambridge, MA (1987)

Casati, F., Shan, M., Dynamic and adaptive composition of e-services. *Information Systems* 26 (2001) 143-163

Cohen, P., Levesque, H., Teamwork. *Special Issue on Cognitive Science and Artificial Intelligence* 25(4) (1991) 487-512

Depke, R., Heckel, R., Küster, J. In: *Agent-Oriented Modeling with Graph Transformation. Springer*, Berlin *et al.* (2001) 120-150

Fischer, K., Elveseater, B., Berre, A.J., Hahn, C., Madrigal-Mora, C., Zinnikus, I., Modeldriven design of interoperable agents. In: *Proceedings of the I-ESA Workshop*

Fischer, K., Florian, M. In: *Contribution of Socionics to the Scalability of Complex Social Systems: Introduction.* Springer- Verlag, Berlin *et al.* (2005)

Fischer, K., Schillo, M., Siekmann, J., Holonic multiagent systems: The foundation for the organization of multiagent systems. *Proceedings of the First International Conference on Applications of Holonic and Multiagent Systems,* Berlin *et al.*, Springer (2003) 71-80

Georgeff, M., Pell, B., Pollack, M., Tambe, M., Wooldridge, M., The belief-desire-intention model of agency. *Proceedings of Agents, Theories, Architectures and Languages.* (1999)

Hahn, C., Fley, B., Florian, M., Self-regulation through social institutions: A framework for the design of open agent-based electronic marketplaces. *Computational and Mathematical Organization Theory* (to appear)

Hahn, C.: A detailed Analysis of Organizational Forms for Holonic Multiagent Systems. Master's thesis, Fachbereich Informatik, Universität des Saarlandes (2004)

Huber, M.J., JAM: a BDI-theoretic mobile agent architecture. In: *Proceedings of the Third International Conference on Autonomous Agents,* (1999) 236-243

Jayatilleke, G., Padgham, L., Winikoff, M. In: *Towards a Component-Based Development Framework for Agents.* Springer-Verlag, Berlin *et al.* (2004) 183-197

Koehler, J., Hauser, R., Sendall, S., Wahler, M., Declarative techniques for model-driven business process integration. *IBM Systems Journal* 44(1) (2005)

Koehler, J., Srivastava, B., Web service composition: Current solutions and open problems. In *ICAPS 2003 Workshop on Planning for Web Services.* (2003)

Koestler, A., *The Ghost in the Machine.* Hutchinson & Co, London (1967)

Luck, M., McBurney, P., Preist, C., Agent Technology: Enabling Next Generation Computing AgentLink (2005). Electronically available, http://www.agentlink.org/roadmap/

McIlraith, S., Son, T., Adopting golog for composition of semantic web services. In: *Proceedings of the International Conference on Knowledge Representation and Reasoning* (KR2002). (2002) 482-493

Perini, A., Susi, A. In: Developing Tools for Agent-Oriented Visual Modeling. Volume 3187 of *Lecture Notes in Artificial Intelligence.* Springer-Verlag, Berlin *et al.* (2004) 169-182

Pires, P., Benevides, M., Mattoso, M. In *Building reliable web services compositions.* Springer-Verlag, Berlin *et al.* (2003) 59-72

Rao, A.S., Georgeff, M.P., BDI-agents: from theory to practice. In Lesser, V., ed.: *Proceedings of the First Intl. Conference on Multiagent Systems,* AAAI/MIT Press (1995)

Sheng, Q., Benatallah, B., Dumas, M., Mak, E.: Self-Serv, A platform for rapid composition of web services in a peer-to-peer environment. *Proceedings of the 28th International Conference on Very Large Databases.* (2002)

Singh, M., Huhns, M., *Service Oriented Architecture: Semantics, Processes, Agents.* Wiley John & Sons, Chichster, West Sussex, UK (2005)

Tambe, M., Towards flexible teamwork. *Journal of Artificial Intelligence Research 7* (1997) 83-124

Wooldridge, M. In: *Intelligent agents.* The MIT Press (2001) 27-77

Models simulation and interoperability using MDA and HLA

Hind El Haouzi

Centre de Recherche en Automatique de Nancy (CRAN UMR 7039), Nancy University, CNRS
F 54506 Vandoeuvre les Nancy, France
Hind.elhaouzi@ cran.uhp-nancy.fr

ABSTRACT: *In the manufacturing context, there have been numerous efforts to use modeling and simulation tools and techniques to improve manufacturing efficiency over the last four decades. While an increasing number of manufacturing system decisions are being made based on the use of models, their use is still sporadic in many manufacturing environments. Our paper advocates for an approach combining MDA (model driven architecture) and HLA (High Level Architecture), the IEEE standard for modeling and simulation, in order to overcome the deficiencies of current simulation methods at the level of interoperability and reuse.*

KEY WORDS: *interoperability, distributed vs. centralised decisions, discrete events simulation.*

1. Introduction

Today manufacturing systems need to be reactive to internal disturbances (e.g. machine breakdown) as well as external disturbances (e.g. economic changes, changing demand, and product adaptation). Consequently research in manufacturing system control has moved away from traditional centralized approaches where decision making is hierarchically broadcast from the higher decisional levels down to the operational units to more distributed architectures. In this way, hierarchical architectures promote production control by distributing every decision capacities in autonomous entities, without any centralized view of the shop floor status. To ensure consistency of decision making, more pragmatic approaches are based on hybrid control which combines the predictability of the centralized control with the agility and robustness against disturbances of the distributed control.

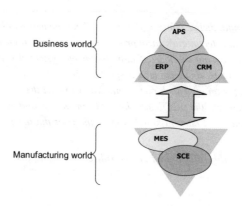

Figure 1. *Business and manufacturing separation*

In this paper, we assume that the enterprise environment is composed of two separated worlds (see Figure 1): *(i)* On one hand, a business world in which centralized decisions concerning the whole enterprise are taken, *(ii)* On the other hand, a manufacturing world responsible of distributed real time decisions in order to control and execute manufacturing processes of shop-floor level. This separation is due to several reasons; the most important is the difference of objectives and rules used in the decision making process. In the figure 1, we tried to position some of the major applications in the enterprise: Manufacturing Execution System (MES), Supply Chain Execution (SCE), Advanced Planning Scheduling system (APS), Enterprise Resource Planning (ERP), Customer Relationship Management (CRM) (Baïna *et al.*, 2005).

The separation of the two worlds implies separation of the models representing each world. Thus, we obtain models representing different universes of discourse (business/manufacturing), and using different concepts, different modeling rules and concerns.

In the manufacturing context, there have been numerous efforts to use modeling and simulation tools and techniques to improve manufacturing efficiency over the last four decades. While an increasing number of manufacturing system decisions are being made based on the use of models, their use is still sporadic in many manufacturing environments. We believe that there is a real need for pervasive use of modeling and simulation for decision support in current and future manufacturing systems. There are several challenges that need to be addressed by the simulation community to achieve this vision.

In this paper, we highlight two major challenges: models interoperability (synchronization, coordination and coherence) and reusability in the decision taking process. To handle these challenges, several issues are to be solved; for example, data integration, time management and synchronization between different simulation models (distributed or centralized).

2. Towards simulation

In fact, models are intended to support management decisions about the system and a single model will often not be capable of supporting all decisions. Rather, different decisions require different models because various aspects of the design and operation of the system will be important for the questions being asked. While spreadsheet and queuing models are useful for answering basic questions about manufacturing systems, discrete event simulation models are often needed to answer more specific questions about how a complex manufacturing system will perform [1]. In general, simulation is a practical methodology for understanding the high-level dynamics of a complex manufacturing system. According to (Yucesan *et al.*, 2000), simulation has several strengths including:

– Time compression: the potential to simulate years of real system operation in a much shorter time.

– Component integration: the ability to integrate complex system components to study their interactions.

– Risk avoidance: hypothetical or potentially dangerous systems can be studied without the financial or physical risks that may be involved in building and studying a real system.

– Physical scaling: the ability to study much larger or smaller versions of a system.

– Repeatability: the ability to study different systems in identical environments or the same system in different environments.

– Control: everything in a simulated environment can be precisely monitored and exactly controlled.

In our context, complex simulations involve individual simulations of several different types of systems (Business and Manufacturing), combined with other aspects of the total environment to be simulated (such as interactions...). Often simulations of some of these components already exist, having been developed for a different purpose, and they could be used in a new simulation. Unfortunately, it is often necessary to make extensive modifications to adapt the component simulation model so that it can be integrated into a new combined simulation. Thus, traditional simulation models often lack two desirable properties: reusability and interoperability.

Reusability, as the name suggests, means that component simulation models can be reused in different simulation scenarios and applications Interoperability implies an ability to combine component simulations on distributed computing platforms of different types, often with real-time operation.

3. The federation mechanism

3.1. *A theoretical approach*

In order to enable the simulation of all different models of the enterprise as a whole, we need to establish a global federated model which will represent the most important aspects and concepts of each specific partial model of the enterprise. This federated model is an instantiation of a federated meta-model where concepts from different universes of discourse can coexist (business, manufacturing, etc.).

Several models interoperability and federation approaches exist; UEML (Berio *et al.*, 2003; Panetto *et al.*, 2004) is one of these approaches. The main problem with the use of UEML in this context is that in order to achieve our first objective which is simulation, we should be able to use UEML models in simulation tools, and this is not possible currently. To encompass this problem, in this section, we introduce a generic approach for interoperability based on a model driven architecture (MDA) (Mellor *et al.*, 2004). Figure 2 shows the four-level ontological approach levels for modeling that are used in the MDA. As it is explained in (Lemesle, 1998, Namenko *et al.*, 2003), the lowest level M^0 presents different subjects for modeling, called universe of discourse. The level M^1 contains different models of each universe of discourse. The next level M^2 presents domain specific meta-models: one meta-model for each of the domains of interest relevant for the M^1 models. And finally, M^3 level presents a meta-meta-model designed to allow the definition of all the existing in the scope of the meta-models.

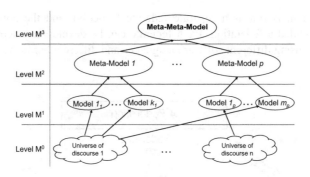

Figure 2. *The four-level ontological approach*

In the case of MDA, each application can be considered as a specific use of a model defined in the M^1 level which is based on meta-model defined in M^2. Application interoperability can then be resolved either by interconnecting applications together using a level M^0 exclusive reasoning, or by establishing a top-down approach for resolving applications interoperability based on the four levels of the MDA. Several research works have been done in order to resolve meta-models mapping problems. (Baïna *et al.*, 2006) explain how models transformation can be resolved by establishing transformation rules between meta-models. Transformation rules define a mapping that guides model transformations from the instances of the source meta-model to instances of the target meta-model.

To ensure interoperability between applications that handle those different meta-models, we should first define mappings that enable transforming one instance of a meta-model in an instance of another meta-model. Let us consider two applications A and B; A and B are interoperable, if and only if there is a mapping from the meta-model of A (M_A) to the meta-model of B (M_B) and a mapping form M_B to M_A. Those mappings ensure that we can build a model compatible with A from a model used by B (and vice versa).

The federation mechanism in the MDA context consists on defining a unified meta-model in the M2 level. This federated meta-model is the interoperability gateway between concepts defined in different universes of discourse, in our case the business and manufacturing worlds.

3.2. *High level architecture*

In this section, we describe an implementation approach of simulation models. As said previously, within the new manufacturing system context, two major problems are encountered by simulation developers; reusability and interoperability. In simulation literature the High Level Architecture (Chance *et al.*, 1997) seems the one partial solution to those challenges. In the HLA, each simulation or other software system is run as a separate federate (process), and the collection of all federates is called a federation. Each federate can be developed independently and implemented using different software languages and different hardware platforms.

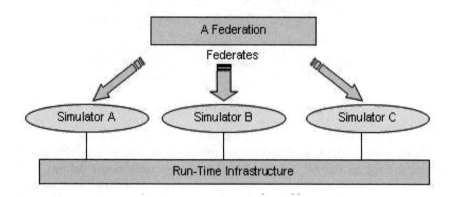

Figure 4. *The four-level ontological approach*

The HLA Baseline Definition was completed in 1996 and was adopted as the Facility for Distributed Simulation Systems 1.0 by the Object Management Group (OMG) in 1998. The HLA was approved as an open standard through the Institute of Electrical and Electronic Engineers (IEEE) - IEEE Standard 1516 (IEEE 2000).

The HLA provides a general framework within which simulation developers can structure and describe their simulation applications. It consists of three components: Federation Rules, Interface Specification, and Object Model Template (OMT).

3.2.1. *Federation rules*

At the highest level, the HLA consists of a set of 10 HLA rules which must be obeyed if a federate or federation is to be regarded as HLA compliant. The HLA rules are divided into two groups consisting of 5 rules for HLA federations and 5 rules for HLA federates. The federation rules establish the ground rules for creating a federation, including documentation requirements, object representation; data interchange interfacing requirements and attribute ownership. The federate rules deal with the individual federates. They cover documentation, control of and transfer of relevant object attributes, and time-management.

3.2.2. Interface specification

The interface specification defines a standard for a Run-Time Infrastructure (RTI). The RTI is software that conforms to the specification but is not itself part of the specification. It provides the software services (Time management, Federation management…), which are necessary to support an HLA compliant simulation. Different versions of the RTI are possible but it difficult to find Open source and free version.

3.2.3. The Object Model Template

Reusability and interoperability require that all objects and interactions managed by a federate, and visible outside the federate, should be specified in detail and with a common format. The Object Model Template (OMT) provides a standard for documenting HLA Object Model information and defines the Federation Object Model (FOM), the Simulation (or Federate) Object Model (SOM) and the Management Object Model (MOM).

4. On-going work

This paper presents ongoing work of the first year PhD student Hind El Haouzi in collaboration with PhD Student Salah Baïna who works essentially on enterprise models interoperability using the MDA approach. The paper does not expose solutions but tries essentially to highlights major problems encountered in the domain of distributed models simulation.

On-going work aims to combining both approaches MDA and HLA to obtain a framework (Analysis and technical tools) for ensuring interoperability between Business and Manufacturing Models. The discrete-event simulation will be used to evaluate decision impacts in both levels. As a case study, the framework will be a useful support to integrate Identification technologies (RFID) in Trane group legacy system.

5. References

Berio G., et al. D3.2:/Core constructs, architecture and development strategy/, UEML TN IST – 2001 – 34229, March 2003.

Baïna S., Panetto H., and Morel G. Holon-oriented B2M process modelling approach for applications interoperability in manufacturing systems environment, Proceedings of the IFAC World Congress, July 4-7, 2005, Prague, Czech Republic, ISBN: 0-08-045108-X.

Baïna S., Panetto H., and Benali K. (2006). A product oriented modelling concept: Holons for systems synchronisation and interoperability. *Proceedings of the 8th International Conference on Enterprise Information Systems (ICEIS'2006)*. May 23-27, 2006 Paphos, Cyprus.

Chance, F., Robinson, J., and J. Fowler, "Supporting manufacturing with simulation: model design, development, and deployment", Proceedings of the 1996 Winter Simulation Conference, San Diego, CA, 1996, p. 1-8.

Lemesle, R. "Transformation Rules Based on Meta-Modelling". *EDOC'98*, La Jolla, California, 3-5 November 1998, p. 113-122.

Mellor S.J., Kendall S., Uhl A. and Weise D. *Model Driven Architecture*, Addison-Wesley Pub Co, March 2004, ISBN: 0201788918.

Panetto H., Berio G., Benali K., Boudjlida N., and Petit M. A Unified Enterprise Modelling Language for enhanced interoperability of Enterprise Models. *Proceedings of the 11th IFAC INCOM2004 Symposium*, April 5th-7th, Bahia, Brazil, Elsevier.

Naumenko, A. Wegmann, A. "Two Approaches in System Modelling and Their Illustrations with MDA and RM-ODP". In *ICEIS 2003, the 5th International Conference on Enterprise Information Systems* (2003), p. 398-402.

The Institute of Electrical and Electronics Engineers, Inc., IEEE Std 1516-2000. IEEE Standard for Modeling and Simulation (M&S) High Level Architecture (HLA) Framework and Rules. 11 December 2000.

Yücesan, E. and Fowler, J., "Simulation Analysis of Manufacturing and Logistics Systems", Encylclopedia of Production and Manufacturing Management, Kluwer Academic Publishers, Boston, P. Swamidass ed., p. 687-697., 2000.

A Study of Aspect-Driven Transformations to Facilitate Model Driven Development

Pulitha Liyanagama

University of Kent
Canterbury
CT2 7NF
United Kingdom
pll4@kent.ac.uk

ABSTRACT: This paper addresses cross cutting concerns in model transformations and identifies a set of requirements for an aspect-driven transformation framework with specific emphasis on non-functional requirements. Model Driven Development (MDD) currently concentrates on mapping platform independent model elements to technology-specific, platform-specific concepts and vice versa. However, while there is much work on transforming models or meta-models along an axis of specialisation/generalization, little emphasis is given for managing cross cutting concerns within these transformations. This paper presents a case study of such a transformation and identifies requirements for future model transformations systems.

KEY WORDS: Model driven architecture, transformation, aspect modelling.

1. Introduction

Although Aspect Oriented Programming (AOP) and Model Driven Development (MDD) were initiated from quite dissimilar viewpoints, with the former emphasising programming while the latter focuses on modelling, there are many facets which are common to them and the two techniques are used as means for almost identical ends. Recent developments in both fields make it even more difficult to distinguish between MDD and AOP. Upon closer inspection it is evident that the two methodologies influence each other in such a way that they are being pushed even closer towards each other. However, model transformations, which arguably forms the core of the MDD initiative (Kalnins *et al.*, 2004) is yet to fully exploit the potential benefits of cross cutting concerns for productivity gains, which usually take the form of higher levels of reusability and interoperability. This paper reports progress in identifying a model transformation methodology that draws on the concepts of aspect-oriented software development in order to realise the benefits of cross cutting concerns in model transformations with specific emphasis on non-functional aspects.

1.1. *Model transformations in MDD*

MDD's potential advantages lie in its ability to shift complexity away from developers and into a tool chain which handles the model transformations. Therefore, a mechanism to perform effective and efficient model transformations is imperative to MDD's success (Kutvonen 2004). While technologies such as the Meta Object Facility (MOF) (MOF 2002) and UML (UML 2004) are well-established foundations on which to build meta-models and models respectively, there is as yet no well-established standard for describing model transformations across and between different levels of abstraction within the MDD modelling cycle. The need for such a standard was the instigating factor behind the OMG's QVT (Queries, Views, Transformations) Request For Proposals (RFP) (DSTC 2004). QVT proposals were intended to be based on MOF to handle transformations between models as well as metamodels. Many transformation frameworks, some academic-driven and others industry-initiated have emerged as a response to these proposals.

1.2. *Separation of concerns through aspects*

The definition of an "aspect" has evolved over time. The current standing definition describes an aspect as a unit that is defined in terms of partial information from other units (Kiczales *et al.*, 1997). Building diverse systems requires simultaneous manipulation of many such aspects. Some of these aspects can be considered as non-functional e.g. security, quality of service, reliability, and manageability while others may be more precise functional concerns such as persistence, concurrency control, caching, and error recovery. The separation of functional from the non-functional can only be determined through a conscious designer decision and may vary from one system to another (Linington 2004).

Since conventional programming techniques are centred on producing a direct sequence of instructions, they require the developer to be aware of all such aspects throughout the programming process (Clark 1997). The developer must explicitly blend the instructions to achieve these concerns with the code for realising the primary application functions. This produces a complex and usually cluttered set of code which in turn leads to systems which are erroneous and difficult-to-maintain.

Emerging software development techniques allow richer specifications of programs and better modularization of these specifications. One of these techniques is Model Driven Development, but Aspect-Oriented Software Development (AOSD) provides another approach. AOSD technologies offer mechanisms for separation of concerns primarily at a linguistic level, along with implementation techniques for weaving these separate concerns into complete systems.

Many projects and tools have emerged to make use of the AOSD paradigm (Kiczales et al., 2005). They provide features to dynamically modify a static model to include the code needed to fulfil the secondary requirements without having to modify the original static model.

1.3. Modelling aspects

Separation of concerns is a fundamental software engineering principle that should be applied throughout all stages of the software development lifecycle. Although aspect oriented programming shows much promise in accommodating this principle, most work in this area has been concentrated on implementation. Although lately the focus has been shifting to other levels of the software development life cycle, very little work exist yet on separation of cross cutting concerns based on aspects at the design level (Moreira et al., 2002). Existing work span from proposed UML profiles to facilitate aspect oriented modelling (Moreno 2004) (Groher et al., 2004) to proprietary modelling standards based mostly on other existing modelling practices with extensions to represent specific aspect information (Moreira et al., 2002). Hardly any of these solutions have been made available as well established frameworks with tangible tool implementations.

Much significance has been given to mapping platform independent model elements to technology-specific, platform-specific concepts and vice versa (OMG 2001) in MDD. However, while there is much work done on transforming models or meta-models along an axis of specialisation vs. generalization, little or no emphasis is given to managing cross cutting concerns within model transformations.

This paper argues that addressing cross cutting concerns would play an integral role in MDD's future. The benefits of such emphasis in model transformations can be substantial. They come in the form of increased interoperability and reuse of models. Hence, there is a need to introduce a process of separating concerns in model transformations. This paper identifies requirements for such a transformation framework through a case study.

2. Simple order processing system with checker based security aspect

A set of case studies has been defined in order to gain a better understanding of the nature of aspect modelling and to build a set of reference points for analysis and future evaluation. The first case study is a simple order processing system with a straightforward authentication or checker based security mechanism. The case study consists of two sets of models, both based on an UML meta-model. The first set describes an order processing system with limited functionality allowing just client login, orders placement and exit. The second will represent a checker based security model. Only a subset of the full requirements of the two aspects will be exposed in the models in order to keep them as simple and as straightforward as possible. The aim in this example is to define an aspect-driven transformation is needed to refine the business model by applying the security controls expressed by the checker model.

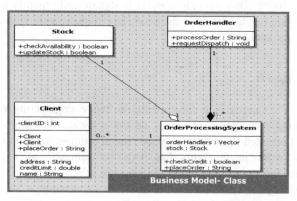

Figure 1. *Class model of the order processing system*

Figure 1 shows the class model of the main business. A client is uniquely identified by a clientID and can place an order on the order processing system through the placeOrder operation which provides the item details and their respective quantities through the operation parameters. The order processing system, then dispatches the order to an available orderHandler which carries out the tasks of updating the stock levels and requesting a dispatch of the items from the suppliers. The sequence of events within an order cycle is illustrated in the sequence model of the business process as shown in Figure 2. The model depicted in Figure 3 is based on the security aspect. The properties of this would subsequently be merged with the business logic through a selected transformation framework to form an aggregate model that represents a more refined design. A checker-based security model was chosen for this purpose due to its relative simplicity. The checker functionality simply dictates that each interaction between two entities with different domain values (hence, a domain boundary between them) would be intercepted by a checker that will check a username and a password.

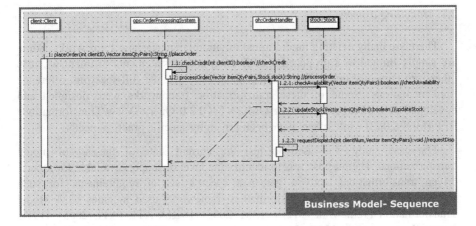

Figure 2. *Sequence model of the order processing system*

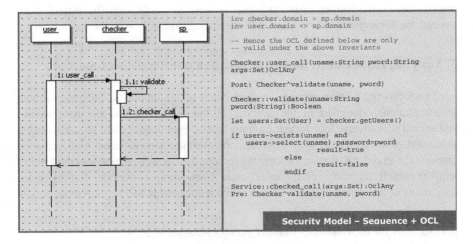

Figure 3. *Sequence model and the relevant OCL constraints*
of the checker based security model

The output of the transformation process should be an aggregate model where each association which crosses a security domain boundary will be redirected through a checker object that acquires its implementation logic from the security model checker class. Further modifications to the parameters of the operations which are involved within the association are also required. Two additional string parameters, username and password, would contain the access information that would be validated by the checker objects. With this scenario in mind, we now look at the practicality of performing such a transformation using existing model transformation frameworks in order to better understand the requirements of aspect-driven transformations.

2.1. *Modelling aspects*

There are many existing model transformation languages and frameworks. Some are simply limited to a proposed specification and/or statements of intent whereas others are currently under development or already provide full-spectrum reference implementations. Some of these transformation frameworks were designed and developed as a direct response for OMG's MOF2.0 Query /View/Transformations RFP (MOF 2002) while others have been driven by specific practical needs.

The case study was used to test the current state of the art of model transformations. The purpose was to identify the level of support available for aspect-driven transformations and so gather a specific set of requirements for such transformations. The model transformation frameworks used includes IBM Model Transformation Framework (MTF) (IBM, 2005), INRIA ATL (ATL 2005), DSTC Tefkat (Lawley *et al.*, 2004), MOLA (Kalnins *et al.*, 2004) and YATL (Patrascoiu 2003). It is not the intention of this paper to give a detailed account of each individual transformation mechanism. And any such summary would soon be out of date. Instead, the subsequent section goes on to extract requirements from the tool analysis.

3. Analysing requirements for an aspect-driven transformation framework

The following section provides a description of requirements, for aspect-driven transformations, identified in the analysis of the QVT-RFP and the case studies considered with diverse transformation frameworks. Each requirement was analysed in detail and cross referenced with different implementations on different transformation frameworks in order to further validate the requirement as well as to assess the level of support which currently exist under each framework. However, due to space limitations of this paper, a generic sketch of the requirements will be presented.

3.1. *Support for many-to-many model transformations*

Model transformations based on functional/non-functional aspects and their reverse transformations tend to involve combining models and separating them respectively. Therefore, the ability to define mappings across multiple inputs and output models is an indispensable requirement in aspect-driven transformations. The transformation language syntax should facilitate importing of multiple models into a single transformation module and subsequent addressing and working with elements of distinct models at a mapping-rule level. Currently available model transformation languages take slightly different paths to dealing with multiple input or output models. The IBM Model Transformation Framework (IBM, 2005) is based on a rule execution pattern based on the ordering of rules starting at an entry rule, very much similar to an imperative language. The source and target models and their meta-models are defined through ecore. The model details are passed into the entry rule of the transformation through standard EMF data structures (DSTC 2004).

A launch configuration provides the mapping between the parameters and the ecore models. A specific model is accessed through the parameter variable which represents it (see Figure 4).

```
import ws "http:///com/ibm/mtf/model/workspace.ecore"

relate simpleEntryRule(ws:IFile model1, ws:IFile model2, ws:IFile model3)
{
            mapClasses(over model1.resource.contents, over model3.resource.contents ),
            ...
            ...
}
```

Figure 4. *Importing and accessing model elements into an entry rule in IBM MTF*

Tefkat utilises a more straightforward approach in defining the type of input-to-output model mapping as well as the meta-model types of each model. Each model defined in the A,B->X,Y style transformation declaration is mapped to corresponding meta models in its launch configuration. The models and the elements within them are accessed through an element@model syntax as shown in Figure 5.

```
TRANSFORMATION simpleTrans : uml1, uml2 -> uml3

//importing metamodel uml -piggybacked on ecore as simpleuml.ecore
IMPORT http://simpleuml

RULE SimpleRule(c1, c2)
 FORALL UMLClass@uml1 c1
 MAKE  UMLClass@uml3 c2
 SET   c2.name = c1.name
; ...
```

Figure 5. *Use of multiple input models and addressing model-specific elements in Tefkat*

ATLAS ATL (ATL 2005) uses a syntactically similar style to Tefkat, although with some variations. Unlike Tefkat it can only provide support for one-to-one or many-to-one style transformations. As a result, currently, ATL is unable to handle most of the transformations involving aspect-separation.

```
module simpleTrans;

create OUT : UML from IN1 : UML, IN2: UML;

rule simpleRule {
 from
 e : UML!Class (UML!Class.allInstancesFrom('IN1')->includes(e))
 to
 out : UML!Class ( ...
 }
```

Figure 6. *Addressing multiple source models in ATL*

Furthermore, as shown in Figure 6, ATL does not provide direct syntactic support for addressing elements of a specific input model and relies on specifying OCL like constraints. This introduces additional overhead in increased constraint checking at the underlying implementation level. However, ATL provides the model to meta-model mappings at the transformation module level. This communicates more useful information about the types of models utilised within the transformation.

Considering the above points an approach that combines Tefkat's versatility in dealing with multiple models with ATL's descriptive header style would be ideal (Figure 7). The ability to handle many-to-many model transformations is a requirement which is also closely related to the requirement of supporting reverse transformations and loop back support.

```
module simpleTrans;

create OUT1:UML, OUT2:UML from IN1: UML, IN2: UML;

rule simpleRule {
from
  e : IN1!Class (...
to
  out : OUT1!Class
  ( ...
  )
}
```

Figure 7. *An example of a modified ATL syntax to better handle*
multiple input and output models

3.2. *Capability to work across many meta-model types*

The transformation framework should be able to work with heterogeneous model types (models which are based on diverse meta-models). For example, the source/target models which serve as input for a transformation might be different from each other. Also the types of the source models and the types of the target models are mutually independent of each other.

One of the main aspirations of the Model Driven Development initiative is to provide unrestricted support for proprietary modelling techniques without binding the modellers to a specific modelling process. It is therefore reasonable to assume that the meta-model types, on which the models that the transformation framework needs to deal with, may vary considerably.

Since aspects may well be designed by different groups with different interests and different modelling techniques, it is likely that in many transformation instances there may be situations where the aspect based model convergence (or divergence in a reverse transformation) should be performed on models that are based on different meta-models. Therefore, the ability to tackle such situations is a very important requirement of the transformation framework.

Most available transformation languages use their own proprietary modelling standard as a base meta-model or use an already available industry standard. An example for such a standard is the MOF1.4 influenced EMF ecore model. Ecore is utilised by Tefkat, MTF and many others transformation languages as the means to bootstrap all other meta-model definitions. Although it is not entirely correct to assume all parties involved in MDE will use meta-models based on a common standard, it is practically difficult if not impossible to support all potential modelling methods, and a compromise must be reached. Within this trade-off between broader support and practical implementability, it would seem that the most sensible arrangement would be to base all meta-models on an already used technically sound meta-meta-model standard such as MOF1.4/2.0. Since ecore is an implementation of these standards, using ecore defined meta-models seem to be the most viable option.

3.3. *Increased support for reverse transformations*

The ability to track upwards or downwards in specialized to generalized states and back is an integral part of the MDE vision. Support for reverse transformations refers to the facility, not only to map elements from source to target models but also to perform a mapping from target to source without any information distortion in the process.

Besides the problems of implementing reverse transformations, integrating them into the modern iterative software development processes is a considerable challenge. In OMG's MDA terms, a Platform Specific Model (PSM) should contain enough information to build an executable application. However, in practice the generated PSMs tend to be skeletons that need to be modified manually and extended to get the end product. It is often necessary in iterative development to switch back to a model of higher abstraction. But to do so requires a mechanism of round-trip engineering build into the transformations; the mechanism usually preferred by existing frameworks tends to be reverse transformation (Weis et al, 2003). This means that all transformations that add specialization or generalization to the source model(s) must as far as possible be reversible. Hence, from an aspect oriented view point an effective transformation framework should be capable of merging models based on aspects (aspect-specialization) as well as separating them based on an aspect (aspect-generalization), so that existing aspects can be "unplugged" from models and new ones be added.

Reverse transformation support is probably one of the more challenging features to support in MDD. Due to the complexities involved in traceability links, rule ambiguities, and difficulty in maintaining synchronization it cannot always be guaranteed, particularly for large scale systems. One of the main issues in reverse transformations is the handling of soft models (i.e. Use case models) that are far less easily derived from a PSM than "hard" models such as class diagrams. And even the hard models are partially soft. This results in far too much detail been produced or produced in the wrong area.

As a result, when a reverse-transformation needs to be done without manual intervention from a model of lower level of abstraction (e.g. PSM) to a model of higher level of abstraction (e.g. PIM), it needs to involve machine-based abstraction. This is a subject area which is closely linked to artificial intelligence. Unfortunately, existing technology in this field does not seem to be mature enough to provide an efficient reverse-transformation mechanism (Weis *et al.*, 2003). Even if lossless reverse transformation mechanism can be implemented it would entail far too much complexity to be used on a generic software development process.

Some the existing model transformation languages such as DSTC Tefkat (Lawley *et al.*, 2004) and YATL (Patrascoiu 2003) provide Track expressions and Trace models that record the exact changes done by the transformation in the exact order in which they were executed and use that trace model as an input to the reverse transformation. Parallels can be drawn between these methods and techniques such as intention lists used in transactions processing. However, this method doesn't solve all the problems of reverse transformation as often there are cases of ambiguities which still exist.

Another noteworthy issue is how to deal with the trace model once it is made. Where does the trace model belong? Between two specific sets of models perhaps; but then if one of the models is modified the trace model would be invalidated. This is a whole new area of concern which has to do with change propagation and model inter-dependencies and would provide an interesting topic of many detailed discussions in itself.

3.4. *Resolving Inter-model dependencies*

A model may be correlated with other models in many facets by explicit or implicit constraint relations. For example, the object model of a particular system must correspond to its class model and vice-versa. Ideally any changes done to a model through a transformation must not contradict these constraints imposed by the related models. However, in transformations in general and aspect-driven transformations in particular, new elements are added to or existing elements removed or modified models. These changes result in inconsistent constraints across the design domain.

Any attempts to resolve such dependencies by transforming all related models is a difficult task that might even be counter productive to the entire modelling process. It would cause a ripple effect across many models and meta-levels that may lead to infinite recursions and loss of information due to unwanted changes. Further research is needed on this subject to deduce whether these dependencies need to be resolved or not. If these dependencies must be maintained across transformations, then all transformations must support not only a reverse transformation strategy but also a mechanism of identifying/listing and resolving cross-model correlations. When all factors are considered, implementing such a dependency resolution system seems a challenging task.

3.5. *Handling the trade-off between separation of concerns and adding aspect support at the model level*

In order to deal with aspect-transformations more effectively than it is done with existing model transformation frameworks, a clear and unambiguous extraction of aspect information from the model is needed. Such a mechanism would allow individual aspects to be dealt with efficiently within the transformation syntax and semantics. Better extraction of aspect detail would involve either adding more model artefacts to represent aspect information or pattern identification and replacement strategy or both. Introducing new model artefacts to represent aspect details is a relatively straightforward solution. However, it would force designers who are only concerned with a particular aspect (e.g. Business aspect) to deal with model elements representing other aspect types (e.g. security, resilience). Some means of encapsulating the unwanted detail from the designer must be introduced. If a design decision of including additional model artefacts to correspond to aspect information is taken, this might be resolvable through a trace model, but that would only devolve the responsibility to the trace model designer.

3.6. *Support for multi-step transformations*

As the case study examples illustrate, certain aspect weaving model transformations must be performed in a multi-stepped manner. Some transformations tend to be naturally multi-stepped while others need to be carried out as a sequence of transformations, largely due to the limitations of the transformation framework. However, there are situations where some of the intermediate steps in a model mapping sequence might violate the constraints defined in the source/target models. For example, if an additional control attribute (e.g. Domain Marker) was introduced to an object model within a transformation rule, the new object model resulting in the transformation will not correspond to the class constraints of the class model. This issue is closely related to the inter-model dependency problem discussed earlier. Even on a rule per rule basis, there needs to be some way of ensuring transitiveness of mappings across the intermediate model states. Research carried out in the area of rule ordering shows completely declarativeness cannot be achieved in practice. Hence, there needs to be some form of compromise. One solution would be to use a prioritisation scheme for rules.

4. Conclusion

This paper has addressed the need for MDD transformation tools to support aspect-driven transformations and compiled a set of requirements for such a mechanism. Based on these requirements a prototype transformations framework is currently being designed and developed with specific support for merging and separation of non-functional aspects. However, there are still basic issues to be resolved and the identification of requirements in itself is an iterative process. The prototype is essential in order to evaluate a pre-defined set of example scenarios as a means of identifying further requirements which would subsequently lead to producing a set of guidelines for a suitable model transformations methodology to promote re-use and interoperability within Model Driven Development.

5. References

http://www.omg.org/cgi-bin/apps/doc?ptc/04-10-02.pdf OMG

ATL, ATL Project Home page. http://www.sciences.univ-nantes.fr/lina/atl/

Clark R., Moreira A. Composition Patterns: An approach to designing reusable aspects *Software Technology and Engineering Practice* pp. 68-75, IEEE Computer Society, Los Alamitos, California 1997

DSTC, *"MOF Quey / View / Transformations: Second revised submission"*: DSTC, IBM, CBOP 2004

Groher I., Baumgarth T. Aspect Orientation from Design to Code *in Proceedings of the Workshop on Early Aspects*: Aspect-Oriented Requirements Engineering and Architecture Design; AOSD, March 2004

IBM *Model Transformation Framework Programmer's guide 1.0.0.* IBM Corp. 2005

Kalnins J. Barzdins E., Celms Basics of Model Transformation Language MOLA. *ECOOP (Workshop on Model Transformation and execution in the context of MDA)*, Oslo, 2004

Kiczales G., *et al. Aspect-Oriented Programming. ECOOP* 1997: 220-242

Kiczales G., Mezini M. Aspect-oriented programming and modular reasoning. *ICSE 2005*: 49-58

Kutvonen L. Relating MDA and inter-enterprise collaboration management. *2nd European Workshop on Model Driven Architecture*, 2004. pp. 84-88, University of Kent, 2004.

Lawley M, Duddy K, Gerber A, Raymond K. *Transformation: The Missing Link of MDA DSTC* 2004

Linington P. F. Model Driven Development and Non-functional Aspects. *Position statement for WMDD 2004 Workshop.*

MOF, *"MOF 2.0 Query/Views/Transformations RFP"*: http://www.omg.org/cgi-bin/doc?ad/ 2002-4-10/ 2002

Moreira A., Araujo J., Brito I, Rashid A. Aspect-oriented requirements with UML. *Workshop on Aspect-Oriented Modelling with UML*, University of Lancaster 2002

Moreno N., Vallecillo A. *What do we do with reuse in MDA?.* Dpto. De Lenguas y Ciencias de la Computacion, Universidad de Malaga

OMG, *"Overview and guide to OMG's architecture omg/03-06-01 (MDA Guide V1.0.1)"* http://www.omg.org/cgi-bin/apps/doc?omg/03-06-01.pdf> OMG

Patrascoiu O. *YATL: Yet Another Transformation Language.* Computing Laboratory, University of Kent 2003

UML2, *"UML 2.0 Superstructure FTF convenience document"* (ptc/04-10-02)

Weis T., Ulbrich A., Geihs K *Model Metamorphosis.* Berlin University of Technology 2003

Session 2:
Business Process Modelling

Workflow Reengineering through Log Event-based Analysis

Walid Gaaloul

LORIA - INRIA - CNRS - UMR 7503
BP 239, F-54506 Vandoeuvre-lès-Nancy Cedex, France

gaaloul@loria.fr

ABSTRACT: Engineering workflow applications are becoming more and more complex, involving numerous interacting business objects within processes. Analyzing the interaction structure of those complex applications will enable them to be well understood, controlled, and redesigned. In this paper, we describe mining techniques, which are able to discover a workflow model, and to improve its transactional behaviour from event based logs. First, we propose an algorithm to discover workflow patterns. Then, we propose techniques to discover activities transactional dependencies that allow us to mine workflow recovery techniques. Finally, based on this mining step, we use a set of rules to improve workflow design. Our approach has been implemented within our prototype WorkflowMiner.

KEY WORDS: workflow patterns, workflow mining, transactional workflow, business process reengineering, log analysis.

1. Introduction

In current organizations and businesses, a continuous push can be witnessed for increased diversification of services and products. This requires increasingly efficient and effective Business Process Management environments. The challenge for the managers and persons responsible for the process is to design a detailed and accurate model and control processes efficiently. However, modelling and controlling a process requires deep knowledge of the business process. And often, when process engineers are faced to the workflow implementing the process to validate the model, it turns out that the system has a different interpretation of the process model than they had expected and the process model as it was modelled is rejected. Indeed, the modelling errors are commonly not detected until the workflow model is performed. To achieve this goal, it is of critical importance to have a good understanding of the business process. Analyzing the interaction structure of those complex systems will enable them to be well understood, controlled and redesigned. Business support systems record different kinds of information for planning, budgeting, bill of materials, distribution, and warehousing flow of work, etc. Based on the running process, process-related data can be collected and certain analysis can be performed. The result of such analysis can provide input for (re)designing and re-engineering the business process. Indeed, Analyzing interactions of those complex systems will enable them to be well understood, controlled, and redesigned.

The work described in this is a contribution to these problems for workflow based process applications. Our aim is to develop a model (theory and tools) that allows the mining of concurrent and transactional workflow behaviour from event-based log. The idea is to reverse the process and to collect data at runtime to support process design and analysis. The information collected at runtime, usually recorded in a process log, can be used to derive a model explaining the events recorded. Our approach is close to reality by using data representing the actual events that took place to (re)design and re-engineer the business process. We based on works in the field of data mining generally, and the field of concurrence discovery specifically.

Our approach starts by collecting log information from workflow processes instances as they took place. Then, it builds, through statistical techniques, a graphical intermediary representation modelling elementary dependencies over workflow activities executions. These dependencies are then refined to discover workflow patterns. After that, as the handling workflow transactional behaviour remains a main problem to ensure a correct and a reliable execution, we have demonstrated in our work that the discovery, and the explanation of this behaviour, would enable to better understand and control workflow recovery. We have provided in our work mining techniques, which are able to improve its transactional behaviour from event based logs. These techniques discover transactional dependencies between activities that allow us to mine workflow recovery techniques. Finally, based on this mining step, we have proposed rules to correct or/and improve these recovery mechanisms to ensure reliable and correct workflow executions. In fact, observing that process activities happen in a way that bypasses the system, we confront man-made models with models discovered by process discovery, to have as deep insight as possible into the process and then to provide tool to correct and improve workflow failures handling and recovery, and finally the application reliability.

2. Mining structural workflow patterns

Concretely, we have developed a new approach to discover workflow patterns by statistically analyzing workflow logs (Gaaloul et al., 2004a, Gaaloul et al., 2005a, Gaaloul et al., 2005b). As we stated before, we start by collecting from workflow instances as they took place 1. Then we build, through statistical techniques, a graphical intermediary representation modelling elementary dependencies over workflow logs. These dependencies are refined by advanced structural workflow patterns. An elementary dependency is an "immediate" dependency linking two activities in the sense that the termination of the first causes the activation of the last. Thus, the event of termination of the first activity is considered as the pre-condition of the activation of the last and reciprocally the activation of the last is considered as a post condition of the termination of the first activity. While an advanced structural workflow pattern is a set of elementary dependencies that defines an advanced structure to express specific behaviour, in terms of control flow, linking these dependencies. As defined in (Gamma et al., 1995), a pattern "is the abstraction from a concrete form which keeps recurring in specific non arbitrary contexts". A workflow pattern (Aalst et al., 2003) can be seen as an abstract description of a recurrent class of interactions based on (primitive) activation dependency.

Our approach is characterised by a "local" workflow patterns discovery covering partial results and a dynamic technique dealing with concurrency. In one hand, this approach brought new mechanisms that allow the analysis of incomplete logs. In an other hand, we can better specify the "join" and the "fork" point and improve the discovery of activities concurrent behaviour by proposing a dynamic mechanism of log "concurrent" window sliding.

3. Workflow recovery mining

Workflow Management Systems (WfMSs) are being increasingly used by many companies to improve the efficiencies of their processes and reduce costs. However, due to the overall complexity of workflows specification, deployment of a process without validation may lead to undesirable execution behaviour that compromises process goals. WfMSs are expected to recognize and handle errors to support reliable and consistent execution of workflows, but as has been pointed out in (Georgakopoulos et al., 1995), up to now, most WfMSs lack such functionalities. The introduction of some kind of transactions in WfMSs is unavoidable to guarantee reliable and consistent workflow executions. In contrast to advanced transaction models, transactional workflows focus on issues of consistency from the business point of view rather than from the database point of view. They are applied in case of failures and define mechanisms supporting the automation of failure handling during runtime. Basically they specify activities transactional interactions in order to resume correctly workflow execution.

The main problem at this stage is how to ensure that the specified workflow model guaranties reliable executions. Generally, formal previous approaches develop, using their workflow modelling formalisms, a set of techniques to analyze and check model correctness (Hofstede *et al.*, 1998, Aalst *et al.*, 1998, Adam *et al.*, 1998). Although powerful, these approaches may fail, in some cases, to ensure workflow reliable executions. Besides, it is neither possible nor intended by most workflow designers to model all failures; the process description will in any case become complex very soon – especially if the original process is more complex (Eder *et al.*, 1996). Furthermore, workflow errors and exceptions are commonly not detected until the workflow model is performed. By gathering and analyzing information about workflow processing as they took place in run time, we can first identify these errors and related recovery techniques and second propose solutions to improve them.

We present a new technique to discover workflow transactional behaviour from logs and to be alerted of design gaps especially about failure handling and recovery techniques (Gaaloul *et al.*, 2005c). This kind of analysis is very useful in showing cause effect relationships.

3.1. *Workflow transactional behaviour*

The motivation behind modelling workflow transactional behaviour is to add the capability in the workflow to handle exceptional circumstances that would otherwise leave the workflow in an unacceptable state. Within transactional workflow behaviour, we distinguish between activity transactional properties and transactional flow (interactions).

Activities transactional properties: During the workflow execution, an activity can pass through several stages defined as activity states (aborted, failed and completed). The transactional properties of an activity depend on the set of its internal states transitions. The main transactional properties that we are considering are retriable and pivot (Elmagarmid *et al.*, 1990). An activity "a" is said to be retriable if it is sure to complete even if it fails. "a" is said to be pivot if once it successfully completes, its effects remain for ever and cannot be semantically undone or reactivated.

Transactional flow: After failure, transactional external transitions are fired by external entities (scheduler, human intervention, etc.) and allow to the failed activity to interact with the outside to recover a consistent state. The goal is to bring the failed process back to some semantically acceptable state. Thus, failure inconsistent state can then be fixed and the execution resumed with the hope that it will then complete successfully.

3.2. *Mining transactional dependencies*

As we have done to discover workflow patterns, we build statistical transactional dependencies that report only events dependencies captured after activities failures. These dependencies provide a convenient way to specify and reason about workflow transactional behaviour expressed in terms of activities transactional properties and transactional flow.

3.2.1. *Discovering activity transactional properties*

Every activity can be associated to a life cycle statechart that models the possible states through which the executions of this activity can go, and the possible transitions between these states. This structure, i.e. life cycle statechart, has an initial state and, on the start transition, moves into the executing state. There could be one or more transitions after this. Thus, the relationships between the significant events of an activity can be represented by a state transition diagram, which serves as an abstraction for the actual activity by hiding irrelevant details of its internal computations. The significant events transitions of an activity depend on the characteristics of its transactional proprieties.

Based on this, retriable and pivot are identified by a unique statechart life cycle. The states/transition diagram of a retriable activity has in addition a transition that specifies a retry operation after observing failure. Indeed, the failure state in retriable activity can not be a persistent state, the activity should be re-executed after each failure until success. Using these specifications we can discover activities transactional properties from statistical transactional dependencies.

3.2.2. *Discovering transactional flow*

Basically, the workflow has to decide, after an activity failure, whether an inconsistent state is reached. Depending on this decision either a complex recovery procedure has to be started or the process execution can continues. The main challenge thereby is to identify and reach a consistent state from where the workflow can be continued. A consistent state point is an execution step of the workflow (equivalent to a save point in database transactions) which represents an acceptable intermediate execution state that is determined to be acceptable from a business perspective and hopefully also a decision point where certain actions can be taken to either fix the problem that caused the failure or choose an alternative execution path to avoid this problem (Du et al., 1997).

The recovery procedure is initialized by an alternative dependency. Depending on the localization of the consistent point, we have identified two kinds of alternative dependencies: backward alternative and forward alternative. Bringing the workflow back to a semantically acceptable state can also entail compensating the already completed activities until the acceptable state is reached through "new" compensation activities which semantically undo the failed activity. Furthermore, an activity failure can cause a non regular, abnormal termination (abort) of one or more active activities. If such a situation happens, the failure of an activity induces the abortion of other activities. This behaviour is described through the abortion dependency.

3.3. *Improving workflow recovery*

The goal of recovery techniques is to minimize the amount of effort resuming the workflow execution. However, the applicability of these techniques depends on the semantics of the process. In this section, we propose techniques giving help for that and correcting potential design errors detected after workflow mining. In fact, we use the transactional behaviour mining as a feed back loop to correct wrong transactional behaviours. By wrong transactional behaviours we mean activity transactional properties and transactional flow initially specified and which do not coincide with the reality. These wrong transactional behaviours can be simply costly but also source of error. We proceed through a set of rules that allow us to:

– correct or remove the wrong transactional behaviour,

– add relevant transactional behaviour for a better failure handling and recovery.

These rules depend on both discovered workflow patterns and discovered transactional behaviour. Indeed, workflow transaction behaviour specification must respect some semantic "regulations" partially depending on the discovered control flow. More details are given in (Gaaloul *et al.*, 2005c).

4. Discussion

In this paper, we discussed issues related to patterns workflow mining from event based Log. Obvious applications of workflow patterns mining exist in model driven business process software engineering, both for bottom up approaches used in business process alignment (Aalst *et al.*, 2004, Benattalah *et al.*, 2004), and for top down approaches used in workflow generation (Baina *et al.*, 2004). The idea of applying process mining in the context of workflow management was first introduced in (Agrawal *et al.*, 1998). This work proposes methods for automatically deriving a formal model of a process from a log of events related to its executions and is based on workflow graphs. Cook and Wolf (Cook *et al.*, 1998a) investigated similar issues in the context of software engineering processes. They extended their work limited initially to sequential processes, to concurrent processes (Cook *et al.*, 1998b). Herbst (Herbst *et al.*, 2000, Herbst *et al.*, 1998) presents an inductive learning component used to support the acquisition and adaptation of sequential process models, generalizing execution traces from different workflow instances to a workflow model covering all traces. Starting from the same kind of process logs, van der Aalst *et al.* explore also proposes techniques to discover workflow models based on Petri nets. Beside analysing process structure, there exist related works dealing with process behaviour reporting, such as (Grigori *et al.*, 2004) that describe a tool that provides several features, such as analysing deadline expirations, predicting exceptions, process instances monitoring.

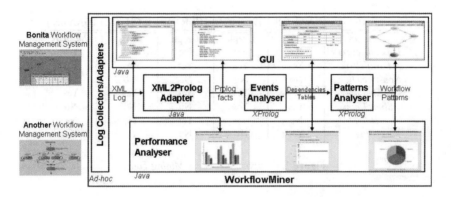

Figure 1. *WorkflowMiner Pipes and Filters mining process*

Our contribution proposes a new approach characterized by a partial discovery of workflow patterns. This approach recovers partial results from log fractions. It discovers more complex features with a better specification of "fork" operator (and-split, or-split, xor-split patterns) and "join" operator (and-join, or-join, and M-out-of-N-Join patterns). It deals better with concurrency through the introduction "concurrent window" that deals dynamically with concurrence. It seems to be more simple in computing. This simplicity will not affect its efficiency in processing the concurrent aspect of workflow.

To apply our process mining techniques, we have proposed to build, at first, a workflow log collecting tool grafted to the workflow management system Bonita. Thereafter, we have implemented our presented workflow patterns mining algorithms within our prototype WorkflowMiner (Gaaloul *et al.*, 2004a, Gaaloul *et al.*, 2005a, Gaaloul *et al.*, 2005b). WorkflowMiner, as seen in Figure 1, is composed of (a) Events Analyser component dealing with causal dependency analysis (producing different SDT tables), (b) Patterns Analyser component using causal dependencies to discover partial workflow patterns and compose them iteratively into a global workflow model, and (c) Performance Analyser exploiting brute event-based log, discovered causal dependencies, and discovered partial and global workflow patterns to measure performance metrics. WorkflowMiner is written in Java and based on BonitaWorkflow Management System2 and XProlog Java Prolog

API. Starting from executions of a workflow, (1) events streams are gathered into an XML log. In order to be processed, (2) these workflow log events are wrapped into a 1st order logic format. (3) Mining rules are applied on resulted 1st order log events to discover workflow patterns. We use a Prolog-based presentation for log events, and mining rules. (4) Discovered patterns are given to the workflow designer so he/she will have a look on the analysis of his/her deployed workflow to restructure or redesign it either manually or semi-automatically.

Tools	[AAL 02]	[WEI 02]	[HER 04]	[SCH 02]	[GAA 05a]
Structure	Graph	Graph	Graph	Block	Patterns
Local discovery	No	No	No	No	Yes
Parallelism	Yes	Yes	Yes	Yes	Yes
Non-free choice	No	No	No	No	Yes
Basic Loops	Yes	Yes	Yes	Yes	Yes
Short Loops	Yes	Yes	No	No	No
Noise	No	Yes	Yes	No	No
Time	Yes	No	No	No	No

Figure 2. *Comparing Process Mining Tools*

Figure 2 compares our WorkflowMiner prototype to workflow mining tools representing previous studied approaches. We focus on seven aspects : structure of the target discovering language, local discovery dealing with incomplete parts of logs (opposed to global and complete log analysis), parallelism (a fork path beginning with and-split and ending with and-join), non-free choice (NFC processes mix synchronization and choice in one construct), loops (basics cyclic workflow transitions, or paths),Short loops (mono- or bi- activity(ies) loops), noise (situation where log is incomplete or contains errors or non-representative exceptional instances), and time (event time stamp information used to calculate performance indicators such as waiting/synchronization times, flow times, load/utilisation rate, etc.). There are others process mining tools (concerning for instance, Social network mining, workflow analysis frameworks), but they are out of the scope of this paper.

5. Bibliography

Aalst W., Van Dongen B. F., "The Application of Petri Nets to Workflow Management", *The Journal of Circuits, Systems and Computers*, vol. 8, no. 1, 1998, p. 21–66.

Aalst W. M. P., Van Dongen B. F., "Discovering Workflow Performance Models from Timed Logs", *Proceedings of the First International Conference on Engineering and Deployment of Cooperative Information Systems*, Springer-Verlag, 2002, p. 45–63.

Aalst W. M. P., Ter Hofstede "Business Alignment: Using Process Mining as a Tool for Delta Analysis", *CAiSE Workshops (2), 2004, p. 138-145*

Adam N. R., Atluri V., Huang W.-K., "Modeling and Analysis of Workflows Using Petri Nets", *J. Intell. Inf. Syst.*, vol. 10, no. 2, 1998, p. 131–158, Kluwer Academic Publishers.

Agrawal R., Gunpolus D., Leymann F., "Mining Process Models from Workflow Logs", Lecture Notes in Computer Science, vol. 1377, 1998, p. 469–498.

Baîna K., Benattallah B., Casati F., Toumani F., "Model-DrivenWeb Service Development", *CAiSE*, 2004, p. 290-306.

Benattalah B., Casati F., Toumani F., "Analysis and Management of Web Service Protocols", *ER*, 2004, p. 524-541.

Cook J. E.,Wolf A. L., "Discovering models of software processes from eventbased data", ACM Transactions on Software Engineering and Methodology *(TOSEM)*, vol. 7, no. 3, 1998, p. 215–249, ACM Press.

Cook J. E.,Wolf A. L., "Event-based detection of concurrency", *Proceedings of the 6th ACM SIGSOFT international symposium on Foundations of software engineering*, ACM Press, 1998, p. 35–45.

Du W., Davis J., Shan M.-C., "Flexible specification of workflow compensation scopes", *Proceedings of the international ACM SIGGROUP conference on Supporting group work: the integration challenge*, ACM Press, 1997, p. 309–316.

Eder J., Liebhart W., "Workflow Recovery", *Conference on Cooperative Information Systems*, 1996, p. 124-134.

Elmagarmid A., Leu Y., Liwin W., Rusiinkiewicz M., "A multidatabase transaction model for InterBase", *Proceedings of the sixteenth international conference on Very large databases*, Morgan Kaufmann Publishers Inc., 1990, p. 507–518.

Gaaloul W., Bbiri S., Godart C., "Discovering Workflow Patterns from Timed Logs", EMISA 2004, *Informationssysteme im E-Business und E-Government, Beiträge des Workshops der GI-Fachgruppe EMISA, LNI,* Luxemburg, October 6-8, 2004, GI, p. 84-94.

Gaaloul W., Baîna K., Godart C., « Towards Mining Structural Workflow Patterns. », *ANDERSEN K. V., DEBENHAM J. K., WAGNER R., Eds., DEXA,* vol. 3588 de Lecture Notes in Computer Science, Springer, 2005, p. 24-33.

Gaaloul W., Godart C., "Mining Workflow Recovery from Event Based Logs", *Business Process Management,* 2005, p. 169-185.

Gamma E., Helm R., Johnson R., Vlisside J., *Design Patterns: Elements of Reusable Object-Oriented Software*, Addison-Wesley, Reading, Massachusetts, 1995.

Georgakopoulos D., Hornick M., Sheth A., "An overview of workflow management: from process modeling to workflow automation infrastructure", *Distrib. Parallel Databases,* vol. 3, no. 2, 1995, p. 119–153, Kluwer Academic Publishers.

Grigori D., Casati F., Castellanos M., Dayal U., Sayal M., Shan M.-C., "Business process intelligence", *Comput. Ind.*, vol. 53, no 3, 2004, p. 321–343, Elsevier Science Publishers.

Herbst J., Karagannis D., "Integrating Machine Learning and Workflow Management to Support Acquisition and Adaptation of Workflow Models", *DEXA '98: Proceedings of the 9th International Workshop on Database and Expert Systems Applications, IEEE Computer Society*, 1998, page 745.

Herbst J., Karagannis D., "A Machine Learning Approach toWorkflow Management", machine Learning: *ECML 2000, 11th European Conference on Machine Learning*, Barcelona, Catalonia, Spain, vol. 1810, Springer, Berlin, May 2000, p. 183–194.

Herbst J., Karagannis D., "Workflow mining with InWoLvE", *Comput. Ind.*, vol. 53, no. 3, 2004, p. 245–264, Elsevier Science Publishers.

Ter Hofstede A. H. M., Orlwaska M. E., Rajapakse J., "Verification problems in conceptual workflow specifications", *Data Knowl. Eng.*, vol. 24, no 3, 1998, p. 239–256, Elsevier Science Publishers

Schimm G., Karagannis D., "Process Miner - A Tool for Mining Process Schemes from Event-Based Data", *Proceedings of the European Conference on Logics in Artificial Intelligence*, Springer-Verlag, 2002, p. 525–528.

Van der Aalst Aalst W. M. P., Ter Hofstede A. H. M., Kiepuszewski B., Barros A. P., "Workflow Patterns", *Distrib. Parallel Databases*, vol. 14, no. 1, 2003, p. 5–51, Kluwer Academic Publishers.

Weijters A. J. M. M., Van der Aalst Aalst W. M. P., "Workflow Mining: Discovering Workflow Models from Event-Based Data", DOUSSON, C., HÖPPNER, F., QUINIOU, R., Eds., *Proceedings of the ECAI Workshop on Knowledge Discovery and Spatial Data*, 2002, p. 78–84.

Dependency based approach for Process Design

Ananda Edirisuriya

Stockholm University/Royal Institute of Technology
Department of Computer and Systems Science
Forum 100, 164 40 Kista
Stockholm
Sweden

si-ana@dsv.su.se

ABSTRACT: *Enterprises that participate in collaborative business needs interoperable business process that run across the borders of the enterprises. To address business process interoperability problems a useful starting point is the analysis of the business model of the enterprise. In this work we will discuss a method that transforms a business model to a process model in a systematic way. We will investigate how to manage dependencies among different events and processes driven by business rules in assisting the design of the executable process model.*

KEY WORDS: *Business Rule, Dependency, Event, Goal, Process, Right.*

1. Introduction

Customer demands are unlimited, changing all the time and change in many ways that increases the complexity of the product or the manufacturing process. Changes in customer demands create new business opportunities that are met by creating new manufacturing or service processes. To meet these demands enterprises could not work alone, but need to put collaborative efforts. To work in collaboration enterprises runs on heterogeneous platforms need interoperable business processes that run smoothly across the borders of enterprises. In addressing business process interoperability problems a useful starting point is the analysis of the business model of the enterprise. A business model state *what* is offered to *whom* by *whom*? It visualize which partners are involved, the value exchanges involved between partners, resources involved in these exchanges. Process model explains how value exchanges are selected, negotiated, contracted and executed at the operational level. It describes ordering of exchanges of resources, additional message flows to facilitate the coordination of value exchanges and communication among the business partners.

The design of a process model itself is not an easy task since, given a particular business model, we can derive alternative process models. The research question we are analyzing in this work is *how to derive a process model from a business model in a systematic way.*

The paper is organized in the following way. Section 2 contains a discussion on Business rules. Section 3 introduces the basic concepts of our ontology use in the methodology. Section 4 outlines the method and section 5 contains expected contribution of the work.

2. The business rules

The business rules controls or influence most of business activities that are guided by business strategy, tradition, culture, policy and experience. "A business rule is a statement that defines or constraints some aspect of an organization. It is intended to assert structure or to control or influence the behaviour of the organization" (Business Rule Group, 2000). The main feature of the business rule technology is that business rules are stored in the business rule engine. The rest of the application is separated from the rule engine. The business rule has been classified differently by different people according to the requirement in hand. The classification used by (Halle, 2002) is given in Table 1.

When analysing business rules finding dependences among rules are very important as they decide the order of execution of the rules. According to (Bühne *et al.*, 2003), most commonly use rule dependency is the requirement dependency. The requirements dependency between two rules means that first rule should be address before the execution of the second rule. See Table 2 for an example. The business rules affect the procedural and provincial aspects of the process model. For instance "Send shipment" event can be execute only after executing the "Receive down payment" event if the customer is not trust worthy.

Type	Definition	Example
Operational Business Rules	*Mandatory Constraint Rules-* Concept/statement that express some aspects of the company. *Action Enabler Rules-* If some condition is true, initiate another business event.	Only preferred customers can send the order without a down payment. If sufficient stocks are available initiate the Accept the sales order.
Supportive Business Rules	*Computational Rules-* A formula to compute one value from other values. *Inference Rules-* Infer additional facts based on other facts.	Employee provident fund is 12% of the Basic Salary. A customer is preferred if savings account balance is more than 90,000 Crowns.

Table 1. *Business rule types*

Rule ID	Rule Type	Rule Description	Depend On
R1	Inference	Type of customer should be known	Nil
R2	Computation	Compute sales discount	R1
R3	Action Enabler	Request a down payment from a new customer before the shipment	R1
R4	Computation	Compute Total Sales amount	R2
R5	Action Enabler	Send the shipment	R3

Table 2. *Requirement dependency among business rules*

3. Ontology of event, process and business rule

The ontology presented in Figure 1 extended the features of established business model ontologies REA(McCarthy, 1982) and e3-value (Gordijn *et al.*, 2000). We will briefly describe it here.

An *Actor* is someone who is able to participate in events. A *Resource* is an object which has a value for some actor. A resource may have properties. This is modelled as *Feature*. For example "weight of a pizza". A *Right* on a resource means that an actor is entitled to use that resource in some way, for example, the ownership of a book. An *Event* changes a feature or a right of a resource. An event could be a *Transfer* or *Conversion*. A transfer means that a right is transferred from one actor to another. A conversion event changes some feature of a resource (Hruby, 2006). A *Process* is a set of Event Types and specifies how to group together transfer and conversion events. This ontology distinguishes between a number of specialized processes interfaces, exchanges, transactions, and transformations. An *Interface* process consists of transfer event types associated with the same actor type. An *Exchange* is a process consisting of a pair of one give transfer event type and one take transfer event type associated to two different actor types. A *Transaction* process consists of a number of transfer event types included in the exchanges. A *Transformation* is a set of conversion event types all associated to the same actor type. A transformation specifies that some resource is produced while other resources are consumed or used. *Goal* is a business achievement that satisfies a certain customer needs. For example, a Distributor goal may be to supply chicken to the customer. To satisfy this goal certain events needs to be fulfilled. Theses goals and events are governed by different business rules.

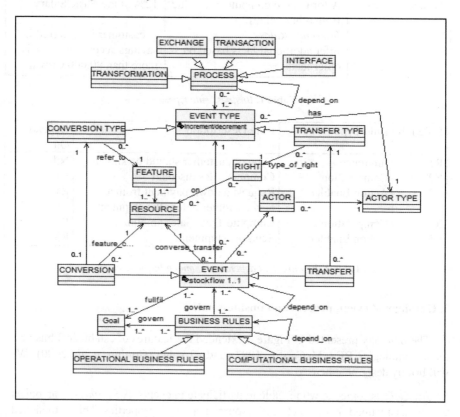

Figure 1. *Event, processes and business rule ontology*

The dependencies among the events and processes need to be taken into account during ordering the activities in designing the processes model. The study presented in (Malone, 1999) suggests that there exist different dependencies between activities and resources consumed by these activities. These dependencies are flow, fit and sharing. A flow dependency is a relationship between two events suggesting that the output produced by one event will be required as an input to another event. Sharing dependency suggest that same resource is shared by two or more events. Fit dependency describes two or more events synchronic to produce a common resource. The activity dependency model of (Andersson *et al.*, 2005), identifies, classifies and relates activities needed for executing and coordinating value transfers. They are flow, trust and duality dependencies. Trust dependency suggests that one event has to be carried out before another as a result of low trust among the partners involved. Duality dependency is the relationship between two reciprocal value transfers.

Our hypothesis is that *"Well organized event, processes and business rule dependencies could use to assist the designing of process model"*.

4. Integrated methodology

When designing the process model, a number of design decisions have to be taken concerning the ordering and decomposition of processes. These design decisions are mainly based on three different types of aspects in a business case, namely logistic, communication and risk aspects (Weigand *et al.*, 2006). *Logistic Aspect:* This aspect concerns the physical flow of resources and the planning of the flow of these resources in time. *Communicative Aspect:* This aspect concerns the coordination between customers and providers that is needed to initiate and complete value exchanges. *Risk Aspect:* This aspect concerns risks that may result in value transactions not being completed or only partially completed.

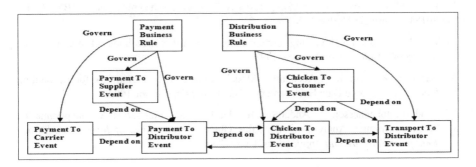

Figure 2. *Dependency diagram*

There are different dependencies among different event types and processes described in section 3. For example there are flow, fit and sharing dependencies among *Interface* Processes and duality dependency among two reciprocal events in an *Exchange* Process. Figure 2 contains the dependency diagram for the well known sample "Chicken Selling" scenario. Our approach involves construction a framework by taking to account above three aspects to organize event and process dependencies driven by business rules to assist the designing of process model.

5. Contribution of the research

The expected contribution of this work is the development of a framework to manage dependencies among different events, processes driven by business rules to facilitate in designing executable process models in a systematic way. These process models can be execute using a business process execution engine in conjunction with a business rule execution engine.

6. References

Andersson B., Bergholtz M., Edirisuriya A., Ilayperuma T., Johannesson P., "A Declarative Foundation of Process Models", *Proceedings of CAISE'05*, Springer-Verlag, LNCS, 2005.

Business Rule Group, GUIDE Business Rules Project, *Defining Business Rules – What are They Really*, 2000, Valid on 2006-01-15, http://www.businessrulesgroup.org.

Bühne S., Halmans G., Pohl K., "Modelling Dependencies between Variation Points in Use Case Diagrams", in *Proceedings of 9th International Workshop on Requirements Engineering: Foundation for Software Quality. In conjunction with CAiSE'03*, Klagenfurt/Velden, Austria, 2003.

Gordijn J., Akkermans J.M., Vliet J.C., "Business Modeling is not Process Modeling", *Conceptual Modeling for E-Business and the Web*, LNCS 1921, Springer-Verlag pp. 40-51, 2000.

Halle B.V., *Business Rules Applied: Building Better Systems Using the Business Rules Approach*, John Wiley & Sons, 2002.

Hruby P., *Model-Driven Design Using Business Patterns*. Forthcoming book. ISBN: 3-540-30154-2. Springer Verlag 2006.

Malone T., "Tools for inventing organizations: Toward a handbook of organizational processes", *Management Science*, 1999.

McCarthy W. E., "The REA Accounting Model: A Generalized Framework for Accounting Systems in a Shared Data Environment". The *Accounting Review* 1982.

Weigand H., Johannesson P., Andersson B., Bergholtz M., Edirisuriya A., Ilayperuma T., "Process Oriented Analysis of the Value Object", *Proceedings of Interoperability for Enterprise Software and Applications*, I-ESA 2006.

A Declarative Approach of Process Models

Tharaka Ilayperuma

Royal Institute of Technology
Department of Computer and Systems Sciences, Sweden
si-tsi@dsv.su.se

ABSTRACT: Interoperable business processes provide great opportunity for business organisations to stand on the ever changing business world. To be able to survive in the business by adapting to dynamic changes that has to be done with the time, a smooth process needs to be carried out when building process models from business model. This can be achieved by considering various aspects like logistic, communicative and risk in a business model which may help to classify various business activities and their relationships and by integrating these identified activity flows into one single model like activity dependency model. In this research we investigate possible linking between these various steps towards developing process model from business model.

KEY WORDS: Process model, risk, business model.

1. Introduction

The rapid development of Information and Communication Technology (ICT) has opened various avenues for companies to jointly work with each other (Osterwalder *et al.,* 2006). As they explain, this has increased the number of stakeholders in the business and made it more and more difficult to understand and communicate with each other. Consequently, with the growing interest of the companies to facilitate business through jointly offering goods, services to customers, many methods to facilitate e-business modelling such as e3-value (Gordijn *et al.,* 2000), Business Modelling Ontology (BMO) (Osterwalder *et al.,* 2005), REA ontology (McCarthy *et al.,* 1982) has emerged.

From business point of view, business model provides design rationale for e-commerce systems (Gordijn *et al.,* 2000). Consequently, in modelling the ways that enterprises do their business, the starting point could be identifying the actors, resources and exchange of these resources among these actors. Ontologies such as e3-value, BMO, REA provide the basis for this. The business models created by these methodologies focus on providing high level view of the agents involved resources and exchange of the resources between agents (McCarthy *et al.,* 1982). The main concern of the business model is to make it clear who are the actors involved in the business and what relationships they would have in terms of exchange of resources among them. The process models on the other hand focus on *how* these activities identified by the business model would be carried out at the operational level and contain additional information like time ordering between these activities.

The issue of building process models from business models taking ever more attraction. Despite the success of the new advents in this area, the process modelling technologies face several shortcomings as explained by (Andersson *et al.,* 2005). As they explain, process models mainly expressed through low level concepts like control flows and message passing. Since the business models expressed in rather high level economic related concepts like value exchanges and resource flows that are more familiar to business users, there is an ontological gap between these two models. This lead to problems like traceability meaning that it makes difficult for designers to trace back their design decisions and convince non technical business users why they made a certain design decision at process level and also makes it difficult for business users to understand the connection between the economic related details in the business model and the technical details in the process model.

Recent research (Andersson *et al.,* 2005) has tried to find a remedy to this problem by bridging the gap between the business model and process model by identifying the possible control flows between the value exchanges identified in the business model and introducing intermediate steps like activity dependency model.

The purpose of this research is to expand this declarative foundation by introducing logistic, communication and risk models to identify and classify activities in the business model and help creating activity dependency model more easily.

2. Research questions

Our research concerns certain aspects related to the following questions.

- What are the methods available to fill the ontological gap between business and process models?
- What could be the main steps towards filling this gap?
- How could we relate these steps one to another and derive process model from business model?

In bridging the ontological gap between a business model and a process model, we might consider logistic flows, communication flows and risk mitigation aspects as explained in (Weigand *et al.*, 2006). But how could we relate these three aspects to each other and make it easier to build the process model? More explicitly, how could we allow designers to introduce and order activities in the process model? Would it be possible to deal these three models mentioned above in parallel or would they affect each other? For example, the risk analysis may suggest that an involving party might needs more communication before taking a decision or a down payment, which has a connection with the logistic model, is needed before accepting an order. In these cases how could designer argue about his design decision? To answer this question we might look into the activity dependency model proposed in (Andersson *et al.*, 2005). Though they have tried to fill the ontological gap between the business model and the process model, their model does not propose a way to identify differences between various activities and relationships. Because of this, even if this model is useful it might not help designers very much. For example, the difference between assignment activity and the production activity may not clear in certain situations like the conference case example that they have used to illustrate the use of the proposed model in bridging the gap between business and process model. One way to overcome this problem could be by building so called activity dependency model based on three models: logistic, communication and risk model. This enables the classification of activities much easier thus by supporting the identification and classification of activities and their relationships in the activity dependency model unambiguously.

3. Proposed solution

In their research, (Weigand *et al.*, 2006) propose a method for analyzing value objects exchanged between various partners involved in a business and to proceed towards the process model by classifying them into various pillars like logistic, communication and risk. The research carried out by, (Berghlotz *et al.,* 2005), introduces means of designing business processes that fit a more strategic business model by linking them with risk mitigation aspects. The activity dependency model proposed by (Andersson *et al.,* 2005) is an intermediate step between the business model and the process model which enables identification and classification of activities and their relationships.

To create this activity dependency model, the three pillars: logistic, communication and risk mentioned by (Weigand *et al.,* 2006) will be useful as they enable us to classify the logistic flows, communication flows and the risk aspects by starting from a business model. To be able to do this, we might need to map various business ontologies like e3-value, REA, BMO onto a common ontology and this work is on progress. The last step would be proposing a possible mapping from business model to the three pillars: logistic, communication and risk and from them to the activity dependency model. As we use these three pillars to classify activities and their relationships in an activity dependency model, we might use patterns as mentioned in (Jayaweera 2004) to fill up the processes identified in the mapping between activity dependency model and process model. The notion used for process model in this research would be BPMN (BPMN 2006). These BPMN process specifications can be used to generate XML based business process execution languages. Figure 1 shows the possible linking between these various steps as explained in this section.

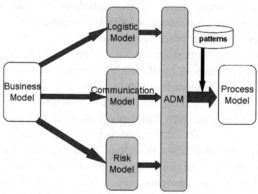

Figure 1. *From Business Model to Process Model*

4. Expected contributions

Classification of business activities into three pillars would help designers to identify various activities and relationships proposed in the activity dependency model by (Andersson *et al.,* 2005). Placing several analytical steps between the business model and the process model will help designers as they will be able to use these steps to describe reasons governed by choosing their design decisions.

The investigation of how to relate the various steps linking business model to process model would be beneficial for developing a common ontology. Identification of the connection between control flow relationships, value exchange activities and risk aspects of these activities would enable to determine at what point a designer should deal with the risk aspects. It would also enable designer to identify possible facts that would hinder the desired goals of the organization.

The main contribution of this research would be linking various steps towards designing the process model. This would help designers to trace back and forth their design decisions and more concretely justify them to the non technical business users. This kind of framework would also beneficial to designers since it would assist them to identify possible points to handle risks in between several business processes where several actors are involved. This would enable integration of several business processes to offer joint services, goods to their environment. Linking various stages from business model to process model would also beneficial in determining how to integrate several systems and coordinate the information flow between them.

5. References

Andersson B., Bergholtz M., Edirisuriya A., Ilayperuma T., Johannesson P., "A Declarative Foundation of Process Models", *Proc. CAISE'05*, Springer-Verlag, LNCS, 2005.

Bergholtz M., *et al.*, "Integrated Methodology for linking business and process models with risk mitigation", *REBNITA 05*.

Business process Modelling Notation (BPMN), Accessed March, 2006, *http://www.bpmn.org/*

Gordijn J., Akkermans J.M. and Vliet J.C. van, "What's in an Electronic Business Model?", *12th Int. Conf. on Knowledge Engineering and Knowledge Management EKAW,* 2000.

Jayaweera P. "A Unified Framework for e-Commerce Systems Development: Business Process Pattern Perspective (BP3)", PhD Thesis (ISBN 91-7265-938-6) September, 2004.

McCarthy W. E., "The REA Accounting Model: A Generalized Framework for Accounting Systems in a Shared Data Environment", *The Accounting Review* 1982.

Osterwalder A., Pigneur Y., "An e-Business Model Ontology for Modeling e-Business", *15th Bled Electronic Commerce Conference*, Bled, Slovenia, June, 2002

Osterwalder A, Pigneur Y., Tucci C., "Clarifying Business Models: Origins, present and Future of the Concept", *CAIS*, Vol. 15, 2005, p. 751-775

Osterwalder A., Parent C., Pigneur Y., "Setting up an ontology of business models", Accessed February, 2006, *http://www.hec.unil.ch/yp/Pub/04-EMOI.pdf*

Weigand H., Johannesson P., Andersson B., Bergholtz M., Edirisuriya A., Ilayperuma T., "Process Oriented Analysis of the Value Object", *I-ESA'06*.

Improving Alignment of Business Models and Business Process Models for Ensuring Strategic Fit of Business Processes

Stéphane Sandron

Institut d'informatique,
Facultés Universitaires Notre-Dame de la Paix,
Rue Grandgagnage 21,
5000 Namur, Belgium
ssn@info.fundp.ac.be

ABSTRACT: *Nowadays, an enterprise must be able to rapidly modify its business model but also its strategy, its organization, its business processes and its supporting ICT systems. All these changes in the models must be coherent with each other. In this paper, we present the problem and we propose a methodology in order to improve the alignment between Business Models and Business Processes Models.*

KEY WORDS: *alignment, business model, business processes model, i*, e³value, e-BMO.*

1. Introduction

Nowadays, we can see more and more networks of enterprises. Enterprises are working together in an environment which is rapidly evolving. One main reason is the generalization of Information Technologies, which led to a growing number of competitors for each enterprise. Their positions on their markets have become more uncertain and they have to innovate to avoid being excluded of the game.

The only possibility for the enterprise to be sure to keep its competitive position is to be able to rapidly modify its business model but also its strategy, its organization, its business processes and its supporting ICT systems. Changes cannot be applied without a due consideration because all these different aspects of the enterprise are interdependent. In (Osterwalder *et al.*, 2005), the authors further characterize the relations between the different viewpoints of the enterprise.

The modifications in a viewpoint of the enterprise should lead to coherent modifications in the others, in order to ensure a good strategic business-IT alignment (Henderson *et al.*, 1993). To understand which kind of modifications belongs to which model, a definition of the models that we consider of interest is necessary.

Firstly, we adopt the following definition of business model by A. Osterwalder, Y. Pigneur and C. L. Tucci (Osterwalder *et al.*, 2005):

A business model is a conceptual tool containing a set of objects, concepts and their relationships with the objective to express the business logic of a specific firm.

Secondly, F. B. Vernadat explains in (Vernadat 1996) that an enterprise model is a representation of a perception of an enterprise. Moreover, the content of this model is whatever the enterprise considers important for its operations. Especially, one of the submodels is the process model describing the business processes for which F. B. Vernadat gives a definition (Vernadat 1996):

A business process is a sequence (or partially ordered set) of enterprise activities, execution of which is triggered by some event and will result in some observable or quantifiable end result.

In order to create models, some ontologies are required. According to (Gruber 1993), *an ontology is the representation of a conceptualisation. It provides a definition of a set of concepts that allow describing a situation under consideration.*

In this paper, we will focus on the relations between a business model ontology (BMO) and a business process model ontology (BPMO). A. Osterwalder and Y. Pigneur proposed in (Ben Lagha *et al.*, 2002) a simple representation of these relations, as you can see in Figure 1.

The authors of the figure explained in (Osterwalder *et al.*, 2003) that there are three levels of abstraction related to the organization of an enterprise. The higher level of abstraction is the Planning level where the global strategy is outlined. In the third level, the business processes implement the logic for creating value in the enterprise (Ben Lagha *et al.*, 2002). They are specified in agreement with the preceding levels. After having understood these different levels of abstraction, it is clear that business processes cannot be modified directly without changes at the higher levels (and particularly in the business model of the enterprise).

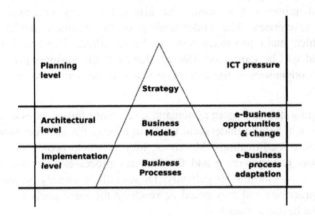

Figure 1. *Relations between models* (Osterwalder *et al.*, 2003)

However, though Figure 1 seems to suggest that a modification of the business model requires a change in the business processes, this is not necessarily always the case. It depends on the type of modification. The enterprise can modify business processes in a way that do not affect its business model. For example, local changes in costumer order processing processes probably do not affect the business logic of the firm. Our hypothesis is that some concepts present in the BMO are from the business strategy, the business organisation (business processes) and the business technology. There are also concepts that we cannot find directly in these three viewpoints of the enterprise. That is normal because each model has different objectives. For example, the segmentation of the customers is a particularity of the business models.

When a modification involves concepts shared by different models, the changes in these must be coherent (no more and no less than what is necessary). But, it is difficult to find where exactly the changes must be implemented. For example, the links between the business model of the enterprise and the business processes model exist, as explained by Osterwalder and Pigneur (Osterwalder *et al.*, 2003), but they are rarely formally expressed. It is problematic because if the enterprise wants to adapt to its changing environment, then it must be possible to locate the appropriate business processes to be changed. In practice, when a modification must be done, the persons in charge forward these from the business model to the business processes thanks to their experience of the way the enterprise is working. They do not have the means to check if their modifications are aligned with the changes at the level of the business model.

Intuitively, it is logical to consider that the business model should be the first viewpoint of the enterprise to be modified because it focuses on the revenue stream, the principal property that would be affected by environmental threats for commercial enterprises. The understanding of the business model is vital to highlight which main processes have to be modified. These will reveal other processes that will be indirectly affected, thanks to the business processes model. This step is compulsory if the enterprise wants to be sure to keep its competing position.

To bring this step to a more systematic level, more formal rules or methods are needed. They will help to understand where to modify the different models and the impacts of these modifications. Moreover, they will help people in charge of the business model re-engineering and the business processes re-engineering to find possible alternatives more systematically. These could be already present at the level of business processes and they could be reaching the same goals as these brought forward by the business model.

The goal of having rules to align the BMOs with the BPMOs is not only to ease the effort of re-engineering, but also to deal with another problem related to modifications of the enterprise. The models rarely take into account the intentionalities of the actors in the enterprise. Most of the time, these are not explicitly expressed but still present. For example, BMOs generally take care of the needs and wishes of the customers, and often describe the advantages of the value proposition for them.

Intentionalities of enterprise actors are important because they drive the way actors behave. Moreover, actors may oppose changes in the business processes of their enterprise if it conflicts with their interests. That is particularly dangerous when changes are implemented in the business processes because it impacts the practical organisation of the enterprise.

To succeed in the implementation of changes, mechanisms which permit to align the business model of an enterprise with its business processes are necessary. Moreover, one or both of them should incorporate the intentionalities of the actors to realize in order to early detect potential problems with the proposed modifications.

2. Proposed methodology in order to improve the alignment between BMs and BPMs

The purpose of the thesis reported to this paper is to propose a modelling framework allowing business models and business processes models alignment facilities, to support their alignment in a more systematic way. The persons in charge of the modifications will have a better understanding of the impacts on each model.

In the modelling framework that we will propose, we will try to take explicitly into account the intentionalities of the agents in one or both ontologies used. The goal is to be sure that the modification will be a success and thus accepted by all the actors of the enterprise.

To define the modelling framework, we will follow the following six steps.

2.1. First step: conducting a survey on BP practices in Wallonia (Belgium)

The survey will target the enterprises with a high probability of having a complex business model and a complex business process model. It will consist in interviews of people in charge of the re-engineering of the business model and the business process model (even if these are not the terms used by the enterprise).

The goal of the first step is to realize if, in current practice, the modifications to the business processes are done (or not) in a systematic way and follow (or do not) well defined rules. By now, our hypothesis is that they are just led by the experience and the feelings of people in charge of the business model re-engineering and the business processes re-engineering.

As the survey requires a lot of work and time, it is not sure that we will conduct enough interviews to have a precise picture of what is necessary for the enterprises.

2.2. Second step: analysis of the literature

The goal of the second step is to analyse the literature on BMOs, BPMOs, and the links and the differences between them, as well as on formalisms usable to represent the relations between concepts of the two ontologies.

This analysis will help us to choose the right ontologies to work on and it will help to see what has already been done.

2.3. Third step: selecting a BPMO or defining a new one

The purpose of the third step is to select a BPMO (or a framework including it) that already has concepts to ease the business process re engineering effort. This ontology or framework should also take into account the intentionalities of the agents related to the enterprise. Business models do not exclude this aspect of actors but concentrate more on the aspects of revenue streams, as we can see in the definition from (Osterwalder et al., 2003).

By now, the modelling framework chosen is i* (Yu 1994). It has the purpose of modelling strategic relationships by taking into account the intentionalities of the actors. Its definition is formal (expressed in TELOS and axiomatically demonstrated) and there are mechanisms allowing to ease the business process reengineering (Yu 1994).

However, i* is more goal-oriented than business processes oriented. Its graphical nature has the disadvantage that the models can become very large compared to other BPMOs. Another drawback is that i* does not allow to represent detailed information about process flows. Therefore, its combination with other BP notations will be envisaged.

2.4. Fourth step: selecting a BMO or defining a new one

The purpose of the third step is to find an ontology for business models that share the same orientations as the modelling framework for business processes. Likewise, it will be easier to establish systematic links between the two.

By now, we chose e-BMO (Osterwalder et al., 2003) (Ben Lagha et al., 2002). The main advantage is that it has been created on the basis of a large amount of literature. Its concepts cover a lot of concepts present in the other BMOs.

Other ontologies will also be investigated such as the eValue BMO (Akkermans et al., 2001).

2.5. Fifth step: identify the concepts shared (and not shared) by the BMO and the BPMO

The first goal of this step is to identify the concepts that are explicitly present in the two ontologies and that can be easily mapped to one another. The second goal is to identify the concepts that are present in one of the two ontologies but not explicitly expressed in the other one.

Intuitively, as we have seen in Figure 1, the business model is at a higher abstraction level (Ben Lagha et al., 2002), a part of the information present in it will probably also be included in the business processes model. But, there will also be information in each model that will not be explicitly represented in the other.

There are at least two possible approaches to identify the correspondences between concepts in BMOs and BPMOs.

The first approach is based on examples and scenarios (as was used for the definition of the UEML 1.0 language (Berio et al., 2003)). The advantage is that it is a fast approach, but we are not sure that we are able to discover all the concepts and the links between them. The second approach is based on the translation of each ontology in a common ontology for semantics (e.g. B.W.W.) (as the one currently used for the definition of the UEML 2.0 (Berio et al., 2005)). The advantage is that we can be sure that we do not forget any concept. The first disadvantage is that the translation needs a lot of work. The second is that it is hard to translate concepts in more generic concepts.

If we keep e-BMO as the business model ontology, the identification will be concentrated on its four pillars: production innovation, customer relationship, infrastructure management, financial aspects.

2.6. Sixth step: formalize the links between the concepts of the ontologies

After the fifth step, we have to formalize the exact relations between the concepts present explicitly or implicitly in the ontologies. This is the purpose of the sixth step.

We do not yet know which formalism we will use to represent the exact links between the concepts. But, the product of this step will be a directory of relationship between the concepts in each ontology and/or guidelines for the use of a precise BMO and a precise BPMO.

3. Results expected from the research

The first contribution expected is that the research will permit a clear and precise identification of the business processes (and the actors) impacted by a modification in the business model of the enterprise.

The second expected contribution is a faster identification of the alternatives while re-engineering the business processes. There is also a hope to decrease the costs related to the acceptance of the modifications by the actors (to put off the failure and the reject of changes).

The third expected contribution is that the research will allow the enterprises to use several coordinated views to reason on the aspects usually present in the business models and in the business processes.

Finally, there is one additional expected contribution which is related to the theoretical field of BPMOs and BMOs. After this research, there is a hope to translate easily the formal links discovered between the chosen BMO and the chosen BPMO in formal links for other relations involving a BMO and a BPMO.

4. References

Akkermans J. M., Gordijn J., "Business Modelling is not Process Modelling", *Conceptual Modeling for E-Business and the Web*, LNCS 1921, p. 40-51, ECOMO 2000, 2000.

Akkermans J.M., Gordijn J., "e³-value: Design and Evaluation of e-Business Models", *IEEE Intelligent Systems, special issue on e-business*, Vol. 16, No. 4, pg 11-17, 2001.

Ben Lagha S., Osterwalder A., Pigneur Y., "An Ontology for Developing e-Business Models", *IFIP DSIage*, 2002.

Berio G. *et al.*, Deliverable D 3.1 Requirements analysis: initial core constructs and architecture. UEML, WP3 – Task 3.1, 3.2, 2003 – available from http://www.ueml.org.

Berio G., *et al.*, Deliverable D5.1. UEML 2.0, WP5, INTEROP, 2005 – available from http://www.interop-noe.org.

Gruber T. R., "A translation approach to portable ontology specifications", *Knowledge Acquisition, 5(2)*, 1993.

Henderson J. C., Venkatraman N., "Strategic alignment: leveraging information technology for transforming organizations", *IBM Systems Journal 32(1)*, pp 4-16, 1993.

Osterwalder A., Pigneur Y, "An ontology for e-business models", Chapter in Wendy Currie (ed) *Value Creation from E-Business Models*, Butterworth-Heinemann, 2003.

Osterwalder A., Pigneur Y., Tucci C. L., "Clarifying business models: origins, present, and future of the concept", *Communications of the Association for Information Systems*, Vol. 15, p. 751-775, 2005.

Vernadat F. B., *Enterprise modelling and integration.* Chapman & Hall, 1996.

Yu E., Modelling Strategic Relationships For Process Reengineering, PhD Thesis, University of Toronto, 1994.

Session 3:
Software Development and Interoperability

An Interactive Multi-Agent Based TV Game Show Implementation

Benjamin Gâteau

Centre de Recherche Public Henri Tudor
29, Avenue John F. Kennedy
L1855 Luxembourg – G.D. Luxembourg
benjamin.gateau@tudor.lu

SMA/G2I/ENSM Saint Etienne
158, Cours Fauriel
42023 Saint Etienne Cedex 02 – France

ABSTRACT: In interactive multimedia applications, the objects composing the scene are increasingly considered as autonomous agents. Although autonomy brings flexibility and realism in the animation, objects' autonomy needs to be controlled. In this purpose we must be able to specify the rights and duties of objects. In this paper we present the $Moise^{Inst}$ meta-model aiming at specifying normative organisations of agents according to four points of view: structural, functional, contextual and normative. We show how this model is used within an application of interactive TV game show where avatars are based on agents.

KEY WORDS: Multi-Agent Systems, interactive TV, normative organisation, electronic institution.

1. Introduction

The research work deals with the iTV domain and concerns the creation of multimedia contents with which a viewer interacts. Multimedia objects involved in this creation are considered as autonomous entities able to adapt and modify their behaviours to the modification of the environment and its related scenario (Renault *et al.* 2004).

We consider here a "questions – answers" TV game show opposing a team of viewers being at home and represented by Avatars and a real players' team. Avatars are directly controlled by their correspondent viewers. In order to define rights and duties of autonomous and generic entities assisting viewers by means of unambiguous specifications, we think that the use of the Electronic Institutions principle (North 1990) based on Multi-Agent System (Luck *et al.* 2003) is in concordance with our needs.

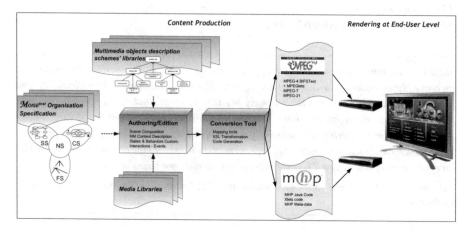

Figure 1. *Simplified version of the iTV content creation chain*

In this paper we talk about our Multi-Agent based Electronic Institution specification model and focus on the implementation of $Moise^{Inst}$, a model for specifying rights and duties of agents within an organisation. We illustrate its use in a real iTV game coming from Cybercultus (Luxembourg) an industrial partner of our research works. Our objective is to add to multimedia objects the capacity to be organised and normed by integrating the $Moise^{Inst}$ meta-model in the iTV content creation chain as displayed on Figure 1. Moreover defining the state and behaviours of multimedia objects we will be able to specify the way they are organised with $Moise^{Inst}$.

This paper is organized as follows: in section 2 we present the $\mathcal{M}$oise^{Inst} meta-model and its use in section 3; section 4 is about the integration of this model in our application; finally we conclude.

2. $\mathcal{M}$oise^{Inst}: an organisational model

We define our Multi-Agent System Interactive Games as an autonomous agents' organisation in which their behaviours are ruled by norms. Agents on which multimedia objects are built are organised according to a model described with the $\mathcal{M}$oise^{Inst} (Model of Organisation for multI-agent SystEm) meta-model. A formal description of this model with the BNF (Backus-Naur Normal Form) language is available in (Gateau *et al.* 2004) for the SS and the FS and in (Gateau *et al.* 2005) for the CS and the NS. $\mathcal{M}$oise^{Inst} is composed of: (i) a Structural Specification (SS) defining roles that agents will play and relations between these roles; (ii) a Functional Specification (FS) defining all goals that have to be achieved in the system; (iii) a Contextual Specification (CS) defining the different contexts influencing the dynamic of the organisation as well as transitions between contexts; (iv) and a Normative Specification (NS) defining clearly rights and duties of roles on missions (set of goals) in specific contexts. These four specifications form the Organisational Specification (OS).

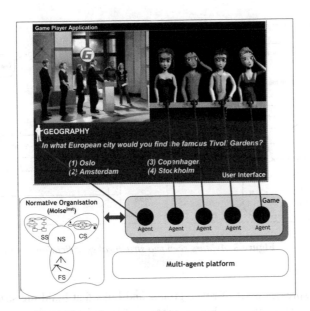

Figure 2. *Multi-agent organisation for iTV global view*

Avatars are multimedia objects involving in an interactive TV game show with the ability to be organised and to follow some norms because they are built on agents (see Figure 2). They are influenced by an organisation definition specified with $\mathcal{M}oise^{Inst}$. That means they are able to interpret the structure of the organisation (in term of groups and roles) and so adopt some role. The same way they can interpret the functioning of the organisation and reach goals in order to achieve the global application goal. At last, they are able to take some norms into account allowing them or not to achieve goals according to the role their play or the group they belong to.

3. Organisation specification of Avatars scenario with $\mathcal{M}oise^{Inst}$

As described in the previous section, we need to organised Avatars and make them respecting some constraints. Avatars are built on multimedia objects on one hand in order to define their multimedia aspect including the transition between rendering behaviours and on Agents on other hand in order to make them sensitive to a $\mathcal{M}oise^{Inst}$ organisation specification. We detail the OS of the iTV game show according to each specification in the following.

3.1. Structural specification

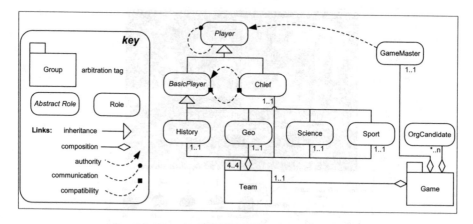

Figure 3. *Avatars scenario structural specification*

The SS expresses a set of roles, groups and links that build the structure of the organisation (see Figure 3). For instance, a "Team" group is composed of the following roles: "History", "Geo", "Sport", "Science" and "Chief". These roles inherit from "BasicPlayer" or "Player" roles that are abstract, i.e. roles that are not adoptable by agents. Cardinality and compatibility links express constraints on the way agents play roles in groups. For instance, cardinality '1..1' on the composition link ensures constraints that, in a "Team" group instance, only one agent can adopt roles at the same time. A compatibility link between "BasicPlayer" and "Chief", allows the same agent to play those two roles or specialization of those roles. Thus, according to this specification, one agent may have the possibility to play at most two of those five roles. Links of communication, authority structures the different roles. For instance, all roles inheriting from "Player" can communicate between them, and the "Chief" has the authority on all "BasicPlayer", which means that all roles inheriting from this role are under the authority of the "Chief". "OrgCandidate" is the first role played by every agents coming in the organisation that's why it could be played by a lot of agents at the same time. "OrgCandidate" does not participate in the game (activity to answer question). According to available roles adoptable in the "Team", agents could change to join the group. "GameMaster" is the role played by the only one presenter assistant.

3.2. Functional specification

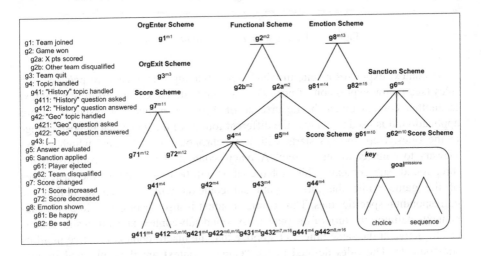

Figure 4. *Avatars scenario functional specification*

The FS specifies the global expected functioning of the system in terms of goals/sub-goals that agents operating in it should achieve (see Figure 4). The goal decomposition trees are organised into different social schemes. For instance, the main social scheme has a goal "X pts scored" that can be achieved by the achievement in sequence of "g4", "g5" and of the "Score Scheme". The "Emotion Scheme" deals with the specification of the emotional behaviour of Avatars as: to show either a happy face or a sad one. The "OrgEnter Scheme" (resp. "OrgExit Scheme") defines the principal behaviours for entering (resp. leaving) an organisation. We also define a scheme relating to the sanctions by specifying that apply a sanction is a choice between the ejection of a player, the disqualification of the team or the modification of the score. We detail further down when this scheme is used.

3.3. *Contextual specification*

To tackle with the situatedness of applications in evolving environment, a CS captures design-time constraints on the evolution of the organisation as a set of contexts and transitions between them (see Figure 5).

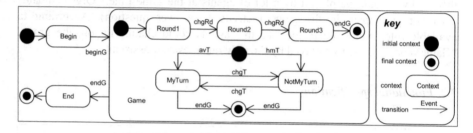

Figure 5. *Avatars scenario contextual specification*

A context expresses a state in which agent playing role have to respect specific rules (see below expression of norms). Transitions define change from one context to another context given the occurrence of different events. For instance, in our application, it is used to express the different rounds of the game that impose change to the rules. Here the CS starts with a synchronous state "Begin" which allows viewers to connect to the system. A macro-context "Game" is decomposed into three rounds sub-contexts. This global context will be used to define the basic rules of the game while the three round sub-contexts will be used to define the corresponding specific rules. The "Game" context is also decomposed into two sub-contexts defining the turn of the players. A round sub-context and a turn sub-context can be active at the same time. Let's notice that the macro-context is active in all its sub-contexts. The rules defined in the "Game" context are thus inherited in sub-contexts and are still valid. Finally the last state is the context in which Avatars quit their team.

3.4. *Normative specification*

Finally, the NS glues all specifications in a coherent and normative organisation. It expresses permissions, obligations and prohibitions of missions referring to the goals of the FS in the context of elements of the SS (roles or groups). Missions groups goals into coherent sets according to the way the designer wants to assign them to roles or groups for their achievement. A norm in NS (see Figure 6) is specified with an *id*, a *context*, a *bearer*, a *deontic operator* referring to a *mission* and a *deadline*. Each norm has three Boolean variable giving information about its activation, its validity and about its respect. A norm is active when the *context* field equals the current organisation context. A norm is valid when the *condition* field result is true. A norm could be respected or violated from the moment it is active and valid.

The Avatars scenario NS displayed on Figure 6 uses functions defined in the $\mathcal{M}oise^{Inst}$ meta-model. The validation condition of N1 (*nb(Team) <max(Team)*) is composed of two functions representing the number of agents already in the Team group and the maximum of agents allowed in the Team. This norm expresses the fact that the Team must not be full in order to allow an agent entry. This specification can define norms as well as their sanction. A sanction is a norm with a violation condition. For instance norms N17 and N18 are sanctions because of the function *violated()* in their condition field. The function return *true* if the norm in parameter is not respected.

context	id	w.	condition	issuer	bearer	deOp	mission	deadline	sanction
Begin	N01	1	nb(Team)<max(Team)	Supervisor	OrgCandidate	O	m1	null	null
End	N02	1	null	Supervisor	Team	O	m3	null	null
Game	N03	1	null	Supervisor	OrgCandidate	F	m1	null	N17
Game	N04	1	null	Supervisor	Team	F	m3	null	null
Game	N05	1	null	Supervisor	Team	O	m2	null	null
Game	N06	1	null	Supervisor	GameMaster	O	m4	null	null
Game	N07	1	null	Supervisor	Team	P	m13	null	null
Game	N08	1	null	Supervisor	Team	F	m16	null	N18
Round1	N09	2	null	Supervisor	Team	O	m16	< answer_delay	null
Round2	N11	1	null	Supervisor	History	O	m5	< answer_delay	null
Round2	N12	1	null	Supervisor	Geo	O	m6	< answer_delay	null
Round2	N13	1	null	Supervisor	Sport	O	m7	< answer_delay	null
Round2	N14	2	null	Supervisor	Science	O	m8	< answer_delay	null
Round3	N10	1	null	Supervisor	Chief	O	m16	< answer_delay	null
NotMyTurn	N15	1	null	Supervisor	Team	F	m16	null	null
NotMyTurn	N16	1	null	Supervisor	Team	F	m14	null	null
Game	N17	1	violated(N02)	Supervisor	GameMaster	O	m9	null	null
Game	N18	1	violated(N08)	Supervisor	GameMaster	O	m11	null	null

Figure 6. *Avatars scenario normative specification*

The norms allow us to define and constrain the functioning of the game as well as what happens at the beginning and at the end of the game. The four first norms in Figure 6 define when it is possible to join and to leave the team. Global rules of game are expressed as functioning norms. For instance Prohibition for "Player" role to answer a question during the game represented by N08 authorizes concerned roles during rounds to answer questions. N09 and N14 oblige the "Player" and the "Chief" roles to answer all questions during the first and third rounds. Four norms for each role in the second round allow concerned roles to answer question.

4. Implementation

The integration of the $\mathcal{M}oise^{Inst}$ meta-model into the chain will allow us to produce content with an authoring tool. With multimedia objects description schemes' libraries and media libraries, the user is able to define a scene composition, the description of multimedia content and the state of objects. With $Moise^{Inst}$, the user can organise the objects and define their behaviours, the events that trigger actions and interactions between them. Consequently, we need to transform the meta-model specification into a computable language. With a XML Document Type Definition (DTD), we can define the meta-model with which we can define XML files representing organisational models. Those XML files permit to define an Organisation Specification (OS). The standard of this format is an advantage in data exchange and interoperability domains. Therefore with help of meta-model and of a compliant model we can either display information by treating data or parse the XML file into programming language. This language is JAVA in our case. We define a JAVA API able to represent an Organisation Specification and its instantiation. The XML DTD file and the JAVA API are available on the $Moise^{Inst}$ web page (http://bnjgat.free.fr/pro/index.php?page=MoiseInst).

Agents don't act directly on an OS. The OS just specify the organisation to obtain a model of organisation that can be instantiate in several real organisations. Namely the OS we describe above define the game principles and each instantiation is a play. An OS instantiation is named a Organisation Entity (OE). The agents act on that. They adopt role, commit on mission and reach goals of structural and functional specification instantiations in the OE by respecting the OS. The instantiation of the contextual and the normative specifications are a set of active contexts and norms.

In order to manipulate a static representation of an organisation and be able to instantiate it, we develop a JAVA API. The moise.os package provides all classes need to specify an organisation and is composed of four sub-packages: moise.os.ss, moise.os.fs, moise.os.cs and moise.os.ns. The OS class representing the Organisation Specification is composed of one and only one class SS, FS, CS and NS representing each one a specification of the organisation. The moise.oe package is based on the moise.os package in order to define the dynamic part of the organisation taking into account the specifications.

In order to make organisation alive, that's mean produce dynamicity, agents have to evolve inside the organisation. That's why the OE class is composed of the OEAgent class as illustrated on the moise.oe package UML class diagram on the Figure 7. An OE is composed of each model specification instantiation (structural, functional, contextual and normative). In JAVA, the structural specification instantiation is expressed by a set of group instances (Group class which doesn't be confused with GrpSpec class which is a reference) and the functional specification instantiation is expressed by a set of schemes (same comment for SCH and SCHSpec). CS and NS instantiations are expressed by references of OE class to a set of contexts (ContextSpec class from moise.os.cs package) and a set of norms (Norm class from moise.os.ns package), which are active at a given time during the organisation lifetime.

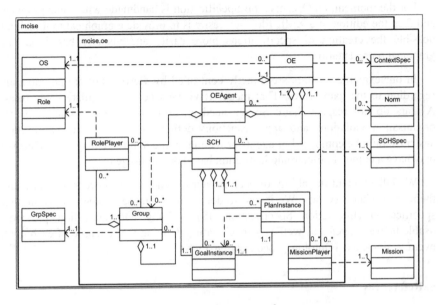

Figure 7. *Moise.oe package for Moise^{Inst} development*

In our iTV game case, an Avatar is composed on one hand by an Agent and on another hand by a multimedia object. This Avatar architecture integrates the ability to behave as a reactive multimedia object and the ability to act as an intelligent agent. The decision allows it to interpret events relating to a Moise^{Inst} organisation and it is able to act on the environment (adopt role, commit on mission, achieve goal, ...) and coordinate it-self with others Avatars by sending events.

By adding organisation abilities in multimedia objects and constraint specifications in the iTV content creation chain, we are able to obtain at the user side reactive and adaptive multimedia objects understanding, interpreting and respecting some rules defined outside each objects. The advantage of this solution is the possibility to change game rules without act on the Avatars behaviours.

5. Conclusion and perspectives

We present in this paper the Moise^{Inst} organisation meta-model allowing the creation of an organisation model constraining a set of agents. This meta-model has been integrated into an iTV content creation chain in order to bring autonomy and constraint. The multimedia content specification being then converted into code, we transform the Moise^{Inst} meta-model into a XML Document Type Definition (DTD). Each XML files is an organisation model. At last we transformed the DTD into a JAVA API.

For the moment, an Organisation Specification is handmade with some graphics and then the edition of a XML file. Our desire is to provide a graphical tool making possible the creation of specifications more easily and visually based on our graphical representation.

In our example Avatars are directly controlled by viewers but are autonomous regarding to the game rules. That means if viewers decide to violate some rules, Avatars do not respect them. So we need an arbitration system able to detect organisation violations and apply sanctions defined in the NS. This arbitration system should be composed of agents providing by the multi-agent system. Thus we may have a complete Electronic Institution based on multi-agent.

We talked about the ability of each Avatar to send event in order to coordinate them with others Avatars. We intend to define in the $Moise^{Inst}$ meta-model another specification (Interaction Specification, IS) defining communication protocols usable between agents as well as a specification defining the semantic of each goal, event, actions, etc. (Ontology Specification, OnS).

6. References

Gâteau, B., Boissier, O., Khadraoui, D., Dubois, E.: "MoiseInst: An organizational model for specifying rights and duties of autonomous agents", *proceedings of CoOrg*, Namur, 2005

Gâteau, B., Khadraoui, D., Dubois, E.: Architecture e-business sécurisée pour la gestion des contrats", *proceedings of SAR*, La Londe-les-Maures, 2004

Luck, M., McBurney, P., Preist, C.: *Agent Technology: Enabling Next Generation Computing* (A Roadmap for Agent Based Computing). AgentLink, 2003

North, D.C.: *Institutions, Institutional Change and Economic Performance*. Cambridge University Press, 1990

OASIS. The Organization for the Advancement of Structured Information Standards, *XLIFF 1.1 Specification*, Committee Specification, 31 October 2003. http://www.oasis-open.org/committees/xliff/documents/xliffspecification.htm (2005)

Renault, S., Meinkohn, F., Khadraoui, D., Blandin, P.: "Reactive and adaptive multimedia object approach for interactive and immersive applications", *proceedings of ICTTA*, Damascus, 2004

Towards Plug and Play Business Software

Andreas Jacobsson

Department of Systems and Software Engineering
School of Engineering
Blekinge Institute of Technology
SE-372 25 Ronneby
Sweden
andreas.jacobsson@bth.se

ABSTRACT: *The ability to realize the potential of innovations is important for societies to be successful. The core of the concept of Plug and Play Business is an integrated set of ICT-tools that support innovators in turning their ideas into businesses. In this paper, we present ongoing research on Plug and Play Business, motivate the research questions and elaborate on the proposed solution. We also specify the expected contributions of this work.*

KEY WORDS: *Interoperability, virtual enterprise, match-making, collaboration, innovation, security.*

1. Introduction

This paper introduces ongoing work on Plug and Play Business software, i.e., an integrated framework of ICT-tools intended to assist enterprises in realizing innovations and conducting business cross organizational boundaries and despite the occurrence of hostile, turbulent and dynamic markets. In this specific context, the ability to locate and collaborate with business partners and customers is vitally important. We envision this set of integrated ICT-tools as a useful measure, especially for small and medium-sized enterprises (SME). Infrastructures for business creation and collaboration are particularly relevant to SMEs, due to their reduced size and high specialization and flexibility. While allowing themselves to maintain their business independence, SMEs are able to reach otherwise unreachable markets and to take advantage of economies of scale.

The paper is organized as follows. We begin by describing the problem background. Thereafter, we pose research questions and discuss a solution direction that addresses the questions. Finally, we conclude by stating the expected contributions of this work and suggest some directions for the future. Sections 2 and 4 are based on previous work within Plug and Play Business (Davidsson *et al.*, 2006; Jacobsson *et al.*, 2006).

2. Background

Today's companies operate in a turbulent and dynamic market with constantly changing conditions. Due to faster and more interconnected information networks, global and local trade is evolving in completely new patterns and organizations are engaging in new types of business alliances. As a consequence, organizations concentrate more and more on their core business processes while outsourcing supporting processes to other organizations, thereby forming Virtual Enterprises (VE). A VE is a temporary alliance of enterprises that come together to share skills or core competencies and resources in order to better respond to business opportunities, and whose cooperation is supported by computer networks (Camarinha-Matos *et al.*, 2003; 2005). The composition of a VE is determined by the need to associate the most suitable set of skills and resources contributed by a number of individual organizations. The general rationale for forming a VE is to reduce costs and time to market while increasing flexibility and access to new markets and resources. Some specific advantages of VEs often emphasized are (Camarinha-Matos *et al.*, 2003):

- Agility: The ability to recognize, rapidly react and cope with the unpredictable changes in the environment in order to achieve better responses to opportunities and higher quality with less investment.

- Complementary roles: Enterprises seek complementarities (creation of synergies) that allow them to participate in competitive business opportunities and new markets.

- Achieving dimension: Particularly for SMEs, being in partnerships with others allow them to achieve critical mass and to appear in the market with a larger "apparent" size.

- Resource optimization: Smaller organizations sharing infrastructures, knowledge, and business risks.

- Competitiveness: Achieving cost effectiveness, by proper division of subtasks among cooperation organizations and timely response by rapidly gathering the necessary competencies and resources.

- Innovation: Being in a network opens the opportunities for the exchange and confrontation of ideas, which can be a basis for innovation.

Most enterprises (and SMEs in particular) recognize the value potential in innovations. The fact that innovations are important to create both private and social values, including economic growth and employment is well-known. However, innovations as such are not sufficient for economic growth; there is also a need to develop the innovation from an idea into a business. From an innovator's perspective there are some common obstacles for realizing the potential of innovations, such as: shortage of time to spend on commercialization activities, lack of business knowledge, underdeveloped business network, and limited financial resources (Tidd et al., 2005). This implies that the innovator requires support to develop the idea into business, something often seen as the specific role of the entrepreneur. As Leibenstein (1968) explains, entrepreneurs are needed to search, discover, evaluate opportunities and marshal the financial resources necessary, among other things. In some but not all cases, the innovator and entrepreneur may be the same person. To play the role as innovator or entrepreneur in the networked economy requires in many instances a global outlook. New trade and production patterns, as well as the emergence of new markets, point towards a more efficient use of global resources. ICT already plays an important role as a facilitator in this development. We believe that better economic growth can be achieved when the innovation and the entrepreneur can compete and solve problems on a global market place.

In a hostile networked surrounding conjured up by strong competition amongst rival companies, complex business processes, new forms of collaboration, and the autonomy and heterogeneity of enterprises, require innovative solutions that are able to manage interorganizational and distributed business partnerships and processes. For this purpose, we propose a new technology – Plug and Play Business Software.

3. Research questions

The overall challenge is to design a system of ICT-tools that support innovators and entrepreneurs to form VEs and collaborate with other enterprises in order to transform a promising idea into a flourishing business. More specifically, the following research questions will be studied within the scope of the overall challenge:

- What are the main market characteristics and what requirements do they imply on the ICT framework?

- What design principles are relevant for an interorganizational framework of ICT-tools?

- What are the main security threats to such a system, and what security-enhancing mechanisms should be included to address them?

So far, our work has mainly been focused on exploring the software requirements and attributes of a Plug and Play Business framework (Jacobsson *et al.*, 2006), information security risk analysis (Carlsson *et al.*, 2005), and examining state of the art technologies that may be useful in constructing the software. The results from this work are presented in the next section.

4. Solution direction

The vision of Plug and Play Business (Davidsson *et al.*, 2006) is to support the creation and management of businesses despite the obstacles mentioned above. The innovations of today are commercialized in the sometimes hostile networked environment of the Internet, engaged in complex business processes, and requiring new forms for collaboration. Together with the autonomy, heterogeneity, and possibly conflicting goals of the involved parties, this requires ICT-solutions that are able to handle turbulent, dynamically evolving and distributed business partnerships and processes that cross the borders of various enterprises. Thus, the interoperability between the information systems of the involved enterprises belongs to the technological core of the concept of Plug and Play Business. Central to Plug and Play Business is the concept of virtual enterprise, or more generally *collaborative networks* (Camarinha-Matos *et al.*, 2005). Other important ideas that can be used for describing the concept of Plug and Play Business are:

- Internet communities: Enterprises dynamically join a Plug and Play Business community by installing and running the Plug and Play Business software and by describing and validating the resources of the enterprise, e.g., production capacity, distribution network, intellectual capital, VAT-number, etc. There may be a need for a specific gate-keeper that regulates the entering and leaving of the community, thus making it a semi-open artificial society.

- Roles: Each member of the community plays one or more roles, e.g., innovator, supplier/provider (of goods, services, expertise, etc.), distributor, marketer, financier, seller, etc. An important role in the life cycle of businesses is the entrepreneur and we make a distinction between this role and that of the innovator. One of the purposes of Plug and Play Business is to automate as much of the entrepreneurial role as possible thus increasing the probability of turning an innovative idea into a business.

- Crystallization: A member of the Plug and Play Business community, typically an innovator, may at any time initiate an attempt to form a collaborative coalition in-between the members. This process may be viewed analogous to crystallization, where a catalyst (innovator) initiates a process resulting in a precise form of collaboration, i.e., the crystal (the VE). The main role of the entrepreneur, which to a large extent is automated by the Plug and Play Business software, is to drive this process.

4.1. *The requirements of Plug and Play Business software*

In order to realize this vision, Plug and Play Business software includes capabilities to enable the different community members to use their resources efficiently and securely within the VEs (crystals). This is specified in two phases where each phase should include a set of functional requirements for the Plug and Play Business software. In the *formation (crystallization) phase*, when the catalyst initiates the VE, the following functions are helpful in forming a successful collaborative coalition:

- Finding: To find candidates suitable for a potential collaboration is an important function. It primarily concerns finding candidates within the community, but possibly also candidates currently outside the community. The finding functionality may include the possibility both for search, based on specific needs specified by criteria, e.g., role, type of products, and business model, as well as for posting general needs or ideas that other members may suggest solutions and/or resources for. Further, the software should also provide the feature of suggesting actors for collaboration based on, for example, content-based recommendation (previous interests of actors) and collaborative recommendations (based on preference of similar actors).

- Evaluation: When a set of potential collaborators has been found they need to be evaluated. This requires support for using track records and potentially support for certification schemes of, for instance, the trustworthiness of the actors. Further, decision support for evaluating trade-offs between a number of characteristics are needed, e.g., between cost of product/service, cost of transportation, and time to delivery of product/service. Which actors to choose for the collaboration (i.e., crystallization) should be based on the evaluation and the estimated value of collaboration with other actors in a crystal.

- Negotiation: When the catalyst has selected actors for the necessary roles of the crystal, agreements between the actors with respect to financial and products/service transfers need to be settled. The Plug and Play Business software should provide support for different types of agreements/contracts including support for intellectual property rights.

When the crystallization phase is finished and a VE is formed, the Plug and Play Business software should also provide support for the *collaboration phase*, i.e., the management of the actual business activities. This support may be on a quite shallow level, e.g., transactions of information between actors. On a deeper level, the Plug and Play Business software should support and facilitate complex coordination and synchronization of activities (resource optimization). A wide range of information types needs to be transferred in an efficient and secure way in order to reduce the administrative costs of the actors, as well as reducing the risk of inaccuracy in information. The management of the crystal requires support for controlling the flow of activities between the involved actors. It concerns activities with potential long-term consequences (e.g., initiating product development) as well as regular business activities (e.g., decisions of production and distribution). With respect to enterprise collaboration, the Plug and Play Business software must support the following (functional) requirements:

- Information resource-sharing: This is related to the content and purpose of the exchanged information with tasks ranging from administrative information exchange to complex operations planning. An example of a simple administrative task is ordering and invoicing, whereas a more complex task may concern making critical information available to the collaborating partners in order to improve operations by better and more efficient planning and scheduling, i.e., resource optimization.

- Multi-lateral collaboration: The more parties involved in the collaboration, the more complex the solutions may be. The simplest case concerns collaboration between only two enterprises, whereas the general case involves a large number of enterprises cooperating with each other in different ways (many-to-many collaboration).

Initially, these functional requirements are used to design a prototype for the Plug and Play Business software. Later on, when defining the architecture, it is recommended to use well defined approaches (such as RUP or UMM from UN/CEFACT) as sources of inspiration. Then, there are some non-functional requirements that are relevant. Even though we have not yet defined the set of requirements needed, we will hereby touch upon them briefly in terms of quality attributes in order to provide a rich picture of Plug and Play Business. A quality attribute can be characterized as an attribute that can be measured, e.g., for comparisons that precede the selection of programs. Apart from common quality attributes, such as scalability, flexibility and performance, there are some security aspects that must be ensured. The attributes of confidentiality, integrity and availability enhances security.

4.2. Implementation issues

The choice of system architecture is closely related to the system's performance in terms of a number of these attributes. Compared to a centralized architecture, a distributed architecture supports many of the quality attributes, e.g., flexibility and scalability. Also, the risk of single point of failure may be avoided increasing the robustness of the system. Another important aspect is software ownership where open source software may support agile operations, which, due to its openness, may present enterprises with the option to speed up software. Some followers of closed source software regard open source software as damaging to the market of commercial software. Others see it as cost avoidance or cost sharing because when many developers need a product it makes sense to share development costs.

A decentralized and open source-based paradigm such as peer-to-peer (P2P) may be preferable for the Plug and Play Business software, because no central authority determines how the participants interact or coordinates them in order to accomplish some task. A P2P infrastructure self-configures and nodes can coordinate autonomously in order to search for resources, find them and interact together. P2P, being a paradigm that allows building dynamic overlay networks, can be used in order to realize an environment that manages a dynamic network of business relations. Dealing with business sensitive assets (e.g., innovators' knowledge), searching and retrieval of contents, as well as discovery, composition and invocation of new services, must be made secure and trustable. The P2P infrastructure realizes an environment in which every organization can make its knowledge and services available to other organizations keeping control over them. In a P2P infrastructure, each organization can autonomously manage this task without having to delegate it to an external central authority that could be perceived as less trusted than the organization itself, and should be the object of an external (to the collaborating network) agreement between all the involved organizations.

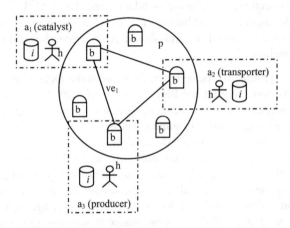

Figure 1. *A Plug and Play Business community (p) consists of a number of actors (a) which may form VEs (ve). Each actor has a specific role in a VE and is represented by a person (h), information systems (i), and the Plug and Play Business software (b)*

In order to make the concept of Plug and Play Business more precise (e.g., so that the requirements of Plug and Play Business software can be crisply defined), we have formalized the most relevant aspects of it (see Jacobsson *et al.*, 2006). As mentioned earlier, there are two main activities (phases) that are supported by the Plug and Play Business software, namely (VE) formation and collaboration. Each enterprise within the Plug and Play Business community is represented by a person, and the Plug and Play Business software. When a VE is formed, each actor takes on a role, e.g., as a producer of a service. Collaboration, which may include the sharing of information resources in-between the collaborating parties, is governed by a set of obligations jointly agreed in the negotiation process. When collaboration is terminated, the VE is dissolved. Figure 1 illustrates the Plug and Play Business community and its associated components.

4.3. *Useful technologies*

Several examinations on current state of the art technologies useful for building ICT infrastructures with the purpose of business creation and management within VEs have been undertaken (see Camarinha-Matos *et al.* (2003; 2005) and Jacobsson (2006)). Some common conclusions are that multi agent technology constitutes a promising foundation for the development of support infrastructures and services. Internet and web technologies, such as web services, represent a fast growing sector with large potential in inter-enterprise collaboration support. However, further support in terms of supporting multi-lateral collaboration is necessary. A number of other emerging technologies, e.g., service-oriented architectures, the semantic web, and countless collections of software standards (see the ebXML framework) are likely to provide important contributions. However, as stated by Camarinha-Matos *et al.* (2005), "publicly funded research should avoid approaches that are too biased by existing technologies".

Based on our review, we believe that there are some technologies that may be useful for the two tasks of Plug and Play Business software. With respect to finding and evaluating partners for a VE, recommendation systems (see Adomavicius *et al.* (2005)) show numerous fruitful examples that can be applied. For the process of establishing an agreement in-between the catalyst and the highest ranked actor in the evaluation process, the Contract Net protocol (Smith 1980) and broker agents (Wiederhold 1992; Wong *et al.*, 2000) may constitute promising alternatives. Software for supporting the collaboration task may be inspired by Microsoft's BizTalk solution, but most likely implemented using wrapper agents (Carlsson *et al.*, 2005; Davidsson *et al.*, 2005) and computational auctions (Rosenschein *et al.*, 1994).

4.4. *Security issues in Plug and Play Business software*

Security (usually defined as the confidentiality, integrity and availability of a system) is a principle feature of Plug and Play Business and security should therefore permeate all aspects of the framework. Violations on ICT infrastructures occur in numerous ways throughout the Internet and both SMEs and large organizations need to consider internal threats (e.g. insiders) and external dangers (e.g. hackers, rival competitors, etc.). Among many things, security problems arise in that the difficulties for guaranteeing that information, which may be sensitive to one party, is not being misused by other parties in a VE. Also, when many companies are involved, access to available information resources is difficult to restrict. More elaboration on security issues of interoperable and interorganizational collaboration can be found in Carlsson *et al.* (2005).

5. Expected contributions

Since the Plug and Play Business framework is intended to be used in real market situations, the forces that govern such markets must be explored. Here, the work may lead to an understanding of the characteristics of market forces such as hostility, turbulence and dynamicity, which the Plug and Play Business community must adjust to. In order to assure the relevance of Plug and Play Business, a business case framing the main market characteristics, with respect to software set to support business creation and management, will be defined.

One important contribution is specifying the design principles and quality attributes that constitute the Plug and Play Business software. Work in this area has partly been undertaken and software requirements have been introduced (see Jacobsson *et al.* (2006)). Another step in approaching Plug and Play Business software is the confirmation of these requirements. Future work will focus on developing an analysis of the components of the Plug and Play Business software and the quality attributes, a validated technological model of the Plug and Play Business software platform, and partial prototypes indicating the viability of the Plug and Play Business concept.

Enhancing security is a critically important factor for enterprises in the Plug and Play Business community. Ensuring security and managing the risks associated with security will aid in guaranteeing the future prosperity of the Plug and Play Business community in that security-enhancing methods enables trust. One important contribution may be that participating enterprises, in particular SMEs, which previously may have dealt with security issues in unprofessional manners, may begin to treat these aspects with greater and more professional care after having deployed the Plug and Play Business software. In further supporting security management, future work will focus on defining proper security-enhancing mechanisms and developing (automated) methods for analyzing threats and valuating risks.

Acknowledgements

This work has been funded by the project "Integration between different SMEs' business systems", financially supported by "Sparbanksstiftelsen Kronan". The author would like to thank all of the members of the project, and in particular; Prof. Paul Davidsson and Dr. Bengt Carlsson.

6. References

Adomavicius, G. and, Tuzhilin, A., "Toward the Next Generation of Recommender Systems: A Survey of the State-of-the-Art and Possible Extensions", *IEEE Transactions on Knowledge and Data Engineering*, vol. 17, no. 6, 2005, pp.734-749.

Camarinha-Matos, L.M. and Afsarmanesh, H., "Collaborative Networks: A New Scientific Discipline", *Journal of Intelligent Manufacturing*, vol. 16, 2005, pp. 439-452.

Camarinha-Matos, L.M. and Afsarmanesh, H., "Elements of a Base VE Infrastructure", *Journal of Computers in Industry*, vol. 51, no. 2, 2003, pp. 139-163.

Carlsson, B., Davidsson, P., Jacobsson, A., Johansson, S.J., and Persson, J.A., "Security Aspects on Inter-Organizational Cooperation Using Wrapper Agents", Proceedings of the Second Workshop on Agent-Based Technologies and Applications for Enterprise Interoperability (ATOP) at the 4th International Joint Conference on Autonomous Agents and Agent Systems, ACM Press, 2005, pp. 13-25.

Carlsson, B., and Jacobsson, A.: Security Consistency in Information Ecosystems – Structuring the Risk Environment on the Internet. To be published in the Journal of Information Systems Security, 2006.

Davidsson, P., Hederstierna, A., Jacobsson, A., Persson, J.A., et al., "The Concept and Technology of Plug and Play Business", to appear in the 8th International Conference on Enterprise Information Systems, 2006.

Davidsson, P., Ramstedt, L., and Törnquist, J., "Inter-Organizational Interoperability in Transport Chains Using Adapters Based on Open Source Freeware", in: D. Konstantas, J.-P. Bourrières, M. Léonard, N. Boudjlida (Eds.) Interoperability of Enterprise Software and Applications, Springer Verlag, Berlin Germany, 2005, pp. 35-43.

Jacobsson, A., and Davidsson, P., "An Analysis of Plug and Play Business Software", in Proceedings of Interoperability for Enterprise Software and Applications Conference I-ESA '06, Springer, 2006.

Leibenstein, H., "Entrepreneurship and Development", The American Economic Review, vol. 58, 1968, pp. 72-83.

Rosenschein, J.S., and Zlotkin, G. Rules of Encounter: Designing Conventions for Automated Negotiation among Computers, MIT Press, Cambridge MA, 1994.

Smith, R.G., "The Contract Net Protocol: High-Level Communication and Control in a Distributed Problem Solver", IEEE Transactions on Computers, C-29, no. 12, 1980, pp. 1104-1113.

Tidd, J., Bessant, J., and Pavitt, K., Managing Innovation – Integrating Technological, Market and Organizational Change, John Wiley & Sons, Chichester West Sussex, 2005.

Wiederhold, G., "Mediators in the Architecture of Future Information Systems", IEEE Transactions on Computers, vol. 25, no. 3, 1992, pp. 38-49.

Wong, H.-C., and Sycara, K.P., "A Taxonomy of Middle-Agents for the Internet", Proceedings of the Fourth International Conference on Multi-Agent Systems, 2000.

Formalising Problem Frames with Ontology

Germain Saval

University of Namur
Institut d'Informatique
rue Grandgagnage, 21
Namur, 5000 (Belgium)
gsa@info.fundp.ac.be

ABSTRACT: *This paper gives a summary of our PhD research started in September 2005 and provides a first PhD schedule. Problem Frames is a method and a notation to structure software requirements analysis and software solution design. It is based on clear separation of concerns between the problem context and the software to be built. To improve traceability and interoperability of models during the requirements analysis and subsequent design phases, the Problem Frames approach needs more formal grounding. We propose an ontology-based formal semantics to Problem Frames. It will be used to relate Problem Frames and other modelling languages using a common ontology. It will ultimately lead to the construction of a tool supporting the Problem Frames approach.*

KEY WORDS: *problem, frame, decomposition, formalisation, ontology, interoperability.*

1. Problem

There are various modelling languages. Some are highly generic and sometimes hard to use in a specific case, others are very domain specific but hard to translate in another domain. Nonetheless, it is obvious that in order to advance in theory and practice of software analysis, we need methods and languages that are both applicable in different domains and translatable in other more specific languages. Software engineering is all about translation. This problem is one of the various topics covered by the term *interoperability*. Here, we are dealing with interoperability of languages and translating constructs and underlying concepts from one to another.

Among the methods to structure and guide requirements and software engineering, the Problem Frames (Jackson, 1995 & 2001) approach is becoming increasingly popular. It aims to separate concerns on the domain (the *givens*) from the software to build (the *machine*). This method identifies shared phenomena (physical or abstract) between domain and machine and thus reduces the interface between these two different states of the world: the givens are a subset of what does exist; the machine belongs to what we must build. It further decomposes the domain and the machine in to smaller elements and the shared phenomena in subsets controlled or observed by these elements. These elements or subproblems are not related in a hierarchical way but are all a different view or *projection* of the problem and the relevant subset of its phenomena.

Problem Frames (PF) notation can be seen as a way of drawing a map of the problem and its context, but they also aim to help identify the solution, not only the problem. To achieve this, the PF approach is equipped with a set of generic *frames* (patterns) to be applied to the problem at hand and its decomposition. These easily recognisable patterns are meant to help the software engineer build and structure the solution while maintaining the coherence with the requirements. In every other engineering discipline, such recognisable patterns are always associated with well-known solutions, built and agreed on by common knowledge and decades of practice. The PF approach is a way to associate partial software solution to specific subproblems. It facilitates the construction of a knowledge base of experience-validated solutions for recognisable problems.

In their state of the art of PF, (Cox *et al.*, 2005) identify four areas on which future research needs to focus:

-   application of the PF approach to realistic case studies,
-   identification of new Problem Frames (new patterns),
-   tool support,
-   teaching and dissemination.

One of the difficulties in the PF approach is to maintain the consistency between models made during the requirements phase, and also between these models and the later phases of design and implementation. This is partially due to a lack of formalisation of the PF language, as reported in (Cox *et al.*, 2005), making hard to maintain traceability between models, design languages and ultimately actual software code. One of the required steps to develop a tool supporting the PF approach is indeed formalisation. We will summarise our claims in the next section, then give an outlook on the proposed solution. In the last sections, we will briefly present our research schedule and expected contributions.

2. Research claims

We claim formalisation will improve the Problem Frames approach, by improving consistency check for problem context decomposition, partially automating the application of Problem Frames (patterns), improving traceability of Problem Frames analysis with respect to other models expressed in different modelling languages, ultimately enabling tool support. Particularly, formalisation will enable checking of problem decomposition, constraints evaluation for PF instantiation and semantic mapping to other modelling languages, relating problem analysis and machine design.

3. Proposed solution

Formalisation can be useful to define and relate different languages. It is especially true for enterprise modelling where one must deal with different models (with various concerns and levels of abstraction). One of the goals of the InterOP European Network of Excellence (INTEROP, 2005) is to define and integrate a new enterprise modelling language called UEML. Quoting INTEROP: "*UEML brings together theories and mechanisms for 'modelling enterprise modelling languages', theories and mechanisms for characterising and finding correspondences between constructs in distinct enterprise modelling languages and, finally, strategies for selecting/classifying such languages.*"

The *UEML approach* to language definition and integration is based on the Bunge-Wand-Weber (BWW) representation model (Bunge, 1977, Bunge, 1979, Wand *et al.*, 1993, Wand *et al.*, 1995), a powerful instrument for understanding modelling languages in general (Evermann *et al.*, 2005, Green *et al.*, 2000, Irwin *et al.*, 2005, Opdahl *et al.*, 2005). In practice, however, many modelling constructs do not map onto just one ontological concept, as assumed by BWW. Instead, they refer to small scenes played by several ontological concepts together. Therefore, a structured template for describing modelling constructs has been built on top of the BWW-model (Opdahl *et al.*, 2004 & 2005).

(Heymans *et al.*, 2006) used this template on the goal modelling language GRL. (Matulevičius *et al.*, 2006) also used this template on the goal modelling language KAOS. These analyses indicate that the UEML approach is difficult to use because it is based on a particular way of thinking. It is sometimes hard to determine exactly which part of a language that constitutes a modelling construct. It is hard to find the appropriate element in the common ontology to use when describing a construct. It is hard to judge when to choose an existing element in the ontology and when to define a new one. The template itself is complex and can be hard to understand. Consequently, the UEML approach, with its ambition to facilitate inter-subjective construct descriptions, can sometimes produce subjective results.

These analyses also highlight several advantages of the UEML approach. It offers more detailed advice on how to proceed when analysing individual modelling constructs. It acknowledges that modelling constructs often represent scenes played by several ontological concepts together. It offers a structured format for storing and managing construct descriptions. It suggests a path towards tool-supported, integrated use of models expressed in different languages, through this structured format in combination with the common ontology.

We will try to apply such a method to define an ontology-based foundation to the PF approach. Specifically, we will use the template to analyse the language constructs of PF. We will then relate this analysis to other modelling languages analyses. Our work will be based on a realistic case study and will try to improve tool support and automatic reasoning. We will try to automate reasoning on ontological concepts with respect to the PF language and other notations, to help discover relations between these modelling languages and the underlying concepts. Ultimately, one will be able to relate concepts expressed in different modelling languages while structuring these models and their relations with the PF approach

4. Schedule

We will focus the first six months of our thesis on a case study. We will apply the PF approach to a realistic case study to improve our knowledge of the approach and possibly discover new Frames. The next six months will be dedicated to the elaboration of a state of art of Problem Frames and ontological approaches. We will study ontologies for information systems, formal semantics and other language description languages. After evaluating the different approaches for PF formalisation, we will try to apply our solution sketched in the previous section to the PF notation. We will implement a tool supporting this approach and evaluate it, using an iterative method during the next two years to refine the tool and the formalisation. The writing of our thesis will take place during the fourth year. Concurrently, we will publish articles and participate to the INTEROP NoE and subsequent projects.

5. Expected contributions

Our research will provide the following outcomes: a realistic software problem analysis using the PF approach, a state of art of the Problem Frames approach with respect to its ontological foundation, an ontology-based formalisation of the PF approach and a tool supporting our approach.

6. References

Bunge M., Ontology I: The Furniture of the World, *Treatise on Basic Philosophy*, vol. 3, Reidel, Boston, 1977.

Bunge M., Ontology II: A World of Systems, *Treatise on Basic Philosophy*, vol. 4, Reidel, Boston, 1979.

Cox K., Hall J. G., Rapanotti L., A Roadmap of Problem Frames Research, *Information and Software Technology*, vol. 47, no. 14, 2005, p. 891-902.

Evermann J., Wand Y., Toward Formalizing Domain Modeling Semantics in Language Syntax, *IEEE Trans. Software Eng*, vol. 31, no. 1, 2005, p. 21-37.

Green P., Rosemann M., Integrated Process Modeling: an Ontological Evaluation, *Information Systems*, vol. 25, no. 2, 2000, p. 73–87, Elsevier ScienceDirect.

Heymans P., Saval G., Dallons G., Pollet I., A Template-based Analysis of GRL, *Advanced Topics in Database Research*, vol. 5, Idea Group Publishing, 2006.

InterOP, Web Page, http://www.interop-noe.org/, November 2005.

Irwin G., Turk D., An Ontological Analysis of Use Case Modeling Grammar, *Journal of AIS*, vol. 6, no. 1, 2005.

Jackson M., *Software Requirements and Specifications: A lexicon of practice, principles and prejudices*, Addison-Wesley, 1995.

Jackson M., *Problem Frames: Analyzing and Structuring Software Development Problems*, ACM Press Books, Addison-Wesley, 2001.

Matulevičius R., Heymans P., Opdahl A. L., Ontological Analysis of KAOS Using Separation of Reference, *To be published in CAiSE'06 International Workshop EMMSAD*, 2006.

Opdahl A. L., Henderson-Sellers B., Understanding and Improving the UML Metamodel through Ontological Analysis, *Software and Systems Modelling*, 1(1), 2002, p. 43–67.

Opdahl A. L., Henderson-Sellers B., A Template for Defining Enterprise Modeling Constructs, *Journal of Database Management (JDM)*, 15 (2), 2004, p. 39–73, Idea Group.

Opdahl A. L., Henderson-Sellers B., Ontologies and Business System Analysis, Green P.Rosemann M., Eds., *Business Systems Analysis with Ontologies*, Idea Group, 2005.

Opdahl A. L., Henderson-Sellers B., A Unified Modelling Language without referential redundancy., *Data Knowl. Eng.*, vol. 55, no. 3, 2005, p. 277-300.

Wand Y., Weber R., On the Ontological Expressiveness of Information Systems Analysis and Design Grammars, *Jour. of Information Systems*, vol. 3, 1993, p. 217–237.

Wand Y., Weber R., On the Deep Structure of Information Systems, *Journal of Information Systems*, vol. 5, 1995, p. 203–223.

Session 4:
Enterprise Modelling
and Knowledge Management

A Proposal for Modelling Enterprise Knowledge in Virtual Enterprises

Reyes Grangel

Grupo de investigación en Integración y Re-Ingeniería de Sistemas (IRIS)
Dept. de Llenguatges i Sistemes Informàtics
Universitat Jaume I
12071 Castelló (Spain)

grangel@uji.es

ABSTRACT: *Enterprise Modelling is defined as the art of "externalising" enterprise knowledge. Many languages, standards and tools have been successfully developed over last few decades to model almost any dimension of an enterprise: process, decision, product, and so forth, and even for modelling Virtual Enterprises. However, some shortcomings of Enterprise Modelling have still not been solved. Some of the most important are related to the interoperability, but also linked to the fact that Enterprise Modelling should be focused on enterprise knowledge, since it provides enterprise models with real value.*

In this context, this paper outlines my PhD thesis, which describes the problematic situation that is the origin of this research and the solutions suggested to solve it, as well as the progress made in the research. The aim of the thesis is to investigate the possibilities of using UML 2 and Profiles mechanism in order to provide a framework in which to solve interoperability problems related to Enterprise Modelling and which takes into account the knowledge dimension in the context of Virtual Enterprises, where interoperability problems are greater.

KEY WORDS: *Enterprise Modelling, Model Driven Architecture (MDA), Computation Independent Model (CIM), Enterprise Knowledge.*

1. Introduction

Enterprise Modelling can be defined as the art of "externalising" enterprise knowledge, which adds value to the enterprise or needs to be shared (Vernadat 2000). In this context, many languages, standards and tools have been developed and used in very different domains and with a number of purposes including requirements engineering, the development of information systems, business process re-engineering, and so forth. Such domains include Virtual Enterprises, where Enterprise Modelling can become very useful in order to achieve their objectives.

However, there still exist some weaknesses in this context for Virtual Enterprises. For instance, the problem of interoperability at a horizontal level as well as a vertical level (see Figure 1), where the main problems are, first, the difficulties involved for exchanging enterprise models among enterprises that use different Enterprise Modelling Languages (EMLs); and, second, the generation of software from these models when different enterprises are involved in this process. Therefore, enterprises, and specially Virtual Enterprises, have troubles for using enterprise models for externalising their enterprise knowledge due to the interoperability problems above described. Some projects attempt to solve these problems. For instance, UEML[1] and POP*[2] provide common exchange formats to make it easy to exchange enterprise models at a horizontal level; and in Model Driven Engineering (MDE), several initiatives have being undertaken, one of the most interesting being Model Driven Architecture (MDA) (MDA 2003) promoted by OMG.

The thesis project presented in this paper has its origin in this framework and its foremost aim is to provide a proposal for a meta-model that enables enterprises to model enterprise knowledge following the MDA approach. The development of this meta-model will be based on previous works carried out in several European Projects, like INTEROP (INTEROP 2003) and ATHENA (ATHENA 2004), in which different meta-models, UEML (UEML 2002, INTEROP 2003) and POP* (ATHENA 2004), have been defined in order to solve interoperability problems at a horizontal level. On the one hand, the objective is to adapt and extend both results to the context of knowledge management systems. On the other hand, the meta-model obtained will be integrated into the Reference Architecture ARDIN (Chalmeta 03) for the integration of Virtual Enterprise, defined by the IRIS Research Group, with the goal of extending its second dimension to enterprise knowledge modelling.

The objective of this paper, then, is to describe my PhD thesis and its current progress state. This section is intended to give an idea about the research question. Section 2 presents the problematic situation that the thesis intends to solve. In the third, the current knowledge and existing solutions related to these problems are

---

1 Unified Enterprise Modelling Language developed first by UEML Thematic Network (UEML 2002), and currently by INTEROP NoE (INTEROP 2003).
2 Acronym of the different enterprise dimensions: Process, Organisation, Product, and so on, represented by a star (ATHENA 2004).

described. Finally, the methodology of work, the main research objectives, and the proposed approach are presented in section 4, section 5 outlines the work carried out so far, together with a discussion on the main contributions provided by the results achieved, and section 6 describes the expected contribution.

2. Description of the problem

Nowadays, there are many languages, methodologies and tools related to Enterprise Modelling, even for modelling Virtual or Extended Enterprises (EXTERNAL 2002). But integrating the models generated with these languages is complicated, since no tools exist with which to integrate models generated with different languages (interoperability problem at horizontal level, see Figure 1).

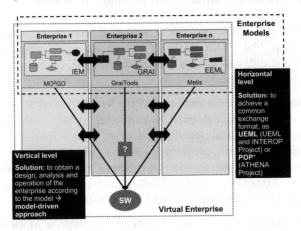

Figure 1. *Interoperability problems and solutions for Virtual Enterprises at the horizontal and vertical level related to Enterprise Modelling*

This kind of languages are defined in proprietary formats and are only implemented by proprietary tools that generally speaking, are only affordable for large enterprises. Therefore, the problem of interoperability is intensified in Small and Medium Enterprises (SME), which have limited resources to successfully adapt innovative technologies existing on the market. Thus, SMEs produce few enterprise models and, moreover, their exchange among partners is very difficult.

On the other hand, SMEs set up Virtual Enterprises in order to establish flexible collaborations with other partners and to take advantage of new market opportunities. The Virtual Enterprise (Browne *et al.,* 1999) can be defined as a temporary network of independent companies, often former competitors, which come together quickly to exploit fast-changing opportunities. The business partners are integrated using Information and Communication Technologies. Therefore, the interoperability problems at different levels, including at the Enterprise Modelling level, can become decisive aspects affecting the achievement of business success.

Furthermore, a vertical interoperability problem arises in the Virtual Enterprise's context when its partners intend to use enterprise models to generate software. Since, it is needed to exchange information at different levels (ontological, business, and technological) in order to achieve full interoperability (Chen *et al.*, 2003, Ducq *et al.*, 2004) between SMEs that make up the Virtual Enterprise. These inconvenients make hard for Virtual Enterprise[3] to use enterprise models to one of their most valuable purposes, to make explicit enterprise knowledge with the objective of improving performance of enterprise.

3. Existing approaches for solving interoperability problems

Regarding interoperability problem at horizontal level, the objective is to achieve a common format, like UEML or POP*, which are valid initiatives to enabling exchange between different models as well to establish an environment allowing existing models to be reused.

On the other hand, different approaches have been proposed to solve the problem of generating software from enterprise models. Such as MDA, which main purpose is to separate the functional specification of a system from the details of its implementation in a specific platform in order to promote the use of models to generate software. Hence, this architecture defines a hierarchy of models from three points of view: Computation Independent Model (CIM), Platform Independent Model (PIM), and Platform Specific Model (PSM) (MDA 2003).

Different works performed on using **UML for Enterprise Modelling** (Marshall 2000, Eriksson 2000, Berio *et al.*, 2003) evaluate the possibilities of using UML for modelling enterprises. Consequently, some of them define different types of specific concepts related to business domain, and use extension mechanisms like stereotypes, tagged values, and so forth provided by UML 1.x. However, the new version and specifications developed by the OMG, such as UML 2 and MDA, call for a review of these proposals again, and the works promoted by OMG with Business Enterprise Integration DTF, like Business Semantics of Business Rules (BSBR), Production Rules Representation (PRR), Business Process Definition Metamodel (BPDM), and Organization Structure Metamodel (OSM) that are currently being carried out show this to be the case. In this sense, it is needed to clarify which is the characterisation of the CIM level and, then, to specify which part of CIM models must be transformed into PIM models, since according to (Berrisford 2004) there must surely be degrees of CIMness.

---

3 The term Virtual Enterprise is used in this paper to concern Virtual Enterprises made up of SMEs.

Furthermore, the new specification of UML 2 provides profiles with a greater degree of completeness than version 1.5. (Fuentes *et al.,* 2004). Therefore, it will be possible to customise UML in a better way. For instance, UML provides many diagrams for modelling dynamic aspects, but not for direct modelling of business processes in a similar way to how they are represented in an IDEF diagram. Business process modelling with UML is therefore complex (Noran 2004) and the use of profiles according to UML 2 can make this task easier.

4. Research objectives and approach proposed

This dissertation project is set within two frameworks. The first one, the distinct research projects related to the Virtual Enterprise in different sectors (transport, tile industry, textile, and so forth) (Chalmeta *et al.,* 2001, 2003, 2003a, 2004, 2005) carried out by the IRIS Research Group at the Universitat Jaume I (Spain). And the second one, the INTEROP NoE in which the IRIS Group is involved and which is focused on interoperability taking into account the following domains: Architecture \& Platforms, Enterprise Modelling, and Ontologies. The methodology used for the research has considered the results obtained in these contexts and it has been performed in an iterative and incremental way following the philosophy of the object-oriented methodologies like UP (Unified Process) (Jacobson *et al.,* 1999).

The research aims to improve the interoperability of SMEs that promote Virtual Enterprises towards enterprise knowledge modelling. The results obtained will allow enterprise knowledge to be modelled in this kind of enterprises. According to (Vail 1999), enterprise knowledge can be seen as information made actionable in a way that adds value to the enterprise. Taking into account this definition, enterprise knowledge is defined in this work as the network of connections among data and information that enables people involved in the enterprise to act and to make decisions that add value to the enterprise. Moreover, the meta-model obtained will be integrated into the Reference Architecture ARDIN (Chalmeta 2003) for the integration of Virtual Enterprises defined by the IRIS Group, with the goal of extending its second dimension to enterprise knowledge modelling.

Therefore, the main research goal is to provide mechanisms that can be used to reduce the interoperability problems related to Enterprise Modelling in a model-driven approach and focused on enterprise knowledge, in the context of Virtual Enterprises. In this regard, the objective is to investigate the possibilities of using UML for Enterprise Modelling in order to solve this kind of interoperability problems. Furthermore, the mechanism provided by UML Profiles, redefined in UML 2, will be analysed in order to extend and adapt UML for the specific domain of enterprise knowledge modelling. The specific objectives of the research work are the following:

– To examine the state of the art in Enterprise Modelling focused on knowledge modelling and UML and UML Profiles focused on Enterprise

Modelling, taking into account the MDA framework defined by OMG and European Projects related to interoperability.

- To obtain a set of requirements for modelling the dimensions (process, product, organisation, etc.) of the whole Virtual Enterprise, especially enterprise knowledge, in order to define a framework for describing the problematic situation.

- To define a meta-model based on UML and its extension mechanism, UML Profiles, that allows the knowledge map of a Virtual Enterprise to be represented.

- To define a methodology for enterprise knowledge modelling including the UML Profiles defined, and set out a series of the guidelines of using these profiles in order to generate interoperable enterprise models.

- To validate the methodological approach and UML extension defined in a real case study, by applying the methodology to a Textile Virtual Enterprise.

5. Discussion

The solution suggested here is focused on enterprise knowledge and its modelling at CIM level, i.e. by following the MDA approach and also taking into account previous works on meta-modelling like UEML and POP*. The main contribution is to combine the following two approaches; traditional Enterprise Modelling (Grangel *et al.*, 2005a), such as GRAI (Doumeingts *et al.*, 1992, 1998), PERA (Williams 1993), GERAM (GERAM 1999), IEM (IEM 2003), EEML (Lillehagen *et al.*, 2002), and so forth, with the framework defined by OMG with MDA and the new version 2.0 of UML (see Figure 2).

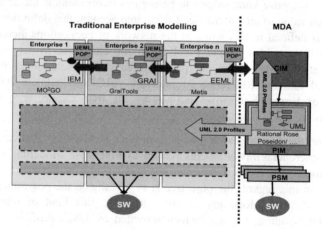

Figure 2. *Research framework: Traditional Enterprise Modelling/MDA*

The idea is to take advantage of strengths of the two approaches in order to provide guidelines and mechanisms, which can be apply to SMEs. Moreover, the originality of this work rests on Enterprise Modelling at the CIM level in the representation of knowledge as a new dimension related to existing enterprise dimensions like process, organisation, decision, and so forth. The main work performed and the results obtained related to this thesis can be summarised in:

 - Conclusions on the state of the art in Enterprise Modelling Techniques, Tools and Standards carried out in INTEROP NoE, from model-driven point of view (Grangel *et al.*, 2005). They state the same difficulties in the context of Enterprise Modelling that have been summarised in this paper, focused especially on interoperability problems due to the great number of languages, frameworks, methodologies and tools concerning Enterprise Modelling that exist. Also, many studies are being performed that deal with PIMs, PSMs, UML Profiles, QVT, and so forth in the MDA framework, but the characterisation of CIMs and the features that an enterprise model must satisfy to be considered a CIM and generate appropriate software are still in progress.

 - During a research stay at the European Software Institute (Spain) to work on the POP* meta-model within the framework of the ATHENA Project , the following work was performed: a comparison among POP*, UEML and other meta-models; participation in the definition of the POP* meta-model; definition of a UML 2 Profiles of POP*; and development of a proof of concept of the POP* meta-model (Grangel *et al.*, 2005b). This work constitutes the basis for future work on the development of an enterprise knowledge meta-model.

 - A general methodology obtained as the result of the current IRIS Research Project related to knowledge management. This methodology guides the process of developing and implementing a knowledge management system that allows knowledge to be collected, modelled and applied, while ensuring the quality, security and authenticity of the knowledge provided. The work presented in this paper is concerning with the third phase of this methodology that deals with knowledge representation.

 - The definition of the target knowledge (Grangel *et al.*, 2006) useful to establish a common conceptual framework in a Virtual Enterprise, while considering each conceptual block of knowledge (enterprise oriented) proposed in the approach for knowledge management defined by IRIS Group, that is to say, organisation, process, product, and resource. The target knowledge defined has been classified taking into account two points of view, in order to provide a basis that can be used as a reference for further representation of knowledge by Virtual Enterprises that need to model their enterprise knowledge.

 - A first proposal for Enterprise Modelling with UML 2 at the CIM level, which takes the model-driven approach into account, is presented in (Grangel *et al.*, 2006a, 2006b). The proposal describes a profile for Enterprise Modelling, only from the organisational structure point of view. This profile is being improved by including other concepts which are essential for a complete enterprise model, such as process, product, and specially knowledge.

6. Expected contributions

Nowadays, the main work in progress is, first, related to the customisation of the UEML/POP* meta-models for enterprise knowledge modelling using UML 2 Profiles and refining the proposal above presented, and second, defining the guidelines for using these profiles in order to generate interoperable enterprise models.

In Figure 3, the current framework proposed to model enterprise knowledge at the CIM level is shown. The framework at the CIM level are divided into three sublevels related to the firsts life-cycle phases defined in GERAM (GERAM 1999), that is to say, "Global Model" linked to *Identification*, "Business Models" linked to *Concept*, and "Business Requirements for Systems" linked to *Requirements*, respectively. Moreover, each model proposed in the framework is being defined at a meta-modelling level in order to provide the UML Profile needed. When this work was finished, the expected contribution will be to provide a practical example applying the defined proposal in a Textile Virtual Enterprise.

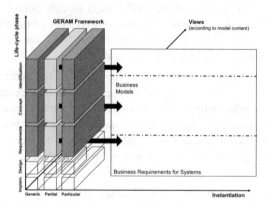

Figure 3. *Relationship between the proposal and the GERAM framework*

Acknowledgments

This work was funded by the EC, Interoperability Research for Networked Enterprises Applications and Software (INTEROP NoE) (IST-2003-508011). The authors are indebted to TG2. It was also supported by CICYT DPI2003-02515.

7. References

ATHENA, "Advanced Technologies for interoperability of Heterogeneous Enterprise Networks and their Applications IP (IST-2001-507849)", 2004, http://www.athena-ip.org.

Berio G., Petit M., "Enterprise Modelling and the UML: (sometimes) a conflict without a case", *Proc. of 10th ISPE International Conf. on Concurrent Engineering: Research and applications*, 2003, p. 26-30.

Berrisford G., "Why IT veterans are sceptical about MDA", *Second European Workshop on Model Driven Architecture (MDA) with an emphasis on Methodologies and Transformations*, Computing Laboratory, University of Kent, Kent, 2004, p. 125-135.

Browne J., Zhang J., "Extended and virtual enterprises - similarities and differences", *International Journal of Agile Management Systems* 1/1, 1999, p. 30-36.

Chalmeta R., Campos C., Grangel, R., "References architectures for enterprises integration", *The Journal of Systems and Software*, 57(3), 2001, p. 175-191.

Chalmeta R., Grangel R., "Performance measurement systems for virtual enterprise integration", *International Journal of Computer Integrated Manufacturing,* 18(1), 2005, p. 73-84.

Chalmeta R., Grangel R., "ARDIN extension for virtual enterprise integration", *The Journal of Systems and Software*, 67(3), 2003, p. 141-152.

Chalmeta R., Grangel R., Campos C., Coltell Ò. "An Approach to the Enterprise Integration", *Open INTEROP Workshop on Enterprise Modelling and Ontologies for Interoperability (EMOI-INTEROP 2004) at CAiSE'04*, 2004, p. 253-256.

Chalmeta R., Grangel R., Ortiz Á., Poler R., "Virtual Integration of the Tile Industry (VITI)", *Conceptual Modeling for Novel Application Domains*, Springer-Verlag, 2003, p. 65-76.

Chen D., Doumeingts G., "European initiatives to develop interoperability of enterprise applications-basic concepts, framework and roadmap", *Annual Reviews in Control*, 27(2), 2003, p. 153-162.

Doumeingts G., Vallespir B., Chen D., *International Handbook on Information Systems*, Springer-Verlag, chapter Decisional modelling GRAI grid, 1998, p. 313-337.

Doumeingts G., Vallespir B., Zanittin M., Chen D., *GIM-GRAI Integrated Methodology, a Methodology for Designing CIM Systems*, Version 1.0, 1992, LAP/GRAI, University Bordeaux 1, Bordeaux, France.

Ducq Y., Chen D., Vallespir B., "Interoperability in enterprise modelling: requirements and roadmap", *Advanced Engineering Informatics*, 18(4), 2001, p. 193-203.

Eriksson H., Penker M., *Business Modeling with UML: Business Patterns at Work*, J. Wiley, 2000.

EXTERNAL, *Extended Enterprise MEthodology*, Final version 1-12-D-2002-01-0 (IST-1999-10091)", 2002, http://research.dnv.com/external/default.htm.

Fuentes L., Vallecillo A., "Una introducción a los perfiles UML", *Novática*, marzo-abril (168), 2004, p. 6-11.

Grangel R., Bourey J-P., Berre A., "Solving Problems in the Parametrisation of ERPs using a Model-Driven Approach", *Interoperability for Enterprise Software and Applications Conference (I-ESA'06)*, 2006.

Grangel R., Bourey J-P., Chalmeta R., Bigand M., "UML for Enterprise Modelling: a Model-Driven Approach", *I-ESA '06*, 2006.

Grangel R., Chalmeta R., Campos C., "Defining of Target Knowledge in VE", *9th BIS*, 2006.

Grangel R., Chalmeta R., "A Methodological Approach for Enterprise Modelling of Small and Medium Virtual Enterprises based on UML. Application to a Tile Virtual Enterprise", *Doctoral Symposium at INTEROP-ESA '2005*, 2005.

Grangel R., Chalmeta R., Campos C., Coltell, Ò, "Enterprise Modelling, an overview focused on software generation", *Interoperability of Enterprise Software and Applications Workshops at INTEROP-ESA '2005*, 2005, Hermes Science Publishing.

Grangel R., Chalmeta R., Schuster S., Peña I., "Exchange of Business Process Models using the POP* Meta-model", *BPM 2005 Workshops*, 2005, Springer-Verlag.

IEM, "Business Process Oriented Knowledge Management", *Knowledge Management. Concepts and Best Practices*, 2003, Springer-Verlag.

IFIP-IFAC, "Generalised Enterprise Reference Architecture and Methodology (GERAM). Technical Report Version 1.6.3", 1999.

INTEROP, "Interoperability Research for Networked Enterprises Applications and Software NoE (IST-2003-508011)", 2003, http://www.interop-noe.org.

Jacobson I., Booch G., Rumbaugh J., *The Unified Software Development Process*, Addison-Wesley, 1999.

Lillehagen F.M., Dehli E., Fjeld L., Krogstie J., Jorgensen H.D., "Utilizing Active Knowledge Models in an Infrastructure for Virtual Enterprises", *PRO-VE*, 2002, p. 353-360.

Marshall C., *Enterprise Modeling with UML. Designing Successful Software Through Business Analysis*, Addison-Wesley, 2000.

Noran O., "UML vs. IDEF: An Ontology-Oriented Comparative Study in View of Business Modelling", *ICEIS (3*, 2004, p. 674-682.

OMG, "MDA Guide Version 1.0.1", 2003, Object Management Group.

UEML,"Unified Enterprise Modelling Language Thematic Network (IST-2001-34229)", 2002, http://www.ueml.org.

Vail E.F., "Knowledge mapping: getting started with knowledge management", Information Systems Management Fall(3), 1999, p. 16-23.

Vernadat F.B., "Enterprise Modeling and Integration: Myth or reality?", *Proc. 2nd Int. Conf. on Management and Control of Production and Logistics (MCPL '2000)*, 2000.

Williams T., "The Purdue Enterprise Reference Architecture", *Proceedings of the Workshop on Design of Information Infrastructure Systems for Manufacturing*, 1993, Elsevier.

Methodology for the development of a tacit knowledge management system for virtual enterprises

Víctor Fernández Pallarés

University Jaume I of Castellón (Spain)
Grupo Integración y Re-Ingeniería de Sistemas www.iris.uji.es
Campus Riu Sec s/n 12006. Castellon. Spain
Tel: +34.964.72.8329. Fax: +34.964.72.84.35
vfernandezpa@gmail.com, victor.fernandez@uji.es
rchalmet@lsi.uji.es

ABSTRACT: *Knowledge management is nowadays one of the great research fields in which several philosophical and theoretical approaches have been proposed, and different technological solutions have also been developed and adapted with in it. However, knowledge management is a concept still evolving, and it faces serious difficulties when attempts are made to implement it in enterprises. The main cause of this situation is the lack of methodologies for guiding the process of development and application of this kind of systems. Moreover, there are few practical cases that can be taken as a reference and none at all when it comes to virtual enterprises. In this context, this paper outlines my PhD thesis proposal for describing this difficult situation, which is the origin of this research and the objectives suggested to solve it. The aim of the thesis is to develop a general methodology for directing the process of development and implementation of a Global Knowledge Management System (including the highly complex tacit part of it) in a virtual enterprise.*

KEY WORDS: *Knowledge management, tacit knowledge, virtual enterprise.*

1. Introduction

This paper describes the background and objectives of my PhD thesis. It is organised in four sections. The first one shows the formulation of the problem. The second one presents the most significant problems within the field of research. The third one shows the suggested solution, in the form of an approach to the problem and the degree of innovation. Finally, the fourth section introduces the research methodology that was applied.

2. Problem formulation

A Virtual Enterprise (or Extended Enterprise) can be considered as a temporary alliance of globally distributed enterprises which intervene in different phases of the life cycle of a product or service, sharing resources, skills and costs. To do so they draw on the new communication and information technologies in order to be able to better utilise market opportunities and design an efficient corporative strategy.

The design and construction of a knowledge management system (KMS) in a virtual enterprise (as a fundamental factor to support the new requirements in the market and obtain a competitive advantage) is a very complex process which includes different strategic, technological, human, organisational and knowledge management elements. Here, we are referring to tacit knowledge in the virtual enterprise. Such knowledge, after its transformation in accordance with the models and flows of the organisation's knowledge conversion management, becomes wholly explicit knowledge, which stimulates the sustainable growth of the organisation (i.e. both virtual and individual enterprises).

This PhD thesis proposal lies within this latter complex framework, that is, tacit and global (integrated tacit and explicit) knowledge management systems, but more specifically within the virtual enterprise. Our objectives will be summarised in the development of a reference architecture and its associated methodology for the integrated and sustainable development of an enterprise system which allows management of tacit knowledge and its application to the virtual enterprise. This framework will be arranged around the elements explained in the next sections of this paper.

Finally, we will apply the specially designed methodology to a Virtual Tile Enterprise to test and validate the results it offers, and in turn this will allow us to reach a number of final conclusions.

3. Significant problems in the field of research

Knowledge management is nowadays one of the great research fields in which several philosophical and theoretical approaches have been proposed. Likewise, different technological solutions have also been developed and adapted to it.

However, knowledge management is a concept that is still evolving, and serious difficulties arise when attempts are made to implement it in enterprises. The main cause of this situation is the lack of formal methodologies (Zack, 1999) (Bueno, 2002) for guiding the process of development and implementation of this kind of systems (Chalmeta, 2001). Moreover, there are few practical cases (Coviello *et al.*, 2001) that can be taken as a reference (Binney, 2001) and **none at all when it comes to the domain of tacit knowledge management in virtual enterprises** (Chalmeta, 2003) (Davenport, 1998).

Formal theories and technological solutions have generally been applied, with varying degrees of success, in an independent manner in order to identify and transfer information and explicit knowledge (basically with documental support). However, the greatest complexity is to be found **in tacit knowledge**, that is to say, implicit knowledge, which is unspoken and located within relationships among people or teams, customers, suppliers, partners, owners or shareholders of different member organisations of the integrated virtual enterprise, etc. Below, we will call these sets of knowledge "domains of knowledge". It is this type of knowledge that will finally give the virtual enterprise its real competitive advantage.

Other types of initiatives, techniques or actions therefore need to be applied. These may include, for example, making a source map of internal experience (which is little more than a DataWarehouse designed for information management and to enable localisation of the uncodified knowledge that exists in the organisation and which is normally embedded in experts' heads), creating networks of knowledge workers or establishing new managerial roles that have to do with knowledge management.

4. Suggested solution: approach to the problem and innovation

To cope with the new market requirements, enterprises and especially the virtual SME need a methodology to achieve integrated and sustainable development using their tacit knowledge. They will therefore be able to confront the market environment with full guarantees of success while maintaining their essence, that is, their intangible knowledge, which is the source of the rest of the knowledge and information generated in corporative information systems.

The suggested solution includes the definition of a reference architecture and its associated methodology in order to allow virtual enterprises to manage their business efficiently from a knowledge point of view. It is very important to note the large, complex problem of tacit knowledge as the centre and core of future interoperability problems.

My approach to this problem about knowledge management in virtual enterprises is organised around the following innovation actions, which define the content of my results. Section 6 includes all my contributions to the resolutions of these problems.

5. Applied research methodology

My experience with information and knowledge management systems, team management, the application of e-business systems and e-commerce technology, the projects carried out throughout my time as a senior-consultant/junior-manager in Accenture and, finally, all my PhD studies conducted parallel to my professional career have enabled me to carry out a complete study of the state of the art in the current research domain. To obtain the results, my thesis was developed using the incremental and iterative methodology outlined below, and which is organised in four different phases:

– Phase I: Review of the state of the art. Definition and input of new requirements.

– Phase II: Approach to/development of a reference architecture and methodology for the integrated and sustainable implementation of a global knowledge management system (including the tacit part as the most important aspect). Definition of an efficient integration strategy that enables results to be achieved.

– Phase III: Application of the methodology thus developed to different virtual enterprises.

– Phase IV: Validation and testing of the methodology, conclusions and future work.

6. Contributions of the applicant to the resolution of the problem: goals and results achieved so far

The specific goals and results achieved in my thesis, which in fact are my contributions as an applicant to the complete resolution of the problem, are the following:

– Analytic study and review of current knowledge (state of the art, which has already been written by me, as introductory point of the thesis) of the problem domain (concerning virtual enterprises), as well as the state of existing solutions, while also focusing strongly on the integration requirements of the virtual enterprise, its reference architecture and its management systems. All this will allow us to continue with the integration of our **vEKM architecture** in them.

– Definition of a Reference **Architecture** for the integrated development of a knowledge management system, which includes the necessary action framework and the associated organisational, technological, human, relational and cultural management aspects.

– Virtual Enterprise Analysis and Identification of Domains of Knowledge/Requirements.

– Definition and development of the methodology to manage, control and coordinate the development and implementation of the highly complex **tacit part associated to the global** (i.e. explicit and tacit) knowledge management system of the virtual enterprise.

All this makes it necessary to define submethodologies like vEKM to customer knowledge management (CKM), business knowledge management (BKM) from the different member enterprises, suppliers and partners, and employee knowledge management (EKM), from the human resources internal to each member enterprise in the global virtual enterprise.

– Development of the final model of the global knowledge management system. This model includes the current information technologies to enable us to achieve the results presented here. There is also a need for the description and design of the **technological components** and **e-business strategy** associated to the development of each of its parts and relations, thus allowing automation of the information flows and relations with customers, suppliers and partners.

This work has been funded by CICYT DPI2003-02515 and INTEROP NoE (IST-2003-508011).

7. Bibliography

Bernus, P. *"Business Evolution and Enterprise Integration-Concept Group"*. Ed. Chapman Hall, 1997.

Binney D. The knowledge management spectrum – understanding the KM landscape, *Journal of Knowledge Management*, 5, 1, 33-42. 2001.

Boisot, M. H. *Knowledge Assets: Securing Competitive Advantage in the Information Economy.* Oxford. University Press, Oxford. 1998.

Borghoff, U., Schlichter, J. *Computer-Supported Cooperative Work: Introduction to Distributed Applications.* Springer, 2000.

Bueno, E. *"Enfoques principales y tendencias en Dirección del Conocimiento"* (Knowledge Management). Ediciones la Coria, Cáceres. 2002.

Bueno, E. *"Gestión del Conocimiento: desarrollos teóricos y aplicaciones"*. Ediciones la Coria, Cáceres. 2002.

Chalmeta, R., Campos, C., Grangel, R.. *Referent Architectures for Enterprise Integration. Journal of Systems and Software* 57 (3), 175-191. Elsevier, 2001.

Chalmeta, R., Grangel, R. ARDIN extension for Virtual Enterprise Integration. *Journal of Systems and Software* 67, 141-152. Elsevier, 2003.

Chalmeta, R. Virtual Transport Enterprise Integration. *Journal of Integrated Design and Process Science* 4 (4), 45-56. IOS Press Publishes, 2000.

Coviello, A. *et al. Standardised KM Implementation Approach.* European KM Forum. IST Project No 2000 – 26393. 2001.

Davenport T., De Long, David, Beer, M. "*Successful Knowledge Management Projects*", Sloan Management Review, Winter, 43-57. 1998.

Fernández, E.; Montes, J.M.; Vázquez, C.J. Tipología e implicaciones estratégicas de los recursos intangibles. Un enfoque basado en la teoría de recursos. *Revista Asturiana de Economía*, no. 11, pp. 159-183, 1998.

Lindvall, M. Rus, I. Sinha, S. Technology Support for Knowledge Management. *Lecture Notes in Computer Science*. Volume 2640. November 2003.

Newman, B.D. and Conrad, K.W., KM Characterization Framework, *The Knowledge Management Theory Papers*, 1999. Also published in the Proc. of the Third Int. Conf. on Practical Aspects of Knowledge Management (PAKM2000) Basel, Switzerland, 30-31. October 2000.

Skyrme, D. Knowledge management solutions - the IT contribution. *ACM SIGGROUP Bulletin* Volume 19, Issue 1. Pages: 34 – 39. 1998.

Zack M.H. Developing a Knowledge Strategy. *California Management Review*, Vol. 41, No. 3, Spring, pp. 125-145, 1999.

Semantic Enrichment of Enterprise Modelling

Nabila Zouggar

LAPS/GRAI, Université Bordeaux 1, ENSEIRB, UMR CNRS 5131
351, cours de la libération
33405 Talence cedex, France

nabila.zouggar@laps.u-bordeaux1.fr

ABSTRACT: *Enterprise modelling and ontology are two separated fields of research. On the one hand, there exist various enterprise modelling languages developed since twenty years, but most of them are considered primarily on a syntactic basis. On the other hand, ontologies have been elaborated, which aim to formally define concepts in order to avoid ambiguities of understanding of knowledge in a specific domain. Problems of application and use of enterprise modelling languages raised are mainly the lack of semantic. So, semantic enrichment of these languages is becoming an essential topic in enterprise integration and interoperability areas.*

KEY WORDS: *Enterprise modelling, Ontology, Semantic Annotation.*

1. Introduction

Considering the semantic lack of the existing enterprise modelling languages, the objective of our research is to allow the semantic enrichment of enterprise modelling using ontologies. The goal of this research is to improve the use of enterprise modelling languages, particularly during their use by several systems.

The rest of the paper is organized as follows. We will firstly present in section 2 a definition and the role of enterprise modelling. We will insist here on the semantic deficit of enterprise modelling languages. Secondly we will briefly review in section 3 the current state-of the-art in Ontology. Finally, we will present in section 4, before concluding the orientations that we consider for the semantic enrichment of enterprise modelling.

2. Enterprise modelling and semantic

Problems of semantic enrichment of the enterprise modelling find its sources in the nature of existing enterprise modelling languages. Indeed, research work on these languages is focused primarily on the syntactic coherence rather than on their semantic contents.

2.1. *Enterprise modelling, languages specialization and conceptual models*

Enterprise is a complex reality which has to be modelled in order to understand it and in the same time allows reasoning on a well defined project. Enterprise modelling aims to formalize the whole or part of an enterprise with the purpose of including/understanding or explaining an existing situation or realizing and then validating a conceived project (Braesch *et al.*, 1995).

In manufacturing engineering, the first work in enterprise modelling was developed in the United States in the 1970s and in particular the development of SADT, SSAD, IDEF0, Data Flow Diagram. In Europe, the programs of the European Commission largely contribute to develop and diffuse enterprise modelling languages and tools since 1980s (Esprit programme for example). We can mention, for example, MERISE, NIAM, M*, CIMOSA, OMT, IEM, IDEFx, METIS or ARIS Toolset (Vallespir *et al.*, 2003), (Vallespir, 2003).

An enterprise model is always associated to finality and it must, according to the needs, be able to take into account the structural, functional and behavioural aspects. In addition to these aspects, it must also be able to represent the particular point of view of an actor. Finally, a specific approach is often associated to each modelling language. This approach clarifies the various phases necessary to the construction and exploitation of the model (life cycle); each phase being often characterized by a level of abstraction (conceptual, organisational or technical). This last, explains why the work undertaken within the framework of the enterprise modelling gave place to many modelling languages and tools corresponding to a modelling finality. When a methodological approach has vocation to have a wide field of modelling, it uses several languages. The latter are structured within a modelling framework which clarifies the relative position of the models, the areas of coverage and the mechanisms of mapping of the one to the other.

Modelling languages are based on conceptual models (or reference models). These conceptual models correspond to coherent valid concepts for the whole of the systems class that language applies. Within this framework, modelling language aims to apply concepts for an operational issue.

In the two cases, precise modelling field or operational variation of a conceptual model, it proves that a modelling formalism corresponds to a defined "semantic field", so it carries this semantics.

2.2. Syntactic dimension of the languages

In spite of this *necessary semantic component* of any modelling language, most of enterprise modelling languages has only the syntactic dimension. This situation is particularly highlighted when we seek to federate different modelling languages. Two approaches are possible, the first is based on an exchange format like PSL, and the other seeks to unify the languages, following the example UEML.

PSL (Process Specification Language) has been designed to facilitate correct and complete exchange of process information among manufacturing systems, such as scheduling, process modelling, process planning, production planning, simulation, project management, work flow, and business process reengineering (Roque, 2005).

UEML (Unified Enterprise Modelling Language) is the consequence of the several existing modelling languages that is difficult for the users to really include/understand them and to choose most adequate one. However, a more detailed study of these languages shows a great similarity in their underlying concepts. The approach which follows is to identify the components (constructs) of languages and to bring them in a single syntax (Vallespir *et al.*, 2003), (Vallespir, 2003), (Roque, 2005), (Roque *et al.*, 2005).

2.3. Semantic lack of enterprise modelling

However, semantics resulting from the subjacent conceptual model to the modelling language is quite present in the model built with this language. Also, we can consider in a first approach that the modelling language ensures a certain syntactic rigour whereas semantic is interpreted by the analyst himself. Thus, the semantic guarantee of the models depends only on the analyst's competences. To avoid the modelling dependency with respect to the analyst's competence, it is necessary to transmit whole or part of semantic by the modelling language itself. This can be possible by the semantic enrichment of the language.

3. Ontology

The development of enterprise ontology was performed by several researchers in the nineties, in particular in the United States and Canada. These researches aim to the knowledge definition and organization about the whole activities of enterprise (process, organizations, strategies, sale, etc.).

Ontology is the study of what exists, i.e. the whole of knowledge of the world. That is the definition used in philosophy. The concept was introduced in Artificial Intelligence (AI) 15 years ago to answer problems of knowledge representation within the data processing systems (Fürst, 2002). Among all the definitions suggested on ontologies, we adopt the one proposed by Gruber: "ontology is an explicit, formal specification of a shared conceptualisation" (Gruber, 2001).

In practice, ontology results in agreeing on the terms meaning employed in an organization, a community, a trade, with a purpose of people and software comprehension. Therefore, we can say that ontology is an organization model of knowledge in a given field. An ontology must propose descriptions for the following concepts:

- object classes to be organized (project, products, commercial documents, contracts, etc.),
- existing relations between objects (object "person" can be connected by a relation "employed by" to an object "organization"),
- properties, or attributes attached to these object (reference, description, address, size, etc.).

3.1. *Anatomy of ontology*

According to Gruber (Gruber, 2001), knowledge in ontologies is mainly formalised by using five kinds of components:

- a class or concept which represents a set of entities within a domain,
- relations which represent the interaction between concepts of the domain,
- functions are a special case of relations in which the n-th element of the relationship is unique for the n-1 preceding elements,
- axioms are used to model sentences that are always true,
- instances are used to represent specific individual elements.

As illustrated in Figure 1, the elements that compose ontology can be seen distributed over three layers (De Nicola *et al.*, 2005):

- upper Domain Ontology (UDO), which incorporates the most general domain concepts,
- application Domain Ontology (ADO), which incorporates the specific concepts of the application domain,

– lower Domain Ontology (LDO), which incorporates attributes and other elementary concepts that are used to compose Application concepts.

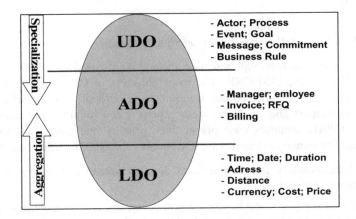

Figure 1. *The ontology layers*

3.2. *Ontology representation*

As for enterprise modelling languages, the representation language of ontologies can be of various degrees of formalization (Uschold *et al.*, 1996):

– informal (natural language text, drawings),
– semi-informal (structured natural language),
– semi-formal (formally defined language),
– formal (formally defined language with a formal semantic).

We can classify ontology languages into graph-based languages, frame-based languages and logical languages. The distinction among these three can be characterized by differences in main "symbols" used to represent the knowledge.

Graph-Based	Frame Based	Logic Based
Semantic networks	Frame Systems	Description Logics (e.g., OIL,
Conceptual graphs	OKBC, XOL	DAML+OIL, OWL)
UML		Rules (e.g., RuleML, LP/Prolog)
		First Order Logic (e.g., KIF)
		Non-classical logics (e.g., Non-mon, probabilistic)

Table 1. *Ontology languages classification*

Graph-based languages use nodes and links. Frame-based languages use frames to represent concepts (classes), which contain slots or properties and they are closely related to object-oriented languages. And Logical languages use logical statements, such as KIF.

3.2.1. OPAL (Object, Process, Actor modelling Language)

OPAL is an ontology representation methodology based on UML and OWL, developed at LEKS, IASI-CNR. The main objective of OPAL is to provide an ontology representation method that incorporates (categorial) elements of the target domain, to support and guide business experts when building and maintaining ontology. OPAL organises concepts in three primary and some complementary categories. The primary categories are (De Nicola et al., 2005), (ATHENA, 2005):

- Business actors: entities of domain, those are able to activate or perform a business process.
- Business objects (and business object documents [BODs]): entities on which a business process operates. A BOD is a further refinement that represents a type of document in the business domain.
- Business processes: business activities aimed at the satisfaction of a business goal, operating on a set of business objects. It can be rather simple, with a limited duration in time, or complex, with parallel branches and phases that last for a long time span.

The complementary categories are:

- Message: it represents the interaction between processes. It is characterized by a content that is a BOD.
- Complex/atomic attributes: in modelling the properties of a concept, we distinguish between structured information, such as address, and elementary information, such as street name. Essentially, a (structured) complex attribute is defined as an aggregation of lower level complex and/or atomic attributes.
- Operation: represents an activity that is not further decomposable. Its use depends on the level of details we are managing.

The OPAL model includes semantic relations defined among categories. The OPAL semantic relations represent well known modelling notions common to (the meta-model of) the majority of Knowledge Representation Languages. They can be organised into two groups: vertical and horizontal relations (De Nicola et al., 2005).

The vertical relations are:

- ISA (refinement): relation among concepts. For instance, an invoice is an accounting document,
- decomposition: part-of relationship among concepts. For instance, a department is a part of an enterprise.

The horizontal relations are:

- predication: it relates attributes to a concept. For instance, an invoice is in predication relation with date, amount, and recipient,
- relatedness: domain specific relationships (named or unnamed) among concepts. For instance, an invoice is related to customer (unnamed).

3.3. Conclusion

Ontology languages aim at the specification of an ontology and are not adapted for the modelling of the structure and the functioning of a particular enterprise. We can note that the existing ontology languages are not adequate to represent manufacturing enterprise concepts (IDEAS, 2003). New solutions are to be developed on the basis of language with an adequate expressive power.

4. Semantic enrichment of enterprise modelling

The solution that we propose to enrich enterprise modelling languages by ontologies consists to use semantic annotation of terms used in a language. That supposes to define an ontology created from the conceptual model of the language (Figure 2) which will be useful in the second time to annotate the language. To enrich the enterprise modelling languages, we propose to follow two steps: ontology creation and semantic annotation.

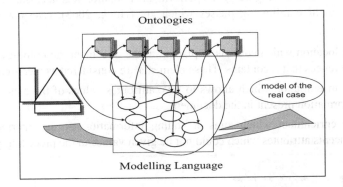

Figure 2. *Enterprise modelling and ontologies*

4.1. Ontology creation

The development of ontology is based on the conceptual model, which identifies and structures the basic concepts implemented by the language. The steps to follow to create ontology are (Fridman Noy *et al.*, 2001):

- Determine the field and scope of the ontology.
- Study the possibility of using existing ontologies, to extend and refine them. Reuse existing ontologies can even constitute a requirement if our system needs to interact with other applications which already use specific ontologies or controlled vocabularies.
- Enumerate the significant terms in ontology. Indeed, it is useful to note in a list form all the terms to be treated or explained to a user, and the properties related to these terms.
- Define the classes and their hierarchy.
- Define the class properties (attributes) and their facets (values types, authorized values, number of values, etc.).
- Create class instances in the hierarchy.

4.2. Semantic annotation

The annotation is one of the most common forms of meta-data in the Web context, it is also graphic or textual information attached to a document and generally placed in this document.

The semantic annotation is a particular case of annotation because it refers to ontology. It can be made in the form of comments, of explanations note, questions or another type of external remark which can be attached to a document or a selected part of this document (Figure 3). To perform an annotation it is necessary to proceed through the three following phases which are (Hung, 2003), (Desmontils *et al.*, 2003).

- the location which consists in placing in the document the ontology concepts references that it contains. These elements are considered as meta-data,
- the instantiation which allows to give attributes values of the concepts using information present in the document,
- the enrichment which aims at adding information by the intermediary of concepts attributes which could not be given values in the preceding phase.

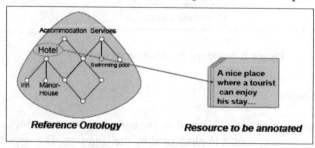

Figure 3. *Semantic annotation example*

We note that in the first two steps, there are not information addition but rather localization and characterization of information already present. They are insertion steps. At the last step, the document is enriched by information which did not exist; it is a step of annotation formalized by meta-data.

5. Conclusion

In this paper, we presented the basic concepts and principles of semantic enrichment of enterprise modelling by ontologies. Research that we carry out uses a bottom-up approach, which consists to enrich existing languages by elaboration of ontology from their conceptual model. We are also interested in another approach known as top-down. It consists first to create an ontology. Based on this ontology, a new enterprise modelling language can be developed.

We can note that there is another research orientation in this field. It is concerned with the enrichment of enterprise models. More precisely it defines the precise meaning of information (process, decisions, resources, etc.) represented in a model. Current research in this direction also focuses on the semantic annotation technique using ontology. The term "enrichment" is used to mean that annotated information can be mapped to other models entities, and consequently allow interoperability between the enterprise models.

It is quite obvious that this research topic is only at its beginnings. A first example will have to be built soon. Then, a full-scale work can start. All these works will be carried out in collaboration with relevant research activities currently running in ATHENA project and INTEROP NoE.

6. References

ATHENA. The Athos specification. Deliverable D.A3.1. http://www.athena-ip.org/. 2005

Braesch Ch, A. Haurat J.-M. Beving. *L'entreprise-système. La modélisation systémique en entreprise*, Paris Hermès.1995.

De Nicola A, Missikoff M, Navigli R. A Proposal for a Unified Process for Ontology Building: UPON. *DEXA 2005*. Copenhagen, Denmark. 2005. Desmontils E, Jacquin C. Annotation sur le web: notes de lecture. Journées de l'AS Web sémantique, http://www.lalic.paris4.sorbonne.fr/stic/. 2003.

Fridman Noy N, McGuinness D-L. Ontology Development 101: A Guide to Creating Your First Ontology. Stanford Knowledge Systems Laboratory Technical. *Report KSL-01-05 and Stanford Medical Informatics Technical Report SMI-2001-0880*, March 2001.

Fürst F. *L'ingénierie ontologique*. Rapport de recherche no. 02-07. Institut de recherche en informatique de Nantes. 2002.

Gruber T. What is an Ontology? Summary statement of Gruber's definition of ontology. http://www-ksl.stanford.edu/kst/what-is-an-ontology.html. 2001.

Hung H-H. Développement d'un outil efficace pour annoter les documents. Mémoire de fin d'études. Institut de la francophonie pour l'informatique. Vietnam. 2003.

Roque M, Vallespir B, Doumeingts G. From a model translation case towards identification of some issues about UEML. *In actes de IFAC TC5.3 workshop on Enterprise Integration, Interoperability and Networking (EI2N)*, Geneva, Suisse, 22 February 2005.

Roque M. Contribution à la définition d'un langage générique de modélisation d'entreprise. PhD Thesis, Bordeaux 1 University, mention productique, 15 November 2005.

Uschold M, Gruninger M. Ontologies: Principles, Methods and Applications. *The Knowledge Engineering Review*. V.11, N.2. 1996.

Vallespir B, Braesch Ch, Chapurlat V, Crestani D. L'intégration en modélisation d'entreprise : les chemins d'UEML. *In actes de la 4ème conférence francophone de Modélisation et Simulation, Organisation et conduite d'activités dans l'industrie et les services, MOSIM'03*, Toulouse, France. 23-25 April 2003.

Vallespir B. Modélisation d'entreprise et architecture de conduite des systèmes de production. Mémoire d'Habilitation à Diriger des Recherches, Bordeaux 1 University. 19 December 2003.

Capability Representation on Increased $\mathcal{ALN}$

Dong Cheng

LORIA-University Henri Poincaré Nancy 1

Campus Sceintifique-BP 239
54506 Vandoeuvre Lès Nancy
France

cheng@loria.fr

ABSTRACT: *Knowledge representation is one of the central concepts in AI, numerous papers have lobbied for varietal representations, where the most fundamental question will be about it "What is it?" A knowledge representation is a substitute for the thing itself; it is some identity descriptions of an entity in a closed knowledge representation world. On the other hand, some application domains as composite software, ranging from search engines, to more general applications, like cooperative and distributed applications or e-business and e-commerce applications, more and more rely on* **capability description**. *In this paper we try to highlight some concepts concerning* **capability description** *and* **discovery**, *and we discuss the relationship between capabilities. Specifically, we propose a capability description language, as and extension of* $\mathcal{ALN}$ **Description Logics** *languages.*

KEY WORDS: *Description Logic, role, transitive closure, capability representation, capability discovery, semantic query.*

1. Introduction

This document provides style guidelines which must be respected by authors in order to ensure the uniform appearance of articles published in Hermes Science journals. This document should be used as a model, particularly for the first page, the headers, sub-titles, headings, etc. Articles should be no longer than 20 to 30 pages, except for some special cases. In the artificial intelligence literature, Randall Davis (Randall *et al.*, 1993) gives some fundamental definitions on *knowledge representation*. Knowledge representation is a substitute for a thing itself to be a set of ontological commitments and to be subject of intelligent reasoning. The definitions give a framework for knowledge representation terminology, where a *knowledge representation* is a surrogate of an entity. Allen Newell (Newell 1982; Wermelinger 1995) has analyzed what he terms the *knowledge level* and he has situated knowledge in the epistemological processes of an observer attempting to model the behaviour of another agent: "The observer treats the agent as a system at the knowledge level, i.e. ascribes knowledge and goals to it.", noting that: "Knowledge is that which makes the principle of rationality work as a law of behaviour", and defining rationality in terms of the principle that: "If an agent has knowledge that one of its actions will lead to one of its goals, then the agent will select that action."

That is, for Newell, knowledge is ascribed to an agent to explain its capabilities, and there is no knowledge without capabilities. In our work, we define a method for capability management, and then we apply the method for capability discovery and composition in a distributed heterogenous knowledge base. The heterogenous knowledge base might use different formal description languages, as Description Logics, Frame-logic, etc.

In our previous work, we defined a mediator-based architecture where heterogeneous systems may work together in the context of semantic queries (Cheng *et al.*, 2005b). We adopted a *Description Logics* (DLs) (Baader 2003) language to represent the semantic query. DLs are a family of knowledge representation languages that is intensively developed and studied in the field of Knowledge Representation. In DLs a description of a world is built using *concepts, roles* and *individuals*. The *concepts* model classes (sets of *concepts*, called Terminologic Box or TBox) of individuals (sets of *individuals* are called Assertion Box or ABox). *Concepts* correspond to generic entities in an application domain. An *individual* is an instance of a concept. *Roles* model binary relationships among the individual classes. A *concept* is specified thanks to a structured description that is built giving *constructors* that introduce the *roles* associated with the *concept* and possible restrictions associated with some *roles*. *Capability* is described on attribute (unitary) and relationship (binary) in this kind of description structure.

In the mediator-based architecture (Boudjlida 2002), one should notice that some cases conduct to a failure of the query when only one mediator is involved. But, if we assume a grouping of mediators (into a federation of mediators); these cases are typical cases where cooperation among the mediators is required. When a mediator partner dissatisfies the query, we need to determine "what is missing?" to the "entities" to satisfy query. That means to determine what part of the query is not satisfied by the found "entities". That part as well as the original query is transmitted then to a mediator of the federation. Conceptually, we can see the query as being addressed to "the union" of by the federated mediators' knowledge bases. The query evaluation and the composition of an answer are performed thanks to the federated mediators, every mediator having its proper Capability KB. This semantic query describes the services or the capabilities an "entity" might offer. The capability of an "entity" is presented under formal concepts. In many situations, it is not possible to find any "entity" which exactly provides the expected capabilities (Cheng et al., 2004). So we need a kind of method to exactly describe the capability itself in the context of semantic queries. In continuation of this work, we extend a DLs language, $\mathcal{ALN}$ with the notion of role. In (Baader et al., 2001), $\mathcal{ALN}$ is extended with the transitive closure of role. It represents capability in formal syntax rule.

In this paper, we will firstly introduce the extended DLs language, and then apply this language to knowledge base management. This paper is structured as follows: The $\mathcal{ALN}_{role+}$ syntax is presented in section 2. We introduce a notion of *capability space* in section 3 that complement the ABox and the TBox. The approach for capability discovery is in section 4 while concluding remarks are in the section 5.

2. Increase $\mathcal{ALN}$ to $\mathcal{ALN}_{role+}$

Before starting with the definition of $\mathcal{ALN}_{role+}$, let us introduce some notational conventions. The letter A will often be used for *primitive concepts* (Baader, F. 2003), and C, D for concept description. Considering *roles*, the letter r will often be used for *primitive role*, the letters R, S for role description, and the letters f, g for functional roles. Nonnegative integers (in number restrictions) are often denoted by n and m, and individuals are denoted a, b, c, d. The higher part in Figure 1 contains a syntax list of $\mathcal{ALN}_{role+}$-concept description, and the lower part is a syntax list of $\mathcal{ALN}_{role+}$-role description.

The part of $\mathcal{ALN}_{role+}$-concept description is exactly as $\mathcal{ALN}$-concept description syntax. Some extended role descriptions were mentioned and proved in (Baader 2003). The added value of transitive closure in individual capability composition is shown in (Baader et al., 2001). For example, an $\mathcal{ALN}_{role+}$-concept description is Flight $\doteq \forall$has-airline*.Airport which intuitively describes all air travel that includes Non-stop flights and Transfers. In particular, $\forall$has-airline* is interpreted as reflexive-transitive closure of the role **has-airline**, thus representing the role "transfers". A simple example of an ABox specified with respect to the TBox depicted is {**Airport(Paris), Airport(Beijing), Airport(Nancy), has-airline(Nancy, Paris), has-airline(Paris, Beijing)**}.

$$
\begin{aligned}
C, D \rightarrow\ & A\ | && \text{(concept name)} \\
& \top\ | && \text{(top-concept)} \\
& \bot\ | && \text{(bottom-concept)} \\
& \neg A\ | && \text{(primitive negation)} \\
& (\geq\ n\ r)\ | && \text{(at-least restriction)} \\
& (\leq\ n\ r)\ | && \text{(at-most restriction)} \\
& C \sqcap D\ | && \text{(concept conjunction)} \\
& \forall R.C && \text{(value restriction on roles)} \\
\\
R, S \rightarrow\ & r\ | && \text{(role name)} \\
& \top_{role}| && \text{(universal role)} \\
& \varepsilon\ | && \text{(identity role)} \\
& \phi\ | && \text{(empty role)} \\
& R \cap S\ | && \text{(role junction)} \\
& R \cup S\ | && \text{(role disjunction)} \\
& R^{-}\ | && \text{(symmetric closure)} \\
& R^{+}\ | && \text{(transitive closure)} \\
& R^{*}\ | && \text{(reflexive-transitive closure)} \\
& R|_{C}\ | && \text{(role concept restriction)} \\
& R f S && \text{(role functional restriction)}
\end{aligned}
$$

Figure 1. *Syntax of $\mathcal{ALN}_{role+}$*

Intuitively, this ABox says that {**Paris, Beijing, Nancy**} have {**Airport**}, and there are {**Airline**} from {**Nancy**} to {**Paris**}, and from {**Paris**} to {**Beijing**}. So we can find that there exist flights from {**Nancy**} to {**Beijing**} with very simple reasoning by composing individuals' capabilities. But the composition of concepts' capability will be of higher value in many applications. The symmetric closure also is an important extension of capability description. As an example, we know that airline companies usually provide round-trip tickets. So we can simply describe this capability by **has-airline⁻**. Let us semantically define this concept description in the usual model-theoretic way, using the notion of interpretation. We define the interpretation function of the complex roles descriptions in Figure 1.

Definition 1. An interpretation $\mathcal{I}$ is a tuple($\Delta^{\mathcal{I}}, \cdot^{\mathcal{I}}$), which consists of a non-empty domain $\Delta^{\mathcal{I}}$ and an interpretation function $\cdot^{\mathcal{I}}$ that assigns to every concept name, A, a set $A^{\mathcal{I}} \subseteq \Delta^{\mathcal{I}}$, to every attribute name, r, a binary relation $r^{\mathcal{I}} \subseteq \Delta^{\mathcal{I}} \times \Delta^{\mathcal{I}}$.

Reflexive-transitive and transitive closures are kinds of role properties. They can be determined for any role. In particular, we will mention the *functional restriction* of a role. These restrictions enforce the interpretations of roles to satisfy certain properties, such as functionality and transitivity. For example, the role composition (denoted as $R \circ S$ in some language $\mathcal{L}$), was the most usual composition between binary relations. It can be defined as:

$$
R \circ S := \{(a, c) \in \Delta^{\mathcal{I}} \times \Delta^{\mathcal{I}} \mid \exists b.(a, b) \in R^{\mathcal{I}} \wedge (b, c) \in S^{\mathcal{I}}\}
$$

$$\mathsf{T}_{role} := \Delta^\mathcal{I} \times \Delta^\mathcal{I},$$
$$\varepsilon := \{(d,d)|d \in \Delta^\mathcal{I}\},$$
$$\phi^\mathcal{I} := \phi,$$
$$(R \cap S)^\mathcal{I} := R^\mathcal{I} \cap S^\mathcal{I},$$
$$(R \cup S)^\mathcal{I} := R^\mathcal{I} \cup S^\mathcal{I},$$
$$(R^-)^\mathcal{I} := \{(b,a) \in \Delta^\mathcal{I} \times \Delta^\mathcal{I}|(a,b) \in R^\mathcal{I}\},$$
$$(R^+)^\mathcal{I} := \bigcup_{i=1}^{\infty}(R^i)^\mathcal{I},$$
$$(R^*)^\mathcal{I} := \bigcup_{i=0}^{\infty}(R^i)^\mathcal{I},$$
$$R|_C := R^\mathcal{I} \cap (\Delta^\mathcal{I} \times C^\mathcal{I}),$$
$$RfS := f \text{ definition}$$

Figure 2. *Role constructors of $\mathcal{ALN}_{role+}$*

Let us move to an example of the application of the role composition for capability composition. We reorganize the knowledge base in the travel domain. We add a definition into the TBox $\mathcal{T}$:

$$
\begin{aligned}
\text{Stopover} &\sqsubseteq \top \\
\text{Airport} &\sqsubseteq \text{Stopover} \\
\text{TrainStation} &\sqsubseteq \text{Stopover} \\
\text{Train} &\doteq \forall\text{has-train}^*.\text{TrainStation} \\
\text{Flight} &\doteq \forall\text{has-airline}^*.\text{Airport}
\end{aligned}
$$

We also add some description of individuals in the ABox $\mathcal{A}$.

```
TrainStation(Beijing), TrainStation(Wuhan),
  has-train(Beijing, Wuhan), Airport(Paris),
     Airport(Beijing), Airport(Nancy),
has-airline(Nancy, Paris), has-airline(Paris, Beijing)
```

The capabilities of the concepts, **Flight** and **Train**, may be composed to satisfy a complex travel requirement using trains and airplanes. Anyway, this composition of concepts' capabilities can be implemented in $\mathcal{A}$: we can find a route from **Nancy** to **Wuhan**, where no direct transportation exists.

By this example we can see that the relationship between roles is important information in some situations for capability discovery and composition. In $\mathcal{ALN}_{role+}$, the symbol f denotes the relationship between roles, as shown in Figure 3.

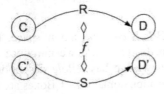

Figure 3. *A model of role functional restriction*

Figure 3 draws a general model of the functional restriction of roles. That functional relation is viewed as a partial function, and thus one can write $f^{\mathcal{I}}(R) = S$ rather than in $f^{\mathcal{I}}(R, S)$. Here we use the letters C and D, C' and D' for two couple concepts. Back to the travel example, it exists relationships **has-way** and **has-airline**. If R identifies the relationship **has-way**, then C and D identify the same concept **Stopover**. S will identify the relationship **has-way**, C' and D' identify the concept **Airport**. It exists a subsumption the relationship f between **has-way** and **has-airline**. Subsumption relationship is the fundamental relationship that may hold among described $\mathcal{L}$-concepts. Intuitively, a concept C subsumes a concept D, if the set of individuals represented by C contains the set of individuals represented by D. More formally, C subsumes D and it is denoted as $D \sqsubseteq C$ (or D is subsumed by C) if and only if $D^{\mathcal{I}}$ for every possible interpretation $\mathcal{I}$. C is called the subsuming concept and D is the subsumed. We can express simple functional restriction definitions (like equivalence and inclusion) by interpretation.

$$R \equiv S := \{a \in \Delta^{\mathcal{I}} \mid \forall b.(a, b) \in R^{\mathcal{I}} \leftrightarrow (a, b) \in S^{\mathcal{I}}\}$$
$$R \sqsubseteq S := \{a \in \Delta^{\mathcal{I}} \mid \forall b.(a, b) \in R^{\mathcal{I}} \rightarrow (a, b) \in S^{\mathcal{I}}\}$$

This formal f is an open model for the relation between descriptions of roles. Many formal relationship descriptions could be accepted by this model, such as equalization, subsumption. One could also count role hierarchies as imposing such restrictions. Here we will treat role hierarchies in the context of a knowledge base.

3. Capability space

As mentioned in section 2, we use *role* to present entities' capability where the *role* is binary relationship between two entities. But many current research work focus on the concept description and proposition reasoning. As we all known that terminological space (TBox) and assertional space (ABox) are the two main components of knowledge base in terminology language. We get a classic definition of TBox in the current literatures.

Definition 2. An $\mathcal{L}$-concept is of the form $A \doteq C$, where $A \in N_C$ (N_C being the Concept Name Space) is a concept name and C is an $\mathcal{L}$-concept description. An $\mathcal{L}$-TBox $\mathcal{T}$ consists of a finite set of $\mathcal{L}$-concept definitions. A concept name is called defined (in $\mathcal{T}$) if it occurs on the left-hand side of a concept definition, otherwise it is called primitive. We require defined names to occur exactly once on the left-hand side of concept definitions in $\mathcal{T}$. The concept description C in the definition $A \doteq C$ of A is called defining concept of A and is referred to by $\mathcal{T}(A)$.

By this definition, $\mathcal{L}$-TBox is *concepts* axiom space. The *role* just is an assisted part of *concept* description. In this work, we introduce a new concept, capability space (T$_r$Box), into the knowledge base. *Role* description is used in a T$_r$Box to define the roles of the application domain. $\mathcal{L}$- T$_r$Boxes are defined as follows.

Definition 3. An $\mathcal{L}$-role is of the form $r \doteq R$, where $r \in N_r$ (N_r being the Role Name Space) is a role concept name and R is an $\mathcal{L}$-role description. An $\mathcal{L}$-T$_r$Box $\mathcal{T}_r$ consists of a finite set of $\mathcal{L}$-role definitions. A role name is called defined (in $\mathcal{T}_r$) if it occurs on the left-hand side of a role definition, otherwise it is called primitive. We require defined names to occur exactly once on the left-hand side of role definitions in $\mathcal{T}_r$. The role description R in the definition $r \doteq R$ of r is called defining role of r and is referred to by $\mathcal{T}_r(A)$.

By the definition of capability space we can imagine a knowledge base as drawn in Figure 4. A capability space, T$_r$-Box, is introduced in this knowledge base: it contains the descriptions of the roles and those of the relationships between roles. In the travel example, the following T$_r$-Box is added to the knowledge.

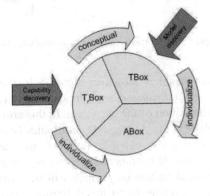

Figure 4. *Request action in Knowledge Base using $\mathcal{T}_{role+}$*

Three relationships, **has-way**, **has-airline** and **has-train**, exist in this T$_r$-Box. As we see, the concepts are often organized into a concept hierarchy by the subsumption relationship in $\mathcal{T}$. Then we may implement some knowledge reasoning services on the concept hierarchy by the *classification* approaches, as subsumption relationship satisfaction (Boudjlida 2002), complement concept determination (Cheng *et al.*, 2004), etc. We may also organize the roles into a hierarchy of roles by the subsumption relationship.

$$
\begin{array}{l}
\text{has-way} \sqsubseteq \top \\
\text{has-airline} \sqsubseteq \text{has-way} \\
\text{has-train} \sqsubseteq \text{has-way}
\end{array}
$$

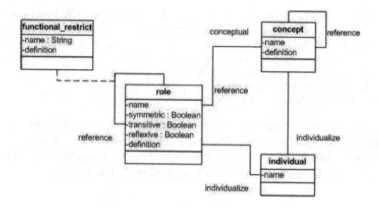

Figure 5. *UML class diagram of Knowledge Base*

The knowledge base model is shown in Figure 5 (expressed as a UML class diagram). The *concept* and *individual* classes are detailed in (Boudjlida 2002). Let's move the focus on the definition of the class *role*. In this article, we extend the *role* class definition to implement the $\mathcal{ALN}_{role+}$. The attributes (*symmetric*, *transitive* and *reflexive*) note the properties of a role. We use an association class, *functional_restric*, to implement the *functional restriction of a role*. This association class includes an attribute *definition* on *f* which will be a first-order logic formula expression. There are six variables under this definition formula, four concepts and two roles, as shown in Figure 3.

4. Capability discovery

There are three connections in this knowledge space: concept-individual, concept-role and role-individual, as drawn in Figure 4. We defined a request action for capability discovery in a federation of mediators based on the subsumption relationship. For example in transport $\mathcal{T}$, **Stopover** subsumes **Airport**, **TrainStation** is subsumed by **Stopover**.

The subsumption relationship organizes the concepts and roles into hierarchy. The classification process aims at determining the position of a new concept/role in a given hierarchy. In this framework, a query is represented as a concept Q to be classified in a given hierarchy. The result of the query is the set of instances of the concepts that are subsumed by Q. The classification is a process that enables discovering whether a subsumption relationship holds between a concept X and those present in a hierarchy $\mathcal{H}$. We use the same method to discover the concept that has a given capability R (formally noted $Q_R \doteq \forall R.\top$).

The classification process for capability discovery is decomposed into two steps:

- Retrieve the most specific subsuming concepts of X (denoted MSSC(X));

- Retrieve the most general concepts subsumed by X (denoted MGSC(X)).

When R is a primitive role, MSSC and MGSC will be a same concept. Such as in Figure 6: if $C_5 \doteq \forall r_1.C_1$ and $Q_R \doteq \forall r_1.\top$, then C_5 is the most specific concept of r_1 in $\mathcal{T}$. C_{10}, which is subsumed by C_5, is also a satisfaction for Q_R.

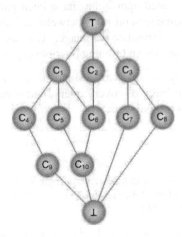

Figure 6. *Concepts hierarchy*

There is a natural dependency structure among capabilities, that possessing one capability, or a combination of capabilities, normally entails possessing another. (Brian R. Gaines 2003) has extended the classification of capabilities as follows: *It is tempting to extend this classification to the knowledge underlying the capabilities but this would be misleading since there is not a one-to-one relationship between knowledge and capabilities--usually, many different sets of knowledge can lead to the same capability.*

In more general situations, the *most specific concept* may be composite concept. The composite concept provides a capability composite to satisfy the query. For example, in Figure 6, we get the query of capability R, and $R \doteq r_1 \circ r_2$, then C_4's definition is $C_4 \doteq \forall r_2.C_1$. The composite concept $C_{Q_R} \doteq C_4 \sqcap C_5$ is the most specific concept of the capability R. For representing the capability R in the concepts hierarchy, we can introduce a concept, named the most specific concept (MSC) for capability R, which is the "best" satisfaction of a query Q_R.

5. The way forward?

We believe that capability discovery and composition will be more and more applied in knowledge discovery and management domains. We believe that the hard problems do not go away even if we solve low-level issues such as defined relationship analysis, complex term mapping, and ontologies integration. Further, we suggest that the capability composition will be between any heterogenous systems.

What can be done about this? Based on our initial experience, there is formal relationship between capabilities and common mathematical logic background knowledge, so two interrelated approaches have been paid attention in our work. The first one is finding some general rules between defined capability relationships which are described in a formulaic language. The second one is defining the capability discovery approaches and finding possible capability compositions.

In the future, we may consider to design and implement a platform, where systems will accept a capability discovery query, and it can support heterogeneous knowledge representation technologies.

6. References

Baader, F., Küsters, R.: Unification in a description logic with transitive closure of roles. In: LPAR '01: Proceedings of the Artificial Intelligence on Logic for Programming, London, UK, Springer-Verlag (2001) 217–232

Baader, F.: Description logic terminology. In Baader, F., Calvanese, D., McGuinness, D., Nardi, D., Patel-Schneider, P.F., eds.: The Description Logic Handbook: Theory, Implementation, and Applications. Cambridge University Press (2003) 485– 495

Boudjlida, N.: A Mediator-Based Architecture for Capability Management. In Hamza, M., ed.: Proceedings of the 6th International Conference on Software Engineering and Applications, SEA 2002, MIT, Cambridge, MA (2002) 45–50

Cheng, D., Boudjlida, N.: An architecture for heterogeneous federated mediators. In Castro, J., Teniente, E., eds.: CaiSE (Conference on Advanced Information Systems Engineering) EMOI'05 (Enterprise Modelling and Ontologies for Interoperability) Open Workshop Volume 2. Porto, Portugal, Springer (2005) 263–271

Cheng, D., Nacer, B.: Federated mediators for query composite answers. In: 6th International Conference on Enterprise Information Systems - ICEIS'2004, Porto, Portugal. Volume 4 (2004) 170–175

Gaines, B.R.: Springer. In: Handbook on Knowledge Management. Volume 1. Springer (2003) Chapter 16: Organizational Knowledge Acquisition

Newell, A.: The knowledge level. *Artif. Intell.* 18(1) (1982) 87–127

Randall Davis, H.S., Szolovits, P.: What is a knowledge representation? *AIMagazine* 14(1) (1993) 1993

Wermelinger, M.: Conceptual graphs and first-order logic. In: *Proceedings of the Third International Conference on Conceptual Structures*, Springer-Verlag (1995) 323–337

INDEX OF AUTHORS